LAKE FOREST LIBRARY
3 1243 00377 0913

P9-DMI-327

MAJOR ACTS OF CONGRESS

EDITORIAL BOARD

MAJOR ACTS OF CONGRESS

VOLUME 3: N-Z

BRIAN K. LANDSBERG
Editor in Chief

MACMILLAN REFERENCE USA™

New York • Detroit • San Diego • San Francisco • Cleveland • New Haven, Conn. • Waterville, Maine • London • Munich

Major Acts of Congress

Brian K. Landsberg, Editor in Chief

For more information, contact Macmillan Reference USA
300 Park Avenue South, 9th Floor
New York, NY 10010
Or you can visit our Internet site at
http://www.gale.com

Cover photographs: Capital dome (PhotoDisc, Inc.); Civil rights march (National Archives and Records Administration); IRS paperwork (PhotoDisc, Inc.); session of Congress (©AP/Wide World Photos. Reproduced by permission).

LIBRARY OF CONGRESS CATALOGING-IN-PUBLICATION DATA

Major acts of Congress / Brian K. Landsberg, editor in chief.
p. cm.
Includes bibliographical references and index.
ISBN 0-02-865749-7 (set hardcover : alk. paper) — ISBN 0-02-865750-0 (v. 1 : alk. paper) — ISBN 0-02-865751-9 (v. 2 : alk. paper) — ISBN 0-02-865752-7 (v. 3 : alk. paper)
1. Law—United States—Encyclopedias. I. Landsberg, Brian K.
KF154.M35 2004
348.73'22—dc22 200301874

This title is also available as an e-book.
ISBN 0-02-865909-0 (set)
Contact your Gale sales representative for ordering information.

Printed in the United States of America
10 9 8 7 6 5

Editorial and Production Staff

Jeff Galas, *Project Editor*
Erin Bealmear, Joann Cerrito, Stephen Cusack, Mark Drouillard, Miranda Ferrara, Kristin Hart, Melissa Hill, Jennifer Wisinski, *Editorial Assistants*
Leitha Etheridge-Sims, Lezlie Light, Michael Logusz, Kelly Quin, *Imaging*
GGS Information Services (York, Pennsylvania), *Tables*
Taryn Benbow-Pfalzgraf, Laurie Di Mauro, Jessica Hornik Evans, Anne Janette Johnson, William L. Peper, *Copyeditors*
Deanna Raso, *Photo Researcher*
Douglas Funk, *Caption Writer*
Paula Kepos, *Sidebar Writer, unless otherwise specified*
Taryn Benbow-Pfalzgraf, Nicolet Elert, Elizabeth Henry, *Proofreaders*
Wendy Allex, *Indexer*
Pamela A. E. Galbreath, *Art Director*
Graphix Group (Fenton, Michigan), *Compositor*
Margaret A. Chamberlain, *Permissions*
Mary Beth Trimper, *Manager, Composition*
Evi Seoud, *Assistant Manager, Composition*
Rhonda Williams, *Manufacturing*

MACMILLAN REFERENCE USA

Jill Lectka, *Director, Publishing Operations*
Hélène Potter, *Director, New Product Development*
Frank Menchaca, *Vice President and Publisher*

Contents

Volume 1

Volume 2

VOLUME 3

O

P

R

S

Topic Outline

CIVIL RIGHTS

Americans With Disabilities Act (1990)
Civil Rights Act of 1866
Civil Rights Act of 1875
Civil Rights Act of 1957
Civil Rights Act of 1964
Equal Pay Act of 1963
Fair Housing Act of 1968
Force Act of 1871
Freedmen's Bureau Acts (1865, 1868)
Indian Civil Rights Act (1968)
Ku Klux Klan Act (1871)
Pregnancy Discrimination Act (1978)
Title IX, Education Amendments (1972)
Violence Against Women Act of 1994
Voting Rights Act of 1965

COMMUNICATIONS

Children's Online Privacy Protection Act (1998)
Communications Act of 1934
Communications Decency Act (1996)
Counterfeit Access Device and Computer Fraud and Abuse Act of 1984
Computer Security Act of 1987
Electronic Communications Privacy Act of 1986
Electronic Signatures in Global and National Commerce Act (2000)
Public Broadcasting Act of 1967

CONSUMER PROTECTION

Bankruptcy Act of 1841
Consumer Credit Protection Act (1969)
Federal Cigarette Labeling and Advertising Act of 1965
Federal Food, Drug, and Cosmetic Act (1938)
Pure Food and Drug Act (1906)

CRIMINAL LAW

Anti-Drug Abuse Act (1986)
Brady Handgun Violence Prevention Act (1993)
Bribery Act (1962)
Communications Decency Act (1996)
Communist Control Act of 1954
Comstock Act (1873)
Controlled Substances Act (1970)
Espionage Act (1917) and Sedition Act (1918)
Federal Blackmail Statute (1994)
Flag Protection Act of 1989
Foreign Corrupt Practices Act (1977)
Gun Control Act of 1968
Hobbs Anti-Racketeering Act (1946)
Juvenile Justice and Deliquency Prevention Act of 1974
Mail Fraud and False Representation Statutes
Mann Act (1910)
Narcotics Act (1914)
National Prohibition Act (1919)
Omnibus Crime Control and Safe Streets Act of 1968
Organized Crime Control Act of 1970
Sentencing Reform Act (1984)
Violent Crime Control Act and Law Enforcement Act of 1994

ECONOMIC DEVELOPMENT/TRADE

Bank of the United States (1791)
Community Development Banking and Financial Institutions Act of 1994
Community Reinvestment Act (1977)
Copyright Act of 1790
Copyright Act of 1976
Economic Cooperation Act of 1948 (Marshall Plan)
Economic Opportunity Act of 1964
Electronic Signatures in Global and National Commerce Act (2000)
Export-Import Bank Act of 1945
Federal Power Acts
Freedmen's Bureau Acts (1865, 1868)
Hill-Burton Act (1946)
Homestead Act (1862)
Housing and Urban Development Act of 1965
Internal Improvements Acts
Merchant Marine Act of 1920
National Industrial Recovery Act (1933)
North American Free Trade Agreement Implementation Act (1993)
Patent Acts
Tennessee Valley Authority Act (1933)
Trade Act of 1974
Trading with the Enemy Act (1917)

ECONOMIC AND FINANCIAL REGULATION

Agricultural Adjustment Act (1933)
Bank of the United States (1791)
Bankruptcy Act of 1841
Bankruptcy Act of 1978
Civil Service Acts
Clayton Act (1914)
Coinage Act of 1792
Coinage Acts
Commodity Exchange Act (1936)
Community Development Banking and Financial Institutions Act of 1994
Community Reinvestment Act (1977)
Consumer Credit Protection Act (1969)
Contract Disputes Act (1978)
Farm Credit Act of 1933
Farmers Home Administration Act (1946)
Federal Deposit Insurance Acts
Federal Employers' Liability Act (1908)
Federal Home Loan Bank Act (1932)
Federal National Mortgage Association Charter Act (1954)
Federal Reserve Act (1913)
Federal Trade Commission Act (1914)
Glass-Steagall Act (1933)
Gold Reserve Act of 1934
Gold Standard Act of 1900
Interstate Commerce Act of 1887
National Bank Act (1864)
Public Utility Holding Company Act of 1935
Pure Food and Drug Act (1906)
Securities Act of 1933
Securities Exchange Act of 1934
Sherman Antitrust Act (1890)
Small Business Act (1953)
Truth in Lending Act (1969)
Walsh-Healey Act (1936)

EDUCATION

Civil Rights Act of 1964
Elementary and Secondary Education Act of 1965
Higher Education Act of 1965
Individuals with Disabilities Education Act (1975)
Morrill Land Grant Act of 1862
No Child Left Behind (2001)
Richard B. Russell National School Lunch Act (1946)
Title IX, Education Amendments (1972)
Vocational Education Act of 1917

ENERGY

Atomic Energy Acts
Department of Energy Organization Act (1977)
Federal Power Acts
National Energy Conservation Policy Act (1978)
Natural Gas Act (1938)
Nuclear Waste Policy Act (1982)
Oil Pollution Acts
Rural Electrification Act (1936)
Tennessee Valley Authority Act (1933)

ENVIRONMENT

Clean Air Act (1963)
Comprehensive Environmental Response, Compensation, and Liability Act (1980)
Emergency Planning and Community Right-To-Know Act (1986)
Endangered Species Act (1973)
Federal Water Pollution Control Act (1948)
Fish and Wildlife Conservation Act of 1980
Food Quality Protection Act of 1996
Hazardous and Solid Waste Amendments of 1984
Highway Beautification Act (1965)
Homestead Act (1862)
Marine Mammal Protection Act (1972)
Migratory Bird Conservation Act of 1929
Mineral Leasing Act (1920)
National Emissions Standards Act (1965)
National Environmental Policy Act (1969)
National Historic Preservation Act (1966)
National Wildlife Refuge System Administration Act (1966)
Nuclear Waste Policy Act (1982)
Oil Pollution Acts
Outer Continental Shelf Lands Act (1953)
Plant Variety Protection Act (1970)
Safe Drinking Water Act (1974)
Solid Waste Disposal Act (1965)
Surface Mining Control and Reclamation Act (1977)
Toxic Substances Control Act (1976)

FOREIGN AFFAIRS/ INTERNATIONAL RELATIONS

Communist Control Act of 1954
Economic Cooperation Act of 1948 (Marshall Plan)
Espionage Act (1917) and Sedition Act (1918)

Export-Import Bank Act of 1945
Federal Civil Defense Act of 1950
Foreign Assistance Act (1961)
Foreign Service Act of 1946
Lend-Lease Act (1941)
North American Free Trade Agreement Implementation Act (1993)
Nonintercourse Act (1809)
Panama Canal Purchase Act (1902)
Trade Act of 1974
Trading with the Enemy Act (1917)
United Nations Participation Act (1945)
United States Information and Educational Exchange Act (1948)

GOVERNMENT STRUCTURE AND PROCESSES

Administrative Dispute Resolution Act (1990)
Administrative Procedure Act (1946)
Balanced Budget and Emergency Deficit Control Act (1985)
Civil Service Acts
Civil Service Reform Act (1978)
Congressional Budget and Impoundment Control Act (1974)
Contract Disputes Act (1978)
Ethics in Government Act (1978)
Federal Advisory Committee Act (1972)
Federal Election Campaign Act (1971)
Federal Tort Claims Act (1946)
Freedom of Information Act (1966)
Government in the Sunshine Act (1976)
Hatch Act (1939)
Judiciary Act of 1789
Judiciary Act of 1801
Legal Services Corporation Act (1974)
Lobbying Disclosure Act (1995)
Negotiated Rulemaking Act (1990)
Paperwork Reduction Act (1980)
Privacy Act of 1974
Public Debt Acts
Regulatory Flexibility Act (1980)
Walsh-Healey Act (1936)
Whistleblower Protection Laws (1978)

IMMIGRATION

Alien and Sedition Acts of 1798
Chinese Exclusion Acts
Immigration and Nationality Act (1952)
Immigration Reform and Control Act of 1986
Naturalization Act (1790)

LABOR

Americans With Disabilities Act (1990)
Civil Rights Act of 1964
Civil Service Acts
Employee Retirement Income Security Act of 1974
Employment Act of 1946
Equal Pay Act of 1963
Fair Labor Standards Act (1938)
Family and Medical Leave Act of 1993
Federal Employers' Liability Act (1908)
Hatch Act (1939)
Keating-Owen Act of 1916
National Labor Relations Act (1935)
Norris-LaGuardia Act (1932)
Occupational Safety and Health Act of 1970
Pregnancy Discrimination Act (1978)
Taft-Hartley Act (1947)

NATIONAL SECURITY/WAR

Alien and Sedition Acts of 1798
Antiterrorism and Effective Death Penalty Act (1996)
Arms Control and Disarmament Act (1961) and Amendments
Atomic Energy Acts
Bonus Bill (1924)
Central Intelligence Agency Act (1949)
Civil War Pensions
Communist Control Act of 1954
Department of Homeland Security Act (2002)
Enrollment Act (1863)
Espionage Act (1917) and Sedition Act (1918)
Federal Civil Defense Act of 1950
First and Second Confiscation Acts (1861, 1862)
Foreign Intelligence Surveillance Act (1978)
Freedmen's Bureau Acts (1865, 1868)
Militia Act (1862)
National Guard Acts
National Security Act of 1947
Neutrality Acts
Nonintercourse Act (1809)
Nuclear Non-Proliferation Act (1978)
Posse Comitatus Act (1878)
Reconstruction Acts
Selective Service Act of 1917
United States Housing Act of 1937
USA Patriot Act (2001)
Veteran's Preference Act of 1944
War Powers Resolution (1973)
Weapons of Mass Destruction Control Act (1992)

NATIVE AMERICANS

Alaska Native Claims Settlement Act (1971)
Indian Civil Rights Act (1968)
Indian Gaming Regulatory Act (1988)
Indian General Allotment Act (1887)
Indian Removal Act (1830)
Indian Reorganization Act of 1934

PUBLIC LANDS/PUBLIC WORKS

Agricultural Adjustment Act (1933)
Federal Land Policy and Management Act (1976)
Federal Power Acts
Freedmen's Bureau Acts (1865, 1868)
Hill-Burton Act (1946)
Homestead Act (1862)
Internal Improvements Acts
National Forest Management Act (1976)
National Industrial Recovery Act (1933)
National Park Service Act (1916)

National Reclamation Act of 1902
National Wildlife Refuge System Administration Act (1966)
Northwest Ordinance (1787)
Soil Conservation and Domestic Allotment Act (1935)
Southwest Ordinance (1790)
Tennessee Valley Authority Act (1933)
Yellowstone National Park Act (1872)

SLAVERY

Compromise of 1850
Freedmen's Bureau Acts (1865, 1868)
Fugitive Slave Acts (1793, 1850)
Kansas Nebraska Act of 1854
Missouri Compromise (1820)
Prohibition of the Slave Trade (1807)
Reconstruction Acts

SOCIAL PROGRAMS/SOCIAL WELFARE

Agricultural Adjustment Act (1933)
Aid to Dependent Children (1935)
Alcoholic and Narcotic Rehabilitation Act (1968)
Antiquities Act of 1906
Bonus Bill (1924)
Born-Alive Infants Protection Act of 2002
Civil War Pensions
Defense of Marriage Act (1996)
Domestic Volunteer Service Act of 1973 (VISTA)
Drug Abuse Prevention, Treatment, and Rehabilitation Act (1980)
Family and Medical Leave Act of 1993
Food Stamp Act of 1964
Freedom of Access to Clinic Entrances Act (1994)
Housing and Urban Development Act of 1965
McKinney-Vento Act (1988)
Medicaid Act (1965)
Medicare Act (1965)
National Housing Act (1955)
Occupational Safety and Health Act of 1970
Peace Corps Act (1961)
Personal Responsibility and Work Opportunity Reconciliation Act (1996)
Social Security Act of 1935
Truth in Lending Act (1969)
Violence Against Women Act of 1994

TAXES

Anti-Injunction Act (1793)
Bland-Allison Act (1878)
Corporate Income Tax Act of 1909
1894 Income Tax and the Wilson-Gorman Tariff Act
Employee Retirement Income Security Act of 1974
Estate and Gift Taxation
Federal Income Tax Act of 1913
Federal Unemployment Tax Act (1939)
Internal Revenue Act of 1954
Medicaid Act (1965)
Medicare Act (1965)
Smoot-Hawley Tariff Act (1930)
Social Security Act of 1935
Tariff Act of 1789
Tax Reform Act of 1986
Taxpayer Bill of Rights III (1998)

TRANSPORTATION

Civil Aeronautics Act (1938)
Federal Aviation Act (1958)
Hazardous Materials Transportation Act (1975)
Highway Act of 1956
Highway Beautification Act of 1965
Highway Safety Act of 1966
Motor Carrier Act (1935)
Mutual Security Act (1951)
National Aeronautics and Space Act (1958)
National Traffic and Motor Vehicle Safety Act of 1966
Rail Passenger Service Act (1970)
Shipping Acts
Staggers Rail Act of 1980
Urban Mass Transportation Acts

PREFACE

In the fall of 2001, Hélène Potter, director of development at Macmillan Reference, asked me to serve as editor in chief of an encyclopedia of major acts of Congress. I found the offer enormously exciting, because the world of reference books had seemingly neglected this area that is so central to American law, government, and history. Moreover, I helped to write, interpret, and enforce laws while at the U.S. Department of Justice Civil Rights Division, and I had taught and written about civil rights legislation. These experiences led me to appreciate how useful a clear and authoritative description of major American legislation could be. My duties as associate dean at the University of Pacific, McGeorge School of Law, initially precluded my undertaking this project. However, the publishing schedule for the encyclopedia changed, and in March of 2002 I enthusiastically signed up.

By the spring of 2002 an outstanding board of editors had agreed to join the project, and we were well underway. Each of the associate editors brings a rich understanding of legislation to the project, but each also contributes a different perspective. Professor Al Brophy of the University of Alabama School of Law is an accomplished and well-recognized legal historian. Professor Thomas Sargentich of American University's Washington College of Law has written extensively about the legal issues of the separation of powers; he serves as codirector of his law school's program on law and government. Professor Nancy Staudt of the Washington University School of Law (St. Louis) teaches and writes on tax law and social programs and has become known for her critical analyses of both tax and social policy.

Courses in American government typically teach students about the roles of the three branches established by the Constitution. Students learn that the Congress makes laws, the executive branch executes laws, and the courts apply laws. Often, however, that lesson may seem abstract. Students may fail to see the connection between these principles and their lives, the lives of their families and friends, or the history of the nation. *Major Acts of Congress* helps make concrete the law-making function of Congress and also casts light on the role of the other two branches in enforcing and applying law. It brings together for the first time, in one work, a selection from the product of the one hundred and seven Congresses which preceded this encyclopedia, as well as the current Congress.

In its first year, 1789, Congress enacted twenty-seven laws. The acts from its first ten years occupy 755 pages, in one volume of the *U.S Statutes At*

Large. By 2002, in the second and last year of the 107th Congress, we find 260 acts, occupying 3115 pages of volume 116 of the *U.S. Statutes*. The laws of the First Congress were mainly devoted to setting up the national government, which must have seemed quite distant to most Americans. By contrast, the 107th Congress enacted laws covering such subjects as agriculture (the names of fourteen laws begin with that word), education, the environment, foreign relations, intelligence, immigration, defense, crime, voter registration, radiation, securities, employment, social security, and so on. Today few aspects of our lives are untouched by federal law.

The acts described in this work demonstrate the range of congressional legislation, from the very first Congress's adoption of the Judiciary Act to the 108th Congress's enactment of legislation regulating so-called partial birth abortions. Described in more detail than one finds in most history books are landmarks of American history, such as the Fugitive Slave Act, the various civil rights acts, legislation from the New Deal and the Great Society, as well as acts that respond to such contemporary issues as terrorism and the rise of electronic technology.

Major Acts of Congress contains entries on 262 acts selected by the editorial board based on such criteria as historical significance, contemporary impact, and contribution to the understanding of American government. Hundreds of other laws are discussed in the entries and can be found through use of the comprehensive index. The entries vary in length from 2500 words down to 300 words. Entries describe the law, but they do much more than that. They typically explain the circumstances that led Congress to consider the law and the issues Congress discussed during its consideration of the law. They also provide information about the subsequent history of the law, including amendments or repeal, enforcement, and court cases.

As the list of contributors reflects, the 159 authors include legal scholars, historians, political scientists, economists, and lawyers from public and private practice. Some played a significant role in the adoption or enforcement of the act they wrote about. Others have literally written the book on the act or area of law.

The essays have been written to make accessible to students and lay persons the frequently complex, technical, arcane concepts and language of legislation. We have included brief excerpts from acts in those entries where a direct quotation would give a flavor of the law. Accessibility is enhanced by the use of sidebars to explain terms and historical allusions, as well as illustrations that help demonstrate the political and human dimension of these laws. Same-page definitions of terms and a glossary in the back matter further enhance access. Entries typically end with a short bibliography of books, articles, and Web sites, for those who wish to delve more deeply. To place the entries in perspective, *Major Acts* begins with an introduction that explains the role of the Congress and other branches. It also contains an in-depth time line in the back matter, showing who was president, the composition of each Congress, and what major events were taking place during the time when each law was enacted.

Major Acts has been a true team effort. The editorial board has worked closely with the publisher. Hélène Potter has skillfully guided the project. Jeff Galas, assistant editor at Macmillan Reference, has been invaluable in helping recruit authors and organize the work. And Kristin Hart has ably supervised the copyediting and the selection of illustrations.

Brian K. Landsberg
September, 2003
Sacramento, California

INTRODUCTION

In a democracy like the United States, congressional action reflects the will of the people. The impetus for acts comes from members of the House of Representatives who stand for election every two years and senators who—after 1916—have stood for election every six years. (Before 1916, they were selected by their state legislature.) The acts discussed in this encyclopedia illustrate the concerns of Americans, from the early national period, through the antebellum period, the Civil War, Reconstruction, the Gilded Age, the Progressive Era, the Great Depression, World War II, and the civil rights eras, right up to the administrations of Presidents Nixon, Ford, and Carter in the 1970s, and Presidents Reagan and Bush in the 1980s, and Presidents Clinton and Bush in the 1990s and 2000s.

At times, the nation is concerned with certain issues—like civil rights—and takes action. That happened in the wake of the Civil War, when Congress proposed and the states ratified three Constitutional amendments, including the Fifteenth Amendment to guarantee all adult males the right to vote, regardless of race. Congress also passed numerous acts to ensure the newly freed slaves had civil rights. Yet, after 1877 those acts lay largely dormant, until the civil rights era of the 1950s.

Examination of the Voting Rights Act of 1965 illustrates how the nation, awakened to the cause of civil rights, again turned to Congress to seek a national solution. Each law described in this encyclopedia went through the process that American students study in increasing detail as they advance through elementary and secondary school, college, and graduate school. The process is established by Article I of the U. S. Constitution. It is not easy to pass legislation, because many actors, representing a range of interests and ideologies, must reach agreement. Rather than simply providing another abstract description of the process in this introduction, we seek to bring the process to life by describing the course of one bill from initial concept to final adoption and enforcement and subsequent amendment. You will find an entry on this law, the Voting Rights Act of 1965, in volume three of this encyclopedia.

Although the Fifteenth Amendment had been added to the Constitution in 1870 in order to forbid official actions abridging the right to vote based on race, by the middle of the twentieth century most Southern states had placed a variety of obstacles in the way of African-American voter registration. The result was that by 1952 only about 20 percent of African Americans of voting age in the Deep South were registered to vote. Congress's first effort to address this problem came in the Civil Rights Act of 1957, the first modern federal civil rights law. It had been brilliantly steered through the United States Senate by Majority Leader Lyndon B. Johnson. It was, however, a bill with few teeth, principally the bare authorization for the Department of Justice to bring suits to remedy discrimination in official voting practices and race-based intimidation against potential voters. Johnson knew that it was not a strong bill, but regarded it as a start. "[I]t's only the first. We know we can do it now." As predicted, the 1957 act did not effectively end racial discrimination in voter registration. Congress tried again, in the Civil Rights Act of 1960, but again it was not politically possible to pass a strong bill. This time, Lyndon Johnson made the pragmatic argument that the legislation was "reasonable" and "the best that the able chairman of the House Judiciary Committee could get." After passage, Thurgood Marshall, the leading black lawyer in the country, said the 1960 act "isn't worth the paper it's written on." Congress made further very minor improvements in voting rights law in the Civil Rights Act of 1964, but that law primarily addressed other matters.

The weaknesses of the 1957 and 1960 acts stemmed largely from the political influence of Southern Democrats, who in those days regularly opposed all civil rights legislation. Though they were a minority in Congress, the availability of the filibuster in the Senate gave them added strength. To pass a bill over their objection required unusual consensus between Northern Democrats and the Republicans. You will see in the descriptions of many of the acts in this encyclopedia that compromises often are necessary in order to win passage and presidential approval of a bill.

Proponents of stronger legislation needed to find a way to convince Congress to abandon the approach of the prior acts. Civil rights groups believed that it would take very strong medicine indeed to effectively insure black voting rights. As you will see in Professor William Araiza's entry on the Voting Rights Act, the act interferes with state voter qualification laws, provides for federal officials to take over the registration process in some counties, and requires some changes in state law to be pre-approved by federal courts or officials before they may be implemented. Not since Reconstruction had such federal intervention into state law occurred.

Civil rights organizations mounted voter registration drives in Alabama, Mississippi, and Louisiana. The Department of Justice brought voter discrimination suits in federal court as Southern registrars turned away thousands of prospective voters. By early 1965, national newspapers and television networks began to report on events in such places as Selma, Alabama. In February 1965 during a civil rights demonstration in Marion, Alabama, Alabama State Troopers shot and killed an African American, Jimmie Lee Jackson, who had unsuccessfully tried in prior months to register to vote. To protest the killing and to dramatize the deprivations of the right to vote, civil rights organizations—the Student Nonviolent Coordinating Committee and Dr. Martin Luther King Jr.'s Southern Christian Leadership Conference—decided to march from Selma to the state capital, Montgomery. As the marchers left Selma and crossed the Edmund Pettus Bridge over the Alabama River, they were set upon by state troopers and sheriff's deputies, many of them mounted on horses. Many were beaten, all were tear-gassed, and they were pursued back to Selma by mounted men swinging billy clubs. The assault on the

Edmund Pettus Bridge in Selma occurred in broad daylight and was broadcast to an outraged nation. The following week President Lyndon Johnson gave a nationwide address in which he announced the outlines of the voting rights bill he was sending to Congress. In the flowery language of presidential addresses, he said that "the cries of pain and the hymns and protests of oppressed people have summoned into convocation all the majesty of this great Government—the Government of the greatest Nation on earth."

President Johnson's speech in the wake of the Bloody Sunday confrontation at the Edmund Pettus Bridge promised the country an effective voting rights act. The administration's interest in a new voting law predated Bloody Sunday by several months. The Department of Justice had begun drafting such a law in November of 1964, at the direction of President Johnson. The attorney general had sent the president a memorandum outlining three possible proposals by the end of December, and the president's State of the Union message on January 4, 1965, had already proposed that "we eliminate every remaining obstacle to the right and the opportunity to vote." However, Johnson had planned to delay the voting rights proposal until his Great Society social bills had passed. The events on Bloody Sunday changed all that.

In the above events we can see four important aspects of the legislative process. First, legislation normally responds to some felt need. It is necessary to mobilize public opinion and demonstrate that the nation faces a problem and that the problem requires legislation. Second, it is not enough to simply place a bill on a president's or a party's legislative agenda. The president and Congress face a myriad of problems that need solving, and they cannot solve them all. So they establish priorities. Unless a bill is given high priority, it is unlikely that Congress will enact it even if it has merit. Third, Congress is not the only player. The president plays an important role in setting the legislative agenda. Even the initial drafting of some laws may be done by executive agencies rather than Congress. Finally, Congress often addresses issues incrementally, with small starts, such as the 1957 and 1960 Civil Rights Acts, later leading to more ambitious legislation.

Within two days of President Johnson's speech, the administration proposal had been introduced in both the House and Senate. Each chamber referred the bill to its judiciary committee. The Committee on the Judiciary of the House of Representatives in turn referred the bill to a subcommittee chaired by Emanuel Celler of New York, with six other Democrats and four Republicans as members. The subcommittee began hearings the following day. It considered 122 bills dealing with voting rights, holding thirteen sessions, including four evening sessions. It then met in executive session for four days and substantially rewrote the administration bill and sent it to the full committee of twenty-four Democrats and eleven Republicans. The committee further rewrote the bill and then sent it to the House of Representatives, with a report and a recommendation that the House pass the bill in its amended form.

Meanwhile, the Senate faced a problem that flowed from the seniority system. The chair of the Senate Judiciary Committee was Senator James Eastland of Mississippi, a strong opponent of all civil rights legislation. And the committee's senior Democrats were also from the Deep South. The Senate responded by sending the bill to the committee with the mandate to report back to the Senate no later than April 9. The full Senate Judiciary Committee held hearings for nine days. It met the April 9 deadline and recommended that the Senate pass the bill, but instead of submitting a committee report submitted sets of "individual views" of the proponents and opponents.

The hearings before both the House and Senate committees began with testimony by Attorney General Nicholas Katzenbach, who presented voluminous exhibits, including the history of the fifty-one suits against voting discrimination and seventeen suits challenging intimidation against black voter registration that the Department of Justice had brought since adoption of the 1957 act. He argued that the litigation approach under these laws had not worked. He noted that the earlier laws "depended, as almost all our legislation does, on the fact that it is going to be accepted as the law of the land and is then going to be fairly administered in all of the areas to which it applies, by States officials who are just as bound as you and I by the Constitution of the United States and by Federal laws." The attorney general continued:

> I think, in some areas, it has become the theory that a voting registrar is not really required to do anything except what he has been doing until his records have been examined and he has been hauled into court and, at public expense, his case has been defended by the State, and all the delaying devices possible have been used, and then it has been taken on appeal, then appealed again with as much delay as possible. Then, when a decree is finally entered, that decree can be construed as narrowly as possible and he can do as little as he can get away with under that decree. Then that decree—what it means—can be questioned again in court, new evidence can be introduced, and meanwhile, election after election is going by.

After delivering his statement, Katzenbach was grilled for a day and half by the House committee and for three days by the Senate committee. Southern senators challenged him at every turn—on the need for legislation, the content of the legislation, and the constitutional basis of the legislation. Civil rights leaders, including the heads of the National Association for the Advancement of Colored People and the Congress for Racial Equality, testified in favor of the bill, as did religious leaders and other federal officials. Southern attorneys general and other public officials testified against the bill.

The hearings, in short, raised issues common to most legislation. First, does Congress have the authority under the Constitution to legislate on this issue? Here, the authority came from section 2 of the Fifteenth Amendment. In most cases Congress' authority is found in Article I, section 8, which contains a laundry list of areas on which Congress may pass laws. Second, why is legislation needed? For example, why isn't existing law sufficient to deal with the problem the bill addresses? Third, what should be the content of the new legislation? It is one thing to say that we need to solve a problem and quite another to agree on what are the appropriate means. For example, the act contains detailed criteria for determining which states will be subject to some of its provisions. One criterion is whether fewer than 50 percent of persons of voting age voted in the 1964 presidential general election. Why 50 percent, as opposed to 40 or 60 percent? Why the general election? These details must be worked out, usually at the committee level.

The Senate was the first chamber to debate the bill. The minority leader, Senator Everett Dirksen, Republican of Illinois, and the majority leader, Senator Mike Mansfield, Democrat of Montana, began the debate by describing the bill and supporting it. Each party had appointed other senators to lead the floor debate, Democrat Philip Hart of Michigan and Republican Jacob Javits of New

York. They spoke at length about the evidence of need. Southern opponents spoke at great length. In addition, Senator Edward Kennedy of Massachusetts proposed an amendment that would outlaw the poll tax, and Senators Robert F. Kennedy and Jacob Javits of New York proposed an amendment designed to protect the right of Puerto Ricans in New York to vote. The poll tax amendment was defeated; the Puerto Rico amendment passed. After over a month of debate, the Senate voted to impose cloture, thus preventing a full filibuster, and on May 26 the Senate adopted the bill with a vote of 79 to 18.

The House considered the bill for three days. It adopted an amendment outlawing the poll tax, and passed the bill on July 9, 328 to 74. Thus, at this point, overwhelming majorities in both chambers supported a voting rights bill, as did the president. However, the two chambers had passed different bills. Therefore the House and Senate appointed a conference committee, charged with the task of reconciling the two bills and agreeing on a final version. For example, what should be done about the poll tax? The conference committee decided that the bill would not outlaw the poll tax but would direct the attorney general to bring litigation challenging this barrier to voting. After almost a month of work, the conference committee reported on its work on August 2, 1965. As Representative Celler told the House of Representatives the next day, "The differences were many, wide, and deep. Mutual concession was essential otherwise there would have been ... no bill." The House adopted the conference bill on August 3, and the Senate did so on August 4. President Johnson signed it on August 6.

President Johnson had presented the legislation as having the highest urgency. Congress did act quickly, but the need for hearings and debates and conference committee meant that the legislative process occupied an enormous amount of the time of the members of Congress during the five months from introduction to passage. We see that, as is often the case, the House and Senate agreed on the general objective but not on the details of the bill. We also see the importance of bipartisan coalition building where, as here, a small group of senators opposes the general objective. And we see once again that compromise is often necessary in order to enact legislation.

This is the end of the story, right? Wrong! The story goes on. The attorney general had to enforce the law. The Southern states challenged its constitutionality, so the Supreme Court had to review the law's validity. Some provisions of the law were to expire after five years. Disputes arose as to the meaning of other provisions. For example, the law was silent as to whether private parties could bring suit to enforce the provision requiring preclearance of changes in voting practices. The Supreme Court therefore had to resolve that question, by trying to determine Congress's intent. Courts have interpreted and applied the act numerous times, while other provisions have been clarified by subsequent legislation, in which Congress has revisited and amended the law several times.

The history of the Voting Rights Act demonstrates that although Congress plays the primary role in enacting legislation, the president and the courts play important roles as well. The president may propose legislation and his signature is normally needed for a bill to become law. The courts may lay a legal and constitutional framework that guides the drafting of legislation, and they apply, interpret, and determine the validity of legislation once it has been enacted.

BIBLIOGRAPHY

"Article I." In *The Constitution and Its Amendments*, ed. Roger K. Newman. New York: Macmillan Reference USA, 1999.

Berman, Daniel M. *A Bill Becomes a Law: The Civil Rights Act of 1960*. New York: Macmillan, 1962.

Hawk, Barry E., and John J. Kirby. "Federal Protection of Negro Voting Rights." *Virginia Law Review* 51 (1965): 1051.

Marshall, Burke. "The Right to Vote." In *The Constitution and Its Amendments*, ed. Roger K. Newman. New York: Macmillan Reference USA, 1999.

Schwartz, Bernard, ed. *Civil Rights*. Statutory History of the United States. New York: Chelsea House, 1970.

Brian K. Landsberg

List of Contributors

Melanie B. Abbott
Quinnipiac University School of Law
Civil Rights Act of 1964
McKinney-Vento Act (1988)

Norman Abrams
University of California, Los Angeles Law School
Violent Crime Control and Law Enforcement Act of 1994

Craig J. Albert
Reitler Brown LLC, New York
Highway Beautification Act (1965)

Ellen P. Aprill
Loyola Law School
Federal Unemployment Tax Act (1939)

William D. Araiza
Loyola Law School
North American Free Trade Agreement Implementation Act (1993)
Voting Rights Act of 1965

Carl Auerbach
University of San Diego School of Law and Northwest University School of Law
Communist Control Act of 1954

Reuven S. Avi-Yonah
University of Michigan Law School
Corporate Income Tax Act of 1909

Steven A. Bank
University of California, Los Angeles School of Law
Federal Income Tax of 1913
Internal Revenue Act of 1954

William Banks
Syracuse University College of Law
Foreign Intelligence Surveillance Act (1978)

Felice Batlan
New York University
Aid to Dependent Children (1935)

Jonathan S. Berck
University of Alabama, School of Law
Foreign Corrupt Practices Act (1977)

Richard K. Berg
Arlington, Virginia
Government in the Sunshine Act (1976)

Neil N. Bernstein
Washington University School of Law
Norris-LaGuardia Act (1932)

Christopher A. Bracey
Washington University School of Law
Civil Rights Act of 1866

Alfred L. Brophy
University of Alabama School of Law
National Historic Preservation Act (1966)

Darryl K. Brown
Washington and Lee University School of Law
Anti-Drug Abuse Act (1986)

Tomiko Brown-Nagin
Washington University School of Law
Elementary and Secondary Education Act of 1965

Alan Brownstein
Davis, California
Religious Freedom Restoration Act (1993)

Richard Buel, Jr.
Wesleyan University
Nonintercourse Act (1809)

Jennifer S. Byram
Orangevale, CA
Central Intelligence Agency Act of 1949
Electronic Communications Privacy Act of 1986
Immigration Reform and Control Act of 1986

Daniel P. Carpenter
Harvard University
Pure Food and Drug Act (1906)

Gilbert Paul Carrasco
Willamette University College of Law
Civil Rights Act of 1957

Federico Cheever
University of Denver College of Law
Endangered Species Act (1973)

Jim Chen
University of Minnesota Law School
Agricultural Adjustment Act (1933)

Gabriel J. Chin
University of Cincinnati
Chinese Exclusion Acts

Ruth Colker
Ohio State University, Michael E. Moritz College of Law
Americans with Disabilities Act (1990)
Individuals with Disabilities Education Act (1975)
Pregnancy Discrimination Act (1978)

Mikal Condon
Electronic Privacy Information Center, Washington, D.C.
Communications Decency Act (1996)

Bo Cooper
Paul, Hastings, Janofsky, and Walter, Washington, D.C.
Immigration and Nationality Act (1952)

Julie Davies
University of the Pacific, McGeorge School of Law
Ku Klux Klan Act (1871)
Title IX, Education Amendments (1972)

Derrek M. Davis
Austin Community College
Computer Security Act of 1987

Charles E. Daye
University of North Carolina School of Law
Housing and Urban Development Act of 1965
United States Housing Act of 1937

David G. Delaney
Brandeis University
Bonus Bill (1924)
Federal Civil Defense Act of 1950
Neutrality Acts

Corey Ditslear
University of North Texas
Public Broadcasting Act of 1967

Charles M. Dobbs
Iowa State University
Economic Cooperation Act of 1948 (Marshall Plan)

Keith Rollins Eakins
The University of Central Oklahoma
Brady Handgun Violence Prevention Act (1993)
Gun Control Act of 1968

Liann Y. Ebesugawa
University of Hawaii, Richardson School of Law
Civil Liberties Act (1988)

Gary J. Edles
American University, Washington College of Law and University of Hull Law School
Government in the Sunshine Act (1976)
Motor Carrier Act (1935)

Jonathan L. Entin
Case Western Reserve University
Balanced Budget and Emergency Deficit Control Act (1985)

Yonatan Eyal
Harvard University
Bank of the United States (1791)

Richard Finkmoore
California Western School of Law
National Wildlife Refuge System Administration Act (1966)

Lucinda Finley
State University of New York at Buffalo, School of Law
Freedom of Access to Clinic Entrances Act (1994)

Louis Fisher
Library of Congress
Congressional Budget and Impoundment Control Act (1974)
Employment Act of 1946
War Powers Resolution (1973)

Justin Florence
Harvard University
Alien and Sedition Acts of 1798

John P. Forren
Miami University, Ohio
Occupational Safety and Health Act of 1970

Julia Patterson Forrester
Southern Methodist University Dedman School of Law
Federal National Mortgage Association Charter Act (1954)

James W. Fox, Jr.
Stetson University College of Law
Naturalization Act (1790)

William Funk
Lewis and Clark Law School
Federal Advisory Committee Act (1972)

Fred Galves
University of the Pacific, McGeorge School of Law
Community Reinvestment Act (1977)

James P. George
Texas Wesleyan University School of Law
Anti-Injunction Act (1793)

Richard Gershon
Texas Wesleyan University School of Law
Estate and Gift Taxation
Taxpayer Bill of Rights III (1998)

Shubha Ghosh
State University of New York at Buffalo, School of Law
Copyright Act of 1790
Copyright Act of 1976
Patent Acts

Michele Estrin Gilman
University of Baltimore School of Law
Personal Responsibility and Work Opportunity Reconciliation Act (1996)

Mark Glaze
Campaign Legal Center, Washington, D.C.
Federal Election Campaign Act (1971)

Linda Gordon
New York University
Aid to Dependent Children (1935)

Brian E. Gray
University of California, Hastings College of the Law
Federal Power Acts
Mineral Leasing Act (1920)
National Park Service Act (1916)
Yellowstone National Park Act (1872)

Pamela L. Gray
Purdue University
Vocational Education Act of 1917

Stuart P. Green
Louisiana State University Law Center
Bribery Act (1962)
Federal Blackmail Statute (1994)

Steven J. Gunn
Yale University Law School
Alaska Native Claims Settlement Act (1971)
Fair Housing Act of 1968
Indian Gaming Regulatory Act (1988)
Indian General Allotment Act (1887)

Daniel W. Hamilton
New York University Law School
Enrollment Act (1863) (The Conscription Act)
First and Second Confiscation Acts (1861, 1862)
Militia Act (1862)
Morrill Land Grant Act of 1862
Reconstruction Acts

Douglas B. Harris
Loyola College in Maryland
Civil Aeronautics Act (1938)
Federal Aviation Act (1958)
National Aeronautics and Space Act (1958)

Philip J. Harter
Vermont Law School
Negotiated Rulemaking Act (1990)

Neil S. Helfand
Washington, D.C.
Department of Homeland Security Act (2002)
Mutual Security Act (1951)
National Security Act of 1947
USA Patriot Act (2001)

James E. Hickey, Jr.
Hofstra University School of Law
Public Utility Holding Company Act of 1935

Thomas M. Hilbink
University of Massachusetts
Omnibus Crime Control and Safe Streets Act of 1968

Arthur Holst
Philadelphia, Pennsylvania
Hazardous Materials Transportation Act (1975)
Oil Pollution Acts

Wythe W. Holt, Jr.
University of Alabama School of Law
Judiciary Act of 1789

Herbert Hovenkamp
University of Iowa
Clayton Act (1914)
Federal Trade Commission Act (1914)
Sherman Antitrust Act (1890)

James L. Huston
Oklahoma State University
Compromise of 1850
Homestead Act (1862)
Kansas Nebraska Act of 1854
Missouri Compromise (1820)

Mark D. Janis
University of Iowa College of Law
Plant Variety Protection Act (1970)

Barry L. Johnson
Oklahoma City University
Hobbs Anti-Racketeering Act (1946)
Mail Fraud and False Representation Statutes
Sentencing Reform Act (1984)

Warren F. Kimball
Rutgers University
Lend-Lease Act (1941)

Andrew R. Klein
Indiana University School of Law—Indianapolis
Rural Electrification Act (1936)

Stephen H. Klitzman
Bethesda, Maryland
Government in the Sunshine Act (1976)

Michael H. Koby
Washington University in St. Louis School of Law
Children's Online Privacy Protection Act (1998)

Thomas C. Kohler
Boston College Law School
National Labor Relations Act (1935)

David A. Koplow
Georgetown University Law Center
Arms Control and Disarmament Act (1961) and Amendments
Nuclear Non-Proliferation Act (1978)
Weapons of Mass Destruction Control Act (1992)

Andrew Koppelman
Northwestern University School of Law
Defense of Marriage Act (1996)

David E. Kyvig
Northern University Illinois
National Prohibition Act (1919)

Julia Lamber
Indiana University School of Law
Age Discrimination in Employment Act (1967)

David J. Langum
Samford University, Cumberland School of Law
Mann Act (1910)

Marc A. Le Forestier
Department of Justice, State of California
Migratory Bird Conservation Act of 1929

Arthur G. LeFrancois
Oklahoma City University School of Law
Fugitive Slave Acts (1793, 1850)
Organized Crime Control Act of 1970

Andreas Lehnert
Washington, D.C.
Federal Reserve Act (1913)

Jennifer Rebecca Levison
Independent Scholar
Narcotics Act (1914)

Alberto B. Lopez
Northern Kentucky University, Salmon P. Chase College of Law
Born-Alive Infants Protection Act of 2002

Kyle A. Loring
Boston College
National Reclamation Act of 1902
Safe Drinking Water Act (1974)
Soil Conservation and Domestic Allotment Act (1935)
Tennessee Valley Authority Act (1933)

Jeffrey S. Lubbers
American University, Washington College of Law

Administrative Procedure Act (1946)
Paperwork Reduction Act (1980)
Regulatory Flexibility Act (1980)

William V. Luneburg
University of Pittsburgh School of Law
Civil Service Acts (1883)
Federal Land Policy and Management Act (1976)
Federal Tort Claims Act (1946)
Hatch Act (1939)
National Environmental Policy Act (1969)
National Forest Management Act (1976)
Toxic Substances Control Act (1976)

Hether C. Macfarlane
University of the Pacific, McGeorge School of Law
Walsh-Healey Public Contracts Act of 1936

Shahla F. Maghzi
University of California, Berkeley Boalt Hall School of Law
Foreign Service Act of 1946
United States Information and Educational Exchange Act (1948)

Michael P. Malloy
University of the Pacific, McGeorge School of Law
Community Development Banking and Financial Institutions Act of 1994
Glass-Steagall Act (1933)
International Emergency Economic Powers Act (1977)
National Banking Act (1864)
Tariff Act of 1789
Trading with the Enemy Act (1917)
United Nations Participation Act (1945)

Jerry W. Markham
University of North Carolina School of Law
Commodities Exchange Act (1936)
Gold Standard Act of 1900
Social Security Act of 1935

Edward J. McCaffery
University of Southern California Law School
Public Debt Acts

Michael D. McClintock
Mcafee & Taft, Oklahoma City
Merchant Marine Act of 1920

Travis McDade
Ohio State University, Michael E. Moritz College of Law
Administrative Dispute Resolution Act (1990)
Legal Services Corporation Act (1974)

W. Eric McElwain
University of the Pacific, McGeorge School of Law
Trade Act of 1974

Robert H. McLaughlin
University of Chicago
Antiquities Act of 1906

Eric J. Miller
Harvard University Law School
Juvenile Justice and Deliquency Prevention Act of 1974

Chandra Miller Manning
Pacific Lutheran University
Internal Improvements Acts

Kelly A. Moore
Washington University School of Law
Federal Cigarette Labeling and Advertising Act of 1965

William S. Morrow, Jr.
Washington Metropolitan Area Transit Commission
Urban Mass Transportation Acts

Mary-Beth Moylan
University of the Pacific, McGeorge School of Law
Highway Act of 1956

Roger K. Newman
Columbia University Graduate School of Journalism
Fair Labor Standards Act (1938)
Hill-Burton Act (1946)

Lawrence H. Officer
University of Illinois at Chicago
Bland-Allison Act (1878)
Coinage Act of 1792
Coinage Acts
Gold Reserve Act of 1934

Todd Olmstead
Yale University School of Public Health
Highway Safety Act of 1966
National Traffic and Motor Vehicle Safety Act of 1966

Craig Oren
Rutgers, The State University of New Jersey, School of Law, Camden
Clean Air Act (1963)

Kevin Outterson
West Virginia University College of Law
Medicare Act (1965)
Prohibition of the Slave Trade (1807)

Thomas Panebianco
Shepherd College; former General Counsel, Federal Maritime Commission
Shipping Acts

Sara M. Patterson
Claremont Graduate University
Indian Removal Act (1830)

Antonio F. Perez
The Catholic University of America School of Law
Foreign Assistance Act

Twila L. Perry
Rutgers, The State University of New Jersey, Center for Law and Justice
Family and Medical Leave Act of 1993

Adam P. Plant
Montgomery, Alabama
Selective Service Act of 1917
Smoot-Hawley Tariff Act (1930)

Ellen S. Podgor
Georgia State University, College of Law
Counterfeit Access Device and Computer Fraud and Abuse Act of 1984

Steve Pollak
Shea and Gardner, Washington, D.C.
Economic Opportunity Act of 1964

James G. Pope
Rutgers University School of Law
National Industrial Recovery Act (1933)

Eric A. Posner
University of Chicago Law School
Bankruptcy Act of 1978

Trevor Potter
Campaign Legal Center, Washington, D.C.
Federal Election Campaign Act (1971)

L.A. Powe, Jr.
University of Texas School of Law
Judiciary Act of 1801

Ann Powers
Pace University School of Law
Federal Water Pollution Control Act (1948)

Steven Puro
St. Louis University
Electronic Signatures in Global and National Commerce Act (2000)
Food Stamp Act of 1964

Steven Ramirez
Washburn University School of Law
Federal Deposit Insurance Acts
Federal Home Loan Bank Act (1932)
Securities Act of 1933
Securities Exchange Act of 1934

Holly A. Reese
Washington University School of Law
Taft-Hartley Act (1947)

Elizabeth Regosin
St. Lawrence University
Freedmen's Bureau Acts (1865, 1868)

Sandra Rierson
Thomas Jefferson School of Law
Comstock Act (1873)

Eugene H. Robinson, Jr.
United States Marine Corps
Hazardous and Solid Waste Amendments of 1984
Solid Waste Disposal Act (1965)

Melissa Rogers
Pew Forum on Religion and Public Life, Washington, D.C.
Religious Freedom Restoration Act (1993)

Stephen C. Rogers
Washington, D.C.
Rail Passenger Service Act (1970)

Sara Rosenbaum
George Washington University
Medicaid Act (1965)

Ross Rosenfeld
Brooklyn, New York
Atomic Energy Acts
Farm Credit Act of 1933
Farmers Home Administration Act (1946)
Force Act of 1871
Interstate Commerce Act of 1887
National Housing Act (1955)
Small Business Act (1953)

Seth Rosenfeld
Atomic Energy Acts
Small Business Act (1953)

William G. Ross
Samford University, Cumberland School of Law
Keating-Owen Act of 1916

Theodore W. Ruger
Washington University in St. Louis School of Law
Federal Food, Drug, and Cosmetic Act (1938)

Steve Russell
Indiana University
Indian Civil Rights Act (1968)

Lawrence Schlam
Northern Illinois University College of Law
Domestic Volunteer Services Act of 1973 (VISTA)
Equal Pay Act of 1963
Higher Education Act of 1965
Indian Reorganization Act of 1934
Peace Corps Act of 1961

Elizabeth M. Schneider
Brooklyn Law School
Violence Against Women Act of 1994

Steven L. Schooner
George Washington University Law School
Contract Disputes Act (1978)

John Cary Sims
University of the Pacific, McGeorge School of Law
Emergency Planning and Community Right-To-Know Act (1986)
Privacy Act of 1974

David A. Skeel, Jr.
University of Pennsylvania Law School
Bankruptcy Act of 1841

Richard Slottee
Lewis & Clark College Law School
Consumer Credit Protection Act (1969)
Truth in Lending Act (1969)

Charles Anthony Smith
University of California, San Diego
Outer Continental Shelf Lands Act (1953)

Donald F. Spak
Chicago-Kent College of Law
National Guard Acts
Posse Comitatus Act (1878)

Michael I. Spak
Chicago-Kent College of Law
National Guard Acts
Posse Comitatus Act (1878)

Andrew C. Spiropoulos
Oklahoma City University School of Law
Flag Protection Act of 1989

Norman Stein
University of Alabama School of Law
Civil War Pensions
1894 Income Tax and Wilson-Gorman Tariff Act

John P. Stimson
United States Marine Corps
Veterans' Preference Act of 1944

Robert N. Strassfeld
Case Western University School of Law
Espionage Act (1917) and Sedition Act (1918)

Thomas Susman
Ropes & Gray, Washington, D.C.
Lobbying Disclosure Act (1995)

Matthew M. Taylor
Georgetown University
Panama Canal Purchase Act (1902)

Joseph P. Tomain
University of Cincinnati College of Law
Department of Energy Organization Act (1977)
National Energy Conservation Policy Act (1978)
Natural Gas Act (1938)
Nuclear Waste Policy Act (1982)
Surface Mining Control and Reclamation Act (1977)

Mark Tushnet
Georgetown University Law Center
Antiterrorism and Effective Death Penalty Act (1996)
Civil Rights Act of 1875

James F. Van Orden
Duke University
Fish and Wildlife Conservation Act of 1980
National Emissions Standards Act (1965)

Robert W. Van Sickel
Indiana State University
Communications Act of 1934

Lynda D. Vargha
Skidmore College
Export-Import Bank Act of 1945

Robert G. Vaughn
American University, Washington College of Law
Civil Service Reform Act (1978)
Ethics in Government Act (1978)
Freedom of Information Act (1966)
Whistleblower Protection Laws (1989)

Wendy Wagner
University of Texas School of Law
Marine Mammal Protection Act (1972)

James Walker
Wright State University
Richard B. Russell National School Lunch Act (1946)

Valerie Watnick
Law Department, Baruch College, Zicklin School of Business
Food Quality Protection Act of 1996

Gregory S. Weber
University of the Pacific, McGeorge School of Law
Comprehensive Environmental Response, Compensation, and Liability Act (1980)

Richard Westin
University of Kentucky College of Law
Tax Reform Act of 1986

Daniel C. Wewers
Harvard University
Northwest Ordinance (1787)
Southwest Ordinance (1790)

Steven Harmon Wilson
Prairie View A&M University
Alcoholic and Narcotic Rehabilitation Act (1968)
Controlled Substances Act (1970)
Drug Abuse Prevention, Treatment, and Rehabilitation Act (1980)

John Fabian Witt
Columbia Law School
Federal Employers' Liability Act (1908)

Kelly A. Woestman
Pittsburg State University
No Child Left Behind (2001)

James A. Wooten
State University of New York at Buffalo, School of Law
Employee Retirement Income Security Act of 1974

Eric Yamamoto
University of Hawaii, Richardson School of Law
Civil Liberties Act (1988)

Diana H. Yoon
New York, New York
Chinese Exclusion Acts

Jeff Zavatsky
New York, New York
Farm Credit Act of 1933
National Housing Act (1955)

Christopher Zorn
Emory University
Staggers Rail Act of 1980

Lynne K. Zusman
Lynne Zusman & Associates, Washington, D.C.
Department of Homeland Security Act (2002)
Mutual Security Act (1951)
National Security Act of 1947
USA Patriot Act (2001)

Narcotics Act (1914)

Jennifer Rebecca Levison

The Narcotics Act of 1914 (38 Stat. 785), also known as the Harrison Act, was one of the first attempts by the federal government to regulate drug consumption. However, it was not mainly concern about drug use at home that spurred passage of the act but rather the United States' desire to improve its relations and trade with China.

Public reaction to the increased spread of drug consumption as well as the need to improve relations with China led to the search for means to control the availability of abused substances, mainly opiates.

Relations between the two countries had deteriorated because of the Chinese Exclusion Acts, which kept Chinese laborers out of the United States, and because of the brutal treatment of Chinese travelers and immigrants in the United States. In response to U.S. policies concerning the Chinese, Chinese merchants organized a voluntary embargo (a stoppage of trade) against American goods in 1905. American traders, who wanted to gain entry into the lucrative China trade, then dominated by the British and other Europeans, were upset about the embargo. Thus, in addition to strained relations with China, the government was also concerned about the grumblings of its own business and trade community.

THE INTERNATIONAL OPIUM PROBLEM

Despite their strained relations, both China (at home) and the United States (in the Philippines) struggled to confront opium use, providing some common ground between the countries. Opium and other opiates are highly addictive drugs derived from the poppy plant. The opium problem had worsened when the United States took control of the Philippines from Spain following the U.S. victory in the Spanish-American War of 1898. For more than half a century, the Spanish had kept strict control over the flow of opium. Following the war, opium began to flow more readily into and out of the Philippines. By 1906 China had made clear their desire to end opium imports and the rampant addiction among China's people.

Charles Henry Brent, an Episcopal bishop, made efforts to help the United States address the opium problem in the Philippines and thus to improve relations with China. In 1906, after the Chinese embargo against trade with the United States had taken effect, Bishop Brent asked President Theodore Roosevelt to convene an international meeting of the United States, Japan, and others with interests in the Far East. Brent argued that such an international effort could stop the flood of opium into China and production of opium in the Philippines. Roosevelt favored Brent's plan because it would ease tensions between the United States and China. The State Department chose Dr. Hamilton Wright, Dr. Charles C. Tenney, and Bishop Brent to act as the United States' delegates to the opium conference in Shanghai in 1909.

At the time, the United States had no federal law limiting or prohibiting the importation, use, sale, or manufacture of opium or coca (the plant from which cocaine is derived) or any other drugs made from these substances.

At the time, the United States had no federal law limiting or prohibiting the importation, use, sale, or manufacture of opium or coca (the plant from which cocaine is derived) or any other drugs made from these substances. Secretary of State Elihu Root believed it was imperative that Congress pass an antidrug measure before the Shanghai meeting. The Smoking Opium Exclusion Act was passed in 1909.

DRUG USE AT HOME

When Wright came home from the Shanghai Opium Commission, he formulated a domestic bill concerning the control and use of drugs. Wright's bill, introduced in 1910 by Representative David Foster of Vermont, chairperson of the House Committee on Foreign Affairs, sought to control drug traffic through federal powers of taxation. The Foster bill required those who handled opiates, cocaine, chloral hydrate (a hypnotic drug), and cannabis (marijuana and hashish) to register, pay a small tax, and record all transactions. Wright told the House Committee on Ways and Means that while the Chinese community had the largest number of opium smokers, use of the narcotic was spreading to other ethic groups. He also warned of cocaine use among the African American population in the South as a way to gain the support of the Southern Democrats. However, the medical and pharmaceutical communities were not strong supporters of the Foster bill, and the bill failed to pass.

In 1911 Wright helped organize the first International Conference on Opium, convened at The Hague. The main topic was finding ways to regulate international narcotic traffic. The conference emphasized that the means to control use and trafficking of narcotics was domestic legislation within individual countries. Wright returned from the conference with a renewed determination to enact domestic drug legislation.

THE HARRISON BILL

Representative Francis Burton Harrison, a Democrat, agreed to sponsor Wright's antinarcotic legislation. The wholesale drug trade, patent medicine makers, pharmacists, and physicians met as part of the National Drug Trade Conference (NDTC) to express their opposition to the Harrison bill. To ensure that the bill would pass in the House, several of the NDTC suggestions were incorporated into the bill. However, the Harrison bill stalled in the Senate.

The Harrison bill gained renewed momentum when President Woodrow Wilson took office in 1913. The new administration directed the State and Treasury Departments to work with the drug trades and medical profession to create an acceptable bill. The NDTC finally signed a draft of the bill, and on December 14, 1914, Congress passed the Narcotics Act. The act imposed registration and record-keeping requirements on the production and sale of opiates and cocaine.

The act imposed registration and record-keeping requirements on the production and sale of opiates and cocaine.

The Harrison Act did not explicitly state how to deal with drug addicts. According to the act, anyone who obtained specified drugs with "a prescription given in good faith" was allowed to possess them. Some doctors prescribed drugs in gradually diminishing amounts as a way to "maintain" addicts. Maintenance was seen as a way to cure addicts of their drug problem. The Treasury Department, which enforced the law, was against this practice and pursued druggists and physicians who maintained addicted patients.

JUDICIAL REVIEW AND LEGISLATIVE REPEAL

In 1916 the U.S. Supreme Court heard a case, *United States v. Jin Fuey Moy*, concerning a doctor whom Treasury agents had arrested for prescribing one-sixteenth of an ounce of morphine sulfate to an addict. The Court ruled in favor of the doctor, finding that it was unlawful for the government to interfere with the practice of medicine.

In 1919 the Court made two important decisions with respect to the Narcotics Act. First, in *United States v. Doremus*, the Court found that the act did not exceed the constitutional powers of the federal government. Then, the Court reversed its earlier position in *Jin Fuey Moy,* ruling in *Webb v. United States* that physicians did not have the right to maintain addicts. In 1922 the Court ruled, in *United States v. Behreman*, that prescribing diminishing amounts of an addictive drug with the intention of curing the addict was an illegitimate medical practice. By this time, opium and cocaine prohibition were firmly in place.

In 1970 Congress enacted the Comprehensive Drug Abuse Prevention and Control Act and repealed the existing drug laws, including the Harrison Act. For more than fifty years, the Harrison Act had served as a central feature of the entire federal legislative scheme of drug control.

See also: Anti-Drug Abuse Act; Chinese Exclusion Acts; Drug Abuse Prevention, Treatment, and Rehabilitation Act; Omnibus Crime Control and Safe Streets Act of 1968; Sentencing Reform Act.

BIBLIOGRAPHY

Epstein, Edward Jay. *Agency of Fear: Opiates and Political Power in America,* rev. ed. London: Verso, 1990.

Inciardi, James A., ed. *Handbook of Drug Control in the United States.* New York: Greenwood Press, 1990.

Jonnes, Jill. *Hep-Cats, Narcs, and Pipe Dreams: A History of America's Romance with Illegal Drugs.* New York: Scribner, 1996.

Krauss, Melvyn B., and Edward P. Lazear, eds. *Searching for Alternatives: Drug-Control Policy in the United States.* Stanford, CA: Hoover Institution Press, 1991.

McLaughlin, Gerald T. "Cocaine: The History and Regulation of a Dangerous Drug." 58 *Cornell Law Review* 537 (1973).

Musto, David F. *The American Disease: Origins of Narcotic Control,* 3d ed. New York: Oxford University Press, 1999.

National Aeronautics and Space Act (1958)

Douglas B. Harris

Excerpt from the National Aeronautics and Space Act

(a) The Congress hereby declares that it is the policy of the United States that activities in space should be devoted to peaceful purposes for the benefit of all mankind.

(b) The Congress declares that the general welfare and security of the United States require that adequate provision be made for aeronautical and space activities. The Congress further declares that such activities shall be the responsibility of, and shall be directed by, a civilian agency exercising control over aeronautical and space activities sponsored by the United States.

The National Aeronautics and Space Act of 1958 (Space Act) (P.L. 85-568, 72 Stat. 426) established a civilian-controlled National Aeronautics and Space Administration (NASA) headed by an administrator as well as a presidential advisory council on aeronautics. The newly created NASA assumed the responsibilities, functions, and many of the employees of the National Advisory Committee for Aeronautics (NACA), while programs related to the military and the development of space-related weapons systems were retained by the Department of Defense with turf battles to be mediated by the President of the United States.

Cold War: a conflict over ideological differences carried on by methods short of military action and usually without breaking off diplomatic relations; usually refers to the ideological conflict between the U.S. and the former U.S.S.R.

The immediate impetus for the Space Act was widespread fear that the United States was losing its **Cold War** with the Soviet Union. On October 4, 1957, the Soviet Union launched the artificial satellite *Sputnik.* This technological achievement and the launch of *Sputnik II* the following month evoked considerable anxiety among policymakers and the American public that the Soviets had gained technological superiority in aeronautics that, coupled with evidence of military superiority (the Soviets had recently tested intercontinental ballistic missiles), portended a Cold War imbalance in the Soviets' favor. Passed as it was in the midst of the Cold War, the Space Act was seen as crucial to the preservation of the United States and its competitiveness with the Soviet Union. Indeed, the constitutional basis cited in the act was Congress's power and obligation, under Article 1, section 8 of the Constitution, to "provide for the common defense and general welfare" of the United States.

Passed as it was in the midst of the Cold War, the Space Act was seen as crucial to the preservation of the United States and its competitiveness with the Soviet Union.

CONSIDERATION OF THE LEGISLATION

While the legislative process is generally slow, remarkably the Space Act was conceived and passed in less than one year. Both the pronounced need for a concerted national effort and both parties' political needs to emphasize, prior to the 1958 elections, their efforts to compete in the space race led to widespread, **bipartisan** support for the Space Act. For its part, the Eisenhower administration, embarrassed by the Soviet advance evidenced by *Sputnik,* hoped to be perceived as proactive in overcoming the technological deficit in the Cold War. In his State of the Union address, delivered January 9, 1958, President Eisenhower announced the creation of the Advanced Research Projects Agency (ARPA) within the Department of Defense to coordinate research into space exploration, satellite technology, and ballistic missiles.

bipartisan: involving members of two parties, especially the two political parties

Skeptical of the Defense Department's ability to meet the needs of the space race, top congressional Democratic leaders sought passage of a Space Act that would establish a civilian-led NASA. From December 1957 to January 1958, Senate Majority Leader Lyndon B. Johnson of Texas, who chaired the

President Dwight D. Eisenhower appointed T. Keith Glennan, right, as NASA's first administrator, and Hugh L. Dryden as deputy administrator. The passage of the National Aeronautics and Space Act was largely in response to the launching of Sputnik *by the Soviet Union less than a year earlier.* (NASA/MARSHALL SPACE FLIGHT CENTER)

Preparedness Subcommittee of the Senate Armed Services Committee, held multiple hearings on space and astronautics. On February 6, the Senate established its Special Committee on Space and Astronautics also to be chaired by Senator Johnson. And, on March 5, the House created its Select Committee on Astronautics and Space Exploration to be chaired by Majority Leader John W. McCormack of Massachusetts. With legislative efforts already underway, on April 2 President Eisenhower acceded to Congress by sending a special message requesting that Congress create a civilian-run NASA. Both the House Select Committee and the Senate Special Committee moved quickly, reporting legislation to their full chambers on May 24 and June 11, respectively.

The content of the legislative debate on both the House and Senate floors reveals the emphasis on the Cold War and military preparedness.

The content of the legislative debate on both the House and Senate floors reveals the emphasis on the Cold War and military preparedness. In the House debate on June 2, Majority Leader McCormack emphasized the future consequences of congressional action, marveling at the quick technological advance and warning that if an "enemy of the free world" were "able to get a decided advantage, that advantage might result in the destruction of the entire world or in the subjugation of the entire world to that particular nation." These sentiments were echoed on the Senate side as Senator Johnson argued to his colleagues in the June 16 legislative debate: "What Congress does with this legislation is of vital importance. The success our country enjoys in space exploration and development depends to a large degree upon the kind of organization and powers which the Congress creates. Unless our success in this new field exceeds that of totalitarian countries, human freedom may perish."

The chief objections to the Space Act, raised during the legislative debate, centered on political turf. Supporters of NACA, ARPA, and other Defense Department programs raised objections to the encompassing nature of NASA's influence. Despite these areas of disagreement, the Space Act enjoyed widespread, bipartisan support, and it passed by voice vote in the House on June 2nd and similarly by voice vote in the Senate on June 16. Differences between House and Senate versions of the bill were reconciled in conference committee and the Conference Report was approved by voice vote in both the House and the Senate on July 16. Congress completed its actions on this legislation by altering House and Senate rules to establish the House Committee on Science and Astronautics on July 21 and the Senate Aeronautical and Space Sciences Committee on July 24 in order to oversee the continuing operations of NASA. On July 29, 1958, President Eisenhower signed P.L. 85-568 into law.

NASA'S IMPACT

The Space Act recommitted the American national government to space research and development and spawned a tremendous growth in the federal government's investment in the study of aeronautics. This is most obvious in a comparison of NASA and its predecessor, the NACA. According to the *NASA Historical Data Book,* whereas the NACA employed 8,000 individuals and had a budget of $100 million in 1958, just a decade later, in 1967, NASA employed 36,000 individuals and had a budget of over $5 billion. This massive effort to engage in high technology research and development generated advances that spilled over into many academic, commercial, and military enterprises.

In addition to raising the very real technological and military stakes in the United States' space race with the Soviet Union, the Space Act's major impact seems to have been symbolic. Without the Space Act, the United States would not have won the space race to the moon. Indeed, perhaps the most significant impact of the Space Act can be found in how the images of NASA's successes and tragic failures have played a central role in the American collective consciousness. From the moonwalk to the *Challenger* and *Columbia* space shuttle disasters, NASA's highs and lows have been nationalizing events that are embedded in America's collective memory.

BIBLIOGRAPHY

Griffith, Alison. *The National Aeronautics and Space Act.* Washington, DC: Public Affairs Press, 1962.

Van Nimmen, Jane, Leonard C. Bruno, and Robert L. Rosholt. *NASA Historical Data Book, Volume 1: NASA Resources, 1958–1968.* Washington, DC: NASA, 1988.

INTERNET RESOURCE

NASA History Office. <http://history.nasa.gov>.

National Bank Act (1864)

Michael P. Malloy

In the 1830s the federal charter of the second Bank of the United States expired. Until the early 1860s, the federal government had no direct involvement in regulating U.S. banking. The national crisis of the Civil War pushed the federal government to reenter bank regulation. The war required vast amounts of money and credit, and difficulties in financing the war were draining the nation's gold supply. As a result, the gold standard, which gave value to the national currency, was eventually abandoned. Borrowing from banks created under state laws was one obvious source of needed credit. By 1861 there were approximately 1,600 state-chartered banks, but no central bank system (like the Federal Reserve) to monitor credit, and no banks directly subject to federal supervision.

Until the early 1860s, the federal government had no direct involvement in regulating U.S. banking.

To help finance the war, in 1861 Treasury Secretary Salmon P. Chase recommended the establishment of a national banking system. National banks could be chartered by the federal government and authorized to issue bank notes secured by U.S. government bonds. Chase's plan would have ensured a market for federal debt, since the new national banks would be required to buy the bonds.

However, the government first tried to finance the war directly by selling U.S. notes to the public, without creating national banks. By early 1862, Congress had authorized the issuance of $150 million in U.S. notes, the first of several issuances, but these sales did not satisfy wartime credit needs. When

Chase's next legislative effort, the 1863 National Currency Act, did not solve the problem, it was amended and reenacted as the National Bank Act (NBA) (13 Stat. 100) in 1864, creating a national banking system on the model originally proposed by Chase. The national bank system, which outlasted the Civil War, became a central feature of the modern U.S. bank regulatory system. It established the federal-state "dual banking system" that has been a characteristic of U.S. commercial banking ever since.

FEATURES OF THE NBA

The NBA created the position of the Comptroller of the Currency as an office within the Treasury Department. The comptroller was authorized to issue national bank charters in legislation that has remained unchanged since 1864:

> Associations for carrying on the business of banking ... may be formed by any number of natural persons, not less in any case than five. They shall enter into articles of association, which shall specify in general terms the object for which the association is formed.... These articles shall be signed by the persons uniting to form the association, and a copy of them shall be forwarded to the Comptroller of the Currency, to be filed and preserved in his office.

This language guided the creation of such powerful nationwide banks as Citibank and the Bank of America, as well as thousands of local banks. The system was originally intended to create a mandatory market for U.S. bonds, since each newly chartered national bank was required to deliver to the comptroller government bonds in an amount equal to $30,000 or one-third of its capital, whichever was greater. However, long after this requirement was revoked in 1913, the role of federally chartered national banks administered by the comptroller has continued to be significant in the national economy.

COURT CHALLENGES

As part of Chase's plan for financing the war, the statutes passed during the early 1860s imposed taxes on the capital and bank notes of commercial banks, both state and national. With the tax on state-chartered banks, Chase was attempting to encourage them to convert to national charters. This plan was challenged in *Veazie Bank v. Fenno* (1869), in which Chase, by then Chief Justice of the Supreme Court, wrote the majority opinion. The Court upheld the constitutionality of the tax, but it did not directly address the constitutionality of the NBA to grant banking charters.

That issue was finally addressed in passing in *Farmers' & Mechanics' National Bank v. Dearing* (1875). The Supreme Court stated that the constitutionality of the NBA rested "on the same principle as the act creating the second bank of the United States." That principle was upheld under the **necessary and proper clause** of Article I, section 8 of the Constitution in *McCulloch v. Maryland* (1819) and *Osborn v. Bank of the United States* (1824). The validity of the NBA has been unchallenged since then.

necessary and proper clause: provision in the U.S. Constitution (Article I, section 8, clause 18) that authorizes Congress to pass laws needed in order to exercise its constitutional powers

FLEXIBLE POWERS OF THE NATIONAL BANKS

Having accepted the constitutionality of the NBA, the Court went on to express the view that the national banks created under the act's authority were to be somewhat favored, and this has largely been their experience ever

This reproduction of a painting, possibly by N. C. Wyeth, depicts President Abraham Lincoln conferring with Secretary of the Treasury Salmon P. Chase about the bill that would become the National Bank Act of 1864. (LIBRARY OF CONGRESS, PRINTS AND PHOTOGRAPHS DIVISION)

since. The national banking system now enjoys, in addition to basic banking powers like lending and accepting deposits, flexible power to engage in a broad range of other activities, including data processing services, lease financing of automobiles, municipal bond insurance, securities activities, and selling variable annuities, among many others.

The national banking system now enjoys, in addition to basic banking powers like lending and accepting deposits, flexible power to engage in a broad range of other activities, including data processing services, lease financing of automobiles, municipal bond insurance, securities activities, and selling variable annuities, among many others.

The Office of the Comptroller, the oldest existing federal bank regulator, is still a bureau of the Department of the Treasury. The comptroller is responsible for administration of virtually all federal laws applicable to national banks, including all banks operating in the District of Columbia. The approval of the comptroller is required for practically any significant action taken by a national bank, including among other things chartering, establishment of branches, and changes in corporate control or structure. In addition, the comptroller has supervisory authority over the day-to-day activities of national banks, including loan and investment policies, trust activities, issuance of securities, and the like. These supervisory responsibilities are carried out, for the most part, through periodic on-site examinations of the banks by national bank examiners. In addition, the Gramm-Leach-Bliley Act of 1999 requires the comptroller to supervise the "financial services activities" of subsidiaries of national banks, the privacy of nonpublic personal information of customers of national banks, and consumer protection with respect to insurance sales by national banks, among other things.

Courts have generally treated the comptroller's decisions under the NBA and other statutes as authoritative. In *Camp v. Pitts* (1973), the Supreme Court held that the comptroller's actions were subject to a very limited standard of judicial review. This means that a party seeking relief in court faces great difficulty, as that party must meet very specific requirements to obtain a favorable ruling. This limited standard, now the basic approach used in judicial review of all federal bank regulators, has no doubt given the comptroller more flexible power to encourage the growth of the national banking system, without much judicial intervention.

The Gold Standard

During the nineteenth century, U.S. currency was backed by both gold and silver—in other words, a dollar in silver, nickel, or copper coins or in paper money was guaranteed by the government to be convertible into a dollar's worth of either metal. As a result of this "bimetallic standard," the valuation of U.S. currency fluctuated wildly. Because the value of the two metals on the open market was constantly changing, speculators were able to turn a profit by selling their coins for more than their face value when the value of the metal exceeded its denomination. When the government flooded the market with silver coins, the price of silver dropped, citizens traded in their silver coins for gold, and federal gold reserves were exhausted. At the same time, prices of wholesale and retail goods saw a steady decline from the end of the Civil War through the 1890s, sending farmers and other providers of goods, whose fixed debts did not decline, into crisis. This chronic monetary instability was a large factor in the 1896 election of President William McKinley, who ran on a platform that included a change to a gold standard. In 1900 McKinley signed the Gold Standard Act, making gold reserves the basis of the monetary system. The gold standard remained in effect until 1933, when the economic pressures of the Great Depression—including gold-hoarding by a panicked citizenry—led the United States to abandon it, and legislation was passed that allowed the Federal Reserve to expand the supply of paper money irrespective of gold reserves.

See also: BANK OF THE UNITED STATES; FEDERAL RESERVE ACT.

BIBLIOGRAPHY

Krooss, H. E., ed. *Documentary History of Banking and Currency in the United States.* New York: Chelsea House Publishers, 1969.

Malloy, Michael P., ed. *Banking and Financial Services Law: Cases, Materials, and Problems.* Durham, NC: Carolina Academic Press, 1999; suppl., 2002–2003.

Malloy, Michael P. *Banking Law and Regulation.* 3 vols. New York: Aspen Law and Business, 1994.

Malloy, Michael P. *Principals of Bank Regulation.* (Concise HornBook Series) 2d ed. St. Paul, MN: West Group, 2003.

McCoy, Patricia A., ed. *Financial Modernization After Gramm-Leach-Bliley.* Newark, NJ: Lexis-Nexis, 2002.

NATIONAL EMISSIONS STANDARDS ACT (1965)

James F. Van Orden

Excerpt from the National Emissions Standards Act

The Secretary shall by regulation, giving appropriate consideration to technological feasibility and economic costs, prescribe as soon as practicable standards, applicable to the emission of any kind of substance, from any class or classes of new motor vehicles or new motor vehicle engines, which in his judgment cause or contribute to, or are likely to cause or contribute to, air pollution which endangers the health or welfare of any persons, and such standards shall apply to such vehicles or engines whether they are designed as complete systems or incorporate other devices to prevent or control such pollution.

The National Emissions Standards Act (P.L. 90-148, 81 Stat. 485), Title II of the Clean Air Act (CAA), represents an evolving federal framework within which automobile pollution has been regulated. Title II was originally called the Motor Vehicle Pollution Control Act when first enacted in 1965. Congress sought to establish national automobile pollution standards, led by the efforts of Senator Edmund Muskie, a Democrat from Maine, who was the chair of the Senate Subcommittee on Air and Water Pollution. A catalyst behind air quality legislation in the 1960s and 1970s, Muskie was nicknamed "Mr. Clean," but his efforts largely paid off in a number of air quality laws that over time reduced air pollution from automobiles.

The National Emissions Standards Act, Title II of the Clean Air Act, represents an evolving federal framework within which automobile pollution has been regulated.

HISTORY OF AIR QUALITY LEGISLATION IN THE 1960S

The original Clean Air Act of 1963 provided federal resources to support state and local air quality protection measures. By the mid-1960s, it was becoming increasingly apparent that air quality was national in scope and that federal actions were necessary to protect human and ecological health. In addition, automobile emissions were particularly significant in degrading the nation's air quality. It had formerly been assumed that air pollution was a state issue, and much of the rest of air pollution legislation turned to the states for implementation. Since 1965 Congress has provided for national emissions standards for automobiles, actions taken under the power provided by the **commerce clause** of the U.S. Constitution, which grants the legislature the authority to regulate commerce among the several states.

Commerce Clause: the provision of the U.S. Constitution (Article I, section 8, clause 3) that gives Congress exclusive powers over interstate commerce—the buying, selling, or exchanging of goods between states

Various states were considering enacting their own emissions standards, and although the auto industry had publicly taken the position that automobile pollution was only an urban problem and did not merit costly national emissions controls, it seems clear in retrospect that the automobile industry preferred a uniform national standard over a patchwork of state standards. The act required that the Secretary of the Department of Health, Education and Environment consider technological feasibility and economic costs and prescribe emissions standards for any pollutant deemed a threat to human health and welfare.

California had previously established emissions standards for automobiles, and the Secretary ultimately applied those standards nationwide for automobiles in model year 1968. In addition, the department granted California the ability to continue to set its own standards because the air quality in that state was especially bad. This distinction raised the objections of the auto industry, which bemoaned the difficulties posed in complying with diverse emissions standards in different markets. However, the California waiver was maintained two years later in the Air Quality Act, which provided that only the federal government could set automobile emissions standards, with the exception of California. California would be allowed to set its own tougher standards so long as they were as stringent as the federal standards because it had done so for decades, and the smog problems the state faced merited even tougher standards. In addition, both the 1965 and 1967 laws called for increased research and development to explore alternative fuel sources and emissions reduction techniques.

California had previously established emissions standards for automobiles, and the Secretary ultimately applied those standards nationwide for automobiles in model year 1968.

CLEAN AIR ACT AMENDMENTS OF 1970

The 1970 CAA Amendments represent a congressional shift in auto pollution law from flexibility to stringency. Senator Muskie opened the debate stating, "Detroit has told the nation that Americans cannot live without the automobile. This legislation would tell Detroit that if this is the case, they can make an automobile with which Americans can live" (quoted in *Congressional Quarterly Almanac,* 1970). Although the automobile industry **lobbied** hard against the bill, Congress enacted stringent new emissions standards. This act vested the power to set regulatory standards in the newly formed Environmental Protection Agency (EPA). Probably the most significant change was the removal of the initial language stating that emissions standards should take into account technological feasibility and economic costs. The statutory language in the 1970 act set forth that the EPA Administrator should set standards based only on whether pollutants from new automobiles endanger the public health or welfare. At a minimum, for all light-duty vehicles in model

lobby: to try to persuade the legislature to pass laws and regulations that are favorable to one's interests and to defeat laws that are unfavorable to those interests year 1975 and after, carbon monoxide and hydrocarbons would have to be reduced by 90 percent, while a similar reduction of nitrogen oxides would be required by 1976. It would be the administrator's duty to decide whether it was possible for automakers to meet these tough new standards. Finally, Title II was expanded by allowing the administrator to regulate and even prohibit fuel additives that endangered health and welfare.

The 1970 developments are important for a couple of reasons. First, they represent the general presumption of the CAA in the modern era; namely, that human health should be protected against the ill effects of air pollution without regard to cost. Next, they are an initial legislative attempt to force necessary new emissions reduction technology since the standards required automakers to equip vehicles with emissions controls that did not yet exist. In fact the auto industry argued during congressional hearings that it would be impossible for them to meet the proposed standards, although Congress ultimately sided with environmentalists and enacted technology-forcing emissions standards. Whereas previous laws had considered cost and feasibility, the 1970 act removed cost considerations from the administrator's decision-making process. Now the question would be whether or not the standards could feasibly be met regardless of cost.

THE IMPACT OF SUBSEQUENT AMENDMENTS

The 1977 and 1990 Clean Air Act Amendments generally retained this structure. Both sets of amendments set even stricter standards for passenger cars

An employee of a car-care business in Rowlett, Texas, performs a mandatory emissions test, April 2002. (© AP/Wide World Photos)

and light-duty trucks for nonmethane hydrocarbons, nitrogen oxides, and carbon monoxide, while the 1990 amendments set standards for particulate matter. Similar standards were put in place for diesel- and gas-powered trucks. Both laws explicitly set forth levels of reduction and timetables for meeting new standards, and they granted the EPA administrator the ability to issue waivers to auto manufacturers if necessary. Overall, Title II of the Clean Air Act vests a good deal of power in the Administrator of the EPA to issue emissions standards regulations based on human health, although at the times Congress has amended the act, it has laid out binding emissions reductions. Also, the 1990 amendments provided for the phase-out of leaded gasoline, which had been shown to adversely affect mental development in children.

Overall, Title II of the Clean Air Act vests a good deal of power in the administrator of the EPA to issue emissions standards based on human health, although whenever Congress amended the act, it laid out binding emissions reductions.

The name "National Emissions Standards Act" is somewhat misleading when the case of California is considered. Congress amended Title II in 1977 to allow other states to enact the tougher California standards, whereas they were preempted from setting their own standards under the act. In short, the "national standards" referred to in the title of the law are actually not applied uniformly throughout the entire nation. Should a state choose to enact the California standards, they have to be exactly the same and must give automakers two years to prepare before they go into effect. Numerous states in the northeast have chosen the tougher California standards rather than the federal standards as a way to meet the National Ambient Air Quality Standards (NAAQS) of the Clean Air Act. The automotive industry has fought the application of California standards in other states in the courts, although they have generally been allowed to go into effect. The California standards are significant because they tend to be tougher and require the development of more new technology than the federal standards, as evidenced by an ongoing mandate for a percentage of all cars sold in California to be zero emissions vehicles. In addition, California's actions tend to be the model for ongoing national standards. Title II represents a form of creative state-federal interaction where Congress has taken an issue with national implications that is under the commerce clause power of the government, and it has granted a state with particular history, expertise, and necessity regarding auto emissions the ability to act as a policy laboratory for the nation. Many of the strides made in auto emissions, including the catalytic converter (which reduces pollutants at the tailpipe) and the gas-electric hybrid car now on the market in some states, can be traced to this type of **federalism.**

Title II of the CAA has led to emissions reductions, although the resulting positive effects have been limited somewhat by an increase in the number of vehicles on the nation's roads, especially of larger vehicles such as SUVs that are much more polluting.

federalism: a system of political organization; a union formed of separate states or groups that are ruled by a central authority on some matters but are otherwise permitted to govern themselves independently

Title II of the CAA has led to emissions reductions, although the positive effects of this progress have been limited somewhat by an increase in the number of vehicles on the nation's roads as well as a rise in larger vehicles such as SUVs that emit higher volumes of pollution. According to a study quoted by Arnold Reitze in *Environmental Lawyer*, in 1997 transportation sources produced 76.6 percent of total national carbon monoxide emissions, 49.2 percent of total nitrogen oxide emissions, 39.9 percent of total volatile organic compound emissions, and 13.3 percent of lead emissions. These are certainly not trivial amounts of pollution, representing the fact that, while some successes have certainly occurred over the last three-and-a-half decades, the automobile continues to pose air quality challenges.

See also: Clean Air Act; Highway Safety Act of 1966

BIBLIOGRAPHY

Bailey, Christopher J. *Congress and Air Pollution: Environmental Policies in the USA.* New York: Manchester Press, 1998.

Dewey, Scott Hamilton. *Don't Breathe the Air: Air Pollution and U.S. Environmental Policies, 1945–1970.* College Station: Texas A&M University Press, 2000.

Reitze, Arnold. "Mobile Source Air Pollution Control." *Environmental Lawyer* 6 (2000): 309–27.

National Energy Conservation Policy Act (1978)

Joseph P. Tomain

The National Energy Conservation Policy Act (P.L. 95-619, 92 Stat. 3206), like much energy legislation in the last half of the twentieth century, came as a result of the energy crisis during the mid-1970s stimulated by the **OPEC oil embargo** in 1973. Previous legislation includes the Energy Policy and Conservation Act signed into law by President Gerald Ford in December 1975, which for the most part addressed fossil fuel energy resources, including coal, oil, and natural gas. The legislative responses to the energy crisis revolved around domestic concerns involving energy reliability and prices as well as international concerns about economic and national security. Energy conservation was one approach, among many, to address both sets of concerns.

OPEC oil embargo: in October 1973, the Organization of Petroleum Exporting Countries (OPEC) banned oil exports to the United States because the United States sold arms to Israel during the Arab-Israeli War of 1973

Conservation can be understood in two distinct senses. Traditionally conservation means the use of fewer nonrenewable natural resources. The second sense in which conservation is used is to increase energy efficiencies, such as increased fuel efficiency for vehicles or in-home heating. The National Energy Conservation Policy Act is directed toward conservation in both senses.

The legislative responses to the energy crisis revolved around domestic concerns involving energy reliability and prices as well as international concerns about economic and national security.

Title II of the act addresses residential energy conservation. Under the act, the secretary of energy is directed to establish procedures for developing and implementing residential energy conservation plans by state utility regulatory authorities. The secretary is authorized to implement and enforce a federal plan in the event of inadequate state action. Specifically addressing residences, for example, the act allows an increase in the eligible income level for weatherization grants as well as establishes a financing program for the installation of weatherization materials.

Title III of the act addresses energy conservation in schools, hospitals, and buildings owned by local governments. The secretary is authorized to make grants to states to conduct energy audits in such facilities as well as to finance conservation projects. Title IV of the act adjusts civil penalties for violations of fuel economy standards, requires fuel efficiency disclosure of certain vehicles, and requires an Environmental Protection Agency report on the accuracy of fuel economy estimates for new automobiles. Title IV also directs the secretary to establish energy efficiency standards for specific household appliances and certain classes of industrial equipment.

Title V of the act addresses federal energy initiatives and amends the Energy Policy and Conservation Act. The Secretary of Energy is directed to establish a program to demonstrate solar heating and cooling technology in federal buildings as well as to set criteria for evaluating federal agency proposals regarding such demonstration programs. Title V also declares it to be the policy of the United States that the federal government has the responsibility to promote the use of energy conservation, solar heating and cooling, and other renewable energy sources in federal buildings. The secretary is likewise to establish energy performance targets for federal buildings. The act also establishes a **photovoltaic** energy commercialization program for federal facilities. Photovoltaic technology turns light into energy.

photovoltaic: relating to the technology used to capture radiation (light) from the sun and turn into electricity

Finally, Title VI of the act expands the industrial energy reporting system to major energy-consuming industries, both those identified by the secretary and industries with at least one trillion BTU's of energy per year.

See also: DEPARTMENT OF ENERGY ORGANIZATION ACT.

BIBLIOGRAPHY

Kelly, Suedeen G. "Alternative Energy Sources." In *Energy Law and Policy for the 21st Century,* ed. The Energy Law Group. Denver, CO: Rocky Mountain Mineral Law Foundation, 2000.

Mansfield, Marla E. *Energy Policy: The Reel World.* Durham, NC: Carolina Academic Press, 2001.

NATIONAL ENVIRONMENTAL POLICY ACT (1969)

William V. Luneburg

Excerpt from the National Environmental Policy Act

To declare a national policy which will encourage productive and enjoyable harmony between man and his environment; to promote efforts which will prevent or eliminate damage to the environment and biosphere and stimulate the health and welfare of man; to enrich the understanding of the ecological systems and natural resources important to the Nation; and to establish a Council on Environmental Quality.

After 150 years of rapid industrialization and urban expansion, along with two world wars, all of which required significant natural resource extraction, the environment of the United States by the end of the 1960s was under considerable stress.

After 150 years of rapid industrialization and urban expansion, along with two world wars, all of which required significant natural resource extraction, the environment of the United States by the end of the 1960s was under considerable stress. Many forested public and private lands had been or were being cleared of trees; industrial water pollution and acid mine drainage made rivers and streams unusable for various purposes, including recreation; many wild and scenic rivers were no longer free-flowing but dammed and silent; smog and other types of air pollution blanketed urban areas; and concrete highways and the developments they encouraged were consuming large areas of rural America, to name just a few of the more obvious sources of concern. At the same time, the increasingly affluent American family that traveled extensively across the continent and was witness to these changes began to put more value on the elimination of these threats to public health and of the destruction and despoliation of the places, vistas, and natural landmarks that had come to symbolize the American wilderness as it presented itself to the explorers, early settlers, and pioneers.

In this context, it was clear to many concerned and knowledgeable observers that agencies of the federal government were themselves significantly responsible for the deteriorating state of the environment within the United States. Federal agencies undertook massive projects themselves (e.g., building dams) or approved work undertaken by state governments or private companies (e.g., interstate highway construction) that involved environmentally destructive consequences. However, confronted with claims that they should consider the potential environmental effects in deciding what actions to take or avoid, federal officials responded by arguing that they had not been authorized by Congress to protect the environment; rather, their respective responsibilities were to build dams, highways or airports, to insure that timber production could meet the demand for new housing construction, and to otherwise carry out the nonenvironmental goals of the legislature.

PROVISIONS OF THE NATIONAL ENVIRONMENTAL POLICY ACT

The National Environmental Policy Act of 1969 (NEPA) (P.L. 91-190, 83 Stat. 852), signed by President Richard Nixon and effective on January 1, 1970, was Congress's attempt to eliminate these pleas of helplessness offered up by the federal bureaucracy. It is a statute that, for its authority, relies on Congress's well-nigh plenary power, or complete authority, to organize the way in which federal agencies go about their work.

The National Environmental Policy Act was the first of the modern federal environmental statutes, shortly followed in the early 1970s by the enactment of those federal laws that now form the bedrock of environmental legislation in the United States. Like those other laws, NEPA responded to the increasing public outcry, symbolized by the first Earth Day in 1970, for protection of the national and global environments. Unlike those other laws, however, NEPA is short and lacks significant detail. Rather, to a great extent, it is composed of ambitious pronouncements of purpose and policy phrased in broad generalities. For example, Section 101 makes it the "continuing responsibility of the Federal Government ... to improve and coordinate Federal plans, functions, programs, and resources to the end that the Nation may ... fulfill the responsibilities of each generation as trustee of the environment for succeeding generations ... [and] assure for all Americans safe, healthful, productive, and esthetically and culturally pleasing surroundings.... "

The National Environmental Policy Act was the first of the modern federal environmental statutes. It was shortly followed in the early 1970s by the enactment of those federal laws that now form the bedrock of environmental legislation in the United States.

The most important specific legislative accomplishments of NEPA are three: (1) the expansion of the legal authority of federal agencies to *require* them, as part of their decision-making processes, to consider the environmental consequences of each action they take; (2) the imposition of a requirement that, prior to making any final decision on a major program, plan, or project, each federal agency prepare and consider a "statement" examining the environmental costs and benefits of action and alternatives to avoid environmental harm (the so-called Environmental Impact Statement [EIS] requirement); and (3) the creation of the President's Council on Environmental Quality (CEQ).

THE LEGISLATIVE HISTORY OF NEPA

The legislative history of NEPA is as remarkable for what it leaves unstated (and perhaps unconsidered) as for what it expressly says. As early as 1959, Congress had considered legislation purporting to offer a national policy on conservation and use of natural resources as well as to establish a presidential advisory counsel on the environment. Nothing came of that legislative effort. However, in 1969 Senator Henry Jackson of Washington and Representative John Dingell of Michigan introduced similar bills in the Senate and the House of Representatives. As originally conceived, there was no "operational" aspect to the proposed bills, that is to say, no specific mechanism to try to insure that environmental protection would be forthcoming. But at a hearing in the Senate, Professor Lynton Caldwell of Indiana University noted the need for "an action-forcing, operational aspect" to the bill being considered. Senator Jackson and his staff then worked with Professor Caldwell to draft what later became Section 102(2)(C) of NEPA, the requirement that, at the time of proposing legislation or a major federal action that might significantly effect the environment, the agency responsible for the action prepare an EIS. With modest changes and little debate or other legislative history to suggest how Congress intended this provision to be implemented, it became law and a keystone of environmental policy as implemented by the federal bureaucracy. Of all the provisions of NEPA, the impact statement requirement has provoked by far the largest amount of attention within and outside the government.

Between 1970 and 1980 federal agencies filed more than ten thousand full environmental impact statements. Nearly two thousand of those were scrutinized by the courts.

Other amendments were attached to the bill enacted as NEPA as it made its way through the legislative process. Two of the most important reflected to some degree a "turf" fight within the Senate over the control of federal environmental policy. Senator Edmund Muskie of Maine chaired the subcommittee that was to produce the Clean Air and Clean Water Acts. He did not want the environmental standards created by or under that or other environmental legislation disregarded or otherwise undercut by NEPA. Nor did he want the views of the federal agencies subject to the oversight of his subcommittee ignored in the decision-making processes required by NEPA. Accordingly, the bill was amended to clarify that NEPA did not trump the environmental obligations imposed by other federal law and that federal agencies preparing Environmental Impact Statements had to solicit comments on draft Environmental Impact Statements from the U.S. Environmental Protection Agency and other federal agencies that possessed the primary responsibility for environmental protection.

THE ROLE OF THE COUNCIL ON ENVIRONMENTAL QUALITY

Both the original bills and the one finally enacted and signed by President Nixon established a Council on Environmental Quality within the Executive

Office of the President. In essence the role of the CEQ, a three-member body, is to gather authoritative information on the state of the environment and assist in the dissemination of that information through preparation of an annual report as well as conduct studies relating to ecological systems and environmental quality, oversee federal agency compliance with the policy and other obligations imposed by NEPA, and recommend to the president national policies for improvement of environmental quality.

Both the original bills and the one finally enacted and signed by President Nixon established a Council on Environmental Quality within the Executive Office of the President.

In connection with these functions the CEQ has adopted a set of elaborate regulations that restate, clarify, and elaborate on the obligations that NEPA imposes on federal agencies. As a practical matter, the most important components of those regulations are the provisions dealing with the need to prepare an EIS, the timing for such preparation, and the contents of an acceptable EIS. These regulations divide agency actions into three categories: actions that generally do not amount to major actions requiring in-depth environmental analysis; actions that are, without question, major ones likely to have significant environmental effects and, therefore, subject to the EIS requirement; and, finally, those for which it is not clear whether an EIS is necessary, so the agency must first prepare an Environmental Assessment (EA) in order to determine the scope and nature of the potential effects and whether they amount to the "significant" effects that trigger full-blown EIS analysis.

CHALLENGES TO THE ACT

In the early years following the enactment of NEPA, there was widespread federal agency resistance to its mandates, not surprisingly since compliance could delay program and project implementation and add significantly to costs. Hundreds of lawsuits were brought against agencies on the grounds that no EIS had been prepared when it should have been or, even if prepared, the EIS was fatally incomplete or otherwise inadequate in addressing relevant environmental impacts and alternatives to avoid those impacts. Many federal actions were stopped in their tracks by courts issuing orders to agencies to comply with NEPA. However, because of the costs of noncompliance with NEPA, increasingly agencies have more seriously considered their NEPA obligations: hundreds of EAs and EISs are prepared every year, and many of those comprise volumes of data and analysis.

While lawsuits continue to be brought on the basis of violations of NEPA, it is increasingly difficult to win them. In part, this is because of a series of Supreme Court cases, including, for example, *Vermont Yankee Nuclear Power Corp. v. NRDC* (1978), that have consistently found that NEPA merely mandates a particular decision-making process; it does not mandate certain results in terms of actions taken or environmental effects avoided. Accordingly, NEPA operates merely as a "stop and think first" statute: before a federal agency acts, it must consider the possible environmental consequences; having prepared an appropriate EA or EIS and having taken it into account, the agency can go right ahead with its plans—despite alternative courses of action that might mitigate or eliminate the adverse environmental consequences that may result from the proposed agency action.

While lawsuits continue to be brought on the basis of violations of NEPA, it is increasingly difficult to win them.

As a result, more than thirty years after the enactment of NEPA, debate continues to rage with regard to whether the statute has resulted in agency decision making that minimizes, to the greatest practicable extent, the adverse impact of federal actions on the natural environment. This debate has not, however, discouraged states, other countries, and the international community from transplanting NEPA's technique of environmental impact assessment into their own distinctive legal systems.

See also: CLEAN AIR ACT; EMERGENCY PLANNING AND COMMUNITY RIGHT-TO-KNOW ACT; FEDERAL WATER POLLUTION CONTROL ACT.

BIBLIOGRAPHY

Anderson, Frederick R. *NEPA in the Courts: A Legal Analysis of the National Environmental Policy Act.* Washington, DC: Resources for the Future, 1973.

Caldwell, Lynton K. *The National Environmental Policy Act: An Agenda for the Future.* Bloomington, IN: Indiana University Press, 1998.

Council on Environmental Quality. *NEPAnet.* July 2003. <http://ceq.eh.doe.gov/nepa/nepanet.htm>.

Mandelker, Daniel R. *NEPA Law and Litigation,* 2nd ed. New York: Clark Boardman Callaghan, 1992.

The National Environmental Policy Act: A Study of Effectiveness after Twenty-Five Years. Washington, DC: Council on Environmental Quality, Executive Office of the President, 1997.

Taylor, Serge. *Making Bureaucracies Think: The Environmental Impact Statement Strategy of Administrative Reform.* Stanford, CA: Stanford University Press, 1984.

NATIONAL FOREST MANAGEMENT ACT (1976)

William V. Luneburg

Excerpt from the National Forest Management Act

In developing, maintaining, and revising plans for units of the National Forest System, ... the Secretary [of Agriculture] shall assure that such plans ... provide for multiple use and sustained yield of the products and services obtained therefrom ... and, in particular, include coordination of outdoor recreation, range, timber, watershed, wildlife and fish, and wilderness.

Today, the federal government owns 192 million acres that comprise the National Forest System. Most of that land is located west of the Mississippi River in the continental United States and in Alaska. It was included among the land acquired by conquest or purchase from various foreign nations during the first seventy years of the nineteenth century. Congress first authorized the withdrawal of this forestland from public entry and disposal in 1891; those withdrawals increased significantly thereafter. There is also national forestland located east of the Mississippi, much of it acquired from private owners. The original purposes of what were first known as "forest reserves" were watershed protection and timber production, and the reserves were regulated for almost eighty years under the Organic Act of 1897 by the U.S. Forest Service located within the Department of Agriculture.

The original purposes of what were first known as "forest reserves" were watershed protection and timber production, and the reserves were regulated for almost eighty years under the Organic Act of 1897 by the U.S. Forest Service located within the Department of Agriculture.

Until the 1940s, national forestland was not extensively used for timber production. However, wartime needs for wood products and the postwar housing boom required significantly increased timber cutting on federal land. At the same time, recreational uses of the National Forest System increased dramatically along with concerns that the timber cutting practices and the forest road building necessary to extract timber were adversely affecting those uses. When Congress enacted the Multiple-Use Sustained-Yield Act in 1960, for the first time it formally recognized recreation as an important, though not an exclusive or dominant, use of national forestland.

In many areas the Forest Service employed clear-cutting as the predominant timber harvesting technique. That is to say, all or most of the trees within a designated area were removed. This practice in the Bitterroot National Forest in Montana and the Monongahela National Forest in West Virginia provoked significant controversy and adverse congressional reaction, including the issuance in 1972 of the so-called Church Report (named after Idaho Senator Frank Church) that called for a decrease in the use of clear-cutting and identified certain types of land (e.g., that with fragile soils) where no timber cutting should be permitted. A lawsuit was also brought by the Izaak Walton League of America to stop the clear-cutting in the Monongahela National Forest on the basis that the 1897 Organic Act did not permit it. When the U.S. Court of Appeals for the Fourth Circuit issued its decision in 1975 agreeing with the league, clear-cutting was effectively barred in all national forests. At that point, given pressures from the timber industry and environmental groups, Congress was compelled to enact a new and comprehensive statute that

The NFMA requires that the Forest Service prepare and revise at fifteen-year intervals a Land and Resource Management Plan (LRMP) for each national forest.

Smokey the Bear

The campaign to prevent forest fires began in the 1940s, during World War II, when protection of the national forests became a matter of significant concern. The War Advertising Council developed posters with slogans such as "Forest Fires Aid the Enemy," and "Our Carelessness, Their Secret Weapon." In 1944, after the release of the motion picture *Bambi*, Disney loaned the main character to the prevention campaign for use on what became a successful poster. When the loan period elapsed, the Forest Service selected a bear as its symbol, and its next poster featured a character called Smokey Bear pouring a bucket of water on a campfire. In 1950 the campaign acquired a living symbol when a black bear cub was rescued from a forest fire in New Mexico. Newswires broadcast the plight of the badly burned cub, eliciting national concern, and the bear eventually found a home at the National Zoo in Washington, D.C., where he served as a symbol for fire prevention and conservation campaigns. In 1952 a jingle was created for Smokey. To maintain the proper rhythm of the lyrics, the composers added the word "the" between Smokey and Bear. The character therefore became commonly known as "Smokey the Bear," although his name was never officially changed. Fifty years later, Smokey continues to warn that only YOU can prevent forest fires.

would attempt to allow continued timber production without, at the same time, unduly compromising recreational and environmental goals. The result was the National Forest Management Act of 1976 (NFMA) (P.L. 94-588, 90 Stat. 2949), adopted in the exercise of Congress's plenary constitutional authority over federally-owned land.

On balance the enactment of NFMA has helped to insure that the Forest Service deals with the National Forest System in a more environmentally-conscious fashion than might otherwise have been the case.

The NFMA requires that the Forest Service prepare and revise at fifteen-year intervals a Land and Resource Management Plan (LRMP) for each national forest. These plans identify what uses are to be made of each part of a forest (e.g., timber production, protection of old growth forest, wildlife protection, recreation) along with the standards and techniques to achieve those uses. Public participation is required in the development and revision of LRMPs. In addition, the NFMA requires that the Forest Service adopt regulations for the management of the national forests to insure that timber production does not undercut non-commodity uses of the land. For example, LRMPs must "provide for diversity of plant and animal communities." Moreover, clear-cutting can be used only where "it is determined to be the optimum method ... to meet the objectives and requirements of the relevant land management plan" and is "carried out in a manner consistent with the protection of soil, watershed, fish, wildlife, recreation, and esthetic resources, and the regeneration of the timber resource."

Despite NFMA's emphasis on ecological and recreational values, the statute's lack of detail leaves the Forest Service great freedom of choice in managing the national forests. While many individuals and groups have sued the Forest Service on the basis of the NFMA to halt plans or projects viewed as environmentally destructive, they have found the courts to be deferential to the agency's implementation based on the generality and ambiguity of the NFMA's language and the alleged technical expertise of the agency. On balance, however, the enactment of NFMA has helped to insure that the Forest Service deals with the National Forest System in a more environmentally-conscious fashion than might otherwise have been the case.

See also: FEDERAL LAND POLICY AND MANAGEMENT ACT.

BIBLIOGRAPHY

Le Master, Dennis C. *Decade of Change: The Remaking of Forest Service Statutory Authority during the 1970s*. Westport, CN: Greenwood Press, 1984.

Lien, Carsten. *Olympic Battleground: The Power Politics of Timber Preservation*. San Francisco, CA: Sierra Club Books, 1991.

Steen, Harold K. *The U.S. Forest Service: A History*. Seattle: University of Washington Press, 1976.

Wilkinson, Charles F. "Forests for the Home-Builder First of All." In *Crossing the Next Meridian: Land, Water, and the Future of the West*. Washington, DC: Island Press, 1992.

INTERNET RESOURCE

U.S. Department of Agriculture Forest Service. <http://www.fs.fed.us/>.

National Guard Acts

Michael I. Spak and Donald F. Spak

The militia, a part of a country's armed forces that is likely to be called to serve only in emergencies, is the product of English **common law** and American colonial customs designed to protect cities and towns in times of emergency and to repel invaders. The Constitution originally created a standing federal army and navy supplemented by state **militias**. These state militias are known as the National Guard.

common law: a system of laws developed in England—and later applied to the U.S.—based on judicial precedent rather than statutory laws passed by a legislative body

militia: a part-time army made up of ordinary citizens

Although some of the Constitution's framers advocated federal control of the militias, others opposed it, fearing that the federal government could use the militias against the states. The Constitution resolved the issue in Article I, section 8, authorizing Congress to fund, support, and regulate the federal land and naval forces, and to provide for calling out the militia, but leaving the states with the power to appoint its own militia officers and train its own soldiers. Congress has the power:

> to raise and support Armies, but no Appropriation of Money to that Use shall be for a longer Term than two Years;
>
> to provide and maintain a Navy;
>
> to make Rules for the Government and Regulation of the land and naval Forces;
>
> to provide for calling forth the Militia to execute the Laws of the Union, suppress Insurrections and repel Invasions;
>
> to provide for organizing, arming, and disciplining, the Militia, and for governing such Part of them as may be employed in the Service of the United States, reserving to the States respectively, the Appointment of the Officers, and the Authority of training the Militia according to the discipline prescribed by Congress.

At the time, each militiaman brought his own infantry weapon and ammunition to militia service and training. The Second Amendment preserved the private ownership of arms, especially for militia purposes: "A well regulated Militia, being necessary to the security of a free State, the right of the people to keep and bear Arms, shall not be infringed." In Article II, section 2, the president was designated the Commander in Chief of the Army and Navy of the United States, and "of the Militia of the several States, when called into the actual Service of the United States."

Accordingly, each militia was funded by Congress when " employed in the Service of the United States" (Article I, section 8), but otherwise funded and trained by the individual states and subject to control of the state governors. There was no standardized militia training, equipment, or organization.

The Constitution originally created a standing federal army and navy supplemented by state militias. These state militias are known as the National Guard.

The Militia Act of 1792 authorized the president to call the militia into federal service under certain circumstances, required all able-bodied men aged eighteen to forty-five to serve, to be armed with a musket or rifle at their own expense, and to participate in annual musters (formal military inspections), with each state legislature to direct the organization of the militia forces into military units. The military units called into "the Service of the United States" during the War of 1812 supported the federal armed forces, primarily in defensive missions.

During the 1800s the militia system fell into disrepair through lack of funding. After the Spanish-American War (1898), the federal government and many militiamen saw the need for a reformed militia. The Militia Act of 1903, better known as the Dick Act after U.S. Representative Charles Dick, a major general in the Ohio National Guard who was instrumental in passing the act, reorganized the militia as a recognized component of the military. The current version of the act (10 U.S.C. § 311) declares that the militia of the United States consists of all able-bodied males at least seventeen years of age and under forty-five years of age, who are citizens or who have declared an intention to become citizens of the United States. The act further divides the militia into two classes: (1) "the organized militia, which consists of the National Guard and the Naval Militia"; and (2) "the unorganized militia, which consists of the members of the militia who are not members of the National Guard or the Naval Militia." The unorganized militia is not further defined.

The Dick Act of 1903 offered federal funds to each state to train and equip its National Guard, provided that the Guard drilled for a certain number of days per year, allowed federal inspections, conformed to federal rules, and met federal standards. The states accepted federal funding and allowed their militias to be standardized and improved. In this fashion, each state National Guard became well-trained, well-equipped, and ready to fulfill its domestic state mission as well as supporting the federal government upon being called into federal service by the president. The 1903 act provided federal funding for five days of annual training, but not for the mandated twenty-four drills each year. Subsequent acts increased the number of days of federal annual training and the number of state drills.

The 1903 act was amended in 1908 to allow Guardsmen to be called up for federal use outside the continental United States, although the attorney general wrote an opinion in 1912 that use of the National Guard outside U.S. territory was unconstitutional. This problem was resolved through later legislation that required Guardsmen to take a dual oath to both the federal and state governments, making each Guardsman a federal reservist available to be called into federal service.

See also: Militia Act; Posse Comitatus Act; Selective Service Act of 1917.

BIBLIOGRAPHY

Donnelly, William M. "The Root Reforms and the National Guard." United States Army Center of Military History. <http://www.army.mil/cmh-pg/documents/1901/Root-NG.htm>.

Dougherty, Chuck. "The Minutemen, the National Guard, and the Private Militia Movement: Will the Real Militia Please Stand Up." 28 *John Marshall Law Review* 959 (1995). Excerpts at the University of Dayton School of Law. <http://academic.udayton.edu/health/syllabi/Bioterrorism/8Military>.

Rothstein, Julius. "The History of the National Guard Bureau." U.S. Army National Guard Bureau. <http://www.neg.dtic.mil>.

INTERNET RESOURCE

Constitutional Charter of the Guard. U.S. Army National Guard. <http://www.arng.army.mil/history>.

National Highway Traffic Safety Administration Act

See Highway Safety Act of 1966

National Historic Preservation Act (1966)

Alfred L. Brophy

The National Historic Preservation Act (P.L. 89-665, 80 stat. 915), first passed in 1966, established the U.S. policy of preserving history, while balancing that preservation with concerns for current, efficient use of property. It was passed at a time of growing cultural awareness of the importance of historic preservation, which was heightened because the nation was undergoing significant economic and social change. It was part of the 1960s movement of urban planners and architects to makes cities and towns livable and preserve some of the character of those places. That revolution in thinking, inspired by such works as *The Death and Life of Great American Cities* by Jane Jacobs, emphasized a cooperation between private landowners, developers, and the federal government. The act was premised partly on the idea that urban development and the creation of highways was destroying historic buildings and was a response to other federal programs, like the Federal Highway Acts. If preservation could be accomplished best by working with landowners, rather than in opposition to them, the act could accomplish that purpose by providing economic incentives for preservation.

If preservation could be accomplished best by working with landowners, rather than in opposition to them, the act could accomplish that purpose by providing economic incentives for preservation.

The act set a framework for national historic preservation policy, including a provision for a National Register of Historic Places, which had more than 76,000 listings by 2003. The register, maintained by the National Park Service, is accessible on its web site. Listing in the register is limited to properties considered "significant" in one or more aspects of American society and culture. It includes all national parks, 2,300 national historic properties designated by the Secretary of the Interior because of their importance to all Americans (like the General Motors Building in Detroit, Michigan, and the Ernest Hemingway House in Key West, Florida), and thousands of other properties nominated by local governments, organizations, and individuals because of their significance to the nation, state, or community.

To be listed, a property must meet rigorous standards, including a demonstration that the property is "of significance in American history, architecture, archeology, engineering, and culture," which is determined through "location, design, setting, materials, workmanship, feeling, and association." Moreover, the property must either be associated with "events that have made a significant contribution to the broad patterns of our history," with "the lives of persons significant in our past," be architecturally significant, or significant as an archeological site.

A property may be nominated to the register by the State Historic Preservation Officer (SHPO) of the state where the property is located, or by the Federal Preservation Officer for federal property, or the Tribal Preservation Officer for tribal property.

A property may be nominated by the State Historic Preservation Officer (SHPO) of the state where the property is located, or by the Federal Preservation Officer for federal property, or the Tribal Preservation Officer for tribal property. Often private citizens prepare the nominations for the SPHO and then the applications are reviewed by a state review board composed of professional historians, architects, archeologists, and other professionals in related fields. If the board and SPHO both approve, the nomination is sent to the National Park Service for its consideration. Throughout the process, property owners are given an opportunity to comment on the proposed designation. When the National Park Service is considering designation, it also solicits public comment.

There are four main benefits to being listed in the National Historic Register. First, it certifies the property as historically significant. Second, there must be special consideration given before the property is altered by any federally funded or assisted projects, which adds an extra level of scrutiny. Many people consider it a burden to develop listed property when federal money is being used because of a cumbersome review procedure. As a result, some

The adobe churches of New Mexico—like the Apostal Santiago shown above—were chosen, collectively, in 1996 for inclusion on an annual list of the eleven most endangered places in the United States. The National Trust for Historic Preservation (NTHP), which compiles the list, was created with legislation signed by President Harry Truman in 1949. It received federal funding under the National Historic Preservation Act of 1966 until 1998, when the funding was terminated with the consent of the NTHP. The NTHP now relies entirely on private contributions. (© AP/Wide World Photos)

property owners resist listing their property. The act's restrictions on development were further expanded in 1996 by President Clinton, who issued Executive Order 13007, which required extra precaution for any federal construction project that might interfere with a Native American sacred site.

There is a twenty-percent investment tax credit for the rehabilitation of income producing property, so the act provides both an incentive for private developers to preserve property and restricts the use of federal money to interfere with historic property.

The third benefit of listing with the National Historic Registry is that the property may be eligible for limited funding for historic preservation. Finally—and most importantly—the property might qualify for federal tax benefits for restoration. There is a twenty-percent investment **tax credit** for the rehabilitation of income-producing property, so the act provides both an incentive for private developers to preserve property and restricts the use of federal money to interfere with historic property.

tax credit: a reduction in the amount an individual or corporation owes in taxes

See also: NATIONAL PARK SERVICE ACT; YELLOWSTONE NATIONAL PARK ACT.

BIBLIOGRAPHY

Duerksen, Christopher J., ed. *A Handbook on Historic Preservation Law.* Washington, DC: The Conservation Foundation, 1993.

Jackson, Kenneth T. *Crabgrass Frontiers: The Suburbanization of the United States.* New York: Oxford University Press, 1985.

INTERNET RESOURCE

National Park Service. <http://www.nps.gov>.

NATIONAL HOUSING ACT (1955)

Ross Rosenfeld and Jeff Zavatsky

The National Housing Act (P.L. 84-345, 69 Stat. 646), also called the Capehart Act, was a **New Deal** measure that Congress adopted with the intent to revitalize the construction industry. The act created the Federal Housing Administration (FHA) to provide long-term, low interest mortgage rates to potential homebuyers. Congress hoped that this federal financing plan would lead to an increased demand for new and remodeled homes, thereby enabling more construction workers to find employment.

New Deal: the legislative and administrative program of President Franklin D. Roosevelt designed to promote economic recovery and social reform (1933–1939)

Great Depression: the longest and most severe economic depression in American history (1929–1939); its effects were felt throughout the world

THE U.S. HOUSING MARKET IN THE EARLY TWENTIETH CENTURY

During the Roaring Twenties housing construction averaged about 900,000 units a year; in 1925 alone, the construction industry built 937,000 new units. By 1933—at the heart of the **Great Depression**—residential construction had dropped to 93,000 units. Moreover, individuals could not repay loans, and banks began to foreclose on homes at a rate of 1,000 units a day. The construction industry was going bankrupt. Prior to the Depression, builders and bankers aligned themselves against government intervention in the real estate industry, but with the decline of the housing market, this trend changed. Many who had at one time feared "socialization" of the

Congress hoped that this federal financing plan would lead to an increased demand for new and remodeled homes, thereby enabling more construction workers to find employment.

While the Home Owner's Loan Corporation worked to rescue homes, the National Housing Act was a law that financed their construction and restoration.

field now welcomed government assistance. Between July 1933 and June 1935, the Home Owner's Loan Corporation—one of the many organizations created by the Roosevelt administration to help provide financing—refinanced one in ten of the nation's owner-occupied homes, successfully coming to the aid of more than a million people.

While the Home Owner's Loan Corporation worked to rescue homes, the National Housing Act was a law that financed their construction and restoration. By preserving a low interest rate, insuring up to 80 percent of a home's value, and extending the mortgage period from three or five to up to twenty years, the FHA made home ownership possible for millions of people. By 1940 the construction workers were back on the job, building more than 500,000 new homes. Within the next forty years, the percentage of Americans owning their own homes would increase dramatically.

HOUSING ISSUES IN THE POSTWAR ERA

After Congress adopted the National Housing Act, it faced another major housing dilemma when six million G.I.s came home from World War II in 1945, followed by another four million in 1946. Hundreds of thousands of these G.I.s became homeless due to the shortage of readily available housing. Two-and-a-half million new or reunited families unable to afford their own homes sought shelter with relatives. Moreover, because twenty million women, employed for the war effort, were forced to give up their jobs and resettle with the return of the men, these housing problems were compounded.

Wisely, Congress began to prepare for this situation when the end of the war came into sight in 1944. It created a mortgage guarantee program that allowed returning veterans to borrow the full value of a home without having to make a down-payment. This was part of the famed G.I. Bill of Rights, arguably one of the finest bills Congress ever passed. A veteran back from the front might have been forced to wait months or even years to get housing for himself and his baby-boom family, but with Congress's financial assistance, the construction industry was able to build more homes faster. Many families waiting for housing were intent on having a new house. In a 1945 *Saturday Evening Post* poll, only 14 percent of the population said that they were willing to live in an apartment or a "used house," and this preference for new homes led to a demand for more than 12.5 million new units.

The government also faced the dilemma of providing housing for a standing army. The world had changed since 1941, and it was evident that a small army would not sufficiently assure the nation's safety in the new era. The new enemy of communism had quickly taken hold in the minds of U.S. officials, and this led to a postwar, peacetime army in the late 1940s that was about seven times larger than that of the 1930s. Congress had adopted the Lanham Act of 1940 to finance the construction of homes for war workers, but these units were meant to be temporary and were not adequate for the number of individuals who needed housing.

PROVISIONS OF THE WHERRY ACT

In 1949 Congress adopted the Wherry Act, named for its sponsor, Senator Kenneth S. Wherry (R-Nebraska). The act depended on the combined efforts of the FHA and the Department of Defense. The Defense Secretary made clear which army bases would remain active, and the FHA would then offer mortgage insurance to businesses from the private sector to provide long-term, low-interest loans to army officers at the bases. The units were capped at an average of $9,000, with the FHA guaranteeing 90 percent of the mortgage ($8,100). The program was voluntary, and the officers' basic allowances would be their means to pay back the mortgages. All married, career personnel were eligible.

The act, named for Republican Senator Homer Capehart, stipulated that private builders be hired out for specific projects to be done on government-owned or government-leased land.

The Wherry program, however, had many faults. The program relied heavily on the private sector, and the FHA could not always guarantee that a project was an "acceptable risk." The projects would go to the best bidder (the one who could meet government standards at the lowest cost), and often builders would try to undercut construction by building under the cap to collect "windfall" profits. Also, as time wore on and **inflation** increased, the $9,000 limit became inadequate for the purpose of building homes, and Wherry homes began to look like small, unappealing bungalows.

inflation: a general rise in the prices of goods and services

PROGRAM MODIFICATIONS UNDER THE CAPEHART ACT

Congress addressed these problems by replacing Wherry's program with the Capehart Act of 1955. The act, named for Republican Senator Homer Capehart, stipulated that private builders be hired out for specific projects to be done on government-owned or government-leased land. The Secretary of Defense would recommend certain sites or facilities for construction projects, and if his recommendation met with FHA approval, the FHA would furnish a loan for 100 percent of the mortgage. Bidding would take place for the con-

A family of six looks at their future home (c. 1930s–1940s). Under a New Deal precursor to the Capehart Act of 1955, ownership of a home became possible for millions of people—putting many construction workers back to work at the same time. (© BETTMANN/CORBIS)

tract, with the understanding that the site would be government—not privately—operated. Congress also raised the average household cap from $9,000 under the Wherry plan to $13,500.

Capehart defended his plan by noting that it would cost the government nothing. The costs of the program, he said, would be covered by "the rents that the men in the service [would] pay." Still, the plan did have its share of detractors, many of whom were uncertain that Capehart's program would be cheaper than a direct funding program. "It's just a question of whether you want to sell bonds to build houses or whether you want to sell mortgages to build them," Capehart remarked. His plan, he argued, would get houses built without any economic pinch.

SHORTCOMINGS OF THE CAPEHART PROGRAM

Yet the Capehart strategy had its flaws too. The $13,500 limit proved too low to match the bids of private contractors, and Congress was forced to raise the limit to $16,500 with the Housing Act of 1956. Size limitations were set by the new act as well, so that builders were forced to keep within price range. A low-ranking enlisted soldier was afforded a 1,080-square-foot house, while a general officer warranted 2,100 square feet. Either way, the newly constructed units were larger than the average 831-square-foot Wherry unit, but still seemed small when compared to the National Homes and Levitt & Sons units being built elsewhere in the nation. Moreover, Wherry sponsors feared, correctly, that buyers would prefer the larger Capehart units to the smaller, though less expensive units. The government eventually acquired the Wherry properties but not at fair market value. The Defense Department, meanwhile, reported that it cost an average of $2,000 to convert a Wherry unit into a Capehart unit.

defaulter: one who fails to comply with the terms of a loan or contract, usually failing to make payments on a debt

lien: the right to take or hold or sell the property of the debtor as security or payment for a debt

The most serious condemnations of the Capehart Act came in 1960. In that year, a scandal erupted involving California developer Hal B. Hayes. Hayes, a consistent **defaulter**, discontinued his construction project due to **liens** placed on the property by his subcontractors and suppliers. Not only did the government lose money when construction projects failed, but the Gener-

Levitt & Sons

Levitt & Sons, founded by Abraham Levitt, was the most important private building firm in America during the housing shortage that followed World War II. In 1929 the Levitts had begun developing residential property, largely for wealthy customers, and by the start of the war there were more than 2,500 Levitt homes in existence. During World War II the firm was contracted to build 2,400 houses for the Navy. Unlike the prewar Levitt homes, the Navy houses had to be completed quickly and at a low cost, prompting the Levitts to develop mass-production building techniques. After the war, the firm used the same techniques to build more than 17,000 homes in the first "Levittown," a planned community in Hempstead, New York, and two more Levittowns followed in New Jersey and Pennsylvania. Simply designed, the houses were built with non-union labor and incorporated cost-saving measures such as concrete slabs rather than basements. The construction process was pared to twenty-six steps, allowing as many as thirty houses to be built in a day. With help from the Federal Housing Administration and Veterans' Administration, the Levitts could offer extremely favorable credit terms to their customers. While the Levittowns were criticized for their drab, uniform appearance, many postwar families jumped at their chance to buy into the dream of suburban homeownership. In 1949, fourteen hundred contracts for Levitt homes were signed in a single day.

al Accounting Office (GAO) criticized the government for wasting government money in other ways. The GAO issued a report that criticized the program for not taking note of housing available in the communities around military bases. Nor, the report suggested, did the Capehart program take note of those soldiers who preferred private housing. Thus the government tended to overestimate housing requirements and funded more units than necessary. The report also observed that an overwhelming number of Capehart units were valued at the $16,500 ceiling, despite the fact that Congress had set such a figure only to make certain that high cost areas were covered—not to encourage construction of such valuable units across the country. The report, combined with various other controversies, helped to signal doom for the act.

Congress held hearings in 1962. One Defense Department witness testified to Congress that "neither you nor we have been satisfied with private financing, since it is the most costly method of acquiring housing and has proven difficult to administer." Senator Capehart continued to defend his plan until it was finally forfeited by Congress that year in favor of appropriated funds. In another sweeping gesture, Congress authorized 1,400 new units and appropriated funds for half that number.

Despite their flaws, both the Wherry Act and the Capehart Act successfully created thousands of units for an army in need of housing. Between the two, approximately 200,000 new housing units were constructed for the Defense Department, and another 60,000 for the army.

Despite their flaws, both the Wherry Act and the Capehart Act successfully created thousands of units for an army in need of housing.

See also: Housing and Urban Development Act of 1965; United States Housing Act of 1937

BIBLIOGRAPHY

Badjer, Anthony J. *The New Deal: The Depression Years, 1933–1940.* New York: Noonday Press, 1989.

Bernhard, Virginia, et al. *Firsthand America: A History of the United States.* St. James, NY: Brandywine Press, 1998.

Burns, James MacGregor. *Roosevelt: 1882–1940: The Lion and the Fox.* San Diego, CA: Harcourt Brace & Co., 1956.

"National Housing Act." *Spartacus Educational.* May 2003. <http://www.spartacus.schoolnet.co.uk/USARhousing.htm<.

"Neighborhood Design Guidelines for Army Wherry and Capehart Era Family Housing." Advisory Council on Historic Preservation. May 2003. <http://www.achp.gov/capehartwherry-guidelines2.pdf<.

Wright, Gwendolyn. *Building the Dream: A Social History of Housing in America.* Cambridge, MA: MIT Press, 1981.

National Industrial Recovery Act (1933)

James G. Pope

When Franklin D. Roosevelt was inaugurated in March 1933, almost 13 million workers—about 25 percent of the workforce—were unemployed. Industrial production was barely half what it had been in 1929. While millions faced starvation, dairy farmers poured fresh milk into the dirt to dramatize the fact that overproduction and cutthroat competition had driven milk prices so low that the farmers could not recover their costs.

To pull the nation out of this crisis, the new administration developed a strategy with two central elements: (1) spreading the available work among larger numbers of employees and (2) increasing the purchasing power of the people. To spread the work available to more workers, the government would limit the number of hours already-employed workers could work, thus reducing the labor performed by these workers and forcing employers to hire new employees from among the unemployed. To increase purchasing power, the government would establish minimum wage rates and launch a public works program (construction projects including schools, hospitals, and bridges) that would pump federal funds into the economy. Instead of restricting hours and wages directly through legislation, the administration proposed to work through private trade associations, which had been unsuccessfully attempting to reduce hours and regulate competition on their own.

Instead of restricting hours and wages directly through legislation, the administration proposed to work through private trade associations, which had been unsuccessfully attempting to reduce hours and regulate competition on their own.

On June 16, 1933, President Franklin D. Roosevelt signed the National Industrial Recovery Act (NIRA) (P.L. 73-67, 48 Stat. 195) into law to counter what the act called the "national emergency" that had resulted in "widespread unemployment and disorganization of industry." The act was intended to encourage

> cooperative action among trade groups, to induce and maintain united action of labor and management under adequate governmental sanctions and supervision, to eliminate unfair competitive practices, to promote the fullest possible utilization of the present productive capacity of industries, ... to increase the consumption of industrial and agricultural products by increasing purchasing power, to reduce and relieve unemployment, [and] to improve standards of labor.

CODES OF FAIR COMPETITION

The NIRA called on private businesses, organized in trade associations, to propose industrial "Codes of Fair Competition" for their industries. Normally, **antitrust** laws would have prohibited such anticompetitive practices, but the act exempted the codes from antitrust restrictions. Upon approval by the president, the codes became legally binding on all participants in the industry concerned. The act gave the president extensive power to shape the codes. If he wished, he could demand that the trade association accept changes as a condition for his approval. In the event that he received no acceptable code for an industry, he could hold hearings and impose a code of his own.

antitrust: laws protecting commerce and trade from monopolistic restraints on competition

Later, the act would be criticized for its alleged lack of effective enforcement mechanisms. But on paper those mechanisms appeared strong. The act commanded the district attorneys of the United States to obtain court orders barring code violations. In addition, violators could be criminally prosecuted and punished by fines of up to $500 per violation. Most impressively, the act empowered the president to require that all businesses in an industry obtain a federal license as a condition of doing business in or affecting interstate commerce. Having done so, he could then revoke the license of any code violator—the business equivalent of a death sentence.

To administer the recovery program, President Roosevelt established the National Recovery Administration (NRA), headed by General Hugh S. Johnson. Early on, Johnson decided to rely on consensus and voluntary consent instead of using the act's mechanisms for imposing and enforcing the fair competition codes. The president embraced this conciliatory policy. Johnson feared that if he attempted to force businesses to cooperate, the courts, which at that time

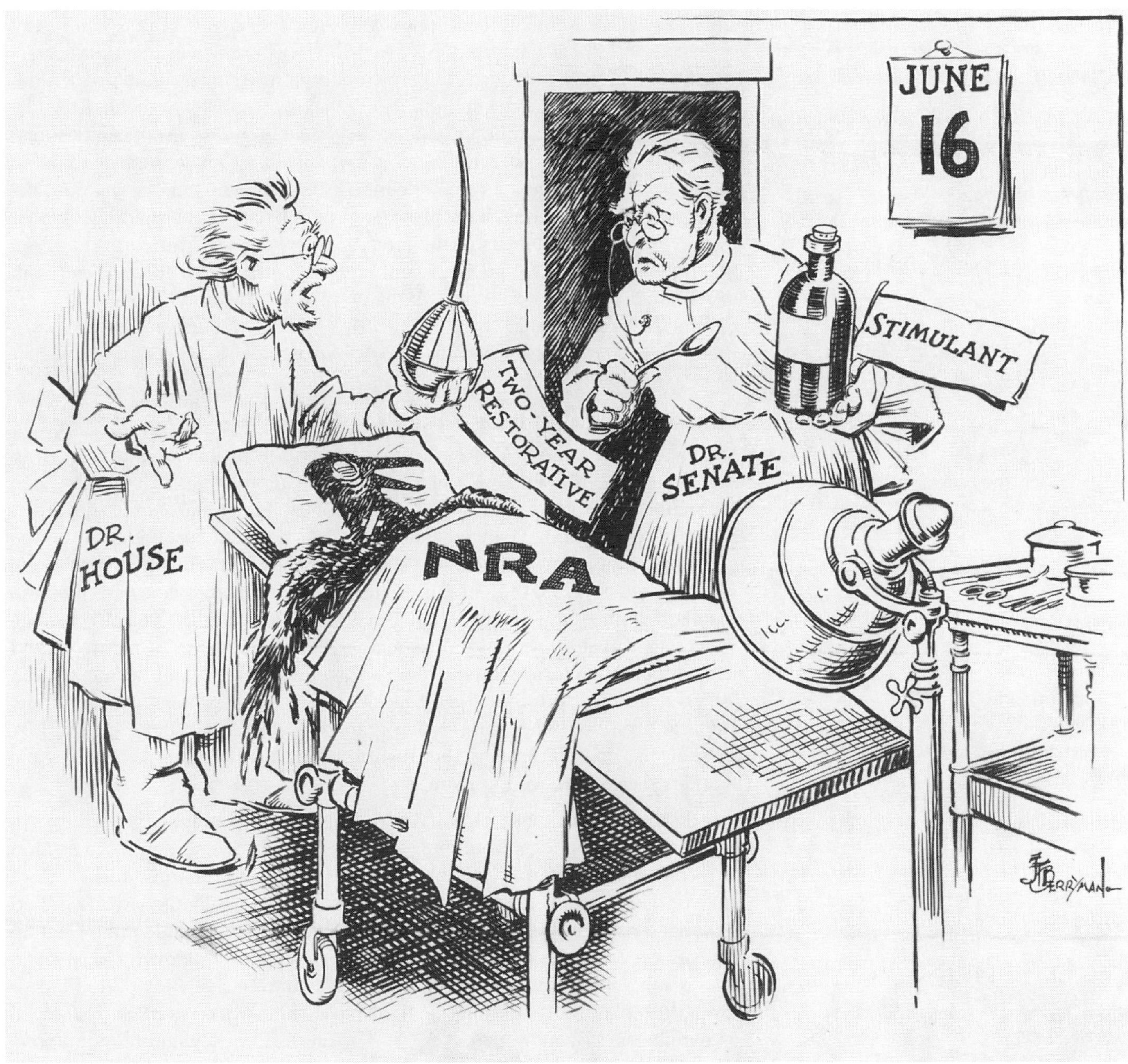

Congress is depicted in this cartoon, published in the Washington Evening Star, *as trying to extend the National Industrial Recovery Act (NIRA) prior to its expiration in June 1935. The National Recovery Administration (NRA) was heavily criticized during its two-year existence (1933–1935); after its emblem, a blue eagle, it is represented here as a beat-up-looking bird. Less than a month before its expiration date, key provisions of the NIRA were declared unconstitutional by the Supreme Court.* (U.S. SENATE COLLECTION, CENTER FOR LEGISLATIVE ARCHIVES)

tended to restrict economic regulation, might declare the act unconstitutional. Instead of using the law to force compliance, Johnson sought to mobilize public opinion in support of the codes. Businesses that complied would display a blue eagle, the emblem of the NRA, on their product labels or in store windows. Violators would be denied this privilege, triggering a consumer **boycott.**

boycott: to refuse to purchase goods or services from a specific company

During the two years of the program's existence, more than 500 codes were enacted. The standard code contained wage and hours provisions, the essential elements of Roosevelt's recovery strategy. In return for accepting these provisions, businesses in many industries insisted on adding production restrictions and price minimums. Unwilling to use the act's compulsory mechanisms, the NRA had no alternative but to go along. In especially disorganized industries, such provisions might have helped to avoid destructive price declines. But historians believe that in most industries these provisions held back recovery and promoted the interests of the largest and most powerful corporations at the expense of others. The maximum hours provisions did force some work sharing, and it is possible that as many as 2 million unemployed workers obtained jobs as a result. On the other hand, it does not appear that the wage minimums were sufficient to offset price increases.

Early on, Johnson decided to rely on consensus and voluntary consent instead of using the act's mechanisms for imposing and enforcing the fair competition codes.

LABOR UNDER THE BLUE EAGLE

Section 7(a) of the NIRA required that each code prohibit employers from interfering with the workers' right to organize unions. This was the first such protection ever to appear in a generally applicable national statute. Regarded by many as a symbolic concession to labor, section 7(a) turned out to be the act's most contentious provision and arguably the most influential in the long run. As of early 1933, the unionized labor was down to fewer than 3 million members from a high of more than 5 million in 1920. But the year 1933 saw a spectacular upsurge in union organizing. In some industries, like coal and garment manufacturing, this recovery was already far along before section 7(a) was enacted. But in the great mass production industries of automobile, steel, and rubber, where previous organizing efforts had been crushed by mass firings and **blacklisting**, the upsurge came only after section 7(a) gave workers the confidence to organize.

blacklist: a list of persons who are to be denied employment

By themselves, these early gains meant little. The unions had yet to win recognition or contracts from their employers. Employers interpreted section 7(a) to permit the establishment of company-dominated unions, and the Roosevelt administration agreed. Many employers also discharged workers and refused to recognize unions in violation of section 7(a), but the administration was reluctant to bring enforcement actions or even to withdraw the blue eagle. As a result, the unions that made lasting gains during the NIRA period did so through **strike** action. For example, the United Mine Workers (UMW) increased its membership by more than 300,000—by far the largest gain of any union—but only after local activists organized a powerful strike movement against opposition not only from the coal operators but also from their own union president, John L. Lewis. Unfortunately for the miners, Lewis, who had hand picked the labor representatives on the NRA coal boards, used the boards to defeat competing unions and to consolidate his dictitorial control over the miners' union. This development contributed to the loss of democracy in other industrial unions, which looked to the mine workers for leadership and support.

strike: to stop work in protest, usually so as to make an employer comply with demands

A provision of the National Industrial Recovery Act required that employers recognize the right of workers to organize. Strikes increased as a result of union organizing, and as this cartoon shows (published July 18, 1934, during the San Francisco General Strike), questions were being asked about whether organized labor was helping the economy recover. (LIBRARY OF CONGRESS, PRINTS AND PHOTOGRAPHS DIVISION)

COURT CHALLENGE AND THE FAILURE OF THE NRA CODES

On May 27, 1935, the day known as "Black Monday" to supporters of the **New Deal**, the U.S. Supreme Court struck down the act's code-making provisions in *A.L.A. Schechter Poultry Corp. v. United States.* Hugh Johnson had been

New Deal: the legislative and administrative program of President Franklin D. Roosevelt designed to promote economic recovery and social reform (1933–1939)

correct to fear the unconstitutionality of forcing industries to accept the codes. After *Schechter,* Congress replaced the NIRA with more narrowly focused statutes. Under these statutes, government agencies, instead of representative boards, carried out regulatory and enforcement functions. Examples include the National Labor Relations Act of 1935, which protected the workers' right to organize unions, and the Fair Labor Standards Act of 1938, which set minimum wages and minimum hours.

Hugh Johnson had been correct to fear the unconstitutionality of forcing industries to accept the codes.

The verdict of historians on the codes has been largely negative. Most agree that they did little to stimulate recovery, and that they tended to benefit large businesses at the expense of consumers and (although this is less clear) small businesses and labor as well. The reasons for failure are disputed. Some historians focus on the absence of strong presidential leadership to counter the demands of special interests and to ensure effective enforcement. Others point to the lack of clear legal directives in the act itself. Such directives could have prevented large corporations from shaping the codes to their benefit. Still others charge that the act embraced an overly ambitious concept of social cooperation and failed to confront the reality that groups with their own special interests tend to conflict with each other. But the act never received a genuine test. From the outset, administrators feared that the Supreme Court would hold the act unconstitutional. To avoid a constitutional confrontation, they refrained from using its strong provisions for shaping and enforcing codes. In a sense, then, the Supreme Court defeated the NIRA long before the *Schechter* decision finished it off.

PUBLIC WORKS

One important piece of the NIRA did survive the *Schechter* decision. The act established an ambitious public works program and created the Public Works Administration (PWA) to administer it. Established barely a decade after the notorious corruption scandals of the Harding Administration (1921–1923), the

New Deal

Alfred L. Brophy

When Franklin Roosevelt ran for president in 1932, the United States was in the midst of the Great Depression. He told delegates at the Democratic Party's nominating convention in Chicago in July 1932 that "I pledge you, I pledge myself, to a new deal for the American people." Roosevelt was elected in a landslide in November and the legislation that followed known as the "New Deal." The legislation was designed to provide jobs and a social safety net, stimulate the economy, and regulate business.

The heyday of the New Deal was 1933–1938. During his first hundred days in office, Congress passed and Roosevelt signed legislation for the National Industrial Recovery Act (NIRA), the Civilian Conservation Corps (CCC), the Tennessee Valley Authority (TVA), the Emergency Farm Mortgage Act, the Federal Emergency Relief Act, the Glass-Stegall Banking Act, and the Agricultural Adjustment Act (AAA). The amount of legislation was staggering and subsequent presidential administrations are always measured against what they do in the "first 100 days." Later New Deal legislation included the National Labor Relations Act, Indian Reorganization Act, Rural Electrification Act, the Gold Standard Act of 1934, Walsh-Healy Act, and the Fair Labor Standards Act. Other legislation established such government agencies as the Security and Exchange Commission, Social Security Administration, the Farm Security Administration, and the Works Progress Administration.

PWA managed to spend more than $6 billion over a period of six years without any serious charges of corruption. Using a combination of direct spending, loans, and grants, the PWA contributed to thousands of construction projects including schools, government buildings, hospitals, subways, and bridges, most of which were built to high standards and many of which are still in service today.

Using a combination of direct spending, loans, and grants, the PWA contributed to thousands of construction projects including schools, government buildings, hospitals, subways, and bridges, most of which were built to high standards and many of which are still in service today.

See also: Agricultural Adjustment Act; Fair Labor Standards Act; Farm Credit Act of 1933; National Labor Relations Act.

BIBLIOGRAPHY

Bellush, Bernard. *The Failure of the NRA.* New York: Norton, 1975.

Brand, Donald R. *Corporatism and the Rule of Law.* Ithaca, NY: Cornell University Press, 1988.

Fine, Sidney. *The Automobile under the Blue Eagle: Labor, Management, and the Automobile Manufacturing Code.* Ann Arbor: University of Michigan Press, 1963.

Hawley, Ellis W. *The New Deal and the Problem of Monopoly: A Study in Economic Ambivalence.* Princeton, NJ: Princeton University Press, 1969.

Irons, Janet. *Testing the New Deal: The General Textile Strike of 1934 in the American South.* Urbana: University of Illinois Press, 2000.

Johnson, Hugh S. *The Blue Eagle from Egg to Earth.* New York: Greenwood Press, 1968.

Schlesinger, Arthur M., Jr. *The Coming of the New Deal.* Boston: Houghton Mifflin, 1959.

National Labor Relations Act (1935)

Thomas C. Kohler

Enacted in 1935, the National Labor Relations Act (NLRA) (49 Stat. 449) is the nation's basic labor relations statute. The act's provisions govern the relationship among employers, employees, and their **labor unions** in the **private sector**. The act also established the National Labor Relations Board (NLRB), an independent federal agency that administers and interprets the statute and enforces its terms.

labor union: an association of workers whose main purpose is to bargain on behalf of workers with employers about the terms and conditions of employment

private sector: the part of the economy that is not controlled by the government

Often described as the "heart" of the act, section 7 of the statute reflects the law's basic purposes. It provides that "employees shall have the right to self-organization, to form, join, or assist labor organizations, to bargain collectively through representatives of their own choosing, and to engage in other concerted activities for the purpose of collective bargaining or other mutual aid and protection," as well as the right to refrain from engaging in any of those activities. Since one of the core purposes of the act is to protect the ability of employees to organize themselves freely and to undertake other activities designed to protect and advance their status, the rights set forth in section 7 are guaranteed to all individuals who come within the statute's definition of being an employee. They are not limited to individuals holding union membership.

THREE ASPECTS OF THE ACT

collective bargaining: a method of negotiations, usually between employees and an employer, in which a representative negotiates on behalf of an organized group of people

In framing the act, Congress did not invent the practices or institutions of **collective bargaining**. Instead, Congress simply adopted a system that had been worked out on a gradual, trial-and-error basis by employers and employees over the decades preceding the act's passage. There are three key principals on which the NLRA rests: 1) the exclusivity principle; 2) the notion of free collective bargaining; and 3) the structural autonomy of the bargaining representative of the employees (in other words, the independence of the employees' labor union from the employer).

Exclusivity Principle. The exclusivity principle is a basic feature of American-style collective bargaining. According to the exclusivity principle, the union representative selected by a majority of employees in a workplace becomes the exclusive (sole) representative of all those employees. The principle is simply an expression of the democratic notion of majority rule. The principle requires the employer to deal with the majority-designated representative of its employees on all issues concerning their "wages, hours, and other terms and conditions of employment." The principle prohibits an employer from making changes in employment terms and conditions without consulting the representative. It also prohibits the employer from attempting to avoid the representative by dealing directly with individuals or groups of employees. The act links privileges with duties: the privileged status that the majority representative enjoys carries with it the legally enforceable duty to represent all employees fairly and even-handedly, regardless of whether they support or are members of the union.

Through the NLRA Congress simply adopted a system that had been worked out on a gradual, trial-and-error basis by employers and employees over the decades preceding the act's passage.

Free Collective Bargaining. Free collective bargaining is the second basic principle of the NLRA. The act leaves the decision whether to organize entirely to employees. Once they do select a bargaining representative, the NLRA requires the employer to bargain in good faith with the representative of the employees. The results of the bargaining process, however, are left wholly to the parties themselves, free from governmental intervention or influence. If the parties are unable to reach an agreement, the law leaves it to market forces—such as the application of economic power through **strikes**, **lockouts**, and other means—to set the terms that will govern the parties' relationship.

strike: to stop work in protest, usually so as to make an employer comply with demands

lockout: the withholding of work from employees by management, to get them to agree to certain terms and conditions

Collective bargaining can best be understood as a private lawmaking system. In the words of the United States Supreme Court, a collective bargaining agreement "is more than a contract; it is a generalized code." This code represents "an effort to erect a system of industrial self-government" through which the entire employer-employee relationship can be "governed by an agreed-upon rule of law." In recognition of the lawmaking character of collective bargaining, the Supreme Court has compared a union's role in the bargaining process with that of a legislature. Not only do the employer and the union make the "law" that governs the employment relationship, they also have the responsibility for administering it. Consequently, collective bargaining agreements typically establish a system to resolve disputes or griev-

The act links privileges with duties: the privileged status that the majority representative enjoys carries with it the legally enforceable duty to represent all employees fairly and even-handedly, regardless of whether they support or are members of the union.

ances through **arbitration,** a process that the union and employer administer together. The arbitration system normally has jurisdiction over nearly every type of dispute that might arise concerning the employer-employee relationship. According to this process, courts do not hear matters that come within the parties' arbitration scheme.

arbitration: the settling of a dispute by a neutral third party

Structural Autonomy. The structural autonomy of the employees' bargaining representative is the third key principle of the collective bargaining system adopted by the NLRA. This principle anchors the system of free collective bargaining. To guarantee employees free choice and freedom of self-organization, the act requires that the employee representative (the union) be solely the agent of the employees and that this representative stand completely independent of the employer. This requirement achieves one of the NLRA's basic goals: to remove barriers to employees' efforts to form autonomous associations, if they so choose, through which employees can engage in the lawmaking process. Section 8(a)(2) of the act forbids employers "to dominate or interfere with the formation or administration of any labor organization or to contribute financial or other support to it." The act broadly defines a "labor organization" as "any organization of any kind, or any agency or employee representation committee or plan, in which employees participate and which exists for the purpose, in whole or part, of dealing with employers concerning grievances, labor disputes, wages, rates of pay, hours of employment, or conditions of work."

HISTORY OF THE ACT AND AMENDMENTS

The version of the NLRA enacted into law in 1935 is often referred to as the Wagner Act, after its chief sponsor, Senator Robert Wagner of New York. The lion's share of the congressional debates over the Wagner Act concerned the language of section 8(a)(2) and the statute's definition of a labor organization. In the years preceding the passage of the NLRA, many large-scale enterprises had appeared and unions had grown. Employers had begun to search for a system of dealing with employees as a group that could act as an alternative to unions and collective bargaining. They came up with a variety of substitute methods for involving workers in managerial decision-making, including semi-autonomous work teams, worker-representatives on company boards, and versions of "unions" sponsored by management. As the participants to the debate understood, the Wagner Act confronted Congress with a clear choice between two distinctly different models of group dealing: on the one hand, self-organized employee associations, and on the other, employer-organized or -sponsored representation schemes.

Congress has made two significant amendments to the NLRA since its enactment. The first set of amendments came through the Taft-Hartley Act in 1947. Among other things, Taft-Hartley added a series of prohibitions against unfair labor practices by unions. These prohibitions largely mirrored those against unfair labor practices by employers that had been set forth in the Wagner Act.

The Taft-Hartley amendments also outlaw most "secondary **boycotts**." In a secondary boycott, a union puts economic pressure on an employer with whom it has no dispute to persuade it to stop doing business with an employer with whom the union does have a dispute. In order to prevent this practice the

boycott: to refuse to purchase goods or services from a specific company amendments call for restricting the audiences to whom unions can make appeals. These amendments also dealt with aspects of strikes and other forms of economic pressure undertaken by unions. Under Taft-Hartley's "secondary boycott provisions," unions could direct their strikes and economic appeals only at certain audiences: employees and customers of the employer with whom the union has its dispute, but not suppliers of the employer.

Like some other provisions of the NLRA, the Taft-Hartley Amendments have been deeply controversial. They suggest strongly that unions and employee associations are a threat to individual status, and thus attempt to contain their activities. Many people oppose this view of unions and the way the amendments affect union activity. The second set of amendments to the NLRA, the Landrum-Griffin Amendments, passed in 1959, consist chiefly of a series of technical amendments designed to close a series of unintended loopholes in the act's Taft-Hartley provisions.

Officials from the National Labor Relations Board watch as employees of the Jones and Laughlin Steel Mill in Pittsburgh, Pennsylvania, vote on whether the Steel Workers Organizing Committee (SWOC) will become their sole bargaining agency, May 20, 1937. The SWOC became the United Steelworkers of America in 1942. (©CORBIS)

JUDICIAL OPINIONS AND THE NLRA

The **commerce clause** of the U.S. Constitution, which gives Congress the power to regulate trade among the states, serves as the constitutional basis for the NLRA. The constitutionality of the statute was sustained by the United States Supreme Court in its 1937 opinion in *National Labor Relations Board v. Jones & Loughlin Steel Corp.* Subsequently, the Court has had many opportunities to construe the statute. One of the most significant occasions came through the set of cases known as the Steelworkers' Trilogy. These cases produced a series of unusually challenging opinions on the issues of statutory interpretation, **separation of powers**, and **federalism**. The Court in these opinions began to fashion a body of law to govern the enforcement of agreements to arbitrate labor disputes.

Commerce Clause: the provision of the U.S. Constitution (Article I, section 8, clause 3) that gives Congress exclusive powers over interstate commerce—the buying, selling, or exchanging of goods between states

separation of powers: the division of the government into three branches: legislative, executive, and judicial, each with distinct powers. This separation supports a system of checks and balances

federalism: a system of political organization; a union formed of separate states or groups that are ruled by a central authority on some matters but are otherwise permitted to govern themselves independently

The Court has heard a second significant line of cases that produced opinions on the NLRA and its amendments. These cases made it necessary for the Court to 1) adjust First Amendment freedom of association issues arising out of the act's requirement that even employees who do not wish to belong to the union are exclusively represented by it, and 2) to resolve conflicts between the act's Taft-Hartley restrictions on union communicative activities and First Amendment freedom of speech guarantees. The union's duty of fair representation was established in the Supreme Court's landmark 1944 opinion in *Steele v. Louisville & Nashville Ry. Co.*, a case that involved discrimination practiced by a union against African-American employees it represented.

A subsequent line of cases involving duty of fair representation concerned the scope of a union's duty to represent individuals in grievances. The first such case produced the Court's 1967 *Vaca v. Sipes* opinion. Now largely resolved, this line of cases led to an unprecedented degree of substantive court review of union decisionmaking. Another very significant line of cases began with the Supreme Court's 1958 opinion in *NLRB v. Wooster Division of Borg-Warner*. There, the Supreme Court held that the NLRA makes a distinction between mandatory and permissive topics of bargaining. A mandatory topic settles an aspect of the relationship between the employer and employees. The parties must bargain over such topics and may use strikes, lockouts, and other economic pressure tactics concerning them. In contrast, the parties may discuss a permissive topic, but they are not required to do so. Moreover, they are forbidden to use economic pressure to achieve consensus over a permissive topic. In some important ways, the mandatory-permissive distinction contradicts the notion of free collective bargaining, and allows the courts a role in a process from which Congress had excluded them.

SOCIAL CONSEQUENCES OF NLRA

By any measure, the NLRA represents one of the landmarks of federal legislation. In passing the act, Congress deliberately opted for a system that would involve minimal government intervention in the employer-employee relationship. This is in sharp contrast to the course taken by the rest of the industrialized world. It is no accident that as the practice of collective bargaining has declined, the level of government regulation and intervention in the employer-employee relationship has substantially increased. In his analysis of the American political system, Alexis de Tocqueville, the great nineteenth-century

In some important ways, the mandatory-permissive distinction contradicts the notion of free collective bargaining, and allows the courts a role in a process from which Congress had excluded them.

French observer of democracy, insisted that for democracies, progress in all areas, including the future of self-rule itself, would depend on the "science of association"—the ways in which groups within democratic societies associate and work together. NLRA's greatest social contribution is the opportunity—and responsibility—it gives to employees to organize themselves and to determine and administer the law that most directly affects the day-to-day conditions of their lives.

See also: FAIR LABOR STANDARDS ACT; TAFT-HARTLEY ACT.

BIBLIOGRAPHY

Derber, Milton. *The American Idea of Industrial Democracy, 1865-1965*. Urbana: University of Illinois Press, 1970.

Dubofsky, Melvyn. *The State and Labor in Modern America*. Chapel Hill: University of North Carolina Press, 1994.

Dulles, Foster Rhea, and Melvyn Dubofsky. *Labor in America: A History,* 4th ed. Arlington Heights, IL: Harlan Davidson, 1984.

Freeman, Richard B., and James L. Medoff. *What Do Unions Do?* New York: Basic Books, 1984.

NATIONAL PARK SERVICE ACT (1916)

Brian E. Gray

On December 19, 1913, President Woodrow Wilson signed the Raker Act, which authorized San Francisco to construct a dam at the mouth of Hetch Hetchy Valley in the Tuolumne River watershed of Yosemite National Park. The Raker Act was preceded by more than a decade of detailed analysis of the city's need for a supplemental supply of water as well as an exhaustive analysis of the alternative sources. Congress passed the act following six months of bitter debate. On one side were progressives, who favored municipal control of water and electric utilities, and conservationists, who believed that the public lands should be used to produce the greatest good for the greatest number of people. On the other side were the preservationists, a new environmental constituency led by John Muir and the Sierra Club. Preservationists argued that the national parks should be preserved and protected for the public's enjoyment and appreciation of scenic beauty and natural wonders. The Hetch Hetchy controversy was the last battle of John Muir's life, and he was devastated by the loss. Friends described him as isolated and despondent. From his home in Martinez, California, Muir wrote to Vernon Kellogg of Palo Alto on December 27, 1913: "As to the loss of the Sierra Park Valley it's hard to bear. The destruction of the charming groves and gardens, the finest in all California, goes to my heart. But in spite of Satan & Co. some sort of compensation must surely come out of this dark damn-dam-damnation." Muir died the following December.

John Muir (1838–1914)

John Muir (1838–1914) was a naturalist who spent a great deal of time studying botanical specimens. From 1880, he campaigned for the establishment of Yosemite National Park, for the preservation of forests, and against the Hetch Hetchy project. Muir was a founder of the Sierra Club. Contemporary protesters adopted his motto against dams, "Free the rivers," and painted it on the Hetch Hetchy Dam in 1987.

THE NEED FOR A NATIONAL PARK POLICY

The Hetch Hetchy debate highlighted two flaws in the prevailing philosophy of national park management. First, although Congress had reserved several million acres of land from the public domain to create fourteen national parks—including Yellowstone (1872), Yosemite (1890), Sequoia and General Grant (1890), Mount Rainier (1899), Crater Lake (1902), Mesa Verde (1906), Glacier (1910), and Rocky Mountain (1915)—it had not set forth a coherent national park policy. For example, Congress established Yellowstone National Park to protect its geothermal resources and wildlife; Yosemite to preserve its granite valleys, meadows, and high peaks; Sequoia to protect its redwood forests; and Mesa Verde for its archaeological resources.

Preservationists argued that the national parks should be preserved and protected for the public's enjoyment and appreciation of scenic beauty and natural wonders.

Second, Congress had failed to answer a variety of important questions about national park management and use:

- Hotels and roads were constructed in Yellowstone, Yosemite, and Glacier, whereas other parks remained relatively undeveloped. Should the special features of the parks be preserved in their natural state or improved for the benefit of tourists?
- Hunting was authorized in Yellowstone. In Mount Rainier National Park, prospectors could stake new mining claims and were allowed to cut timber as needed to supply operations. Sheep and cattle were driven from the San Joaquin Valley each summer to feast on the meadows and other forage in Yosemite Valley and Tuolumne Meadows. Does the reservation of land for use as a national park necessarily rule out other uses?
- The Hetch Hetchy controversy had focused Congress's attention on the tension between preservation and conservation more than had any previous conflict. Is it possible to protect the scenic wonders for which the national parks were created while also putting the resources of the parks to use to produce the greatest good for the greatest number?

CREATION OF THE NATIONAL PARK SYSTEM

In an effort to answer at least some of these questions, Congress enacted the National Park Service Act of 1916 (39 Stat. 535), which created the national park system. Although Muir did not live to see it, this act partly compensated for the loss of Hetch Hetchy Valley and turned his vision of protected lands into reality. The act gathered into a single system the fourteen national parks and twenty-one national monuments and created a National Park Service to manage that system. In defining the land and resource management responsibilities of the Park Service, Congress adopted the preservationists' vision for the national parks, declaring that the fundamental purpose of the national park system is "to conserve the scenery and the natural and historic objects and the wild life therein and to provide for the enjoyment of the same in such manner and by such means as will leave them unimpaired for the enjoyment of future generations."

In defining the land and resource management responsibilities of the Park Service, Congress adopted the preservationists' vision for the national parks, declaring that the fundamental purpose of the national park system is "to conserve the scenery and the natural and historic objects and the wild life therein and to provide for the enjoyment of the same in such manner and by such means as will leave them unimpaired for the enjoyment of future generations."

Over the next two decades, Congress significantly expanded the national park system, adding, among others, Mount McKinley (now Denali National Park, 1917); the Grand Canyon, Acadia, and Zion (1919); Bryce Canyon (1924); the Great Smoky Mountains and Shenandoah (1926); Grand Teton (1929); Carlsbad Caverns (1930); Isle Royale (1931); the Everglades

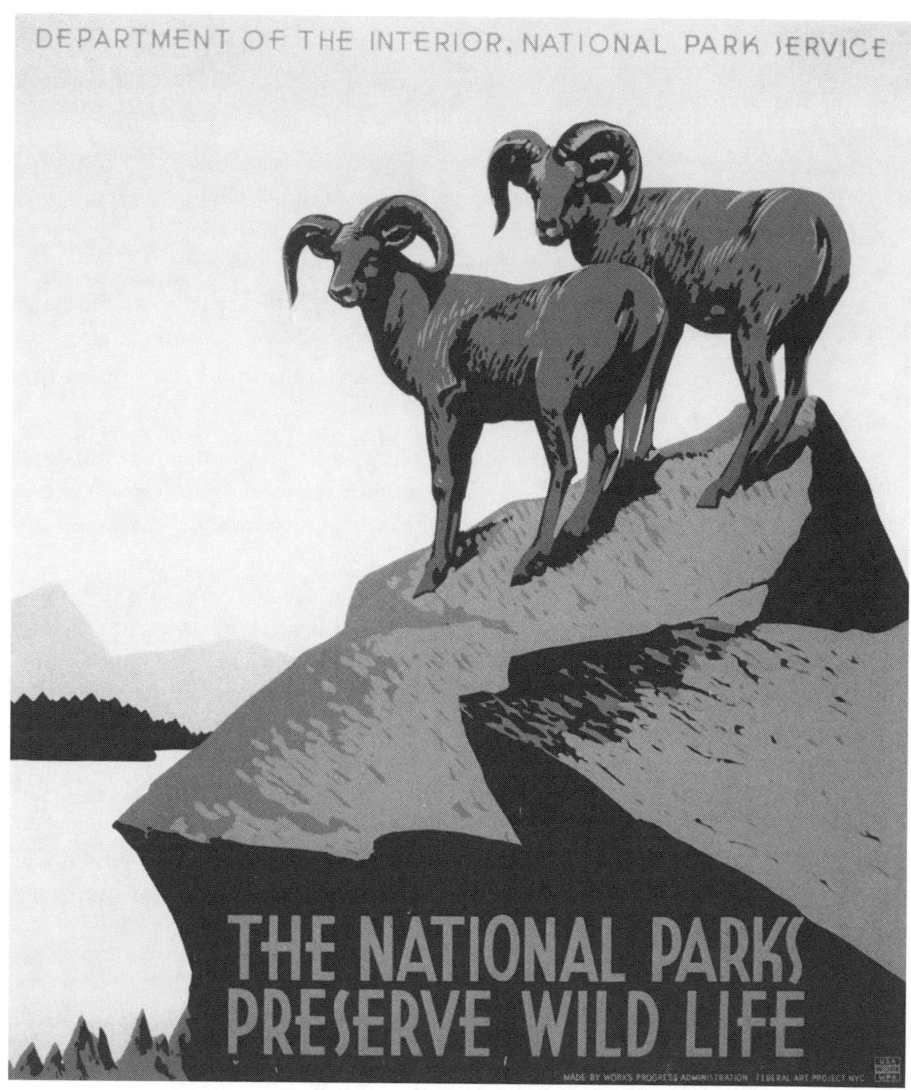

A 1939 poster, created by the Works Progress Administration Federal Art Project, promoting travel to National Parks. (LIBRARY OF CONGRESS, PRINTS AND PHOTOGRAPHS DIVISION)

(1934); Big Bend (1935); and Olympic (1938). Under the leadership of its first directors, Stephen Mather and Horace Albright, the National Park Service managed its lands for the protection and preservation of the unique features that caused the lands to be set aside in the first place. Although many parks remained open to preexisting activities such as grazing and mining, neither the Park Service nor Congress was willing to authorize new uses that would be inconsistent with the preservationists' goals.

Although many parks remained open to preexisting activities such as grazing and mining, neither the Park Service nor Congress was willing to authorize new uses that would be inconsistent with the preservationists' goals.

THE PARK SERVICE TODAY

Today, the National Park Service manages 383 parks, monuments, recreation areas, battlefield preserves, memorials, historic sites, lakeshores, seashores, scenic trails, and wild and scenic river corridors—more than 80 million acres of land. The national park system extends from the islands of Acadia

National Park in Maine to the Hawaii Volcanoes in the Pacific, and from the Gates of the Arctic in Alaska to Florida's Everglades. It includes North America's highest peak (Denali) and its lowest elevation (Death Valley). The system embraces the vast and remote wilderness of the Alaska parks and preserves; the summer crowds of Yellowstone, Yosemite, and the Grand Canyon; the urban refuges of the Golden Gate and New York Gateway recreation areas; the still waters of Crater Lake; the powerboats of Lake Mead and Lake Powell; the monoliths of Mount Rainier and Devil's Tower; the remnants of the Anasazi; the symbols of the Revolution at Valley Forge and Philadelphia; and the solemn memorials of Gettysburg, Arlington, and the Capitol Mall.

Despite tensions and management conflicts, the national parks system is an essential American institution, evoking and preserving our grandest mountains, most majestic canyons, verdant forests, and cherished cultural artifacts.

The National Park Service has not yet resolved the tensions that were present at its creation. Traffic jams in Yosemite Valley and the South Rim of the Grand Canyon, snowmobiles in Yellowstone and Grand Teton, and stresses on fragile ecosystems in Mesa Verde and Carlsbad increasingly pose conflicts between the twin goals of the National Park Service Act—to preserve the parks and their natural resources while also providing for their use and enjoyment. Clear cuts on national forest land along the edge of Redwood National Park, oil exploration adjacent to Arches, and pollution flowing into the Everglades expose the parks as "helpless giants"—affected by human activities outside their borders but lacking clear legal authority to protect their lands and resources. And the Park Service has struggled with the question of whether the national parks should provide accommodations and entertainment similar to those found in the communities from which their visitors have come (hotels, fast food, and structured recreational activities, for example) or instead offer a unique wilderness (or at least quasi-wilderness) experience—what Professor Joseph Sax, a national park scholar, has called "Mountains without Handrails."

Yet despite these tensions and management conflicts, the national parks system is an essential American institution, evoking and preserving our grandest mountains, most majestic canyons, verdant forests, and cherished cultural artifacts. To quote Wallace Stegner, one of the American West's greatest writers, our national parks remain "the best idea we ever had."

See also: NATIONAL HISTORIC PRESERVATION ACT; YELLOWSTONE NATIONAL PARK ACT.

BIBLIOGRAPHY

Ise, John. *Our National Parks Policy: A Critical History*. Washington, DC: Resources for the Future, 1961.

Nash, Roderick. *Wilderness and the American Mind,* 3d ed. New Haven, CT: Yale University Press, 1982.

Runte, Alfred. *National Parks: The American Experience,* 3d ed. Lincoln: University of Nebraska Press, 1992.

Sax, Joseph L. *Mountains Without Handrails: Reflections on the National Parks*. Ann Arbor: University of Michigan Press, 1980.

Simon, David J., ed. *Our Common Lands: Defending the National Parks*. Washington, DC: Island Press, 1988.

Stegner, Wallace. *Marking the Sparrow's Fall*. New York: Henry Holt, 1998.

National Prohibition Act (1919)

David E. Kyvig

The National Prohibition Act (P.L. 66-66, 41 Stat. 305), also known as the Volstead Act, was adopted by Congress in 1919 to implement the recently ratified Eighteenth Amendment to the Constitution of the United States. For nearly a century, **temperance** crusaders had attempted to impose abstinence from alcohol on American society, and the Volstead Act became the fullest expression of their effort. The act became as well known as the constitutional amendment on which it rested. In April 1933 Congress relaxed the terms of the Volstead Act, and for many Americans this represented the end of National Prohibition even before states completed the repeal of the Eighteenth Amendment eight months later.

temperance: moderation in or abstinence from the consumption of alcohol

The Eighteenth Amendment approved by Congress in December 1917 and eventually ratified by well over three-fourths of the states declared a national ban on the manufacture, sale, transportation, importation, and exportation of intoxicating liquors for beverage purposes to take effect one year after the amendment's **ratification**. A definition of intoxicating beverages as well as arrangements for enforcing their prohibition remained for Congress to establish. Because of the amendment's rapid ratification, completed January 16, 1919, federal legislators had reason to believe that the American public would welcome strong provisions for enforcement of Prohibition.

ratify: to formally approve; three-fourths of all states in the Union must approve an amendment for it become part of the Constitution

PROVISIONS OF THE ACT

Representative Andrew J. Volstead, a Minnesota Republican and chairman of the House Judiciary Committee, proposed that Congress adopt a Prohibition enforcement act. Both Volstead and Wayne Wheeler, legal counsel for the Anti-Saloon League of America, later claimed authorship of the act. Many of the act's provisions reflected standard Anti-Saloon League thinking. The first section of the act continued temporary wartime prohibition until the Eighteenth Amendment could go into effect. Preventing an orgy of drinking as soldiers returned from World War I was a prime Anti-Saloon League concern. The third section of the act regulated industrial and scientific use of alcohol. To prevent its diversion to drinkers, industrial alcohol was to be denatured, a process that renders it unfit for human consumption. The second section of the Volstead Act focused directly on implementing the constitutional beverage liquor ban.

median: the middle value in a distribution above and below which lie an equal number of values

forfeiture: the loss of something (property, assets) as a result of breaking the law

The Volstead Act's central section concentrated on preventing the manufacture, sale, and distribution of beverage alcohol. Violations were to be punished by fines of up to $1,000 (at time about two-thirds of **median** annual family income), imprisonment for up to six months, and **forfeiture** of vehicles used in the commission of the crime. However, the law did not directly forbid the consumption of intoxicating beverages. In fact, the Volstead Act specifically exempted wine used for religious sacraments and liquor prescribed by a physician as medicine. Over Anti-Saloon League objections, Congress also permitted continued private possession of alcoholic beverages purchased before Prohibition took effect as well as the home fermentation of fruit juices to produce cider or wine for personal use.

For nearly a century, temperance crusaders had attempted to impose abstinence from alcohol on American society, and the Volstead Act became the fullest expression of their effort.

Some members of Congress were determined to make the United States "wet," as Representative John Philip Hill (R-Md.) demonstrates, 1926. (LIBRARY OF CONGRESS, PRINTS AND PHOTOGRAPHS DIVISION)

The Eighteenth Amendment granted states concurrent power with the federal government to enforce the so-called "dry law," which meant that states could independently enforce an equivalent or more strict Prohibition but could not relax the terms of the law within their borders. Many Prohibition sympathizers thought it desirable to limit expansion of federal enforcement authority. Congress, therefore, entrusted to state and local police much of the responsibility for upholding the liquor ban. Federal enforcement authority was delegated primarily to the Treasury Department's Internal Revenue Service because of its experience in dealing with the liquor industry. Although the Volstead Act established only a small federal policing unit, the 1,500-member Prohibition Bureau was at the time the largest federal law-enforcement agency ever created. The

However, the law did not directly forbid the consumption of intoxicating beverages.

bureau's modest $2 million budget as well as the $100,000 set aside for the Justice Department to prosecute violations reflected congressional assumptions that states would embrace their concurrent power and implementing national Prohibition would not greatly burden the federal government.

DEFINING AN INTOXICATING BEVERAGE

The most notable feature of the Volstead Act was its definition of intoxicating liquor. During the long campaign for the Eighteenth Amendment much attention had focused on "demon rum," an umbrella term for all varieties of distilled spirits (such as whiskey, gin, rum, and vodka) with high alcoholic content. Distilled spirits were also known as "hard liquor," as opposed to fermented beverages such as wine and beer, which have a much lower alcohol content. Producers of fermented beverages, in particular commercial brewers and wine makers, thought they might escape the ban and even prosper from the elimination of competition from hard liquor.

veto: when the president returns a bill to Congress with a statement of objections

Andrew Volstead's measure, however, defined as intoxicating any beverage containing more than 0.5 percent alcohol. President Woodrow Wilson, who thought that the public would be more willing to give up distilled liquor if permitted to continue drinking beer, regarded the standard as too severe. He **vetoed** the National Prohibition Act, objecting in particular to the continuation of wartime prohibition after hostilities had ended. But Congress was determined to enforce a total ban on even mildly intoxicating beverages. By a vote of 175 to 55 in the House on October 27, 1919, and 65 to 20 in the Senate on the following day, Congress overrode the presidential veto. The Volstead Act took effect immediately, even before the Eighteenth Amendment went into force on January 17, 1920.

President Woodrow Wilson, who thought that the public would be more willing to give up distilled liquor if permitted to continue drinking beer, regarded the standard as too severe.

Al Capone

During Prohibition, the bootleg distribution of "demon rum" became a multimillion-dollar business, making notorious gangsters into very rich men. The most famous of these was Al Capone, a ruthless criminal whose larger-than-life persona and generosity toward those in need nevertheless endeared him to the public. Based in Chicago, Capone commanded a powerful organization that stretched as far as New York, dominating the bootleg liquor trade by bribing politicians and police and murdering rivals. He was the acknowledged mastermind behind the St. Valentine's Day Massacre, in which his partner, Jack McGurn, took revenge on a rival who had tried to kill him. Disguising his men as police officers, McGurn staged a raid on the rival's bootleg operation and slaughtered seven members of the rival's gang, who had thought they were being arrested. The resulting notoriety brought attention from the administration of President Herbert Hoover and the Justice Department, which selected Eliot Ness to bring Capone to justice. As Ness made strides against Capone, the gangster counterattacked with more bribery and violence. By the time Ness had secured indictments against Capone and his associates for Prohibition violations, the Treasury Department had also obtained indictments for tax evasion, and it was on the latter charge that Capone was eventually convicted and sentenced to eleven years in prison. When he was released, after serving eight years of his sentence, Capone's organization and health were both in ruins, and he died of syphilis in 1947. The power of his image remained undiminished, however, and he was immortalized in books, movies, and comic strips as the iconic American gangster.

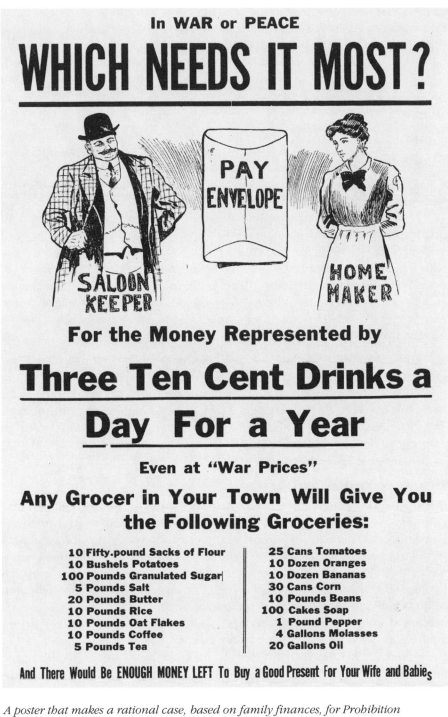

A poster that makes a rational case, based on family finances, for Prohibition (c. 1917–1918). (LIBRARY OF CONGRESS, PRINTS AND PHOTOGRAPHS DIVISION)

ENFORCING THE ACT

In the *National Prohibition Cases* (1920), the U.S. Supreme Court ruled that, because the Eighteenth Amendment granted the states concurrent power of enforcement, it also required states to adhere to the federal definition of intoxicating beverage. However, the amendment did not require states to take any particular enforcement action. With the exception of Maryland, states did at first participate in the policing effort, but the burden of Prohibition enforcement increasingly fell upon the federal government much more than the creators of the Volstead Act had anticipated. Resistance to the liquor ban grew, particularly in urban areas where recent immigrants as well as middle- and upper-class drinkers proved unwilling to abandon alcohol. Especially as some state enforcement efforts slackened, obtaining compliance with the Volstead Act became increasingly difficult.

By the late 1920s neither the Prohibition Bureau nor cooperating state and local law enforcement officials proved able to cope with the volume of Volstead Act violations.

By the late 1920s neither the Prohibition Bureau nor cooperating state and local law enforcement officials proved able to cope with the volume of Volstead Act violations. By 1929 over 500,000 federal arrests had been made under the Volstead Act. Overall, the annual volume of federal criminal cases had quadrupled since 1916, and nearly two-thirds of new prosecutions involved Volstead Act violations. Federal courts found themselves unequipped to deal with the number of slow and costly jury trials and so provided "bargain days" on which defendants agreed to plead guilty in exchange for a light fine or short sentence. While two-thirds of convicted Volstead Act violators were merely fined, by 1930 federal prisons were filled to nearly twice their capacity, and the overflow crowded state prisons and county jails.

With violation of the Volstead Act becoming more commonplace, Congress in 1929 adopted the so-called Jones Five-and-Ten Law, increasing penalties for first offenses to five years in prison, a $10,000 fine, or both. Even these severe consequences did not induce compliance with the law, and thus pressures on the judicial and prison systems increased. As the nation entered the **Great Depression**, Volstead Act enforcement began to drop off.

Great Depression: the longest and most severe economic depression in American history (1929–1939); its effects were felt throughout the world

ENDING NATIONAL PROHIBITION

In 1932 the Democratic Party platform endorsed the repeal of Prohibition. In February of 1933, following a sweeping Democratic victory the previous November, a bipartisan two-thirds majority of the outgoing Congress proposed a repeal amendment. Before any states had acted to ratify the amendment, the new Seventy-Third Congress overwhelmingly endorsed a proposal by the Franklin Roosevelt administration to change the Volstead Act definition of intoxicating beverage to allow manufacture and sale of beer at a low 3.2 percent alcohol. Put into effect on April 7, 1933, the Beer Bill was celebrated as the end of the Volstead Act's heavy-handed "bone dry" Prohibition. On December 5, 1933, the Twenty-First Amendment was ratified, finishing the dismantling of the National Prohibition Act.

See also: MANN ACT.

BIBLIOGRAPHY

Blocker, Jack E., Jr. *American Temperance Movements: Cycles of Reform.* Boston: Twayne, 1989.

Hallwas, John E. *The Bootlegger: A Story of Small Town America.* Urbana: University of Illinois Press, 1998.

Hamm, Richard F. *Shaping the Eighteenth Amendment: Temperance Reform Legal Culture, and the Polity, 1880–1920.* Chapel Hill: University of North Carolina Press, 1995.

Hamm, Richard F. "Short Euphorias Followed by Long Hangovers: Unintended Consequences of the Eighteenth and Twenty-first Amendments." *Unintended Consequences of Constitutional Amendment.* Ed. David E. Kyvig. Athens: University of Georgia Press, 2000.

Kyvig, David E. *Repealing National Prohibition,* 2d ed. Kent, OH: Kent State University Press, 2000.

Murchison, Kenneth M. *Federal Criminal Law Doctrines: The Forgotten Influence of National Prohibition.* Durham, NC: Duke University Press, 1994.

Pegram, Thomas R. *Battling Demon Rum: The Struggle for a Dry America.* Chicago: Ivan R. Dee, 1998.

Solomon, Rayman L. "Regulating the Regulators: Prohibition Enforcement in the Seventh Circuit." *In Law, Alcohol, and Order: Perspectives on National Prohibition.,* ed. David E. Kyvig. Westport, CT: Greenwood, 1985.

NATIONAL RECLAMATION ACT OF 1902

Kyle A. Loring

On June 17, 1902, Congress enacted the National Reclamation Act (P.L. 57-161, 32 Stat. 388), also known as the Newland Act, to "[a]ppopriat[e] the receipts from the sale and disposal of public lands in certain States and Territories to the construction of irrigation works for the reclamation of arid lands." With this act, Congress intended to harness the intermittent precipitation in seventeen western states and use it to encourage individual families to settle in the West by converting arid federal land into agriculturally productive land. The act created a Reclamation Service with the technical expertise to construct monumental water projects to irrigate the West, and established a Reclamation Fund to finance these expensive ventures. A century later, with every major river but the Yellowstone dammed, the Bureau of Reclamation has been forced to shift its focus from massive construction projects to the operation and maintenance of these facilities.

With this act, Congress intended to harness the intermittent precipitation in seventeen western states and use it to encourage individual families to settle in the West by converting arid federal land into agriculturally productive land.

BEFORE THE RECLAMATION ACT

In 1888, Francis G. Newlands arrived in Nevada and began to advocate for an irrigation system that would divert water from the Truckee and Carson Rivers to local family farms. Newlands suggested that his proposal could be funded through the sale of federal lands. When Nevada elected him to the House of Representatives, he worked with Frederick Newell, the chief hydrographer of the U.S. Geological Survey (USGS), to pursue this idea on a national scale.

During this period, demand for water from expanding western farms began to exceed the supply from intermittent precipitation, and farmers sought to capture rain and snow runoff as an alternative source for water. When their private and state-sponsored irrigation programs failed due to inadequate funding and technical expertise, these farmers pressed the federal government for aid. Because the federal government had already become involved itself in other local infrastructure subsidies for roads, river naviga-

Notwithstanding eastern and midwestern opposition, Congress passed the Reclamation Act when western legislators filibustered and delayed votes on eastern rivers and harbors projects.

tion, harbors, canals, and railroads, both Republican and Democratic candidates believed they could convince Congress to aid irrigation programs, and so campaigned on pro-irrigation platforms. Notwithstanding eastern and midwestern opposition, Congress passed the Reclamation Act when western legislators filibustered and delayed votes on eastern rivers and harbors projects.

PASSAGE OF THE RECLAMATION ACT

As initially promulgated by Congress, the Reclamation Act encouraged western settlement by selling federal lands to individual farmers and then supplying them with inexpensive water, for which the farmers would repay the government. These payments and the proceeds from land sales would be placed in a Reclamation Fund to finance the construction of the water projects. In addition, water sales were to be limited to those individuals farming one hundred and sixty or fewer acres and residing on the land. By the start of the twenty-first century, however, the acreage limitation had been relaxed and the residency requirement had been abolished completely.

The Reclamation Act created the United States Reclamation Service as the agency to implement Congress's mandate, and the Reclamation Fund as the financial mechanism that would finance the program. The Reclamation Service investigated potential water projects in each of the seventeen western states with federal lands. The Reclamation Service later became the independent Bureau of Reclamation (BOR) within the Department of the Interior.

Congress created the Reclamation Fund on the premise that fees collected from water purchased from reclamation projects would create a self-sustaining endeavor, repaying construction and operation costs. The projects' immense construction costs soon proved the premise unrealistic. For example, earlier self-supporting projects created by local initiatives had cost less than twenty dollars an acre. The federal reclamation projects, by contrast, cost an average of eighty-five dollars an acre. Thus, the farmers' share of the federal expenses proved too great a sum for their repayment.

DEVELOPMENTS UNDER THE RECLAMATION ACT

Congress responded to farmers' inability to pay water costs first with extended repayment periods, and then a decreased obligation to repay the funds. In 1926, Congress passed the Omnibus Adjustment Act to extend the terms of repayment from ten annual installments to forty annual payments. Then, when Congress realized that farmers still could not repay the project costs, it passed the Reclamation Project Act of 1939 that conditioned repayment only on a farmer's "ability to pay."

When Congress realized that farmers still could not repay the project costs, it passed the Reclamation Project Act of 1939 that conditioned repayment only on a farmer's "ability to pay."

This lack of repayment by farmers forced Congress to look elsewhere to fund the reclamation projects. In June 1910 Congress advanced $20 million from general treasury funds and $5 million in March 1931 for these projects. After that time, appropriations for individual projects drew funding from both the Reclamation Fund and the general treasury fund. Additional funding sources included receipts from the Mineral Leasing Act, proceeds from the lease and sale of products from withdrawn lands, and money from the sale of surplus lands.

During its heyday, the BOR erected such impressive public works as Hoover Dam, Shasta Dam, and Grand Coulee Dam, each the largest concrete structure in the world at the time of its construction.

During its heyday, the BOR erected such impressive public works as Hoover Dam, Shasta Dam, and Grand Coulee Dam, each the largest concrete structure in the world at the time of its construction. These dams provided benefits including electricity production, irrigation, water storage, flood control, and public recreation in the form of fishing, water skiing, and swimming. In raising these monuments to human ingenuity, however, BOR subtly shifted its mission from constructing dams for society's benefit to merely constructing dams. Led primarily by BOR efforts, 75,000 public and private dams were built in the United States during the twentieth century. President William J. Clinton's secretary of the interior, Bruce Babbitt, in assessing this figure, recognized that BOR had gone too far, noting that it

The Roosevelt Dam on the Salt River, Arizona, 1915. Construction of the Roosevelt Dam, the first dam built as part of the Salt River Project, began in 1903. The Salt River Project was the first major undertaking under the Reclamation Act of 1902. Seen behind the dam is Roosevelt Lake, which holds enough water to irrigate fields for two years, even without any rainfall. (© AP/WIDE WORLD PHOTOS)

This man holds sugar beets grown with irrigation from the Klamath Reclamation Project in Oregon, 1910. (© AP/WIDE WORLD PHOTOS)

amounted to an average of one dam a day, including weekends, built since the signing of the Declaration of Independence.

Since the 1970s, the dam-building fervor has slowed dramatically. The last major authorization for a project occurred in the late 1960s. Since then, the combined effects of the Administrative Procedure Act (1946) and the National Environmental Policy Act (1969) have forced federal agencies to justify economically and environmentally their major projects. With cost overruns of completed water projects exceeding estimates by at least 50 percent, and with major disruption as well as destruction of riparian ecosystems, such justifications have not been easily found. One study has even pointed to dam construction as a major factor in the degradation of aquatic habitats, with 67 percent of freshwater mussels, 64 percent of crayfish, 36 percent of fish, and 20 percent of dragonfly species extinct, imperiled, or vulnerable as a result.

Even though the Reclamation Act has led to unintended adverse economic and environmental impacts, it continues to serve as the basis for the operation and maintenance of current facilities. Indicating awareness that some of its projects no longer serve useful purposes, a congressional committee in 1994 even discussed the demolition of Glen Canyon Dam. Thus, the BOR's mission may realign itself with Congress's initial goals for the agency, that of constructing water projects where necessary to best serve all interests involved.

Even though the Reclamation Act has led to unintended adverse economic and environmental impacts, it continues to serve as the basis for the operation and maintenance of current facilities.

See also: National Environmental Policy Act; Surface Mining Control and Reclamation Act.

BIBLIOGRAPHY

"The Bureau of Reclamation: A Brief History." Bureau of Reclamation. <http://www.usbr.gov/history/borhist.htm>.

Center for Columbia River History. "Reclamation Act/Newlands Act of 1902." <http://www.ccrh.org/comm/umatilla/primary/newlands.htm>.

Collier, Michael, et al. "Dams and Rivers: A Primer on the Downstream Effects of Dams." *U.S.G.S.* Circular 1126 (1996).

Devine, Robert S. "The Trouble with Dams." *Atlantic Monthly* 276, no. 2 (1995): 64–74.

Fernley Nevada Chamber of Commerce. "The National Reclamation Act of 1902: The Newlands Irrigation Project." <http://www.fernleynvchamber.com/Water%20History.htm>.

Klein, Christine A. "On Dams and Democracy," *Oregon Law Review* 78, no. 3 (1999): 641–93.

McCully, Patrick. *Silenced Rivers, the Ecology and Politics of Large Dams*. London: Zed Books, 1996.

National Security Act of 1947

Lynne K. Zusman and Neil S. Helfand

The United States emerged victorious from World War II but with the realization that a major reorganization of its national security policy was essential. Japan's surprise attack on Pearl Harbor in 1941, which dealt a crippling blow to the nation and forced our entry into the war, highlighted the need for greater intelligence resources and coordination to prevent similar future disasters. Furthermore, during the course of the war our ground, sea, and air forces operated autonomously, with insufficient communication between them and without uni-

The United States emerged victorious from World War II but with the realization that a major reorganization of its national security policy was essential.

fied direction. Coordination of their operations by a united department became essential. Another important consequence of the war was the growth in power of the Soviet Union, which posed an ever greater threat to U.S. security. To cope with security challenges, the United States would need to modernize its organizational structure. The president would have to be supplied with the information necessary to make informed decisions to deal with future threats.

During the war President Franklin Roosevelt had addressed security and intelligence needs by creating the Office of Strategic Services (OSS), the first organized effort by the United States to implement a centralized system of strategic intelligence. The OSS was responsible for collecting and analyzing information about countries at war with the United States, as well as for espionage and sabotage within those countries. By the end of the war the OSS had become legendary, both for its agents' feats and for the role it played in directly aiding the military with essential information to conduct its campaign. However, the OSS was disbanded after the war, and legislators recognized the need for a permanent intelligence agency capable of operating independently from other governmental departments. The result would be the National Security Act of 1947 (P.L. 80-235, 61 Stat. 496), signed by President Harry Truman, and its subsequent amendment through the National Security Act of 1949 (63 Stat. 579).

MAJOR FEATURES OF THE ACT

The National Security Act of 1947 is a historic piece of legislation. It single-handedly created a modern military organization, comprised of four institutions that operate effectively to this day: the Department of Defense, the United States Air Force, the Central Intelligence Agency, and the National Security Council.

Department of Defense. The Department of Defense (DoD) unified the United States Army, Navy, and Air Force under a single cabinet-level secretary, the secretary of defense. This integration into one department was revolutionary for the time. (The National Security Act of 1949 amended the 1947 act by reorganizing certain aspects of the new department.) The secretary of defense has carried on as head of the unified army, navy, and air force to the present day. The law provided that the secretary of defense would report directly to the president. The secretary's primary tasks were to coordinate defense matters among the separate services and to develop general policies for the military.

The National Security Act of 1947 single-handedly created a modern military organization, comprised of four institutions that operate effectively to this day: the Department of Defense, the United States Air Force, the Central Intelligence Agency, and the National Security Council.

United States Air Force. The 1947 act established the United States Air Force as an independent armed service within the Department of Defense. Until that time, the air force was an entity of the army, and traced its roots to the founding of the Aeronautical Division of the Army Signal Corps (1907).

Central Intelligence Agency. The Central Intelligence Agency (CIA) became the successor to the OSS, and the 1947 act reorganized, centralized, and streamlined the intelligence community. The act provided for the creation of a director of central intelligence (DCI) who is responsible for protecting intelligence sources and methods. The National Security Act charges the DCI through the CIA with coordinating the nation's intelligence activities and correlating, evaluating, and disseminating intelligence that affects national security. The CIA is responsible for providing accurate, comprehensive, and timely foreign intelligence on national security topics to the president and the National Security Council. It further conducts counterintelligence activities, special activities, and other functions related to foreign intelligence and national security, as directed by the president.

National Security Council. The National Security Council (NSC) was given the task of coordinating and advising the president on the integration of domestic, foreign, and military policies relating to national security. The CIA was to provide the necessary intelligence and analyses to the NSC so that it could keep pace with trends and events and thus effectively advise the president. The NSC is made up of senior members of the U.S. government, the armed forces, and the intelligence community. This includes, among others, the president, vice president, secretary of state, secretary of the treasury, secretary of defense, national security advisor, chairman of the joint chiefs of staff, and director of central intelligence. Given its role as an advisory body to the president, the NSC is a flexible organization, to be used as each president sees fit.

The importance of the reorganization of the country's national security institutions, as set forth by the National Security Act of 1947, cannot be overstated.

HISTORICAL IMPACT OF THE ACT

Today, the importance of the reorganization of the country's national security institutions, as set forth by the National Security Act of 1947, cannot be overstated. The military's unified commands have achieved a remarkable degree of integration in organization and operations. The U.S. military is thus able to operate as one of the greatest fighting forces ever assembled. The CIA, through its enhanced intelligence-gathering techniques and coordination, has enabled presidents to have before them the most accurate and up-to-date information necessary to make informed decisions on national security issues.

Finally, the NSC, by incorporating the knowledge and talents of both the DoD and the CIA, provides the president with an invaluable forum for the deliberation and coordination of domestic, foreign, and military policies related to national security. Without the reorganization of the country's security infrastructure in 1947, America would not be prepared to face today's challenges to our national security.

See also: Central Intelligence Agency Act; Department of Homeland Security Act.

National Traffic and Motor Vehicle Safety Act of 1966

Todd Olmstead

Excerpt from the National Traffic and Motor Vehicle Safety Act of 1966

An Act to provide for a coordinated national safety program and establishment of safety standards for motor vehicles in interstate commerce to reduce accidents involving motor vehicles and to reduce the deaths and injuries occurring in such accidents.

The National Traffic and Motor Vehicle Safety Act of 1966 (P.L. 89-563, 80 Stat. 718) was enacted to reduce traffic accidents as well as the number of deaths and injuries to persons involved in traffic accidents. The act required regulators to establish federal motor vehicle safety standards to protect the public against "unreasonable risk of accidents occurring as a result of the design, construction or performance of motor vehicles" and also against "unreasonable risk of death or injury ... in the event accidents do occur."

The act required regulators to establish federal motor vehicle safety standards to protect the public against "unreasonable risk of accidents occurring as a result of the design, construction or performance of motor vehicles" and also against "unreasonable risk of death or injury ... in the event accidents do occur."

MOTOR VEHICLE SAFETY ISSUES IN THE 1960S

The act was motivated by a variety of factors. First and foremost, the public was growing increasingly concerned over the rising number of traffic fatalities on the nation's roads. Such fatalities had increased by nearly 30 percent between 1960 and 1965, and experts forecasted 100,000 such deaths annually by 1975 unless something was done to improve traffic safety. Adding fuel to the fire, Ralph Nader's *Unsafe at Any Speed,* published in November 1965, criticized the automobile industry for neglecting safety in favor of "power and styling" when designing new vehicles.

Nader's criticism was later substantiated during hearings held by the Senate Commerce Committee in which committee members reported "disturbing evidence of the automobile industry's chronic subordination of safe design to promotional styling, and of an overriding stress on power, acceleration, speed, and 'ride' to the relative neglect of safe performance or collision protection." Committee members remarked that new vehicle models had shown little improvement in safe design or in the incorporation of safety devices until industry had been subjected to the prod of heightened public interest and governmental concern. Members also noted that even basic safety design features such as safety door latches did not become standard equipment until ten years after their desirability and feasibility had been established. In short, Congress decided that the industry had been neglecting vehicle safety long enough, and in August 1966 both houses unanimously passed the National Traffic and Motor Vehicle Safety Act, which was signed the following month by President Lyndon B. Johnson.

PROVISIONS OF THE ACT

Administration of the act evolved considerably during its first several years. Initially, the act was to be administered by the Secretary of Commerce through a newly created National Traffic Safety Agency. In October 1966, however, when the Department of Transportation was created, Congress declared that the act would be carried out by the Secretary of Transportation through a National Traffic Safety Bureau. In June 1967, Executive Order 11357 terminated the National Traffic Safety Bureau and transferred its responsibilities to the National Highway Safety Bureau (NHSB). The NHSB was originally established as a National Highway Safety Agency by the Highway Safety Act of 1966 and renamed a "Bureau" by the Department of Transportation Act. In December 1970 the Highway Safety Act of 1970 established the National Highway Traffic Safety Administration (NHTSA) to succeed the NHSB in carrying out the safety programs developed under the National Traffic and Motor Vehicle Safety Act.

The National Traffic and Motor Vehicle Safety Act of 1966 gave regulators until January 31, 1967, to develop federal motor vehicle safety standards that were practical, stated in objective terms, and met the need for motor vehicle safety.

The National Traffic and Motor Vehicle Safety Act of 1966 gave regulators until January 31, 1967 to develop federal motor vehicle safety standards that were practical, stated in objective terms, and met the need for motor vehicle safety. In addition, the initial federal standards were required to be based on existing safety standards, such as those developed by the Society of Automotive Engineers. New and revised federal standards (that did not need to be based on existing standards) were required by January 31, 1968. Violators of the standards were subject to a $1,000 civil penalty for each offense, up to a maximum of $400,000 for a related series of violations (the maximum penalty was increased to $800,000 in 1974).

Regulators issued twenty standards for passenger cars by the initial deadline, including rules requiring installation of seat belts for all occupants, impact-absorbing steering columns, padded dashboards, safety glass, and dual braking systems. In time, federal motor vehicle safety standards have expanded to cover many other aspects of motor vehicle safety, including everything from windshield wipers, lights, and rearview mirrors to door locks, head restraints, and fuel tanks. In addition, federal motor vehicle safety standards have been developed for trucks, buses, trailers, and motorcycles.

AMENDMENT TO THE ACT IN 1974

In 1974 the act was amended to require manufacturers to remedy safety-related defects at no cost to consumers. Prior to the 1974 amendment, the act merely empowered the Secretary of Transportation to declare that a safety-related defect existed and to require that manufacturers notify the owners of the defective vehicles—the act did not require the manufacturers to fix the defect for free. In fact, a "repair at no cost" amendment had been considered as early as 1969, but was dropped when manufacturers promised Congress that all safety-related defects would be remedied at their expense, regardless of whether legislation required it. However, the industry broke its promise in 1971 and again in 1972, and so Congress responded by formally requiring manufacturers to fix all safety-related defects at no charge to consumers. A flurry of recalls took place in the years following the amendment, and the number of cars recalled for repair between 1977 and 1980 surpassed the number of new cars sold.

Although it is reasonable to conclude that the National Traffic and Motor Vehicle Safety Act of 1966 has improved traffic safety, it is difficult to estimate with certainty the precise impact of the act. Traffic fatalities and the fatality rate (measured in fatalities per million vehicle miles traveled) declined 17 percent and 71 percent,

Although it is reasonable to conclude that the National Traffic and Motor Vehicle Safety Act of 1966 has improved traffic safety, it is difficult to estimate with certainty the precise impact of the act.

respectively, between 1967 and 2001. Undoubtedly, at least some of this improvement in traffic safety is due to the motor vehicle safety standards promulgated under the act. However, it is impossible to isolate the impact of these motor vehicle safety standards from the effects of changes in the myriad other factors that contribute to motor vehicle crashes, including changes in state laws governing speed limits, driver education, driver licensing, seat belt usage, drunk driving, and vehicle inspection as well as overall improvements in emergency response, medicine, highway design, and traffic control techniques.

See also: HIGHWAY SAFETY ACT OF 1966.

BIBLIOGRAPHY

Graham, John D., ed. *Preventing Automobile Injury: New Findings from Evaluation Research*. Dover: Auburn House Publishing Company, 1988.

Mashaw, Jerry L., and David L. Harfst. *The Struggle for Auto Safety*. Cambridge, MA: Harvard University Press, 1990.

Nader, Ralph. *Unsafe at Any Speed*. New York: Grossman Publishing, 1965.

National Highway Traffic Safety Administration, U.S. Department of Transportation. *National Traffic and Motor Vehicle Safety Act of 1966: Legislative History*. Washington, DC: Government Printing Office, 1985.

NATIONAL WILDLIFE REFUGE SYSTEM ADMINISTRATION ACT (1966)

Richard Finkmoore

United States wildlife refuges are one of several systems of federally owned land, including the national forests and the national parks. The National Wildlife Refuge System Administration Act (1966, P.L. 89-669, 80 Stat. 927) establishes the mission of the refuge system, provides guidance to the U.S. secretary of the interior on refuge management, requires refuge planning, and gives refuge managers directions for making decisions about proper uses of the refuges. As of January 1, 2003, the refuge system comprised more than 95 million acres in 538 refuges and over 3,000 small waterfowl breeding and nesting areas. National wildlife refuges are located in all fifty states and several U.S. possessions. Because almost all refuge lands are owned by the federal government, constitutional authority for the Refuge Administration Act is found in the property clause of the U.S. Constitution (Article IV, section 3). This clause provides that Congress has the power to make "all needful Rules and Regulations respecting the Territory or other Property belonging to the United States...."

BACKGROUND

America's first refuge was created in 1903 when President Theodore Roosevelt set aside Pelican Island in Florida to protect herons and egrets from overhunting. During the next several decades, other presidents and Congress established scores of refuges, many as "inviolate sanctuaries" where wildlife could not be hunted or otherwise disturbed. Refuges were established for a variety of purposes, in some instances to protect a single species, in others to protect particular groups of animals, and sometimes for very general purposes. Many refuges were created to conserve migratory waterfowl, and in the mid-1900s a significant number of refuges were opened to hunting. Because refuges were established without any overall strategy, but rather as needs and opportunities presented themselves, the refuges became a diverse and rather haphazard collection of lands.

America's first refuge was created in 1903 when President Theodore Roosevelt set aside Pelican Island in Florida to protect herons and egrets from overhunting.

The National Wildlife Refuge System Administration Act was enacted to create a system from this loose network of refuges. The act consolidated the refuges under the jurisdiction of the Interior Department's Fish and Wildlife Service. The act also permitted any uses of refuge lands that were "compatible" with the purposes of individual refuges.

AMENDMENTS TO THE ACT

Under the 1966 statute, many refuges suffered from numerous uses that were harmful to wildlife, such as farming, livestock grazing, recreational activities, and in many instances even oil and gas production and military training exercises. Environmentalists and others urged that the refuges be given greater protection from such abuses and that conservation of the nation's wildlife be declared the first priority of the refuge system. At the same time, some hunting groups sought greater access to more refuges.

Congress responded in 1997 by passing the National Wildlife Refuge System Improvement Act, which made significant amendments to the 1966 act. Section 4 of the 1997 act sets forth for the first time one mission for all refuges: "to administer a national network of lands for the conservation, management, and ... restoration of the fish, wildlife, and plant resources and their habitats within the United States for the benefit of future generations." The act also establishes a hierarchy of uses allowed on refuges. The dominant use is wildlife conservation, and priority public uses are recreational activities, including hunting, fishing, wildlife observation, and environmental education. Uses that are "compatible" with wildlife conservation are still permitted on refuges, but the act specifies standards and procedures intended to prevent uses that are harmful to wildlife. Finally, the 1997 legislation requires the secretary of the interior to prepare comprehensive conservation plans for all refuges through a process that ensures public participation.

See also: FEDERAL LAND POLICY AND MANAGEMENT ACT; NATIONAL FOREST MANAGEMENT ACT.

BIBLIOGRAPHY

Bean, Michael J., and Melanie J. Rowland. *The Evolution of National Wildlife Law,* 3d ed. Westport, CT: Greenwood Publishing, 1997.

Reed, Nathaniel, and Dennis Drabelle. *The United States Fish and Wildlife Service.* Boulder, CO: Westview Press, 1984.

INTERNET RESOURCE

U.S. Fish and Wildlife Service. "America's National Wildlife Refuge System." <http://refuges.fws.gov>.

Natural Gas Act (1938)

Joseph P. Tomain

Together with the Federal Power Act of 1935, the Natural Gas Act of 1938 (NGA) (P.L. 75-688, 52 Stat. 821) was an essential piece of energy legislation in the first half of the twentieth century. These statutes regulated interstate activities of the electric and natural gas industries, respectively. The acts are similarly structured and constitute the classic form of command-and-control regulation authorizing the federal government to enter into a regulatory compact with utilities. In short, the Natural Gas Act enabled federal regulators to set prices for gas sold in interstate commerce in exchange for exclusive rights to transport the gas.

The Natural Gas Act enabled federal regulators to set prices for gas sold in interstate commerce in exchange for exclusive rights to transport the gas.

The impetus behind the NGA was a 1935 Federal Trade Commission Report finding that interstate pipelines exercised abusive monopoly power. The NGA conferred on the Federal Power Commission (now the Federal Energy Regulatory Commission) the authority to set rates that were just, reasonable, and nondiscriminatory. Interstate pipelines then dedicated natural gas to interstate commerce and had a federally protected service territory. The constitutionality of the NGA was upheld in the cases of *FPC v. Natural Gas Pipeline Co.* (1942) and *FPC v. Hope Natural Gas* (1944).

At the time of the NGA's enactment, gas regulation was divided generally between the federal government and the states. The federal government had jurisdiction over wholesale sales by interstate pipelines as well as transportation by interstate pipelines. The states exercised regulation over retail sales and intrastate transactions.

The scheme worked relatively well as the Federal Power Commission asserted jurisdiction over interstate pipelines but did not assert jurisdiction over producers. Yet this limited jurisdiction caused certain problems because interstate sales were defined to exclude the price that producers in the field charged to the pipeline (the wellhead price). The wellhead prices that were charged by producers were automatically passed on to consumers. Hence, any protection afforded consumers could easily be thwarted by excessive prices at the wellhead. In 1947 the U.S. Supreme Court ruled that the Federal Power Commission had jurisdiction over the prices that producers charged to affiliated pipelines in *Interstate Natural Gas Co. v. FPC.* Federal jurisdiction over nonaffiliated producer prices was extended in 1954 in the case of *Phillips Petroleum v. Wisconsin* to regulate excessive prices being charged in interstate commerce. A direct consequence of the *Phillips Petroleum* case was that the Federal Power Commission was unable to conduct all the individual hearings necessary to review producer prices. Instead of individual rate hearings for pipelines or producers, the Federal Power Commission first set area rates for natural gas in the case of the *In Re Permian Basin Area Rate* (1968), and then it set national rates in *Shell Oil Co. v. FPC* (1975).

The NGA worked relatively smoothly until the early 1970s when the natural gas market collapsed.

The NGA worked relatively smoothly until the early 1970s when the natural gas market collapsed. Federal ratemaking to set natural gas prices was based on average historic costs of pipelines and producers. At the same time, however, world prices were rising above average historic costs, and a dual market was created. Pipelines and producers who had dedicated gas to interstate commerce were selling gas much below the world market price, and they sought to extract themselves from the interstate market to sell their gas in intrastate markets where prices were higher and set more closely to the world level. A gas shortage was the effective end of the Natural Gas Act as it previously had been administered. The dual market was addressed in the Natural Gas Policy Act of 1978 as deregulation of the natural gas industry began and continues to this day.

See also: ATOMIC ENERGY ACT; FEDERAL POWER ACTS.

BIBLIOGRAPHY

Breyer, Stephen G., and Paul W MacAvoy. "The Natural Gas Shortage and Regulation of Natural Gas Producers." *Harvard Law Review* 86 (1973): 941–87.

Kelly, Suedeen G. "Natural Gas." In *Energy Law and Policy for the 21st Century,* ed. Energy Law Group. Denver, CO: Rocky Mountain Mineral Law Foundation, 2000.

MacAvoy, Paul W. *Natural Gas Market: Sixty Years of Regulation and Deregulation.* New Haven, CT: Yale University Press, 2000.

Tomain, Joseph P. *Energy Law.* St. Paul, MN: West Publishing Co., 1981.

Natural Gas Pipeline Safety Act

Passed in 1968, the Natural Gas Pipeline Safety Act gave the federal government authority over interstate pipelines transporting hazardous liquids and natural gas. The Office of Pipeline Safety (OPS) was formed under the Department of Transportation (DOT) to set minimum safety standards for design, construction, inspection, testing, operation, and maintenance, as well as to perform inspections and enforce regulations. Today the OPS is responsible for more than 2.2 million miles of pipeline. Hazardous liquid lines transport mainly gasoline and fuel oil, while gas pipelines transport 22 trillion cubic feet of gas.

NATURALIZATION ACT (1790)

James W. Fox, Jr.

Naturalization is the process by which people can become citizens of a country they were not born in. The United States Constitution grants Congress the power "to establish an uniform Rule of Naturalization" (Article I, section 8, clause 4). Soon after the Constitution was ratified Congress passed the Naturalization Act of 1790 (1 Stat. 103). The act provided

This act reveals one of the deepest ambiguities in American citizenship.

> that any alien, being a free white person, who shall have resided within the limits and under the jurisdiction of the United States for the term of two years, may be admitted to become a citizen thereof, on application to any common law court of record, in any one of the States wherein he shall have resided for the term of one year at least, and making proof to the satisfaction of such court, that he is a person of good character, and taking the oath or affirmation prescribed by law, to support the Constitution of the United States....

This act reveals one of the deepest ambiguities in American citizenship. In requiring a period of residence prior to naturalization, members of Congress emphasized that foreigners should spend sufficient time in the United States to appreciate American democracy; Congress viewed America as a school for equality and democracy. But by preventing foreign-born people of color from becoming citizens, the act established that American citizenship contained its own aristocracy, that of race.

The violence of the French Revolution in the early 1790s, dramatically exemplified by the Reign of Terror of 1793, raised fears that violent French revolutionaries (the Jacobins) would come to America. In response, Congress extended the residence requirement for citizenship in the 1795 Naturalization Act from one to five years. At first Thomas Jefferson's Democratic-Republican Party supported the extended residence requirement. Although Republicans favored admission of European revolutionaries, who generally supported the Democratic-Republican Party, they also feared an influx of merchants who would oppress the common farmer-citizens and support the Federalist Party.

Republicans, however, opposed the longer restrictions of fourteen years implemented by a Federalist Congress with the Naturalization Act of 1798. This act, as part of the infamous Alien and Sedition Acts, was designed to restrict the political power of persons sympathetic to Jefferson's Republicans. When Republicans wrested control of Congress from the Federalists in the election of 1800, they returned the residence requirement to five years in the Naturalization Act of 1802.

The increased residence restrictions implemented during the 1790s reflected a nativism, a policy that favors native-born citizens over immigrants, through which current citizens expressed a fear of foreigners and attempted to preserve what they saw as the uniqueness of American citizenship. Federalists and Republicans were each affected, in different ways, by this nativist rejection of foreigners. Throughout the nation's history, nativism has been behind exclusions of people based on race, country of origin, and political ideology.

The history of naturalization also reveals that citizenship was centered around men. While the 1790 act naturalized all "persons" and so included women, it also declared that "the right of citizenship shall not descend to persons whose fathers have never been resident in the United States...." This prevented the automatic grant of citizenship to children born abroad whose mother, but not father, had resided in the United States. Citizenship was inherited exclusively through the father. Congress did not remove the inequity until 1934.

Citizenship was inherited exclusively through the father. Congress did not remove the inequity until 1934.

The Civil War changed American ideas of citizenship. The Fourteenth Amendment guaranteed citizenship to all people born in the United States regardless of race, class, or gender. Congress then passed the Naturalization Act of 1870, which extended naturalization to people of African descent. Throughout the late nineteenth and the twentieth centuries, however, restrictions on immigration and naturalization based on countries of origin continued. Naturalization was limited for groups thought suspect, such as Chinese nationals, perpetuating a racial idea of citizenship. The tension between the ideals of equality and freedom and the realities of race, gender, and politics evident in the history of the naturalization laws of the first century of the United States set the stage for the debates about immigration and immigration laws during the twentieth century.

See also: Alien and Sedition Acts of 1798; Chinese Exclusion Acts; Immigration and Nationality Act; Immigration Reform and Control Act of 1986.

BIBLIOGRAPHY

Foner, Eric, and John A. Garraty, eds. *The Reader's Companion to American History*. Boston: Houghton Mifflin, 1991.

Kerber, Linda K. *No Constitutional Right to Be Ladies: Women and the Obligations of Citizenship*. New York: Hill and Wang, 1998.

Kettner, James H. *The Development of American Citizenship, 1608–1870*. Chapel Hill: University of North Carolina Press, 1978.

Smith, Rogers M. *Civic Ideals: Conflicting Visions of Citizenship in U.S. History*. New Haven, CT: Yale University Press, 1997.

Negotiated Rulemaking Act (1990)

Philip J. Harter

When passing a new law, Congress generally sets the basic policy but then directs the agency charged with implementing the law to issue rules that provide the detail of what must be done. The traditional process is for the agency to study the subject and draft a proposed rule that it publishes in the ***Federal Register,*** a daily newspaper that contains notices of the activities of the federal government. This is called a "Notice of Proposed Rulemaking." Anyone who is interested can submit comments, which the agency will take into account. The agency then makes the appropriate revisions and publishes the final rule.

Federal Register: a newspaper published daily by the National Archives and Records Administration to notify the public of federal agency regulations, proposed rules and notices, executive orders, and other executive branch documents

For most rules, this process works fairly well. But since so much can be at stake, sometimes the process becomes adversarial and contentious. At other times an agency may lack the expertise necessary to write the rule. In still other instances, an agency may consider it important for those groups who will be directly affected by a rule to participate in the development of the policies that the rule will implement. One way to meet these needs is to assemble representatives of those groups who will be significantly affected by a proposed rule to consider the relevant issues, develop the required facts, and come to an agreement on a proposed rule. This process, called "negotiated rulemaking," is commonly referred to as regulatory negotiation or "reg-neg."

One way to meet these needs is to assemble representatives of those groups who will be significantly affected by a proposed rule to consider the relevant issues, develop the required facts, and come to an agreement on a proposed rule, a process called "negoatiated rulemaking."

Congress enacted the Negotiated Rulemaking Act in 1990 (P. L. 101-648, 104 Stat. 4,969, amended 1996, P. L. 104-320, 110 Stat. 3,870) to encourage agencies to use this process and to provide the explicit blessing of Congress for its use. Under the act, a person called a "convener" identifies (1) the interests that will be significantly affected by the proposed rule; (2) the issues that must be resolved by the agency in the new proposed rule; and (3) people who are willing and able to represent the affected interests.

If the agency agrees with the convener's assessment and recommendations, it appoints its own representative and publishes a notice in the *Federal Register* as well as other, more widely read publications inviting anyone who feels significantly affected but not represented to come forward to participate on the committee. The Notice of Intent, as it is called, ensures that no interest will be left out. Thus, the process is highly democratic, with the representatives being chosen by interest instead of by arbitrary geographical areas. The committee then meets in open meetings and develops an agreement on a

Most of the empirical research shows that reg-neg saves time and significantly improves the substance of the rules.

proposed rule, which the agency, after review and any necessary modifications, publishes as a Notice of Proposed Rulemaking.

Most of the empirical research shows that reg-neg saves time and significantly improves the substance of the rules. Although some contend that the process is not democratic because some individuals may be left out, others point out that reg-neg is far more inclusive than traditional rule making and that anyone who is interested can still comment on the Notice of Proposed Rulemaking. Overall, negotiated rulemaking has been highly successful in writing some enormously complex and controversial rules.

See also: ADMINISTRATIVE DISPUTE RESOLUTION ACT; ADMINISTRATIVE PROCEDURE ACT.

BIBLIOGRAPHY

Harter, Philip J. "Negotiating Regulations: A Cure for Malaise." *Georgetown Law Journal* 71 (1981).

NEUTRALITY ACTS

David G. Delaney

Between 1935 and 1939 Congress passed four neutrality acts to limit America's involvement in foreign conflicts. The political debate surrounding the neutrality acts reflected the evolving view of America's role in the world. Public opinion was shifting away from **isolationism** toward **interventionism** and collective security and the belief that America's best defense lay in cooperative efforts with other nations and international organizations. The acts also signify a power shift from the legislative to the executive branch in international affairs. Whereas Congress previously controlled the details of foreign policy programs, the acts increasingly granted the presidency and executive agencies leeway to implement new laws.

isolationism: a policy of not getting involved in international affairs

interventionism: a policy of getting involved in international affairs through membership in international organizations and multinational alliances

President Franklin D. Roosevelt signed the Neutrality Act of 1935 (P.L. 74-76, 49 Stat. 1081) into law on August 31. The act banned all arms and ammunition shipments to belligerent nations and placed America's armaments industry under federal control for six months. Following Italy's invasion of Ethiopia on October 3, 1935, Roosevelt declared the United States neutral and invoked the act to place a blanket ban on all weapons shipments to both countries and to prohibit Americans from traveling on ships registered in either nation.

Between 1935 and 1939 Congress passed four neutrality acts to limit America's involvement in foreign conflicts.

The policy of American neutrality was ineffective in shaping the outcome of that conflict. Also, it disfavored Ethiopia because the act did not prohibit the significant trade in raw materials that Americans conducted with Italy. The State Department drafted broader neutrality legislation to address this imbalance, giving the president authority to implement **embar-**

embargo: a prohibition on commerce with a particular country for political or economic reasons goes selectively. Such authority would better reflect the administration's position toward warring countries. However, congressional isolationists rejected the measure as giving the president too much control over American trade. In the Neutrality Act of 1936, Congress simply extended the 1935 act by fourteen months and added a provision to prohibit private loans to belligerents.

CONTINUITY AND CHANGE IN THE 1937 ACT

The Neutrality Act of 1937 made the 1936 act permanent and included the basic provisions of its predecessors:

> Whenever the President, or the Congress by concurrent resolution, shall find that there exists a state of war between foreign states, and that it is necessary to promote the security or preserve the peace of the United States or to protect the lives of citizens of the United States, the President shall issue a proclamation naming the states involved.... It shall

President Franklin D. Roosevelt asks Congress to repeal neutrality legislation, September 26, 1939. (© HULTON/ARCHIVE BY GETTY IMAGES)

> thereafter be unlawful for any American vessel to carry any passengers or any article or materials to any state named in such proclamation ... [and] it shall be unlawful for any person to export, or attempt to export, from the United States to any other state, any arms, ammunition, or implements of war....

But the 1937 act also added a two-year "cash-and-carry" provision permitting Americans to trade with belligerents who paid cash and transported the goods on non-U.S. vessels following a declaration of neutrality:

> It shall thereafter be unlawful to export or transport, or attempt to export or transport, or cause to be exported or transported, from the United States to any state named in such proclamation, any articles or materials (except copyrighted articles or materials) until all right, title, and interest therein shall have been transferred to some foreign government, agency, institution, association, partnership, corporation, or national.

Cash-and-carry gave the president the authority he had sought in 1935 to declare limited rather than blanket embargoes. The plan permitted the president to tailor the U.S. approach to the circumstances of unique conflicts and perhaps better reflect America's interests. However, critics noted that cash-and-carry would unequally benefit nations like Japan, England, and France, capable of paying cash and protecting their ships with strong navies.

THE SHIFT AWAY FROM NEUTRALITY

In response to the Sino-Japanese War of August 1937, Roosevelt avoided the issue of cash-and-carry altogether by not invoking the Neutrality Act. U.S. trade would therefore continue unrestrained with China and Japan. This decision and the president's Quarantine Speech on October 5, 1937, are perhaps the earliest outward signs that the Roosevelt administration viewed neutrality legislation as unrealistic, ineffective prescriptions for America's involvement in closely interconnected issues of international politics, trade, and law. If anything, neutrality

Excerpt from Franklin D. Roosevelt's "Quarantine Speech," October 5, 1937

Without a declaration of war and without warning or justification of any kind, civilians, including vast numbers of women and children, are being ruthlessly murdered with bombs from the air. In times of so-called peace, ships are being attacked and sunk by submarines without cause or notice. Nations are fomenting and taking sides in civil warfare in nations that have never done them any harm. Nations claiming freedom for themselves deny it to others.

Innocent peoples, innocent nations are being cruelly sacrificed to a greed for power and supremacy which is devoid of all sense of justice and humane considerations.

To paraphrase a recent author, "perhaps we foresee a time when men, exultant in the technique of homicide, will rage so hotly over the world that every precious thing will be in danger, every book, every picture, every harmony, every treasure garnered through two millenniums, the small, the delicate, the defenseless—all will be lost or wrecked or utterly destroyed."

If those things come to pass in other parts of the world, let no one imagine that America will escape, that America may expect mercy, that this Western hemisphere will not be attacked and that it will continue tranquilly and peacefully to carry on the ethics and the arts of civilization....

If those days are not to come to pass—if we are to have a world in which we can breathe freely and live in amity without fear—then the peace-loving nations must make a concerted effort to uphold laws and principles on which alone peace can rest secure.

legislation had encouraged Germany and Italy to pursue their political interests knowing that the United States would likely not act to stop them.

In March 1939, after Germany marched into Czechoslovakia, Roosevelt sought to revise or eliminate neutrality legislation. In response to Germany's September 1, 1939, invasion of Poland, the president declared neutrality under the 1937 act but lobbied Congress to repeal the mandatory arms embargo. Over continued isolationist opposition from Senators William E. Borah, Arthur H. Vandendurg, Gerald P. Nye, and Robert M. La Follette, Jr., the Neutrality Act of 1939 gave the president this authority and laid the groundwork for the future Lend-Lease Act.

The neutrality acts had failed to achieve their primary goal of keeping the United States out of war, but they evolved into less restrictive measures that authorized the executive branch to respond to rapidly changing global events. Following World War II, Congress largely rejected the isolationism that had spawned neutrality legislation. The United States would thereafter play a leading role in international organizations like the United Nations and the North Atlantic Treaty Organization and the nation's foreign and defense policy would embrace an international outlook.

The neutrality acts had failed to achieve their primary goal of keeping the United States out of war, but they evolved into less restrictive measures that authorized the executive branch to respond to rapidly changing global events.

See also: LEND-LEASE ACT.

BIBLIOGRAPHY

Divine, Robert A. *The Reluctant Belligerent: American Entry into World War II,* 2d ed. New York: Knopf, 1979.

NEWLAND ACT

See NATIONAL RECLAMATION ACT OF 1902

NO CHILD LEFT BEHIND (2001)

Kelly A. Woestman

No Child Left Behind (NCLB) (P.L. 107-110, 115 Stat. 1425) is a major revision of the 1965 Elementary and Secondary Education Act (ESEA). The key components of the new version of this legislation, passed with significant **bipartisan** support, are two goals associated with accountability and the closing of the achievement gap between students of different socioeconomic backgrounds. Critics of the original 1965 legislation argued that the law provided federal funding to schools but did not mandate accountability for academic results; NCLB does both. In contrast, critics of the current legislation, including the National Educational Association, have claimed that adequate funding is not provided to satisfy the more stringent accountability requirements included in NCLB.

bipartisan: involving members of two parties, especially the two political parties

Critics of the original 1965 legislation argued that the law provided federal funding to schools but did not mandate accountability for academic results; NCLB does both.

To satisfy NCLB requirements, schools must prove that each one of its students is *proficient,* or on grade level, in key educational areas, such as reading and math, by 2014 in order to continue to receive federal funding. Beginning in 2002–2003, NCLB requires school districts to prepare annual reports for families and the public at large describing academic achievement in the aggregate (for the entire district), by individual schools, and by grade level. Since the federal government provides only about seven percent of the total funding for public elementary and secondary schools, however, it may have trouble demanding the level of accountability that NCLB seeks.

SCHOOL ACCOUNTABILITY AND NCLB

The federal government plans to make the results from the accountability tests available in annual report cards so parents can measure school performance and statewide progress, and evaluate the quality of their child's school, the qualifications of teachers, and their child's progress in key subjects. In addition, statewide reports will show progress for all student groups in closing achievement gaps between disadvantaged students and other groups of students.

Under NCLB, each state sets its own benchmark for purposes of demonstrating that it has achieved "adequate yearly progress." This is part of a larger trend in education that focuses on the collection of data and the analysis of that data in relation to student learning. Adequate yearly progress is measured overall for each school as well as disaggregated, or reported separately, for students from major ethnic and racial groups, economically disadvantaged students, students with disabilities, and students with limited English proficiency. No Child Left Behind clearly provides that states must raise their target goals over time and that the federal government expects increasing numbers of students to meet them. More important, states are to evaluate all students, and each subgroup is to make adequate yearly progress or the school fails in its entirety. Schools that do not consistently meet these requirements may eventually have to reorganize and/or surrender to state control. The requirements of NCLB, however, do not apply to private schools or to students who are home-schooled.

No Child Left Behind clearly provides that states must raise their target goals over time and that the federal government expects increasing numbers of students to meet them.

"Scientifically based research" is a key element to the accountability standard established by NCLB. Scientifically based research means research that involves the application of rigorous, systematic, and objective procedures to obtain reliable and valid knowledge about education activities and programs and involves rigorous data analyses that are adequate to test the stated hypotheses and justify the general conclusions drawn. Mentioned 111 times in the pages of the legislation, "scientifically based research" nevertheless is not defined within the act in such a way that schools and school districts clearly understand how to apply it to their various educational settings. Teachers are most concerned that the actual implementation of the proposed research methodology would mean that they would have trouble actually using these methods in a classroom, and these NCLB provisions might also severely limit classroom teaching methods and materials. Critics also assert that increased standardized testing is too expensive, too restrictive, and impossible to administer effectively.

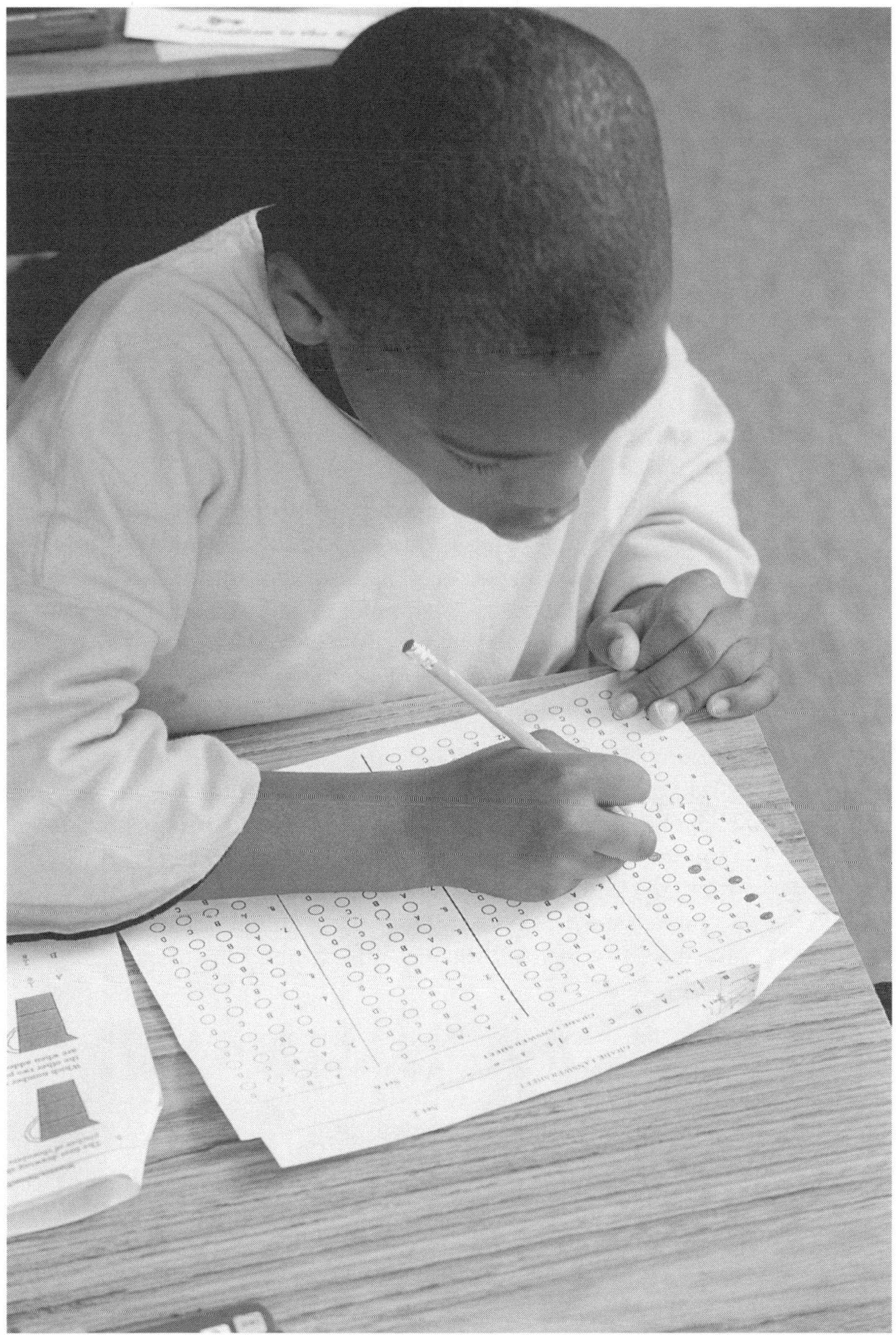

The No Child Left Behind Act will increase the use of standardized tests in key subjects, the results of which will eventually determine whether or not a school will continue to receive federal funding. (©Will & Deni McIntyre/Corbis)

TEACHER ACCOUNTABILITY AND NCLB

In addition to measuring student achievement, the law requires that an increased accountability standard be applied to the nation's teachers. It mandates that all teachers who teach core academic subjects must be *highly qualified* by 2005–2006. In the past, teachers were able to obtain teaching certificates labeled as *temporary, provisional,* or *emergency*; now NCLB prohibits this practice. Existing teachers at all levels must demonstrate sufficient content knowledge in the subjects that they teach. Elementary teachers entering the profession must possess full state certification, have earned at least a bachelor's degree, and have passed a rigorous state test demonstrating subject knowledge and teaching skills in curriculum areas such as reading, writing, and math. New teachers in the middle and secondary schools must also have full state certification, at least a bachelor's degree, and have passed a rigorous state test in the subjects he or she teaches or have successfully completed an academic major (or equivalent course work), graduate degree, or advanced certification in each subject taught.

SOCIAL ISSUES AND THE FUTURE OF NCLB

Other NCLB provisions simplify federal support for bilingual education and allow students to change schools if their school is deemed *persistently dangerous.* In the area of sex education, schools may not use federal funds to operate a program that distributes condoms or other contraceptives in the schools—the school must emphasize abstinence. Furthermore, public school districts must certify each year that none of their policies prevent or deny participation in constitutionally protected prayer in elementary and secondary schools.

Proponents of NCLB believe that this new legislation will allow individual schools more choices regarding the students they teach. As an ideal, states are to set their own standards, or benchmarks, of performance to fulfill the needs of their students. In certain critical curriculum areas—reading, math, and science—the law will measure students and schools in comparison to the performance of students throughout the country in annual testing by 2013–2014.

Students without essential support systems outside of school may have trouble meeting the ambitious goals of NCLB despite a massive increase in efforts made by his or her teachers.

Numerous factors, however, determine a student's academic success, and no amount of legislation can effectively control the student's home life, his or her socioeconomic background, whether or not he or she lives in a bad neighborhood, or whether he or she is personally motivated to succeed. Students without essential support systems outside of school may have trouble meeting the ambitious goals of NCLB despite a massive increase in efforts made by his or her teachers. Finally, critics assert that many schools that are thought to be *failing* are not—they are simply serving poor neighborhoods and are underfunded and that the proposed "adequate yearly progress" system cannot tell the difference between a learning gain and random noise created by a large number of statistics.

See also: Elementary and Secondary Education Act of 1965.

INTERNET RESOURCE

U.S. Department of Education Official Web Site. No Child Left Behind. <http://www.nclb.gov/>.

Nonintercourse Act (1809)

Richard Buel, Jr.

During the Napoleonic Wars of 1803 to 1815, Great Britain and France sought to strangle each other's commerce by seizing the ships of neutral nations carrying their adversary's trade. As the world's leading neutral carrier, the United States was the principal sufferer from this manner of waging war. In December 1807 Congress laid an embargo, a ban on commerce that made it unlawful for American ships to leave American ports. Congress wanted to protect the nation's maritime resources from being seized. The embargo's sponsors also hoped that depriving Britain and France of the benefit of the American carrying trade would lead the belligerent nations to stop seizing U.S. ships.

The embargo caused economic distress at home. The Federalist Party, centered in New England, used that distress to recover political control of the New England states from their rivals, the Republicans. The opposition of the Federalist state governments to the embargo encouraged commercial traders to evade its provisions. Massachusetts, which at that time included present-day Maine, even threatened to make it unlawful to enforce the embargo within the state. New England Federalists also threatened to withdraw from the union with the other states if the embargo was not repealed.

The Republican majority in Congress was divided over how to defend the republic against foreign pressures in the face of such opposition from the New England Federalists. Some wanted to repeal the embargo and go to war against both European powers, despite being almost totally unprepared for hostilities. Others preferred to maintain the embargo even though it was destroying the Republicans' political position in New England and attempts to enforce it threatened to provoke civil conflict. Eventually a Republican majority in Congress agreed to modify the embargo with the Nonintercourse Act of 1809, though this was no one's first choice.

The Republican majority in Congress was divided over how to defend the republic against foreign pressures in the face of such opposition from the New England Federalists.

The act prohibited commercial intercourse with Great Britain and France. It excluded the public (armed) vessels of both belligerent nations (Great Britain and France), together with their merchant vessels, from American waters; it made it unlawful to import goods from either of them or their **dependencies** directly or through third parties; and it repealed the embargo of 1807 (as amended before March 1, 1809).

dependency: a territory under the jurisdiction of a sovereign nation

Although the Federalists opposed the Nonintercourse Act, they preferred it to war with Britain, with whom they desired good relations no matter what the cost in United States relations with France. British naval superiority also allowed Great Britain access to American trade though third parties that it could deny to France. But this feature of Nonintercourse made it seem to the Republican majority like **capitulation** to Britain. Republicans, both in Congress and the nation, favored accommodating France at the expense of good relations with Britain and felt they had been humiliated by the Federalist minority.

capitulate: to surrender under specific conditions; to give up resistance

For a brief period after James Madison's inauguration in March 1809 it looked as though the Nonintercourse law might please both parties. Section

11 of the statute authorized the president to revoke its provisions as they applied to any nation that lifted its restrictions against American commerce. David Erskine, the British ambassador, promised President Madison that Britain would revoke its restrictions against the commerce of the United States if Madison, under section 11, released Britain from the effect of Nonintercourse. Madison obliged on April 19, 1809, allowing the swarm of vessels that had sailed with the repeal of the embargo (March 15) to make for British destinations. Soon afterward Madison learned that the British government had disavowed Erskine's agreement. Although Madison reinstated Nonintercourse against Britain, the Republicans felt their attempt to use commercial pressures rather than war to shape the nation's foreign relations had been sabotaged.

For a brief period after James Madison's inauguration in March 1809 it looked as though the Nonintercourse law might please both parties.

Though the Republicans viewed Nonintercourse as a modified embargo, the new law proved no more effective or less difficult to enforce than the original embargo. For this reason the next Congress allowed the Nonintercourse Act to expire in May 1810. However, Nonintercourse was reimposed against Britain in February 1811 under a subsequent statute, after France exempted American commerce from its commercial restrictions. Thereafter relations with Britain deteriorated until war was finally declared in June 1812. Hostilities might still have been avoided had not the Federalists justified every action of the British government, including its rejection of the agreement between Madison and Erskine and its refusal to match France's commercial concessions on the grounds that they were bogus. Federalist behavior persuaded the Republicans that the United States confronted not just a foreign enemy but a dangerous faction within the nation's midst that was in league with Britain.

BIBLIOGRAPHY

Brown, Roger H. *The Republic in Peril: 1812.* New York: Columbia University Press, 1964.

Rutland, Robert A. *The Presidency of James Madison.* Lawrence: University of Kansas Press, 1990.

Spivak, Burton. *Jefferson's English Crisis: Commerce, Embargo, and the Republican Revolution.* Charlottesville: University Press of Virginia, 1979.

Stagg, J. C. A. *Mr. Madison's War: Politics, Diplomacy, and Warfare in the Early American Republic, 1783–1830.* Princeton, NJ: Princeton University Press, 1983.

NORRIS-LAGUARDIA ACT (1932)

Neil N. Bernstein

When it adopted the Norris-LaGuardia Act (47 Stat. 70), Congress liberated organized labor from the crippling restraints of federal court injunctions. Prior to the act's passage, a federal judge, persuaded that a potential or actual strike, picketing, or boycott might violate the law, would issue an injunction to halt a union's activities. Although the injunc-

Fiorello H. LaGuardia (1882–1947), Republican of New York, and sponsor of the Norris-LaGuardia Act in the House of Representatives. (LIBRARY OF CONGRESS, PRINTS AND PHOTOGRAPHS DIVISION)

tions remained in effect for only a few days, they would break the momentum of the employees, thereby terminating the activity permanently. Moreover, an employer could frequently secure an injunction without notice to the union, with no proof other than questionable affidavits, and with language barring many forms of employee conduct which were probably lawful.

To end these abuses, the Norris-LaGuardia Act:

Prior to the act's passage, a federal judge, persuaded that a potential or actual strike, picketing, or boycott might violate the law, would issue an injunction to halt a union's activities.

(1) Declared any "yellow dog" contract (under which an employee promised not to become a member of any labor organization) to be unenforceable in any court of the United States.
(2) Deprived federal courts of jurisdiction to issue injunctions against peaceful striking, assembling, patrolling, or publicizing facts in connection with a labor dispute.
(3) Defined "labor dispute" as broadly as possible to encompass any controversy concerning the terms and conditions of employment or representation.
(4) Provided that in any dispute where an injunction might be issued (when harm to person or property is threatened), the federal courts must comply with stringent procedural safeguards, including a prior hearing under oath in open court with cross examination.

LEGISLATIVE HISTORY

Enactment of the statute occurred only after a long, bitter struggle. A group of five lawyers and economists, led by Professor Felix Frankfurter of Harvard Law School originally drafted a bill in 1928 but the document they produced would not become law until 1932. The draft bill was reported to the Senate Judiciary Committee, with a recommendation that it be reported favorably to the Senate. The Committee, however, took no action on the proposal and it died upon the **adjournment** of the Seventieth Congress. Reintroduced in the Seventy-first Congress in 1930, the bill was the subject of extensive hearings before a judiciary subcommittee. This time, the Judiciary Committee did report the bill to the full Senate, but with a recommendation that it not be enacted. The Senate took no action, and the bill again died when Congress adjourned.

adjournment: the closing, or end, of a session

In the meantime national sentiment shifted to the side of the legislation, occasioned by the economic depression and the plight of working men. Both political parties had adopted planks in their national platforms calling for legislation to eliminate the abuses of injunctions in labor disputes. In the Seventy-second Congress, the Senate Judiciary Committee finally reported the bill favorably to the full Senate. The legislation had little opposition in Congress itself, passing the Senate 75 to 5 and the House of Representatives by a vote of 363 to 13.

President Herbert Hoover signed the bill on March 23, 1932, and simultaneously released a letter from the attorney general indicating that while some questioned the bill's constitutionality, he nevertheless recommended that the president sign it so the objections "can be set at rest by judicial decision." The courts, however, have never questioned the constitutionality of the legislation.

SUBSEQUENT LEGISLATION

Congress enacted the Norris-LaGuardia Act before the New Deal era and intended the act to remove the federal government from any involvement in relations between unions and employers in the private economy. Basically, it left the parties free to carry on their struggles using all the economic weapons at their disposal, with no holds barred. The legislation removed judicial obstructions impeding the efforts of unions to organize, strike, picket, and boycott, but did not commit the government in any way to intervene on the side of the unions.

Congress enacted the Norris-LaGuardia Act before the New Deal era and intended the act to remove the federal government from any involvement in relations between unions and employers in the private economy.

The reign of Norris-LaGuardia as the labor policy of the federal government was short-lived. In 1935 Congress passed the National Labor Relations Act, which established a new national policy in favor of collective bargaining and union organizing. The statute protected union organizing tactics and deprived employers of the economic weapons they had utilized against unions, such as firing union organizers and **adherents**. Government policy changed again in 1947 with the enactment of the Taft-Hartley amendments to the National Labor Relations Act. Taft-Hartley regulated the economic activities of unions for the first time and prohibited the use of secondary boycotts and lengthy organizational picketing.

adherent: a follower of a leader or party, or a believer in a cause

Massachusetts militia were called to control a massive strike, involving tens of thousands of workers, in Lawrence, Massachusetts, January 1912. Throughout the first half of the twentieth century, organized labor would gain increasing rights. The Norris-LaGuardia Act prevented federal court injunctions from halting a union's activities. (LIBRARY OF CONGRESS)

The most important impact of Norris-LaGuardia was its utilization as the justification for an antitrust exemption for organized labor.

Congress, nevertheless, never repealed the Norris-LaGuardia Act and it has retained a significant role in U.S. labor law. The most important impact of Norris-LaGuardia was its antitrust exemption for organized labor. Prior to 1932 many federal courts regarded unions as "conspiracies in restraint of trade" and were willing not only to enjoin their activities, but also to grant substantial damages at the behest of their target employers. Congress originally sought to remove unions from antitrust scrutiny through a special exemption in the 1914 Clayton Act, but the Supreme Court limited the exemption to disputes between employers and their direct employees. The Norris-LaGuardia Act by its explicit language only barred injunctions and said nothing about private treble damages suits or criminal prosecutions. In a later decision, *United States v. Hutcheson* (1941), the Supreme Court's Justice Frankfurter (who was one of the drafters of Norris-LaGuardia before he became a Supreme Court Justice) held that Norris-LaGuardia should be read broadly to provide a total antitrust exemption for labor unions, "so long as a union acts in its self-interest and does not combine with non-labor groups."

IMPACT OF THE STATUTE

Norris-LaGuardia was also significant as a limitation on injunctions against violations of no-strike provisions in collective bargaining agreements. Most collective bargaining agreements contained a pledge by the union not to strike for the life of the agreement but to submit all disputes to binding **arbitration**. Yet from time to time, employers refused to arbitrate a disagreement, or employees went on strike in spite of contract promises. In these cases, the courts were willing to grant injunctions on the theory that the policy in favor of arbitration was more important than Norris-LaGuardia.

arbitration: the settling of a dispute by a neutral third party

In *Buffalo Forge v. United Steelworkers* (1976), however, the Supreme Court held that this exception to Norris-LaGuardia was a "narrow" one applied only when there was an underlying dispute that was arbitrable. In all other cases, even though the legality of the strike itself may be arbitrable, Norris-LaGuardia barred an injunction until an arbitrator had ruled that the strike was an actual contract violation.

Another important area of Norris-LaGuardia concerned labor disputes under the Railway Labor Act, which governs labor relations in the railroad and airline industries. Conflicts in those industries have been divided into "major disputes," which relate to the negotiation of new agreements or provisions, and "minor disputes," which concern the application or meaning of labor agreements. Under the Railway Labor Act, minor disputes must be resolved by mandatory arbitration, while major disputes were channeled through a lengthy negotiation process.

If a major dispute is not settled during the negotiation period, the employer is free to change the terms of the agreement unilaterally and the union is free to strike or picket.

If a major dispute is not settled during the negotiation period, the employer is free to change the terms of the agreement unilaterally and the union is free to strike or picket. The courts have accommodated the seemingly conflicting provisions of the Railway Labor Act with Norris-LaGuardia by holding that the mandatory provisions for resolving minor disputes should prevail over Norris-LaGuardia and that injunctions may be issued against any party who fails to follow the prescribed procedures. So far as major disputes are concerned, however, once the parties have exhausted the steps of the negotiating procedures, Norris-LaGuardia bars the issuance of injunctive relief against economic pressure whether or not that pressure is allowable under the Railway Labor Act.

Norris-LaGuardia has been read in the broadest terms to permit unions and civil rights groups to use picketing and boycotts in controversies not normally categorized as "labor disputes." The case of *New Negro Alliance v. Sanitary Grocery Company* (1938) concerned picketing by an association of African Americans to induce companies to employ more African American clerks. The Supreme Court held that because the controversy was over employment, it was a "labor dispute" and federal courts could not prevent the picketing.

Similarly, in *Marine Cooks & Stewards v. Panama S.S. Company* (1960), the union picketed foreign ships in U.S. waters to protest the employment of foreign crew members. The Supreme Court ruled that this picketing also concerned employment and wages, was a "labor dispute" under the Norris-LaGuardia Act, and could not be enjoined. Finally, in *Jacksonville Bulk Terminals v. International Longshoremens Association* (1982), employers tried to enjoin union members who had refused to load or unload goods bound to or from the Soviet Union to protest the Soviet invasion of Afghanistan. The Supreme Court held that because the dispute between the parties concerned work stoppages and whether they violated a collective bargaining agreement, it was a "labor dispute" and could not be prohibited.

The Norris-LaGuardia Act was originally passed to set a policy for the indefinite future, but as events actually occurred, that policy was abandoned by the federal government after a very short period of time. The statute has survived major policy reevaluations and has remained a vital component of present law.

In conclusion, although the Norris-LaGuardia Act was originally passed to set a policy for the indefinite future, as events actually occurred that policy was abandoned by the federal government after a very short period of time. The statute has survived major policy reevaluations and has remained a vital component of present law.

See also: NATIONAL LABOR RELATIONS ACT; TAFT-HARTLEY ACT.

BIBLIOGRAPHY

Berenson, Michael A. "Comment: Labor Injunctions Pending Arbitration," *Tulane Law Review* 63 (1989): 1681.

Frankfurter, Felix, and Nathan Greene. *The Labor Injunction*. New York: Macmillan, 1930

Gorman, Robert A. *Basic Text on Labor Law*. St. Paul, MN: West Publishing Company, 1976.

Gregory, Charles O. *Labor and the Law*. Revised, enlarged ed. New York: Norton, 1949.

Koretz, Robert F., ed. *Statutory History of the United States: Labor Organization*. New York: Chelsea House, 1970.

Lawry, Matthew C. "Jacksonville Bulk Terminals: The Norris-LaGuardia Act and Politically Motivated Strikes." In *Ohio State Law Journal* 44 (1983): 821.

Norris, George W. *Fighting Liberal*. New York: Collier Books, 1961.

Vance, Catherine A. "Note: Secondary Picketing in Railway Labor Disputes." In *Fordham Law Review* 55 (1986): 203.

North American Free Trade Agreement Implementation Act (1993)

William D. Araiza

Excerpt from the North American Free Trade Agreement Implementation Act

[T]he Congress approves—

(1) the North American Free Trade Agreement ... with the Governments of Canada and Mexico ....

(b) CONDITIONS FOR ENTRY INTO FORCE OF THE AGREEMENT.—The President is authorized to exchange notes with the Government of Canada or Mexico providing for the entry into force, on or after January 1, 1994, of the Agreement for the United States with respect to such country at such time as—

(1) The President—

(A) determines that such country has implemented the statutory changes necessary to bring that country into compliance with its obligations under the Agreement ... and

(2) the Government of such country exchanges notes with the United States providing for the entry into force of the North American Agreement on Environmental Cooperation and the North American Agreement on Labor Cooperation for that country and the United States. (19 U.S.C. § 3311)

tariff: a tax imposed on goods when imported into a country

The leaders of the United States, Mexico, and Canada signed the North American Free Trade Agreement (NAFTA) on December 17, 1992. NAFTA created a "free trade zone" through the elimination and reduction of **tariffs** and barriers to trade. President William Jefferson Clinton signed NAFTA without consulting Congress. Congress later approved and implemented NAFTA on December 3, 1993, with the passage of the North American Free Trade Agreement Implementation Act (P.L. 103-182). The act provided a series of laws to enforce NAFTA's provisions within the United States.

CIRCUMSTANCES LEADING TO THE ACT

By the late 1980s the United States had entered into a free trade agreement with Canada. As part of the Reagan Administration's commitment to free trade, plans had been made eventually to extend this free trade area to Mexico and, ultimately, to the rest of the Western hemisphere. The first step in this expansion was Mexico, which in the early 1990s led to the negotiation of NAFTA.

POLITICAL DEBATE

NAFTA was the subject of heated political debate in the United States.

NAFTA was the subject of heated political debate in the United States. Business interests and mainstream economists generally supported the idea of freer trade, especially with close neighbors such as Canada and Mexico, with whom American business had historically enjoyed close ties. On the other hand, labor and environmental groups, among others, were concerned that NAFTA, and especially the prospect of freer trade with Mexico, would lead to (1) the loss of manufacturing jobs to the lower-paying Mexican economy, and (2) to the relaxation of labor and environmental protections as part of NAFTA's overall requirements of free trade and the elimination of non-tariff barriers. Free trade can often result in the relaxation of those protections, if those protections are alleged to be nothing more than attempts to impose non-tariff trade barriers. In addition, if the free trade agreement is between a country with strict standards and one with less strict standards, firms in the former nation will be tempted to shift operations to the less strict country to circumvent the stricter standards. Because of the free trade agreement, they would still have complete access to the markets of the nation with the stricter standards. Ross Perot, an independent presidential candidate, made NAFTA a central issue of his 1992 campaign. He argued that it would lead to a large-scale loss of employment in the United States. But because both major parties supported NAFTA, it was largely to be expected that the United States would sign the agreement.

In the congressional debate on NAFTA, an issue of major importance was the provision of assistance (called "transition adjustment assistance") to American workers whose jobs were lost because of the effects of free trade. Congress provided for such assistance in title V of the act.

The Court of Appeals for the Eleventh Circuit held that the workers who brought that suit and claimed to be adversely affected by NAFTA did have standing to sue.

CONSTITUTIONAL ISSUES

The 2001 case *Made in the USA Foundation v. United States* (242 F.3d 1300, 11th Cir.) raised constitutional issues concerning NAFTA. The first issue concerned whether workers displaced as a result of NAFTA can sue based on a claim that the act is unconstitutional. The Court of Appeals for the Eleventh Circuit held that the workers who brought that suit and claimed to be adversely affected by NAFTA did have standing to sue. The court reasoned that a favorable judgment in such a lawsuit would result in a reimposition of trade barriers eliminated by NAFTA. This would in turn be likely to raise import costs, thus making domestic manufacturing more profitable and providing jobs to the plaintiff-workers.

The second issue concerned whether NAFTA satisfied the requirements for treaty ratification set out in the **treaty clause** of the Constitution (Article II, section 2). If NAFTA did in fact fail to satisfy these requirements, it would be unconstitutional. The Eleventh Circuit held that this was a political question that could not be settled in a court of law.

treaty clause: provision of the U.S. Constitution (Article II, section 2, clause 2) that grants the power to make treaties with foreign nations to the president, which are subject to approval by the Senate

EXPERIENCE UNDER THE ACT

In the period since congressional enactment of the NAFTA Implementation Act, American trade with both Canada and Mexico has increased significantly. For example, from 1993 to 1998, trade between the United States and Canada increased by 80 percent. Investment across borders by the countries that signed NAFTA has also increased significantly. For example, from 1993 to 1998 direct U.S. investment in Canada increased by 63 percent, while Canadian investment in the United States increased 86 percent. It could be argued that expansion in trade and investment was primarily a consequence of the economic boom of the 1990s. However, lower trade barriers presumably ensured that some of this increased economic activity took the form of trade with Canada and Mexico. Mexico's peso crisis of the mid-1990s also muddies the picture of NAFTA's effect on American trade with Mexico.

The overall effect of NAFTA on jobs in the United States is also a matter of dispute. However, because of the small size of the Canadian and Mexican economies in relation to that of the United States, any such effect will most likely be minor. (By contrast, the United States is Mexico's largest trading partner, with Mexico shipping almost 90 percent of its exports to the United States and receiving 70 percent of its imports from the U.S.) President Clinton's 1997 report to Congress on NAFTA estimated that the agreement had a "modest positive effect" on U.S. exports, income, investment, and export-oriented jobs. One result of NAFTA's reduction of trade barriers has been the continued expansion of *maquiladora* plants, that is, assembly plants located in Mexico near the United States border. These plants take advantage of low Mexican wage rates and nearness to the U.S. market to assemble and manufacture goods destined for that market.

Dispute Resolution. NAFTA states that certain disputes, such as those concerning antidumping claims, will be resolved not by national institutions, such as the United States Court of International Trade, but instead by a sys-

Trucks transporting goods from the United States to Mexico line up at customs in the border town of Nuevo Laredo, Mexico, December 1998. Since NAFTA's implementation, this has been a common sight. (© AP/Wide World Photos)

tem of binational review panels involving the affected nations. It also states that disputes over investment will be resolved by arbitration.

AMENDMENTS

In response to concerns from American labor and environmental groups, the United States negotiated "side agreements" with Mexico and Canada on labor standards and environmental protection. For example, the environmental side agreement required that each country agree to maintain and enforce high levels of environmental protection. Each country promised not to weaken those protections in the hope of attracting foreign investments. The labor side agreement requires each government to establish an office to receive public complaints about nonenforcement of that country's labor law. These agreements, however, do not provide for significant trade sanctions against participating countries that violate the side accords.

Expansion of NAFTA to include all of the Western hemisphere remains official United States policy, but progress on that front has been slow.

See also: TRADE ACT OF 1974.

BIBLIOGRAPHY

Folsom, Ralph. *NAFTA in a Nutshell.* St. Paul, MN: West Group, 1999.

Hufbauer, Gary, and Jeffrey Schott. *NAFTA: An Assessment.* Washington, DC: Institute for International Economics, 1993.

INTERNET RESOURCE

Home page for the NAFTA Secretariat. <http://www.nafta-sec-alena.org>.

NORTHWEST ORDINANCE (1787)

Daniel C. Wewers

Excerpt from the Northwest Ordinance

Sec. 13. And, for extending the fundamental principles of civil and religious liberty, which form the basis whereon these republics, their laws and constitutions are erected; to fix and establish those principles as the basis of all laws, constitutions, and governments, which forever hereafter shall be formed in the said territory: to provide also for the establishment of States, and permanent government therein, and for their admission to a share in the federal councils on an equal footing with the original States, at as early periods as may be consistent with the general interest....

The Northwest Ordinance, approved on July 13, 1787, organized the "Territory of the United States Northwest of the River Ohio" into one district, delineated rules for its interim governance by Congress, and established the

Continental Congress: the first central governing body of the United States (1774–1789)

Articles of Confederation: first constitution of the United States (in effect 1781–1789); it established a union between the thirteen states, but with a weak central government

process for territories to enter the United States as states. Passed by the **Continental Congress** as one of the final provisions of the **Articles of Confederation**, the Northwest Ordinance was reenacted, with minor modifications, after ratification of the Constitution by the first Congress on August 7, 1789. While the ordinance applied solely to the "Old Northwest"—the area lying west of Pennsylvania, north of the Ohio River, and east of the Mississippi River to the border with British Canada—it shaped congressional action regarding federal territories long after 1787. Considered one of the most important acts passed by Congress under the Articles of Confederation, the Northwest Ordinance ranks with the Declaration of Independence and the Constitution as the three most significant founding documents in American history.

ordinance: a law

Debate over expansion into western territories occupied the new nation in the 1780s, and the Continental Congress passed three separate **ordinances** for territorial governance during that critical decade. Thomas Jefferson was the principle author of the Ordinance of 1784, written after a major 1784 Virginia land cession. The act articulated a general statement of democratic principles, recommending the evolution of the territories toward statehood in stages of increasing self-government. The Ordinance of 1784 advocated the division of the region into sixteen new states (with names like Polypotamia and Pelisipia), each possessing the same powers as the original thirteen states. The Ordinance of 1784 also prohibited slavery in the western territories after 1800, but its enforcement met delays for various reasons. In the meantime, the Land Ordinance of 1785 addressed the land-sale issue. It directed that the territory's land be surveyed in six-mile-square townships, each containing thirty-six one-mile square (640 acre) "sections" to be sold at auction for a dollar an acre. The ensuing grid pattern from this legislation still dominates the region's landscape to this day.

The Northwest Ordinance of 1787 filled the void left by the ineffectual 1784 Ordinance. Originally intended as an amendment to Jefferson's legislation, Massachusetts Representatives Rufus King and Nathan Dane completely redrafted the bill in the final days of Congress's session. The drafting committee also received contributions from Reverend Manasseh Cutler, an agent for the Ohio Company, a group of Massachusetts speculators prepared to purchase five million acres in the territory. Pressured by land speculators anxious to preserve private property on the frontier, the act represented a general movement toward law, order, and stability in the new nation that expressed itself in the simultaneous drafting of the Constitution. As Abraham Lincoln pointed out to a Cincinnati audience in 1859, "Our fathers who made the government, made the ordinance of 1787."

Fourteen preliminary "sections" and six solemn "articles of compact" comprised the text of the Northwest Ordinance. The opening section established one district in the Northwest Territory "for the purposes of temporary government" that Congress might subdivide if it deemed necessary. The second section contained provisions for conveying real property, making wills, and settling estates of persons dying without wills.

Debate over expansion into western territories occupied the new nation in the 1780s, and the Continental Congress passed three separate ordinances for territorial governance during that critical decade.

The ordinance then outlined a three-stage process for the transition from territorial status to statehood. In the first stage, Congress would appoint a governor, a secretary, and a court of three judges to administer the territory. To achieve its ends, this first-stage legislature of five officials was authorized to "adopt and publish" criminal and civil laws from existing states, as necessary for governance of the territory. The governor would serve a three-year term as commander in chief of the militia and appoint magistrates and other civil officials in the territory. He would also enjoy the power to establish counties, townships, and other civil divisions until the organization of the second-stage legislature, as well as to convene, suspend, or dissolve the general assembly as he saw fit. The governor would even enjoy absolute veto power over acts of the assembly.

Fourteen preliminary "sections" and six solemn "articles of compact" comprised the text of the Northwest Ordinance.

Once the district reached a population of five thousand free males of "full age," the governor, an elected lower house, and an appointed legislative council would assume responsibility for administration. Male inhabitants of the territory meeting the property qualifications for voting could elect one representative for every five hundred free males in the district. These representatives would form the lower house of a general assembly and, in conjunction with the governor, nominate members for the legislative council (or upper house/senate). This second-stage legislature could enact any laws necessary for governing the territory not repugnant to the 1787 Ordinance or the Constitution; it also could send one non-voting member to Congress. When the district reached a population of sixty thousand free inhabitants, it entered the third stage of the process. It then could adopt a "republican" state constitution and apply to Congress for full statehood. Upon approval by Congress, the state would enter the federal union "on an equal footing with the original States in all respects whatever."

The second portion of the ordinance included six "articles of compact between the original states and the people and states in the said territory," to be forever "unalterable, unless by common consent." Similar to the bills of rights included in many contemporary state constitutions, Articles I and II of the ordinance guaranteed freedom of religion, the writ of **habeas corpus**, trial by jury, proportionate representation in the legislature, and judicial proceedings under common law. Article III provided for public support of education in the territory and pledged (at least in theory) the "utmost good faith" in relations with Native Americans. Article IV made the territory's inhabitants responsible for their share of the federal debt and government expenses, while Article V established the provisional boundaries of "not less than three nor more than five States," as well as the third-stage threshold of sixty thousand free inhabitants. The sixth and final article prohibited slavery and involuntary servitude in the territory, although it did allow for the recovery of fugitive slaves. Despite its lasting fame as the first piece of national legislation to limit the expansion of slavery—Article VI became an icon of the mid-nineteenth-century Free Soil movement—the ordinance contained no enforcement mechanisms, and slavery persisted in parts of the region as late as the 1840s.

habeas corpus: (Latin, "you should have the body") a written order to bring a prisoner in front of a judge, to determine whether his or her detention is lawful

The ordinance's blueprint for continental expansion and its provisions for territorial evolution from colonial dependency to equal statehood were perhaps its most important legacies. While the Northwest Territory's relatively short administrative history ended with the admission of Ohio to the United States in 1803, the original grant of territory eventually fashioned four other states: Indiana (1816), Illinois (1818), Michigan (1837), and Wisconsin (1848), as well as part of Minnesota (1858). Altogether, this landmark legislation, establishing the basic framework for U.S. territorial governments, eventually served in related forms in the establishment of thirty-two states, one common-

While many have showered acclaim on a document that married territorial expansion with republican self-government, others have pointed out its tragic consequences for the Native American population that faced decimation and exile in the wake of white settlement of the Northwest Territory.

wealth, and one republic. Senator Daniel Webster declared in an 1830 speech, "We are accustomed to praise the lawgivers of antiquity; ... but I doubt whether one single law of any lawgiver, ancient or modern, has produced effects of more distinct, marked, and lasting character than the Ordinance of 1787." Modern historians might add a degree of caution to Webster's remarks. While many have showered acclaim on a document that married territorial expansion with republican self-government, others have pointed out its tragic consequences for the Native American population that faced decimation and exile in the wake of white settlement of the Northwest Territory.

See also: SOUTHWEST ORDINANCE.

BIBLIOGRAPHY

Onuf, Peter S. *Statehood and Union: A History of the Northwest Ordinance.* Bloomington: Indiana University Press, 1987.

Taylor, Robert M., Jr., ed. *The Northwest Ordinance, 1787: A Bicentennial Handbook.* Indianapolis: Indiana Historical Society, 1987.

Williams, Frederick D., ed. *The Northwest Ordinance: Essays on Its Formulation, Provisions, and Legacy.* East Lansing: Michigan State University Press, 1988.

NUCLEAR NON-PROLIFERATION ACT (1978)

David A. Koplow

The Nuclear Non-Proliferation Act (P.L. 95-242, 92 Stat. 120) is the central act in a family of statutes intended to control the spread of nuclear weapons materials and technology. Congress found that the dissemination of such items "poses a grave threat to the security interests of the United States and to continued international progress toward world peace and development." This complex and controversial act relies on a variety of legal strategies to stop the spread of the most hazardous weapons-related items while allowing access to nuclear power used for peaceful purposes.

Many nuclear fuels, facilities, components, and technologies are "dual capable." In other words, they can be useful (indeed, essential) in peaceful civilian applications of nuclear energy, such as electrical power generation, and in potentially aggressive or hostile military applications, including explosive weapons. The challenge for policy makers—especially in the United States, traditionally the world's leading supplier of these items—is to develop a method of promoting the peaceful atomic uses while preventing or at least inhibiting hostile uses.

This complex and controversial act relies on a variety of legal strategies to stop the spread of the most hazardous weapons-related items while allowing access to nuclear power used for peaceful purposes.

BACKGROUND

In the 1970s many countries, reeling from the shock of the 1973 Arab oil embargo, were exploring non-fossil fuel sources with renewed interest. Some turned toward the promise of safe, cheap, reliable, and clean nuclear energy. At the same time, the dangers of nuclear weapons proliferation were never more apparent. In 1974 India announced a test detonation of a nuclear device, expanding the "club" of states acknowledged to possess nuclear weapons.

Congress also recognized another fundamental political and economic reality: the importance of enhancing the reputation of the United States as a reliable supplier of nuclear materials. For countries that have chosen to adopt nuclear power plants as a component of their national energy production plans, stability of access to fuels, replacement parts, and expertise is essential. If the United States threatens to restrict or cut off supplies, those countries will be driven to greater reliance on their own sources. In the short run, this fallback plan might inhibit a country's nuclear ambitions. But in the longer term, such a strategy might lead to greater independence in nuclear matters, reducing America's ability to steer nuclear programs toward exclusively peaceful directions.

Finally, Congress was aware that the United States would soon no longer hold total control as a supplier of nuclear materials. Additional countries were entering the market. If the United States were to attempt to impose strict unilateral controls for non-proliferation or other reasons, potential purchasers would readily switch to other, less careful sources. International cooperation among all suppliers, therefore, had to be a hallmark of future policies. Some efforts had already been undertaken in that direction, such as the convening of the London Suppliers Group in 1974 to coordinate export policies.

FEATURES AND GOALS OF THE ACT

The Nuclear Non-Proliferation Act (NNPA), championed by Senators John Glenn, Democrat of Ohio, and Charles Percy, Republican of Illinois, addressed all these concerns in several ways. First, Congress endorsed the International Nuclear Fuel Cycle Evaluation (INFCE) program of study, which had been initiated by President Jimmy Carter shortly before the NNPA was passed. With forty-one countries participating over three years, the INFCE was a major international assessment of ways to reduce opportunities for the diversion of materials and technology from civilian to weapons purposes.

Next, Congress committed itself to strengthening the International Atomic Energy Agency (IAEA), a watchdog on nuclear safety and security. The act pledges additional financial and technical assistance for IAEA's safeguards programs, as well as cooperation in data-sharing and other areas. In succeeding years, the annual U.S. Program on Technical Assistance to Safeguards has contributed more than $150 million in support of the IAEA.

On the domestic side, the NNPA revised the existing hodgepodge of U.S. law related to export controls on nuclear facilities, equipment, materials, and technology. For example, several executive branch agencies (the Departments of State, Defense, Energy, and Commerce, the Arms Control and Disarmament Agency, and the Nuclear Regulatory Commission, among others) all provide input on nuclear matters. The NNPA formalized the process of coordinating the information provided by these agencies, making it quicker and more efficient.

"AGREEMENTS FOR COOPERATION"

The NNPA also mandated the renegotiation of most existing "agreements for cooperation." These agreements (there were 22 at the time the NNPA was enacted) are the basic device through which the United States exports nuclear-related items to purchaser countries. Each individual agreement for cooperation is a legally binding treaty that specifies the rights and responsibilities of each country, and details, in particular, the assurances against diversion of the transferred materials into weapons uses. By 1978, Congress was dissatisfied with the strictness of some of those assurances, and demanded an across-the-board toughening. This process has required several years of painstaking country-by-country negotiation.

One key feature of the revised agreements for cooperation is consent to "full scope safeguards." This means that the international protections against diversion to weapons uses must apply not only to the specific materials, equipment, and other items supplied by the United States, but to *all* peaceful nuclear activities undertaken in the country, regardless of their

A protester wearing a mock radiation suit stands next to a burning sign criticizing North Korean leader Kim Jong-Il at a demonstration in Seoul, South Korea, November 15, 2002. In October 2002, North Korea announced that it had a clandestine nuclear weapons program in violation of the 1968 Nuclear Nonproliferation Treaty. On January 10, 2003, North Korea withdrew from the treaty altogether. (©REUTERS NEWMEDIA INC./CORBIS)

origin. These safeguards, typically administered by the IAEA, have not proven to be "airtight" in thwarting a recipient's nuclear weapons ambitions (as revealed by the violations detected in the 1990s in Iraq and North Korea). Nonetheless, they are the best and most up-to-date means we have of ensuring non-proliferation. Under the act, if the president finds that a recipient country has violated the IAEA safeguards, all U.S. cooperation with that state is to be terminated (with the possibility of a presidential waiver of termination).

"SUBSEQUENT ARRANGEMENTS"

The NNPA also regulates "subsequent arrangements," covering a wide variety of actions such as retransfers (shipping nuclear items from the original recipient to someone else); storage or disposal of nuclear fuel after irradiation in a power reactor (demanding a U.S. approval right for storage of U.S.-supplied items); and appropriately strict standards for the physical protection and security of facilities and materials (often a sensitive matter, considered to infringe on a recipient country's control over security operations inside its own territory).

One important category of subsequent arrangements is the "reprocessing" of spent fuel. Reprocessing offers the potential of extracting additional energy from the fuel and perhaps reducing the cost of generating electrical power. But it does so at the price of creating additional quantities of plutonium, a particularly dangerous substance with direct weapons applications. The NNPA explicitly states that a condition of U.S. supply of nuclear materials is a U.S. veto over any reprocessing.

As an enforcement measure, the NNPA also terminates nuclear cooperation with any country that has conducted a nuclear explosion or "engaged in activities involving source or special nuclear material and having direct significance for the manufacture or acquisition of nuclear explosive devices."

ENSURING COMPLIANCE BY NUCLEAR NATIONS

As an enforcement measure, the NNPA also terminates nuclear cooperation with any country that has conducted a nuclear explosion or "engaged in activities involving source or special nuclear material and having direct significance for the manufacture or acquisition of nuclear explosive devices." In essence, these provisions virtually require each recipient country to join the 1968 Non-Proliferation Treaty (NPT), under which they would renounce possession of nuclear weapons. In 1978 the majority of countries in the world had accepted the obligations of the NPT. By the beginning of the twenty-first century, virtually all states (with the conspicuous exceptions of North Korea, India, Israel, and Pakistan) have done so. The global consensus against the further spread of nuclear weapons has been repeatedly reaffirmed at the highest levels.

The NNPA also calls for multilateral negotiations and cooperation among suppliers (such as the INFCE). In addition, the act aims to unite the supplier countries behind a program of enhanced export controls and, through the coordination of international efforts, to preempt a dangerous competition among sellers that could lead to looser constraints. The act therefore directs the president to "take immediate and vigorous steps to seek agreement from all nations" to apply full-scope safeguards requirements as conditions for their nuclear exports. Similarly, the NNPA calls for negotiation among all nations with nuclear capabilities to strengthen physical security standards.

THE ROLE OF CONGRESS IN SECURITY MATTERS

The NNPA requires that the executive branch keep Congress more fully informed about non-proliferation activities and dangers. In particular, section 601 calls for a wide-ranging annual report covering ongoing U.S. non-proliferation policy and accomplishments, including the negotiations toward improved agreements for cooperation, an assessment of the success of U.S. policy, and information on which countries have complied with American and IAEA standards. These reports allow the executive branch to review the year's non-proliferation successes and failures. They have also proven quite useful in advising the Congress and the general public about unfolding events.

The NNPA also gave Congress a more important role alongside the executive branch in security matters. Injecting itself directly into the international arena, Congress called for negotiation or renegotiation of a whole series of important international agreements. After the NNPA was enacted, Congress monitored more closely than before both the internal and the international operations of the U.S. government in this critically important security area.

THE IMPORTANCE OF NON-PROLIFERATION

The NNPA made the United States much more assertive in combating the spread of nuclear weapons capability. Although this issue had always been a significant American concern, the technical and diplomatic complexity of the task had frustrated many policy makers. Competing priorities had sometimes required compromise of non-proliferation policies. Through the NNPA, the United States elevated non-proliferation as a fundamental policy goal and emphasized the importance of the problem. Non-proliferation became an issue that the United States cared even more about, and to which the country was prepared to devote more technical and political resources.

See also: Arms Control and Disarmament Act and Amendments; Weapons of Mass Destruction Control Act.

BIBLIOGRAPHY

Bettauer, Ronald J. "The Nuclear Non-Proliferation Act." *Law and Policy in International Business* 35 (1978): 1105–1180.

Franko, Lawrence. "U.S. Regulation of the Spread of Nuclear Technologies through Supplier Power: Lever or Boomerang?" *Law and Policy in International Business* 35 (1978): 1181–1204.

Nuclear Waste Policy Act (1982)

Joseph P. Tomain

Regulation of nuclear power was transferred from military to civilian control with the passage of the Atomic Energy Act of 1954. Although the dangers of radioactivity were known before the act, it was not until the passage of the Nuclear Waste Policy Act (NWPA) (P.L. 97-425, 96 Stat. 2201) that the back end of the fuel cycle was addressed.

HAZARDS OF NUCLEAR WASTE

The central problem of nuclear waste derives from the facts that radioactivity may last for many thousands of years and must be contained so it no longer presents a significant risk to human health or to the environment. Nuclear waste is generated from many sources. The mining and milling process generates radioactive debris known as mill tailings, which constitute a low-level source of radioactivity. Mill tailings are addressed in the Uranium Mill Tailings and Radiation Control Act of 1978. Radioactive materials are also generated from medical and industrial uses. Certain low-level wastes are addressed in the Low-Level Radioactive Waste Policy Amendments Act of 1985. By far the largest source of radioactive waste results from the generation of electricity by commercial nuclear reactors, which produce tens of thousands of tons of spent nuclear fuel. The primary problem at commercial nuclear power sites is that temporary storage facilities for spent fuel are full and require expansion until a permanent disposal site is completed. In addition, thousands of tons of nuclear waste are generated through military uses.

The central problem of nuclear waste derives from the facts that radioactivity may last for many thousands of years and must be contained so it no longer presents a significant risk to human health or to the environment.

The NWPA requires the Department of Energy (DOE) to dispose of nuclear waste safely and with environmentally acceptable methods in a geologic formation with the intent to bury designated waste at underground disposal sites. The National Academy of Sciences began looking for disposal sites in the mid-1950s. Preliminary screening identified four large potentially promising regions of either salt domes or bedded salt mines. These formations offer relatively safe space for nuclear waste because they restrict the flow of water that can spread radioactivity.

In 1970 the Atomic Energy Commission identified specific disposal sites, and in the late 1970s, the National Waste Terminal Storage Program helped develop the technology necessary for repository licensing, construction, operation, and closure. In 1980 the Department of Energy, after engaging in an environmental impact statement process, selected mined geologic repositories as the preferred storage space for spent commercial nuclear fuel. All of those efforts culminated in the Nuclear Waste Policy Act of 1982.

PROVISIONS OF THE NWPA

Although the federal government has the primary responsibility for permanent disposal of such waste, the costs of disposal are intended to be the responsibility of generators and owners of the waste and spent fuel. The act also recognizes an important role for public and state participation. The reason for the

Although the federal government has the primary responsibility for permanent disposal of such waste, the costs of disposal are intended to be the responsibility of generators and owners of the waste and spent fuel.

broad participation of other sovereigns is because repositories must be located somewhere and choosing a site is, as correctly predicted, controversial. Thus, the statute involves the secretary of energy, the president, Congress, the states, Native American tribes, and the general public in the site selection process.

In 1983 the Department of Energy located nine sites in six states as potential repository sites. Based on initial studies, the president approved three sites in Hannaford, Washington; Defsmith County, Texas; and Yucca Mountain, Nevada. In 1987 Congress amended the Nuclear Waste Policy Act, directing the Department of Energy to study only Yucca Mountain, which is now the designated site awaiting NRC approval. The selection of Yucca Mountain has not been without controversy. In *Nevada v. Watkins* the United States Court of Appeals for the Ninth Circuit rejected the state's challenge of legislative authority for this decision. Pursuant to NWPA, Nevada exercised a veto over site selection, and that veto was overridden in both houses of Congress.

CHALLENGES TO THE ACT

Since the passage of the NWPA, the siting program has faced a number of challenges, including legislative mandates, regulatory modification, fluctuating funding levels, and the evolving and often conflicting needs and expectations of various and diverse interest groups. The challenges from scientists, citizens, legislators, and governors all complicated the process, generating increased Congressional dissatisfaction.

The identification and scheduling of disposal sites have not been finalized as of the date of this writing. In 1997 Congress directed the DOE to complete a "viability assessment" of the Yucca Mountain site. The viability assessment was codified into law by the Energy and Water Development Appropriations Act, which directed that no later than September 3, 1998, the secretary of energy provide to the president and Congress a viability assessment of the Yucca Mountain site. The viability assessment must include:

(1) preliminary design concept of the repository and waste package
(2) total system performance assessment describing the probable behavior of the repository relative to overall system performance
(3) plan and cost estimate for remaining work required to retain a license
(4) an estimate of costs to construct and operate the repository

The NWPA envisioned that site selection would be completed in 1998 and that a facility would then be available to accept waste. That date, of course, has passed. The site characterization process and the politics involved have become increasingly complex. In 1987 the DOE announced an opening date in 2003, a date that also was not met. In 1989 a further delay was announced by the Department of Energy to 2010.

In December 1998 the DOE submitted its assessment to the president and Congress. The viability assessment indicated that the site required further study, although it supported a recommendation of the site to the president. The Department of Energy now seeks final authorization from the Nuclear Regulatory Commission to develop the site as a repository. Consequently, Yucca Mountain is currently earmarked for receipt of waste upon Nuclear Regulatory Commission approval.

Nuclear wastes are currently located in 129 sites in thirty-nine different states, which include seventy-two commercial nuclear reactor sites, a commercial storage site, forty-three research sites, and ten Department of Energy sites. Once the major disposal site is finalized, the secretary of energy is authorized to enter into contracts with owners and generators of spent nuclear fuel for storage. In addition, transportation plans must be undertaken in an environmentally safe and sound manner. Although the commercial nuclear power market has been stagnant for nearly two decades, nuclear waste disposal issues continue to be an important part of the nation's energy planning.

Nuclear wastes are currently located in 129 sites in thirty-nine different states, which include seventy-two commercial nuclear reactor sites, a commercial storage site, forty-three research sites, and ten Department of Energy sites.

See also: ATOMIC ENERGY ACTS; HAZARDOUS MATERIALS TRANSPORTATION ACT.

BIBLIOGRAPHY

Bosselman, Fred, Jim Rossi, and Jacqueline Lang Weaver. *Energy, Economics and the Environment*. New York: Foundation Press, 2000.

Carter, Luther J. *Nuclear Imperatives and Public Trust: Dealing with Radioactive Waste*. Washington, DC: Resources for the Future, Inc., 1987.

Tomain, Joseph P. *Nuclear Power Transformation*. Bloomington: Indiana University Press, 1987.

Union of Concerned Scientists. *Safety Second: The NRC and America's Nuclear Power Plant*. Bloomington: Indiana University Press, 1987.

Zillman, Donald N. "Nuclear Power." In *Energy Law and Policy for the 21st Century*, ed. The Energy Law Group. Denver, CO: Rocky Mountain Mineral Law Foundation, 2000.

Occupational Safety and Health Act of 1970

John P. Forren

With the Occupational Safety and Health Act of 1970 (OSHA) (84 Stat. 1690), Congress triggered a rapid and unprecedented expansion of the federal government's role in protecting worker health and well-being. For most Americans, the concerns that had prompted passage of this landmark law were hardly unfamiliar or new. Journalists and progressive reformers for nearly a century had highlighted—often with grisly tales of disfigurement and death—how accidents in America's factories and mines had ruined thousands of workers' lives. Federal statistics compiled since 1911 had also documented a growing epidemic of work-related illness and disease. Still, Congress throughout the industrial period had done little to stem this tide. The broadest early federal reform measures—legislation establishing the U.S. Department of Labor in 1913 and banning exploitative child labor in 1938—intentionally left most regulatory power over industrial working conditions with the states. Stronger federal laws, such as the Esch Act of 1912 (which effectively outlawed the production of white phosphorus matches) and the Walsh-Healey Public Contracts Act of 1936 (which barred federal contracts for companies operating hazardous worksites), applied only to targeted industries or small segments of the private sector.

New Deal: the legislative and administrative program of President Franklin D. Roosevelt designed to promote economic recovery and social reform (1933–1939)

By the late 1960s, however, prospects for a broader federal regulatory role had improved in several respects. For one thing, Americans in the wake of the **New Deal** and the civil rights movement had largely grown accustomed to federal oversight of activities—like industrial production—once controlled primarily by the states. For another thing, the federal judiciary had substantially adjusted the Constitution's balance of state and federal powers since the late 1930s so as to accommodate more aggressive national regulation. Most significantly, decades of regulatory failure had made clear to most observers that the nation's faith in state laws to protect workers' health and safety had long been tragically misplaced. On-the-job accident rates had continued to rise unabated; as the Secretary of Labor reported in 1969, disabling work-related injuries had increased by 20 percent—up to 2.2. million per year—just since 1958. State governments struggled constantly to pay for vigorous enforcement of their health and safety laws. And states, competing with each other to attract and retain manufacturing jobs, faced ever-stronger incentives to water down their safety standards in order to reduce the costs of businesses operating within their borders.

THE ENACTMENT OF OSHA

Citing a national crisis, President Lyndon B. Johnson submitted a comprehensive occupational safety and health bill to Congress in January 1968. Under Johnson's proposal, the U.S. Department of Labor would have been charged with establishing mandatory safety standards for most worksites throughout the nation. Employers also would have been assigned a new "general duty" to prevent on-the-job accidents and illnesses. What is more, to ensure compliance—long a problem under existing state laws—Johnson proposed a new corps of federal inspectors, to be armed with broad authority to investigate

A steelworker rests on the eighty-sixth floor of the unfinished Empire State Building in New York, September 24, 1930. This would certainly be a violation of OSHA standards, had the law been in effect then. (© AP/Wide World Photos)

worksites and penalize violators. Labor groups immediately applauded Johnson's initiative and promised political support; yet in the end, the Johnson bill failed to come to a vote in either house of Congress in 1968. Industry groups lobbied vigorously against it from the outset, joined by pro-business legislators and "states' rights" activists fearing an expansion of federal regulatory authority. President Johnson, distracted by the Vietnam War, domestic upheaval, and election-year politics, never mounted an aggressive legislative campaign in response.

Despite this initial setback, workplace safety legislation emerged again in Congress the following year. Newly elected Republican President Richard M. Nixon, seeing an opportunity to siphon blue-collar voters away from opposition Democrats, announced his support for a modified occupational safety and health bill early in August 1969. Under Nixon's plan, the Labor Department would have carried out the task of workplace inspections in much the same way that President Johnson had envisioned; yet in a key change, Nixon sought to assign the power of establishing national safety and health standards to a new five-person board to be appointed by the president. Nixon also called for lighter penalties against violators and exemptions from the law for small employers. Business groups, led by the U.S. Chamber of Commerce, this time came out solidly in support of Nixon's division-of-power approach. Organized labor, however, rejected any watering down of Labor Department authority and rallied behind an alternative Senate Democratic bill instead.

Amidst this labor-management conflict, both legislative proposals bogged down in Congress for more than a year. But congressional Republicans broke the logjam in November 1970 when they agreed to lodge standards-making authority in a new agency—the Occupational Safety and Health Administration—within the Department of Labor. Democrats, in turn, agreed to dilute Occupational Safety and Health Administration's enforcement power by creating a separate appointed body, the Occupational Safety and Health Review Commission, to judge cases involving possible industry violations. With this compromise in hand, both houses of Congress quickly agreed to a final version of the bill in a lame-duck December session. President Nixon dropped his remaining objections, and in a Labor Department ceremony attended by labor union and business leaders alike, Nixon signed the Occupational Safety and Health Act into law on December 29, 1970.

Downfall of the OSHA

OSHA quickly became one of the federal government's most disliked agencies. Small-business owners complained that they were subject to voluminous and petty rules, as well as to arbitrary inspections. The problem resided in the fact that OSHA adopted a range of "consensus standards" previously defined by federal agencies, trade associations, and safety organizations. Some of these standards were ancient and deemed irrelevant, making OSHA the object of much scorn.

In its final form OSHA established a multifaceted federal approach toward improving workplace conditions. One set of provisions in the act established procedures aimed at promoting cooperation between OSHA regulators and state public health agencies. Another set of provisions created the National Institute for Occupational Safety and Health—now part of the Centers for Disease Control and Prevention—to carry out research into job-related accidents and diseases. Additional sections of the act required the Occupational Safety and Health Administration to collect and distribute up-to-date health and safety information to employers in high-risk industries. Extensive funding and outreach mechanisms were also established to assist small businesses and industries with outmoded technologies in their efforts to meet OSHA-**promulgate** workplace standards.

promulgate: to make the terms of a law known by formal public announcement

Beyond those measures, the act most notably granted to the Occupational Safety and Health Administration the direct authority to promulgate and enforce specific safety and health rules for almost every place of employment in the United States. The Occupational Safety and Health Administration's primary mission, the act declares, is "to assure so far as possible every working man and woman in the Nation safe and healthful working conditions." To that end, the agency must ensure that employers take any measures "reasonably necessary and appropriate" to protect workers' long-term health and safety. Mandatory OSHA standards may thus include extensive requirements of protective equipment, employee training, and monitoring of dangerous job sites. Agency compliance efforts may entail unscheduled worksite inspections and extensive record-keeping requirements. OSHA inspectors may impose sanctions and remedial measures on employers found in violation of promulgated standards. And in the event of "imminent" threats to worker safety or health, the agency may bypass its ordinary rule-making process and seek immediate **injunctive relief** in a federal district court.

injunctive relief: a court order that requires a person to refrain from doing something; the order guards against future damages rather than remedies past damages

OSHA'S IMPACT IN THE WORKPLACE

By arming the agency with such broad regulatory and enforcement authority, OSHA's main architects in Congress clearly hoped for dramatic and lasting

Construction is a particularly dangerous occupation. Falls from elevations are among the leading causes of death of construction workers. Of the 37,493 federal inspections performed by OSHA in fiscal year 2002, 21,347 were in the construction industry. (© AP/Wide World Photos)

improvements in the health and well-being of American workers. Indeed, as one leading senator predicted during final floor debate, the Occupational Safety and Health Act would stand as "one of the truly great landmark pieces of social legislation in the history of [the] country." Yet over three decades later, reviews of the act and the administrative apparatus it created continue to be mixed at best. OSHA supporters point to compelling evidence of success: since 1970, workplace fatalities in the United States have decreased sharply, debilitating occupational diseases such as "brown lung" and asbestosis have virtually disappeared, and workers in American factories and mills now experience greatly reduced levels of exposure to such dangerous substances as cotton dust, lead, arsenic, beryllium metal and vinyl chloride. Yet critics of the agency question whether OSHA should be assigned significant credit for these achievements; technological advances and global economic changes, they say, have been the primary forces behind improvements in American worker safety and health. Further, critics from across the ideological spectrum attack the agency for failing to execute its mission with what they see as appropriate zeal. Naysayers on the political right complain that OSHA regulators too often ignore market remedies and impose workplace rules without adequate consideration of cost. Those on the left, meanwhile, sometimes fault the agency for watering down standards in the face of industry pressure and for failing to exercise sufficient independence during periods of pro-business Washington leadership.

bipartisan: involving members of two parties, especially the two political parties

Despite such criticisms, attempts to enact major revisions of OSHA since 1970 have consistently failed. Moreover, given the current **bipartisan** consensus about the need for active federal leadership in occupational safety and health, significant alterations of the act in the near future seem unlikely.

See also: FAIR LABOR STANDARDS ACT OF 1938; WALSH-HEALEY ACT.

BIBLIOGRAPHY

Berman, Daniel M. *Death on the Job: Occupational Health and Safety Struggles in the United States.* New York: Monthly Review Press, 1978.

Lofgren, Don J. *Dangerous Premises: An Insider's View of OSHA Enforcement.* Ithaca, NY: ILR Press, 1989.

McGarity, Thomas O., and Sidney A. Shapiro. *Workers At Risk: The Failed Promise of the Occupational Safety and Health Administration.* Westport, CT: Praeger, 1993.

Rosner, David, and Gerald Markowitz, eds. *Dying for Work: Workers' Safety and Health in Twentieth-Century America.* Bloomington: Indiana University Press, 1989.

United States Department of Labor. *All about OSHA.* Washington, DC: OSHA Publications Office, 2000.

United States Senate Committee on Labor and Public Welfare. *Legislative History of the Occupational Safety and Health Act of 1970.* Washington, DC: Government Printing Office, 1971.

Viscusi, W. Kip. *Risk by Choice: Regulating Health and Safety in the Workplace.* Cambridge, MA: Harvard University Press, 1983.

White, Lawrence. *Human Debris: The Injured Worker in America.* New York: Seaview/Putnam, 1983.

INTERNET RESOURCE

Occupational Safety and Health Administration Home Page. <http://www.osha.gov/>.

Oil Pollution Acts

Arthur Holst

The Oil Pollution Act of 1990 (OPA) (P.L. 101-380 104 Stat. 484) established **liabilities** for polluters and recovery methods for areas affected by oil spills. It was preceded by the Oil Pollution Act of 1924 (43 Stat. 604) and the Oil Pollution Act of 1961 (P.L. 87-167). The 1924 act prohibited the discharge of oil into U.S. coastal waters and was regulated by the U.S. Coast Guard. The 1961 act forbade the discharge of oil in any waters within fifty miles of the U.S. coast, extending the area regulated by the previous legislation.

liability: an obligation, responsibility, or duty that one is bound by law to perform

In 1980 the Oil Pollution Act of 1961 was superceded by the Act to Prevent Pollution from Ships of 1980 (P.L. 96-478), which forced ships in U.S. waters, or U.S. ships anywhere, to follow the pollution prevention guidelines established by the International Convention for the Prevention of Pollution from Ships of 1973. This convention, a reaction to the environmental damage caused by the oil spill off the ship *Torrey Canyon* in the English Channel in 1967, set guidelines that regulated oil, chemical, sewage, and garbage discharges into the sea.

Oil pollution prevention legislation was further strengthened by OPA, signed into law on August 18, 1990. The new legislation was enacted soon after the *Exxon Valdez* ran aground on Bligh Reef in the Prince William Sound of Alaska in March of 1989, spilling over eleven million gallons of oil. Although Congress was in favor of the legislation, opposition came from the oil industry executives who were concerned about the costs of implementing the OPA's stricter requirements. The act enabled the Environmental Protection Agency (EPA) to better regulate, prevent, and respond to devastating oil spills. The purpose of the OPA was to "amend [section] 311 of the Clean Water Act to clarify federal response authority for oil spills, increase penalties for spills, require tank vessel and facility response plans, and provide for contingency planning in designated areas."

The act enabled the Environmental Protection Agency (EPA) to better regulate, prevent, and respond to devastating oil spills.

Under the OPA, liability for oil spills is placed on the owner or operator of the ship. The responsible party must pay the costs of environment recovery, repair of damage to natural resources, and compensation to people affected by the spill. In addition, parties that use oil tankers or have certain facilities that could pose a threat to the local environment must create acceptable contingency plans (plans to cover possible spills). These plans must be approved by the EPA. The OPA establishes the Oil Spill Liability Trust Fund, which can provide up to $1 billion for oil spill recovery efforts and is financed primarily by a per barrel tax on oil.

Other important provisions of the OPA include revoking a mariner's registries and licenses on the grounds of alcohol and drug abuse, the maintenance of U.S. Coast Guard units specialized in oil spill cleanup, the establishment of a study on tanker navigation and tanker safety, and the requirement of double-hulled tank vessels. Assessments of the legislation have shown that many oil companies have yet to convert to double-hulled oil

Under the OPA, liability for oil spills is placed on the owner or operator of the ship.

The Exxon Baton Rouge *(smaller ship) attempts to off load crude oil from the* Exxon Valdez, *March 29, 1989. The* Exxon Valdez *ran aground on a reef in the Prince William Sound, off the coast of Alaska, in the largest oil spill in American history.* (©AP/WIDE WORLD PHOTOS)

tankers. The Department of Justice has used the OPA to prosecute oil spills, including the *New Carissa* spill in Coos Bay, Oregon, in 1999, the *Scandia* and *North Cape* spill at Moonstone Beach, Rhode Island, in 1999, and the cruise ship line *Royal Caribbean* for illegal oil dumping from 1990 to 1994.

BIBLIOGRAPHY

National Research Council. *Double-Hull Tanker Legislation: An Assessment of the Oil Pollution Act of 1990.* Washington, DC: National Academy Press, 1998.

"Oil Pollution Act of 1990: Summary Overview." Cook Inlet RCAC. <http://www.circac.org>.

"Prevention of Pollution by Oil." International Maritime Organization. <http://www.imo.org/environment>.

INTERNET RESOURCES

Environmental Protection Agency. <http://www.epa.gov>.

Omnibus Crime Control and Safe Streets Act of 1968

Thomas M. Hilbink

Excerpt from the Omnibus Crime Control and Safe Streets Act of 1968

Congress finds that the high incidence of crime in the United States threatens the peace, security, and general welfare of the Nation and its citizens. To prevent crime and to insure the greater safety of the people, law enforcement efforts must be better coordinated, intensified, and made more effective at all levels of government. Congress finds further that crime is essentially a local problem that must be dealt with by State and local governments if it is to be controlled effectively.

The late 1960s were years of great social and political upheaval in the United States. Crime policy reflected struggles over race and poverty, perhaps most clearly in the Omnibus Crime Control and Safe Streets Act of 1968 (OCCSSA) (P.L. 90-351, 82 Stat. 197). This legislation bears the marks of divergent visions of the causes and cures of crime in America.

HISTORICAL BACKGROUND

There was little debate over one matter in the mid-1960s: the United States was experiencing a nationwide upswing in crime. One barometer, the homicide rate, was approximately 10 murders per 100,000 in 1932. The homicide rate fell over the next two decades, settling around 5 per 100,000 throughout the 1950s. It began climbing around 1963, as did all major types of crime.

There was little debate over one matter in the mid-1960s: the United States was experiencing a nationwide upswing in crime.

May 1965 marked the first time that a majority of people responding to nationwide polls named crime as the most important problem facing the nation. Such fears can be tied to forces beyond crime itself. **Civil disobedience** and marches by Southern blacks were met by widespread violence in the form of beatings, bombings, and murders by or with the approval of local police and government, most famously during the Birmingham protests of 1963. Broadcast over the nation's televisions, images of protests and police reaction gave many Americans the impression that lawlessness was epidemic. Urban riots only intensified such feelings.

civil disobedience: nonviolent protest

Beginning in Harlem, a section of New York City, in 1964, and Watts, a section of Los Angeles, in 1965, summers came to be marked by urban unrest. Often sparked by incidents and allegations of police brutality, civil disorders occurred in over 100 cities by 1968, accompanied by looting, arson, and clashes with police and the National Guard. Reactions to crime, protest, and riots carried with them strong undercurrents of racism, a consistent facet of American law and politics in this period.

Whereas crime was not a concern in the 1960 presidential race between John F. Kennedy and Richard M. Nixon, the issue rose to prominence in 1964.

Whereas crime was not a concern in the 1960 presidential race between John F. Kennedy and Richard M. Nixon, the issue rose to prominence in 1964. Candidates George Wallace and Barry Goldwater called for "law and order" in challenging President Lyndon Johnson. Johnson won the 1964 election, after which he seized on the crime issue by creating the President's Commission on Law Enforcement and the Administration of Justice. The Katzenbach Commission, as it was known, issued dozens of studies on crime and criminal justice over the next two years. Pointing to the socioeconomic roots of crime, the commission's recommendations fit with the policy approaches of Johnson's **Great Society**. The commission called for more education, better training of law enforcement officers, and increased research on crime. The commission's proposals served as a blueprint for the OCCSSA, the crime bill Johnson sent to Congress in 1967.

Great Society: broad term for the domestic programs of President Lyndon B. Johnson, in which he called for "an end to poverty and racial injustice"

FEATURES OF THE ACT

The OCCSSA contained four major elements designed to address the crime problem:

(1) It created the Law Enforcement Assistance Administration (LEAA) to provide financial assistance to state and local government law enforcement.
(2) It included provisions regarding the admissibility of confessions in criminal trials (through an amendment to the act in the Senate).
(3) It established procedures to allow wiretapping by law enforcement authorities.
(4) It included provisions that placed regulations on firearm sales and possession.

The LEAA constituted the core of Johnson's anticrime policy. Government grants supported state and local coordination and planning on crime fighting, education and training of law enforcement officers, surveys and advisory services relating to the operation of law enforcement agencies, development of demonstration programs, the creation and funding of institutes for research and training, and aid for equipment and infrastructure. Though state and local governments were straining to cover law enforcement budgets, throughout the legislative debate supporters and opponents of the bill expressed concerns that federal grant-making to state and local authorities could serve as the first step in creating a federal police force. These concerns stemmed from conflicts between federal, state, and local governments over the enforcement of civil rights laws and controversies relating to federal control of local programs under the Economic Opportunity Act. Thus, Congress removed provisions allowing for grants to pay officers' salaries and approved amendments giving state governors veto power over any grant.

Though state and local governments were straining to cover law enforcement budgets, throughout the legislative debate supporters and opponents of the bill expressed concerns that federal grant-making to state and local authorities could serve as the first step in creating a federal police force.

EXPERIENCE UNDER THE ACT

In its first year, the LEAA granted $300 million, primarily to police for equipment purchases. Over the years the LEAA funded, among others, programs to train local bomb squads, pilot programs studying alternatives to incarceration, drug treatment programs, and state court organization and training. Significantly, the LEAA was responsible for developing national training programs for state and local law enforcement officers and lawyers, bringing modern techniques to many departments for the first time. By 1981, when the LEAA shut down and federal crime policy shifted toward direct federal involvement in law enforcement, the LEAA had granted over $8 billion. While some see the LEAA's shuttering as a sign of failure, states adopted 70 percent of LEAA-sponsored programs in one form or another. It thus made a significant contribution to the modernization and standardization of local law enforcement. More enduring was the act's creation of the National Institute of Law Enforcement and Criminal Justice (now the National Institute of Justice). The institute revolutionized the gathering, interpretation, and dissemination of crime studies and statistics.

Title III of the act related to use of electronic surveillance (wiretapping) as a law enforcement practice. Although the Communications Act of 1934 made wiretapping a crime (even by law enforcement officers), police and others regularly engaged in such activity. The Supreme Court's decisions in *Berger v. New York* (1967) and *Katz v. United States* (1967) held that the gathering of evidence through electronic surveillance methods constitutes a "search and seizure" under the Fourth Amendment and is thus subject to Constitutional requirements. Reacting to those decisions, Congress established court procedures regulating law enforcement's use of electronic surveillance. (It otherwise made wiretapping a crime with limited exceptions.) Nowhere has the impact of the wiretapping provision been felt more acutely than in the world of organized crime. In trials since the act's passage, the government has relied heavily on wiretap evidence to convict organized crime figures at every level.

Nowhere has the impact of the wiretapping provision been felt more acutely than in the world of organized crime.

The regulation of firearms became a national issue in the wake of the assassinations of Martin Luther King, President Kennedy, and Senator Robert F. Kennedy. But congressional debate on this matter reflected an apparently unfounded fear that African-Americans were stockpiling weapons. Prior to 1968, gun owners were required to register guns with the government as set out in the National Firearms Act of 1934, but the OCCSSA marked the first major restrictions on handgun purchase and ownership (the Gun Control Act of 1968 would extend restrictions to rifles and other firearms). The act required licensing of firearms manufacturers, dealers and importers; criminalized interstate transportation and sales of handguns by those not licensed; and banned sales to and possession of guns by indicted or convicted felons, veterans dishonorably discharged, undocumented immigrants, and the mentally ill, among others.

Finally, the act aimed to overturn Supreme Court decisions as to the admissibility of evidence obtained in violation of the Constitutional rights of the people under the Fourth Amendment. The Supreme Court's decision in *Miranda v. Arizona* (1966) barred the use at trial of any voluntary confession if the confessor was not informed of his rights to remain silent and right to have an attorney assigned prior to questioning. Thus, Title II of the act allowed for the admission of such voluntary confessions, even if the police failed to inform the suspect of his rights. On this issue the legislation had little effect, as federal courts retained the power to determine the scope and applicability of the Constitution. The Supreme Court affirmed this view (and declared Title II unconstitutional) in *Dickerson v. United States* (2000).

OCCSSA also marked a shift from liberal crime policies focused on societal causes of crime to conservative policies focused on individual guilt and retribution.

The OCCSSA represented a major step toward federalization of crime policy and control. It also marked a shift from liberal crime policies focused on societal causes of crime to conservative policies focused on individual guilt and retribution. Both visions of crime control were present in the OCCSSA. However, the politics of "law and order" would dominate federal crime policy in the remaining decades of the century.

See also: Anti-Drug Abuse Act; Organized Crime Control Act of 1970; Sentencing Reform Act; Violent Crime Control and Law Enforcement Act of 1994.

BIBLIOGRAPHY

Fagan, Jeffrey. "Continuity and Change in American Crime: Lessons from Three Decades." *The Challenge of Crime in a Free Society: Looking Back ... Looking Forward,* ed. U.S. Department of Justice, Office of Justice Programs. Washington, DC: U.S. Department of Justice, 1997.

Feeley, Malcolmx, and Austin Sarat. *The Policy Dilemma: Federal Crime Policy and the Law Enforcement Assistance Administration.* Minneapolis: University of Minnesota Press, 1980.

Finckemauer, James O. "Crime as a National Political Issue, 1964–76: From Law and Order to Domestic Tranquility." *Crime and Delinquency* 24 (1978): 13–27.

Friedman, Lawrence. *Crime and Punishment in American History.* New York: Basic Books, 1993.

President's Commission on Law Enforcement and Administration of Justice. *The Challenge of Crime in a Free Society: A Report.* Washington, DC: U.S. Government Printing Office, 1967.

Scheingold, Stuart. *The Politics of Law and Order.* New York: Longman, 1984.

Walker, Samuel. "Reexamining the President's Crime Commission: The Challenge of Crime in a Free Society After Ten Years." *Crime and Delinquency* 24 (1978): 1–12.

Wilson, James Q. *Thinking about Crime.* New York: Vintage Books, 1985.

Organized Crime Control Act of 1970

Arthur G. LeFrancois

In the early 1950s, Senator Estes Kefauver of Tennessee led a committee of the U.S. Senate in investigating organized crime in the United States. The Special Senate Committee to Investigate Organized Crime in Interstate Commerce concluded that organized crime was a threat to America's economy and security. At about the same time, the American Bar Association, at the request of Senator Kefauver, created its Commission on Organized Crime. Other groups studied the issue of organized crime as well, in 1967 the President's Commission on Law Enforcement and the Administration of Justice issued a report that examined the problem of organized crime.

These efforts reflected a growing concern in the nation about the influence of organized crime, which involves people coming together in syndicates to conduct illegal business like narcotics trafficking or to infiltrate legal businesses. People were concerned that these crime syndicates were draining the economy and threatening people's safety. So lawmakers sought to devise ways to address the problem of organized crime. These efforts led to the passage of the Organized Crime Control Act (OCCA) (P.L. 91-452, 84 Stat. 922) in 1970. On October 15 of that year, President Richard M. Nixon signed the OCCA, saying that the new law would allow law enforcement to "launch a total war against organized crime."

FEATURES OF THE ACT

The OCCA says that its purpose is "to seek the eradication of organized crime in the United States by strengthening the legal tools in the evidence-gathering process, by establishing new penal prohibitions, and by providing enhanced sanctions and new remedies to deal with the unlawful activities of those engaged in organized crime."

The OCCA has thirteen parts, or titles. Titles that relate to the evidence-gathering process are, for example, those that allow the creation of special grand juries (panels of citizens with powers to investigate) and those that provide special rules to make it easier to get information from witnesses. These special rules include:

- Allowing witnesses to be jailed if they refuse, without good reason, to comply with court or grand jury orders.
- Allowing witnesses to be jailed and fined for providing false information to a court or grand jury.
- Limiting the ability of witnesses to refuse to testify on the basis that their testimony might incriminate them (the Fifth Amendment privilege).
- Providing safe housing for those who fear that their testimony might endanger their safety.

Two titles of the OCCA concern the creation of "new penal prohibitions." These titles establish the crimes of syndicated gambling and crimes relating to explosives. Another title concerns "enhanced sanctions" to deal with organized crime, and another allows for increased criminal sentences in cases of "dangerous special offenders."

RICO

The most controversial part of the OCCA is commonly called RICO, for Racketeer Influenced and Corrupt Organizations. Critics claim that RICO threatens civil liberties and that, although it was designed to deal with problems of organized crime, it is used in cases having nothing to do with organized

The most controversial part of the OCCA is commonly called RICO, for Racketeer Influenced and Corrupt Organizations.

crime. RICO's defenders argue that it provides important tools to prosecutors. They also say it was designed only in part to attack the problem of organized crime but was also intended to apply to other kinds of enterprise criminality, such as white-collar (business) crime.

RICO allows the government to bring criminal prosecutions against people or "entities." This is called criminal RICO. An entity is a person or group of persons capable of having a legally recognized interest in property. RICO also allows the government to pursue civil remedies (such as compelling someone to do or refrain from doing something) against people or entities. Finally, it authorizes private civil suits for damages by a person or entity. This is called civil RICO.

To make out a RICO claim, the government must allege that:

(1) A "person" (as defined by the statute to include certain entities) has used
(2) a "pattern of racketeering activity" or proceeds from such activity
(3) to infiltrate an interstate "enterprise"
(4) by investing in the enterprise any income derived from the pattern of racketeering activity, by gaining or keeping an interest in the enterprise through the pattern of racketeering activity, by using the pattern of racketeering activity to conduct the affairs of the enterprise, or by conspiring to do any of these three things (investing, acquiring, or conducting).

A private person or entity bringing a civil suit under RICO must claim the elements listed above, and in addition must claim injury to their business or property.

RICO thus aims at enterprise-oriented criminality. It condemns certain crimes against, by, or through enterprises. "Enterprise" covers criminal organizations and legitimate businesses. Although RICO has been used against organized crime, it has also been used in cases of political corruption, white-collar crime, terrorism, and small criminal enterprises. An enterprise, under RICO, can be an "individual, partnership, corporation, association, or other legal entity," as well as a group of people who do not form a legal entity, so long as they are "associated in fact." RICO has been applied to businesses, law firms, unions, mob families, and government offices and agencies.

RICO: Applications for the Internet

In 2003 Senator Bill Nelson of Florida introduced a bill that would make Internet spam prosecutable under the Racketeer Influenced and Corrupt Organizations (RICO) section of the Organized Crime Control Act. Noting that nearly half of all e-mail received in the United States is unsolicited advertising, Nelson sought to target spammers who use e-mail in deceitful or illegal ways. The proposed legislation would require recipients of unsolicited e-mail to be able to opt out of receiving future advertisements and prohibited messages that concealed the identity of the sender. Victims would be able to sue for damages in civil court. Critics of the proposed bill argued that it was an inappropriate use of RICO that was unlikely to hold up in court.

FORBIDDEN ACTIVITY

RICO seeks to punish and prevent the infiltration of enterprises by those who engage in a "pattern of racketeering." This pattern element requires two or more acts of racketeering, one of which occurred after the date RICO became law, and the last of which occurred within ten years after a prior act of racketeering activity. Courts continue to determine just what, beyond this minimum, constitutes a pattern.

The "racketeering activity" condemned by RICO includes acts of "violence, the provision of illegal goods and services, corruption in labor or management relations, corruption in government, and commercial fraud" (Blakey 1990, p. 854). More specifically, it includes acts or threats punishable under state law involving "murder, kidnapping, gambling, arson, robbery, bribery, extortion, or dealing in narcotic or other dangerous drugs." Racketeering activity also includes acts that violate a wide range of federal laws, including those prohibiting fraud, gambling, obstruction of justice, embezzlement, and counterfeiting.

RICO provides several criminal penalties for violations of its provisions. Each RICO violation is punishable by a fine of not more than $25,000, imprisonment of not more than twenty years, or both. RICO convictions can also result in the defendant losing certain property. Forfeiture of property to the government upon criminal conviction was a new punishment enacted by RICO.

CIVIL REMEDIES

RICO also authorizes civil remedies. The government can seek court orders to prevent and restrain RICO violations, to compel persons to divest themselves of any interest in an enterprise, and to restrict persons' future activities or to dissolve enterprises. Additionally, the statute enables private parties to sue for RICO violations that injured their business or property. This part of RICO provides for "treble damages," meaning that any award of damages will be tripled. This part also allows the private party suing to recover the cost of

Joseph M. Valachi, a New York City gangster, sitting at the witness table facing the Senate Investigation subcommittee, reveals the inner workings of a major crime syndicate, October 8, 1963. As the problem of organized crime was examined throughout the 1960s, it became clear that it was a threat to the security and economy of the United States, requiring additional law enforcement measures. (© AP/WIDE WORLD PHOTOS)

the suit, including attorney's fees. This private right of action part of RICO has become perhaps its most controversial.

Civil RICO was a late addition to the bill that was ultimately passed by Congress in the midst of an election campaign in which law and order was a prominent feature. Originally ignored, civil RICO came to be used in the early 1980s in a wide variety of cases. Legislation thought by many to have been targeted toward organized crime and its infiltration of legitimate business was suddenly being used as a routine matter against banks, insurance firms, corporate executives, and government officials.

RICO, and the OCCA of which it is a part, give powerful tools to government prosecutors. The law creates new crimes, new penalties, and new investigative and prosecutorial weapons. In part because of the right of private action—civil RICO—the law has developed in some surprising ways. Courts will continue to be faced with difficult issues, particularly those regarding the proper reach of RICO.

See also: ANTI-DRUG ABUSE LAW; OMNIBUS CRIME CONTROL AND SAFE STREETS ACT OF 1968; SENTENCING REFORM ACT.

BIBLIOGRAPHY

Abrams, Douglas E. *The Law of Civil RICO.* Boston: Little, Brown, 1991.

Sixteen members of the Luchese crime family were arrested on November 14, 2002, on Long Island, New York, for operating a racketeering ring. Officials said they made nearly $1.5 million through activities such as loansharking, gambling, construction payoffs, and restaurant extortion. (© AP/WIDE WORLD PHOTOS)

American Bar Association, Criminal Justice Section. *A Comprehensive Perspective on Civil and Criminal RICO Legislation and Litigation*. Washington, DC: American Bar Association, 1985.

Blakey, G. Robert, and Thomas A. Perry. "An Analysis of the Myths that Bolster Efforts to Rewrite RICO and the Various Proposals for Reform: 'Mother of God—Is This the End of RICO?'" *Vanderbilt Law Review* 43 (1990): 851–1101.

Rakoff, Jed S., and Howard W. Goldstein. *RICO: Civil and Criminal Law Strategy*. New York: Law Journal Press, 2000.

Outer Continental Shelf Lands Act (1953)

Charles Anthony Smith

Excerpt from the Outer Continental Shelf Lands Act

It is hereby declared to be the policy of the United States that —the subsoil and seabed of the outer Continental Shelf appertain to the United States and are subject to its jurisdiction, control, and power of disposition ... the right to navigation and fishing therein shall not be affected ... the outer Continental Shelf is a vital national resource reserve held by the Federal Government for the public, which should be made available for expeditious and orderly development, subject to environmental safeguards, in a manner which is consistent with the maintenance of competition and other national needs.

The Outer Continental Shelf Lands Act of 1953 (OCSLA) (67 Stat. 462) provides a mechanism for the federal government to establish ownership of and jurisdiction over the subsoil and seabed of the Outer Continental Shelf. The Outer Continental Shelf is the submerged edge of land that slopes towards the bottom of the ocean. The purpose of establishing ownership and jurisdiction is to allow for the exploitation and conservation of the land and extractable resources contained there. The main extractable resources that are the concern of the OCSLA are oil and natural gas, although it contemplates jurisdiction over any minerals discovered. The geographic jurisdiction of the OCSLA begins where the state boundaries end and continues until the end of the Continental Shelf. The OCSLA first was enacted in 1953 along with the Submerged Lands Act and has been amended numerous times throughout the years. The OCLSA reaffirmed the claim of federal supremacy over the seabed and subsoil asserted by President Harry Truman in Proclamation 2667 on September 28, 1945.

The Outer Continental Shelf Lands Act provides a mechanism for the federal government to establish ownership of and jurisdiction over the subsoil and seabed of the Outer Continental Shelf, the submerged edge of land that slopes towards the bottom of the ocean.

The original political motivation of the proclamation and the subsequent enactment of OCSLA had two dimensions. First, the shortages of fuel during World War II led the federal government to view access to energy resources as a security issue. Second, as World War II ended and the **Cold War** began, the assertion of sovereignty over the extended seabed served as a signal to the Soviet Union and others that the United States had no intention of disengag-

Cold War: a conflict over ideological differences carried on by methods short of military action and usually without breaking off diplomatic relations; usually refers to the ideological conflict between the U.S. and the former U.S.S.R.

ing from world affairs simply because the war was over. Originally, OCSLA was not a contentious bill although there was some debate about possible infringement on states' rights and about which administrative agency would direct future activity affected by the legislation.

The subsequent amendments to OCSLA have been more controversial than the original bill. Specifically, beginning in the 1970s, conservation became a more salient political issue, while beginning in the 1980s, state sovereignty was resurrected as an important political issue. Conservation of the resources and the environment in which those resources are found frequently conflicts with the exploitation of those resources. Similarly, federal jurisdiction over the resources and land inherently reduces state jurisdiction.

Despite its politically benign origins, virtually every aspect of OCSLA is now controversial. Much of the environmental controversy involves the valuation of the resources at issue and the impact of exploitation of those resources on the surrounding environment. Of special concern is the cleanup and valuation of damages arising out of oil spills. The jurisdiction controversy frequently is focused on whether state or federal laws should apply in disputes including labor laws, contract enforcement, and torts. Additionally, the competing interests of the extraction industries and the fishing industries led to a series of amendments, contained in Title IV of the act, to establish the Fisherman's Contingency Fund to compensate those in the fishing industry when they are damaged by some extraction activity.

Despite its politically benign origins, virtually every aspect of OCSLA is now controversial.

See also: MINERAL LEASING ACT.

BIBLIOGRAPHY

Environmental Management in Oil and Gas Exploration and Production. London: E&P Forum/UNEP, 1997.

Farrow, R. Scott. *Managing the Outer Continental Shelf: Oceans of Controversy.* New York: Taylor and Francis, Inc., 1990.

P

Panama Canal Purchase Act (1902)

Matthew M. Taylor

Excerpt from the Panama Canal Purchase Act

"An Act to provide for the construction of a canal connecting the waters of the Atlantic and Pacific oceans. Be it enacted, ... that the President of the United States is hereby authorized to acquire, for and on behalf of the United States, at a cost not exceeding forty millions of dollars, the rights, privileges, franchises, concessions, grants of land, right of way, unfinished work, plants, and other property, real, personal, and mixed, of every name and nature, owned by the New Panama Canal Company, of France, on the Isthmus of Panama.... That the President is hereby authorized to acquire from the Republic of Colombia, for and on behalf of the United States, upon such terms as he may deem reasonable, perpetual control of a strip of land, the territory of the Republic of Colombia, not less than six miles in width, extending from the Caribbean Sea to the Pacific Ocean, and the right to use and dispose of the waters thereon, and to excavate, construct, and to perpetually maintain, operate, and protect thereon a canal..."

The Panama Canal Purchase Act (P.L. 57-183, 32 Stat. 481), enacted on June 28, 1902, provided for the construction of a canal connecting the Atlantic and Pacific Oceans. The act authorized (1) the purchase of the French New Panama Canal Company at a cost not exceeding $40 million; (2) negotiation with the Colombian government for "perpetual control" of a strip of land at least six miles wide on either side of the canal, as well as rights to operate the canal; and (3) the building and operation of the canal "for vessels of the largest tonnage and greatest draft" in use at the time of the act's passage.

The canal across Panama has involved a long list of treaty ratifications and large sums of public money, making Congress a major player in relations with that Central American country.

Interest in a trans-isthmus canal was longstanding, and deeply affected by U.S. relations with European powers. Many believed that a canal would (1) reinforce U.S. domination of the Caribbean, especially in light of U.S. victory in the 1898 Spanish-American war; (2) ensure naval defenses on both oceans; and (3) significantly ease commerce. But before a canal could be built, the U.S. needed to overcome its obligations to Great Britain under the Clayton-Bulwer Treaty of 1850, which prevented either country from "exercising any dominion" over Central America or from acquiring "sole control" of a canal in the region. The friendly neutrality of the British during the Spanish-American war encouraged Congress to negotiate the Hay-Pauncefort Treaty, by which both nations agreed to U.S. control of a canal but on the condition that all nations would be allowed equal peacetime access.

The location of the new canal was the second obstacle to the passage of a canal act.

The location of the new canal was the second obstacle to the passage of a canal act. The recommendations of the Walker Commission, appointed by President William McKinley in 1899 to report on the best trans-isthmus route, were to build the canal through Nicaragua, rather then Panama. This route was closer to the United States and less expensive. Following these recommendations, the House of Representatives overwhelmingly approved the Hepburn Bill (named after Representative William Hepburn of Iowa), which called for construction of a Nicaraguan canal. But passage of that bill led the owners of the French New Panama Canal Company, most notably Philippe Bunau-Varilla, the majority shareholder, to lower their sale price from $109 million to $40 million, making the Panama route more attractive in terms of both

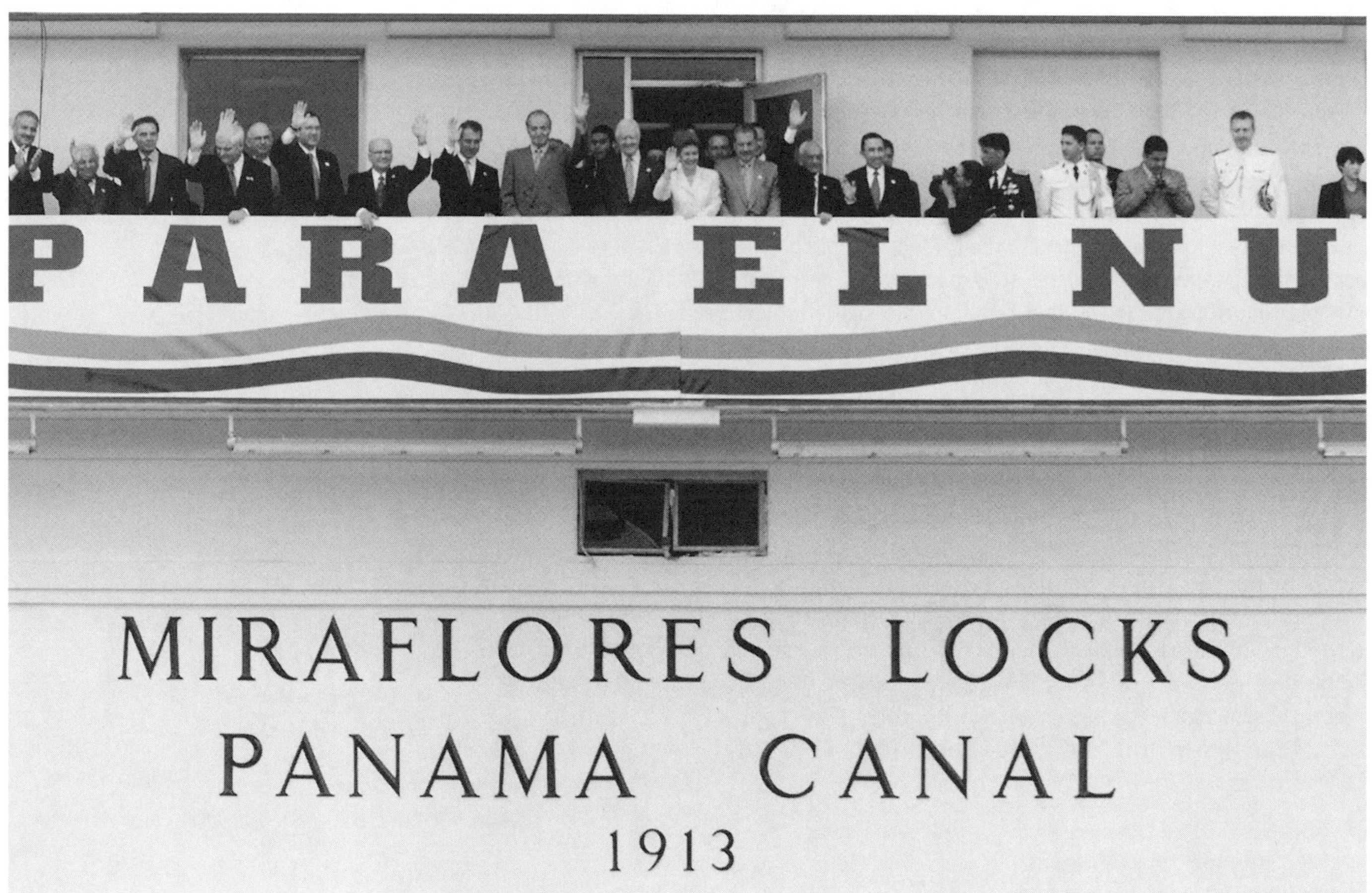

A ceremonial gathering on the control tower of the Miraflores Locks of the Panama Canal, December 14, 1999. As stipulated in the Carter-Torrijos Treaties, the United States transferred control of the canal to Panama on December 31, 1999. (© AP/WIDE WORLD PHOTOS)

length and cost. With Republican Party support, as well as the successful tactic of playing up volcanic activity in the Nicaraguan canal route, Bunau-Varilla was able to ensure the passage of an amendment (known as the Spooner Amendment after Senator John Spooner of Wisconsin) to the Hepburn Bill on June 28, 1902, authorizing President Theodore Roosevelt to purchase the company's rights for $40 million and negotiate with Colombia over land cession.

The purchase of the New Panama Canal Company was quickly undertaken. The Colombian government, however, having just emerged from a civil war, was less flexible. The Colombians, fearing political damage and the potential loss of their northernmost province, hoped to use their reluctance as a financial bargaining chip. In January 1903 the Colombian minister in Washington agreed to the Hay-Herrán Treaty, which would allow the ceded land to be sold to the United States for $10 million, plus an annuity (a yearly payment). But in Colombia the treaty was a politically sensitive issue. When U.S. communications appearing to bully the Colombian government were revealed in 1903, the Colombian lower house unanimously rejected the treaty.

Under the terms of the Spooner Amendment, this setback suggested the canal would now be built in Nicaragua. But President Roosevelt, Bunau-Varilla, and a group of Panamanian nationalists were insistent on the Panama route. The U.S. Navy was sent to Panama to prevent arrival of Colombian troops, and the United States declared and recognized Panamanian independence in early November. Bunau-Varilla became the first Panamanian ambassador to the United States and signed the Hay-Bunau-Varilla Treaty on November 18 (ratified on February 25, 1904). By means of this treaty, the United States acquired a ten-mile strip of land through Panama in perpetuity, as well as rights of intervention in the main cities, in exchange for $10 million and a $250,000 annuity.

Work on the canal began in 1904 and was completed, at a cost of over $350 million, in 1914.

Work on the canal began in 1904 and was completed, at a cost of over $350 million, in 1914. In 1977 President Jimmy Carter signed the Carter-Torrijos Treaties, providing for the return of the Canal to Panama in 2000. These were ratified in 1978, and the canal was returned to Panama on December 31, 1999.

BIBLIOGRAPHY

McCullough, David. *The Path Between the Seas: The Creation of the Panama Canal.* New York: Simon and Schuster, 1977.

Miner, Dwight Carroll. *The Fight for the Panama Route: The Story of the Spooner Act and the Hay-Herrén Treaty.* New York: Columbia University Press, 1940.

Paperwork Reduction Act (1980)

Jeffrey S. Lubbers

Excerpt from the Paperwork Reduction Act

[E]ach agency shall ... consult with members of the public and affected agencies ... to—

(i) evaluate whether the proposed collection of information is necessary for the proper performance of the functions of the agency, including whether the information shall have practical utility;

(ii) evaluate the accuracy of the agency's estimate of the burden of the proposed collection of information;

(iii) enhance the quality, utility, and clarity of the information to be collected; and

(iv) minimize the burden of the collection of information on those who are to respond, including through the use of automated collection techniques. [44 U.S.C. § 3506]

The Paperwork Reduction Act (PRA) of 1980 (P.L. 96-511, 94 Stat. 2812) was intended to minimize the amount of paperwork the public is required to complete at the behest of federal agencies. At the same time, because the PRA also recognizes that good information is essential to agencies' ability to serve the public successfully, it gives the Office of Management and Budget (OMB) the responsibility to weigh the practical utility of the information to the agency against the burden its collection imposes on the public. The act requires federal agencies to request the approval of the OMB before collecting information from the public.

The act requires federal agencies to request the approval of the OMB before collecting information from the public.

GENERAL STRUCTURE OF THE ACT

The act established the Office of Information and Regulatory Affairs (OIRA) in OMB, and authorizes and requires it to perform an array of oversight functions relating to information resources in the federal government. More specifically, OIRA is given responsibility for coordinating government information policies, including the approval of agency collections of information (CIs). The act provides that agencies "shall not conduct or sponsor the collection of information" without first obtaining the go-ahead of OMB. The act applies to all agencies in the executive branch, including the independent regulatory agencies. OMB's general clearance procedures are, however, subject to the PRA's provision that independent regulatory agencies may, by majority vote, override an OMB decision disapproving a proposed information collection. The act also contains the only statutory definition of "independent regulatory agency."

Only certain functions are exempted from the PRA's coverage, such as intelligence activities, criminal enforcement matters, civil and administrative actions, and investigations. This coverage gives OIRA a tremendous amount of clout within the federal government—even beyond what it already has with its budgetary and regulatory oversight roles. Failure to obtain OMB approval of a collection of information triggers the PRA's "public protection provision," which provides that "no person shall be subject to any penalty for failing to comply" with a CI that is subject to this chapter if the CI does not display a valid control number assigned by OMB.

Agencies must publish their proposed information collection in the *Federal Register* for a sixty-day public comment period. After reviewing the public comments and revising the proposed collection as appropriate, agencies submit the proposal to OMB for review, discussion, and approval (or disapproval). In seeking OMB's approval, the agency needs to demonstrate that the CI is the most efficient way to obtain information necessary for the proper performance of the agency's functions, that the information would not duplicate other information that the agency already maintains, and that the agency will make practical use of it. The agency also must certify that the proposed CI "reduces to the extent practicable and appropriate the burden" on respondents. The act applies to freestanding CIs (such as tax forms) as well as those embedded in proposed rules (such as reporting requirements).

In seeking OMB's approval, the agency needs to demonstrate that the CI is the most efficient way to obtain information necessary for the proper performance of the agency's functions, that the information would not duplicate other information that the agency already maintains, and that the agency will make practical use of it.

The act requires the head of each agency, supported by his or her chief information officer, to be responsible for the agency's information collection activities. This includes reducing the amount of paperwork required of the public.

CIRCUMSTANCES LEADING TO THE ADOPTION OF THE ACT

The PRA was originally enacted in 1980, but it had precursors going back to the **New Deal**. President Franklin Roosevelt's concerns over the large number of statistical reports that federal agencies were requiring from business and industry led to a review of such reports and, ultimately, the enactment of the Federal Reports Act in 1942. That act gave the Bureau of the Budget (the precursor to OMB) the responsibility to review agency information requests. However, in 1974 Congress responded to continuing constituent complaints about paperwork burdens by creating a Commission on Federal Paperwork. The commission undertook numerous studies to determine the nature of the federal paperwork problem and to make recommendations for changes in statutes, regulations, and procedures. The final report was submitted in 1977, and Congress responded in 1980 by enacting the Paperwork Reduction Act.

New Deal: the legislative and administrative program of President Franklin D. Roosevelt designed to promote economic recovery and social reform (1933–1939)

EXPERIENCE UNDER THE ACT

Since the passage of the act, agencies have had to be much more careful about unnecessary paperwork burdens. For its part, OMB must produce an annual Information Collection Budget report, made available on the Internet, that contains examples of burden reduction achieved by its reviews. The act's goal of attaining an annual 5 percent government-wide reduction of paperwork burden is somewhat beyond OMB's control, because new laws contain new CIs, and also because over 80 percent of this burden is produced by the Treasury Department (chiefly, the Internal Revenue Service).

Conflicts over the interpretation of certain provisions of the act resulted in amendments. The 1986 amendment clarifies the relationship between the procedures required for clearance of information collections in proposed rules and other proposed information collections.

The 1995 amendments updated, strengthened, and recodified the act. It also settled the important question of whether the act covers agency rules that require businesses or individuals to maintain information for the benefit of third parties or the public (rather than for the government). In 1990 the Supreme Court had ruled in *Dole v. United Steelworkers* that the act did not so require, but the 1995 amendments make clear that it does now. This means that many agency rules containing such requirements not previously reviewed by OIRA are subject to review.

RELATIONSHIP WITH OTHER LAWS

The act, in effect, serves as an amendment of the Administrative Procedure Act in that it adds additional OMB clearance procedures for proposed rules that contain CIs. It also shares the approach of the Regulatory Flexibility Act in requiring consideration of alternatives that produce fewer paperwork burdens on small entities.

See also: ADMINISTRATIVE PROCEDURE ACT.

BIBLIOGRAPHY

Funk, William F. "The Paperwork Reduction Act: Paperwork Reduction Meets Administrative Law." *Harvard Journal on Legislation* 24 (1987): 1-116.

Lubbers, Jeffrey S. "Paperwork Redux: The (Stronger) Paperwork Reduction Act of 1995." *Administrative Law Review* 49 (1997): 111-121.

PATENT ACTS

Shubha Ghosh

Imagine inventing a gizmo that people have only dreamed of. You probably would want to keep others from stealing your invention. Patent law is the area of law that allows you to protect your invention from theft.

EARLY VIEWS ABOUT PATENTS

Ever since the founding of the American Republic, patent law has been a source of debate. In England patents were granted by the crown to reward inventors for their creations. The patent gave the inventor a monopoly in the form of an exclusive right to practice the invention and keep others from using it. Many of our founding fathers worried about the granting of such monopolies, especially ones that had been associated with the King of England.

Ever since the founding of the American Republic, patent law has been a source of debate.

Thomas Jefferson, for example, was highly suspicious of a patent system. His views were famously expressed in a letter to Isaac McPherson, a Baltimore inventor, in 1813: "That ideas should freely spread from one to another ... for the moral and mutual instruction of man ... seems to have been peculiarly and benevolently designed by nature when she made them ... expansible over all space, ... incapable of confinement or exclusive appropriation. Inventions ... cannot, in nature, be a subject of property." In another letter, Jefferson was quite blunt in stating that it would be unwise for Congress to meddle in "matters of invention." Jefferson, however, was not at the Constitutional Convention, whereas James Madison and James Iredell were. They had the final word on patents. Madison asserted that "the utility [of Congress' power to grant patent[s] will scarcely be questioned." Referring to George Mason, who was critical of too much congressional power except for the granting of patents, James Iredell, the first North Carolinian to serve on the United States Supreme Court wrote: "He is a gentleman of too much taste and knowledge himself to wish to have our government established upon such principles of barbarism as to be able to afford no encouragement to genius."

CONSTITUTIONAL POWER

Congress' ability to encourage genius was made possible by Article I, section 8, clause 8 of the United States Constitution, which gave to Congress the power "to promote the progress of science and the useful arts by securing for limited times to authors and inventors the exclusive right to their respective writings and discoveries." Pursuant to this power, Congress passed the first Patent Act in 1790, with amendments in 1793, 1836, 1839, 1870, 1897, 1903, 1928, and 1939, and with a complete revision in 1952. The 1952 Patent Act is the current law of patents, and it in turn has been amended several times, with the most recent amendments in 1999.

Current Patent Act

According to the current Patent Act (35 U.S.C. § 101): "Whoever invents or discovers any new and useful process, machine, manufacture, or composition of matter, or any new and useful improvement thereof, may obtain a patent therefor."

THE VARIOUS PATENT ACTS

The 1790 act created a system for patent review and grant that was administered by the secretary of state, the secretary of war, and the attorney general. Under this system, an invention would be submitted to these three officials for review. If two out of three determined that the invention was "sufficiently useful and important," a patent would be granted to the inventor. The patent gave the inventor the exclusive right to make, use, and sell the invention for fourteen years from the time the patent was granted.

In 1793 the system was changed radically to a registration system. Under this system, an inventor would register his invention with the secretary of state, who would instruct the attorney general to grant a patent for fourteen years to the inventor. Remember that the first secretary of state was Thomas Jefferson. It is ironic that the first patent act was administered largely by a man who, being an inventive genius in his own right, not only never sought a patent but also was critical of a patent system.

It is ironic that the first patent act was administered largely by a man who, being an inventive genius in his own right, not only never sought a patent but also was critical of a patent system.

The 1836 Patent Act which created the Patent Office as part of the Department of State. The 1870 act moved the Office to the Department of Interior. The Patent Office was renamed the United States Patent and Trademark Office and moved to its current home in the Department of Commerce as a result of changes to the law in the 1940s.

PATENTS TODAY

To obtain a patent today, an inventor must go through a review process by a patent examiner, an employee of the United States Patent and Trademark

Office (USPTO). The process, which takes on average two years, involves a determination that the invention is new and useful. Once the patent is granted, a description of the invention is published for everyone to read and the inventor is given an exclusive right to make, use, sell, and offer to sell the invention. If someone does make, use, sell, or offer to sell the invention without the patent owner's permission, the patent owner can sue for infringement and obtain money damages from the infringer.

Several controversies riddle contemporary patent law. Criticisms about the granting of improper patents have been raised against the office. Newspaper accounts document patents given for seemingly frivolous items. In 1998 the online retailer Amazon.com brought suit against Barnesandnoble.com for allegedly infringing on its patent for the "One-Click Shopping Method," by which customers can easily and quickly submit their order information by clicking the mouse once in the appropriate area of Amazon's Web site. The lawsuit remained in the courts until 2001, when it was determined that the patent granted to Amazon was invalid.

The One-Click patent has been cited as an example of a patent that wastes economic resources and is used only to hurt one's competitors in the marketplace. Reform proposals include expanding the USPTO to allow for more thorough patent review, disallowing patents for certain inventions altogether, and even returning to a registration system for patents as it existed in 1790 because the USPTO arguably has not been able to carry out its mission. Although it is unlikely that we will return to a pure registration system, more moderate reforms are certainly on the horizon.

INTERNATIONAL ISSUES

The major challenge to the U.S. patent system comes from international law. The biggest international questions are who is the inventor and what can be patented. The United States is unique in the world for having a first-to-invent system. Under U.S. law the first person to actually think of and make use of a new invention is entitled to the patent. In the rest of the world, the patent goes to whoever is the first to file his or her invention. This difference has been a source of contention, but it is unlikely that the United States or the rest of the world will change.

The biggest international questions are determining who is the inventor and what can be patented.

WHAT CAN BE PATENTED?

The question of what can be patented has been a difficult problem from the beginning of the United States patent system. One problem is the patent of importation, a source of controversy originating with the first Patent Act. A patent of importation is a patent granted to an invention that is taken (imported) from another country and brought into the United States. The person seeking the patent may not actually have invented the subject of the patent but may simply have discovered it. Thomas Jefferson strongly opposed patents of importation, whereas Alexander Hamilton felt they were an important way for United States citizens to obtain and disseminate inventions from other countries.

United States law allows patents of importation in very narrow ways through the legal definition of a "new" invention. Under United States law, an invention is new if it is not known or used in the United States or written about in a published form in the United States or anywhere else in the world. Notice that this definition of "new" allows a patent to be granted for something that is known outside the United States but not written about outside the United States.

The debate over patents of importation continues today with patents for drugs and therapeutic techniques based on traditional medicines. Some United States pharmaceutical companies travel to developing countries, learn traditional uses of plants and herbs, and return to the United States with this knowledge for patenting purposes. Developing countries complain that this is theft of knowledge. The U.S. companies argue that they

Patent examiners at work in the Patent Office, Washington, D.C. This illustration was published in Harper's Weekly, *July 10, 1869.* (Library of Congress, Prints and Photographs Division)

are entitled to the patent because the use of the plants and herbs is new, as the word is defined by the law, to the United States. Some developing countries have been successful in challenging United States patents on traditional medicines by showing that the knowledge had been written about and published in ancient scriptures and texts. The result of challenging the patent successfully is that the United States companies lose the right to practice the medicine exclusively. However, because much traditional knowledge exists in oral cultures, this strategy cannot be always be used to challenge the patents.

BIOTECHNOLOGY

The most controversial issue in patent law is raised by biotechnology and the patenting of life forms. In 1980, in *Diamond v. Chakravarty,* the United States Supreme Court ruled that a patent can be granted on a genetically modified bacteria. The USPTO denied the patent because of longstanding policy that natural phenomena, such as plants and animals, are not patentable. The Supreme Court ruled that a genetically modified organism is not a natural phenomenon but is manmade, and that patents can be granted to "anything under the sun that is manmade." In 1988 a patent was granted on an oncomouse, a mouse genetically modified to carry human cancer cells. The rest of the world has been hesitant to expand patent protection to biotechnology. For example, Canada did not recognize a patent on the oncomouse until 2000, and many European and developing countries deny patents on biotechnological products for moral reasons. As advances in genetics and research in cloning continue, the question of how far patent protection reaches will become ever more important.

The most controversial issue in patent law is raised by biotechnology and the patenting of life forms.

Despite Jefferson's warning, Congress has meddled with the "matters of invention" in enacting the Patent Acts. Following Madison and Iredell, the Patent Acts have served as an encouragement of genius that has expanded from the seemingly trivial (One-Click Shopping) to the very edges of our biological and natural existence (the oncomouse). This seemingly technical area of the law has provided and will continue to provide an important stage for international and domestic debates about the conduct of life and life itself.

See also: Copyright Act of 1790; Copyright Act of 1976.

BIBLIOGRAPHY

Koch, Adrienne, and William Peden, eds. *The Life and Selected Writing of Thomas Jefferson.* New York: Modern Library, 1993.

"Patently Problematic." *The Economist.* September 14–20, 2002, pp. 75–76.

Ryan, Michael P. *Knowledge Diplomacy: Global Competition and the Politics of Intellectual Property.* Washington, DC: Brookings Institution Press, 1998.

Slater, Dashka. "huMouse." *Legal Affairs* (November/December 2002): 21–28.

Walterscheid, Edward C. *To Promote the Progress of Useful Arts: American Patent Law and Administration, 1787–1838.* Littleton, CO: F. B. Rothman, 1998.

Warshofsky, Fred. *The Patent Wars: The Battle to Own the World's Technology.* New York: John Wiley and Sons, 1994.

INTERNET RESOURCE

United States Patent and Trademark Office. <http://www.uspto.gov>.

Peace Corps Act of 1961

Lawrence Schlam

In his 1961 inaugural address, President John F. Kennedy stated, with regard to those impoverished and in need abroad, "we pledge our best efforts to help them help themselves." On March 1, 1961, President Kennedy signed **Executive Order** No. 10924, establishing the Peace Corps as an agency in the U.S. Department of State, and later that same year Congress adopted the Peace Corps Act (P.L. 87-293):

executive order: an order issued by the president that has the force of law

> to promote world peace and friendship through a Peace Corps, which shall make available to interested countries and areas men and women of the United States qualified for service abroad and willing to serve, under conditions of hardship if necessary, to help the peoples of such countries and areas in meeting their needs for trained manpower, particularly in meeting the basic needs of those living in the poorest areas of such countries, and to help promote a better understanding of the American people on the part of the peoples served and a better understanding of other peoples on the part of the American people.

These commitments, coupled with the goal of facilitating mutual understanding between the United States and developing and underdeveloped countries, were the underlying themes of the act—and of President Kennedy's efforts to create a global community. The Peace Corps Act also encourages other countries, countries interested in hosting volunteers, to develop and participate in international and domestic voluntary service programs and activities of their own.

Commitments to peace and progress as well as facilitating mutual understanding between the United States and the developing world were the underlying themes of the act—and of President Kennedy's efforts to create a global community.

A LEGAL MECHANISM TO FACILITATE INTERNATIONAL WORK

The president, under the Peace Corps Act, is authorized to "carry out programs in furtherance of the purposes." He is also authorized to "appoint, by and with the advice and consent of the Senate, a Director of the Peace Corps and a Deputy Director of the Peace Corps." To ensure that the Peace Corps best serves American foreign policy, the Secretary of State is responsible for continuous supervision and general direction of programs authorized by the act.

The Peace Corps Act also creates a Peace Corps National Advisory Council consisting of fifteen voting members, at least seven of whom are required to be former volunteers, who the president appoints with the advice and consent of the Senate. The council, legislatively established in a 1985 amendment to the act, advises, consults, and conducts onsite inspections to evaluate the accomplishments of the Peace Corps. The council also assesses the potential capabilities and the future role of the Peace Corps and makes recommendations to the president.

Since its inception, more than 168,000 people have served as volunteers in the Peace Corps and its programs, beginning in only six countries in 1961, and having reached a total of 136 nations by the twenty-first century.

Since its inception, more than 168,000 people have served as volunteers in the Peace Corps and its programs, beginning in only six countries in 1961, and having reached a total of 136 nations by the twenty-first century. Current Peace Corps activities involve projects in agriculture, environment, health, education, business, community development, as well as some areas of special concern, such as HIV and AIDS education and prevention, as well as computer skills training courses to assist developing nations in acquiring competent workers to help those nations become economically self-sufficient.

The Peace Corps strives to maintain, at any given time, a volunteer corps of at least 10,000 individuals. "Volunteer leaders," who receive benefits similar to those of volunteers, are responsible for managerial and supervisory duties. Qualified citizens and nationals of the United States are eligible to enroll in the Peace Corps and must undergo a security investigation. In addition, volunteers assigned to a particular country must be able to speak that language with reasonable proficiency.

The law provides these volunteers with living, travel, and leave allowances, as well as housing, clothing and health care in order to perform effectively. They also receive a monthly readjustment allowance and vocational counseling upon returning to the United States. In 2001, $298 million was allotted to the Peace Corps, with this figure rising to $365 million in 2003.

SUBSEQUENT LEGISLATION AND COURT LITIGATION

Amendments to the Peace Corps Act have generally only involved matters of administration and execution, leaving unaltered the fundamental policies behind the act. Some policy changes, however, have occurred in response to

Applying for "The Toughest Job You'll Ever Love"

Step 1: Complete the written application, which asks for detailed information about your work and volunteer experience, education, and hobbies. Step 2: Provide references from an employer, a volunteer supervisor, and a friend. Step 3: Interview with a recruiter, either in person or by telephone. The recruiter will assess your flexibility, adaptability, cultural awareness, motivation, and commitment. Step 4: Successful candidates will be "nominated" for entry into the Peace Corps. Step 5: Pass a medical screening. Step 6: Pass a legal screening. Your eligibility may be affected by previous arrests or convictions, bankruptcy, financial obligations, past association with U.S. intelligence agencies, or current military obligations. Your personal data and fingerprints will be submitted to the FBI for a background check. Step 7: Your placement officer will make a final match between your skills and needs in the field. Step 8: An invitation packet will be mailed to you that includes the description of your assignment, passport and visa applications, and a volunteer handbook. You have ten days to decide whether to accept. Step 9: Meet your fellow trainees, complete your pre-departure orientation, and head out into the world to make a difference.

The first group of Peace Corps volunteers before they left for Ghana and Tanzania, August 1961. (© AP/Wide World Photos)

changing domestic and international political climates. For example, in a 1978 amendment, Congress, repudiating the **Cold War** philosophy, struck a provision of the act that required Peace Corps training to include "the philosophy, tactics and menace of communism."

Cold War: a conflict over ideological differences carried on by methods short of military action and usually without breaking off diplomatic relations; usually refers to the ideological conflict between the U.S. and the former U.S.S.R.

The same amendment also explicitly requires the Peace Corps to recognize the significant role of women in today's society, and mandates that special attention be given to projects which integrate women into the national economies of developing countries. Another group given special attention by the Peace Corps Act is disabled persons. Under the act, the Peace Corps must assist the disabled population to become involved in the economies of developing countries, which will in turn improve the status of disabled persons and assist the development effort.

Litigation relating to the Peace Corps has often involved alleged civil rights violations on the part of the agency's administration in the selection and termination of Peace Corps volunteers and employees. Issues related to the act have also arisen in federal prosecutions under the Military Selective Service Act of 1967 of Peace Corps volunteers refusing to submit to induction into the military.

In general, the Peace Corps has made a significant positive contribution toward creating good will for America throughout the world.

In general, the Peace Corps has made a significant positive contribution toward creating good will for America throughout the world.

See also: DOMESTIC VOLUNTEER SERVICES ACT OF 1973 (VISTA).

BIBLIOGRAPHY

Cobbs Hoffman, Elizabeth. *All You Need Is Love: The Peace Corps and the Spirit of the 1960s.* Cambridge, MA: Harvard University Press, 1998.

Rice, Gerard T. *The Bold Experiment: JFK's Peace Corps.* Notre Dame, IN: University of Notre Dame Press, 1985.

PENDLETON ACT

See CIVIL SERVICE ACTS

PERSONAL RESPONSIBILITY AND WORK OPPORTUNITY RECONCILIATION ACT (1996)

Michele Estrin Gilman

Excerpt from the Personal Responsibility and Work Opportunity Reconciliation Act

The purpose of this [act] is to increase the flexibility of States in operating a program designed to—

(1) provide assistance to needy families so that children may be cared for in their own homes or in the homes of relatives;

(2) end the dependence of needy parents on government benefits by promoting job preparation, work, and marriage;

(3) prevent and reduce the incidence of out-of-wedlock pregnancies and establish annual numerical goals for preventing and reducing the incidence of these pregnancies; and

(4) encourage the formation and maintenance of two-parent families.

On August 22, 1996, President William Jefferson Clinton signed the Personal Responsibility and Work Opportunity Reconciliation Act (PRWORA) (P.L. 104-193, 110 Stat. 2105) into law, thus fulfilling his campaign promise to "end welfare as we know it." The PRWORA changed both the substance and administration of the national welfare system. The act eliminated the prior welfare system, which had been attacked for decades by policymakers, the press, and the public for increasing government spending while making the poor dependent on government charity.

The PRWORA changed both the substance and administration of the national welfare system.

The stated purposes of the PRWORA were to reduce welfare dependency and out-of-wedlock births and to encourage the formation of two-parent families. In line with these goals, the PRWORA required welfare recipients to work within two years of receiving assistance, and it put a five-year lifetime limit on the receipt of benefits. It also ended the entitlement status of welfare benefits. In addition, the act made other, less publicized changes to several social welfare programs, both restricting the availability of benefits (making it harder for disabled children to qualify for assistance, limiting eligibility for food stamps, denying welfare benefits to most legal immigrants) and strengthening programs that aid children (reorganizing and increasing funding for child care, toughening the enforcement of rules for child support).

In addition to the act's primary emphasis on putting welfare recipients to work, the PRWORA also radically altered the way government delivers welfare benefits in three important ways:

(1) *Increased role of states.* To fund welfare the PRWORA provided the states with fixed block grants called Temporary Assistance to Needy Families (TANF) to fund welfare, totaling $16.5 billion annually over six years. Congress also included a provision in the act that would result in TANF funding cuts if the states failed to move a required percentage of recipients into the workforce and off welfare. Nevertheless, TANF gave states extensive discretion to design and operate their own programs. This transfer of authority from the federal government to the states is called "devolution." Under devolution, states have many choices to make in shaping their welfare policies—including being more stringent than federal law requires. For instance, some states have chosen to limit the receipt of benefits to less than five years, to cut benefits to families with truant children, or to mandate that parents take parenting classes.

(2) *Increased role of local entities.* The PRWORA allowed states to devolve their authority even further to counties, local governments, or even private entities. The private entities involved in welfare administration include a wide range of for-profit companies, **nonprofit** companies, and religious groups. As a result, welfare programs vary widely not only from state to state but also within local jurisdictions.

nonprofit: an organization whose business is not conducted or maintained for the purpose of making a profit, but is usually aimed at providing services for the public good

This transfer of authority to private providers, an approach called "privatization," has raised questions about accountability. In other words, some critics argue that PWROWA has made it more difficult for the government to oversee programs so as to ensure quality service to recipients. The accountability of for-profit entities is of particular concern, because the incentive to earn profits can lessen the quality of services provided.

Critics also charge that privatization may cause private providers to lose their independent character as they become increasingly bureaucratic and reliant on government funding. In addition, there has been sharp debate over whether religious groups should receive government funding for delivering social services. Opponents charge that this violates the separation between church and state. Proponents hold that a spiritual approach to the delivery of social services is more effective than secular approaches.

(3) *Changes in the role of welfare workers.* The work-first emphasis of the PRWORA has dramatically changed the role of front-line workers, those low-level welfare office workers who interact directly with welfare clients. Before the PRWORA, front-line workers focused on two tasks: (1) verifying whether applicants met objective criteria to become eligible for assistance, and (2) issuing checks in a timely manner. By contrast, under the PRWORA these front-line workers must perform a variety of tasks, including evaluation and

counseling, designed to put people to work. As a result, they have a much bigger say in decisions affecting applicants than they had previously.

WELFARE HISTORY

New Deal: the legislative and administrative program of President Franklin D. Roosevelt designed to promote economic recovery and social reform during the 1930s

Great Depression: the longest and most severe economic depression in American history (1929–1939); its effects were felt throughout the world

The PRWORA eliminated the existing welfare program, Aid to Families with Dependent Children (AFDC). AFDC was begun in 1935 as part of the **New Deal** response to the **Great Depression**. Under AFDC, welfare benefits were an entitlement. In other words, families who met objective eligibility criteria had a right to receive benefits for as long as they needed them. Moreover, the federal share of funding for AFDC rose and fell with caseload levels. Initially, federal welfare benefits were seen as a way to help impoverished, "deserving" widows stay home and raise their children. However, as time passed, critics attacked AFDC for encouraging dependency among a growing class of unmarried mothers, as well as creating a bloated and inefficient bureaucracy.

By the 1970s women had entered the workforce in large numbers. Americans were becoming increasingly hostile to aid for single mothers, who were no longer viewed as "deserving." In addition, the welfare rolls had grown dramatically, as had the cost of the program. Racial issues also played into the debate over welfare, as politicians and the media inaccurately stereotyped welfare mothers as predominantly African-American.

In the 1980s the federal government began to grant waivers, or exceptions, from AFDC requirements to states that wanted to experiment with their welfare programs. These states imposed work requirements and time limits, and they attempted to shape the behavior of welfare recipients by awarding or withholding benefits in line with the particular goals of their programs. During this time, influential conservative intellectuals such as Charles Murray argued that welfare not only failed to help poor people but also increased poverty by encouraging a culture of dependency.

After his election in 1992, President Clinton, eager to prove that he was tough on social policy issues, continued to grant states waivers from AFDC. In 1994 Republicans took control of Congress and proposed a legislative agenda called the Contract with America, which promised to enact conservative values into law. This put increased pressure on President Clinton to pass substantial welfare reform legislation and to demonstrate his credentials as a centrist politician.

Nevertheless, in 1995 President Clinton vetoed two Republican welfare reform bills that he deemed too harsh. In 1996 both political parties were under pressure to seize the initiative on welfare reform and to show results on the issue before the upcoming national elections. As a compromise, Congress presented President Clinton with the PRWORA, and the President signed it into law despite his concerns over some of its provisions. Several high-ranking administration officials subsequently resigned in protest, fearing that the PRWORA would increase poverty, homelessness, and hunger, especially in times of recession.

HAS WELFARE REFORM WORKED?

Before 1996 the number of people on welfare was already falling. After the PRWORA's enactment, the number continued to drop dramatically. Between

1996 and 2000, the number of people receiving welfare dropped by half, although caseloads in most states started to rise again slightly by 2001 and then to continue to fluctuate mildly. In addition, poverty rates fell to their lowest recorded levels (from 22 percent in 1994 to 19 percent in 1999), although the poverty rate never fell as dramatically as the number of welfare recipients. The dire consequences predicted by many welfare advocates did not come to pass, in part because of a robust economy and low unemployment throughout the period.

Despite the encouraging numbers, it was less clear whether welfare families were better off under the PRWORA. By the end of 2002, many former welfare recipients were working in low-wage jobs with few benefits and were no longer receiving food stamps or Medicaid coverage, even where eligible. Often, income gains from employment were reduced by the loss of public benefits. Many former welfare recipients thus remained below the poverty line. Up to a third of those who left welfare for work were back on welfare within a year, unable to obtain steady work or reliable child care.

By the end of 2002, and despite the encouraging numbers, it was less clear whether welfare families were better off under the PRWORA.

Moreover, about 40 percent of families who left welfare were not working at all. Some of these families were discouraged from applying for benefits, many had their benefits reduced or eliminated for failing to meet program requirements, and others simply disappeared from the system. In addition, a core of TANF recipients had severe barriers to work, such as illiteracy, lack of education, health problems, or drug or alcohol dependency. Although the PWRORA offered no clear policy approaches to help families and individuals cope with or overcome such barriers, these recipients faced set time limits on assistance.

LEGAL CHALLENGES

Given the breadth of the changes wrought by the PRWORA, it is not surprising that the law and its implementation have faced numerous legal challenges. The Supreme Court has heard one case arising out of the PRWORA. In *Saenz v. Roe* (2001), the Court ruled that it was unconstitutional for a state to provide lower TANF benefits to new state residents, because such provisions violated the constitutional right to travel between states.

In addition, several lawsuits have successfully challenged welfare offices that engaged in unfair practices, such as discouraging and deterring needy persons from applying for benefits, denying welfare beneficiaries fair hearings after their benefits were terminated or reduced, or imposing excessive sanctions on families who failed to comply with work requirements. However, other challenges have been less successful. For instance, there are court rulings upholding drug testing of welfare applicants, barring client advocates from welfare offices, and denying employment discrimination protections for employees who are working as a condition of receiving benefits.

Other lawsuits have challenged aspects of Charitable Choice, the PRWORA's requirement that states choosing to contract out welfare administration must include religious groups in the process. In 2002 a federal district court in Wisconsin struck down state funding of a faith-based, long-term residential alcohol and drug rehabilitation program, although the court did not address the constitutionality of the PRWORA.

REAUTHORIZATION

The PRWORA required that Congress reauthorize the legislation in October 2002 or it would expire altogether. In May 2002, President George W. Bush proposed to increase the minimum work hours required of adult recipients. In addition, under his plan states would have to increase the number of recipients in the workforce from 50 percent to 70 percent by 2007. Also, President Bush proposed to fund state programs that promote marriage and encourage unwed teenagers to abstain from sex. In May 2002 the Republican-controlled House passed President Bush's proposal.

In June 2002 the Senate Finance Committee passed a more generous bill that increased child care spending, expanded the definition of work activities, and permitted states to give welfare to legal immigrants. However, the full Senate never voted on that bill. Unable to come to a consensus on these issues, Congress passed a continuing resolution to maintain TANF until March 2003, thus leaving it to the 108th Congress to bridge the divide.

See also: Aid to Dependent Children.

BIBLIOGRAPHY

Blank, Rebecca M., and Ron Haskins, eds. *The New World of Welfare*. Washington, DC: Brookings Institution Press, 2001.

Caraley, Demetrios James. "Ending Welfare As We Know It: A Reform Still in Progress." *Political Science Quarterly* 116, no. 4 (2001): 525.

Congressional Quarterly News Features. "After 60 Years, Most Control Sent to States." In *Congressional Quarterly Almanac*. Washington, DC: 1996.

Glazer, Sarah, "Are Former Welfare Recipients Better Off Today?" *CQ Researcher* 11, no. 27 (Aug. 2001).

Trattner, Walter, I. *From Poor Law to Welfare State: A History of Social Welfare in America*. 6th ed. New York: Free Press, 1999.

Weil, Alan, and Kenneth Finegold, eds. *Welfare Reform: The Next Act*. Washington, DC: Urban Institute Press, 2002.

Plant Variety Protection Act (1970)

Mark D. Janis

The Plant Variety Protection Act (PVPA) (P.L. 91-577, 84 Stat. 1542) provides intellectual property protection for seed-grown plants. "Intellectual property" refers to patents, copyrights, and other types of rights in intangibles. For example, intellectual property rights might protect the innovative concept that makes a computer work or the creative expression in a book or song. Plant variety protection (PVP) is generally weaker than patent protection, and PVP certificates are granted by the PVP Office of the U.S. Department of Agriculture, not the U.S. Patent and Trademark Office.

In the early twentieth century, plant breeding became recognized as a "science," and plant breeders argued that plants should be recognized as patentable inventions. In 1930 Congress passed a Plant Patent Act, but it only awarded patent protection to plants that were reproduced asexually—that is, by cuttings. As a practical matter, plant patents benefited nursery operators who propagated fruit trees, ornamentals, and roses primarily through cuttings, but did not benefit breeders who propagated new crop varieties (such as grain crops or cotton) through seed.

In the early twentieth century, plant breeding became recognized as a "science," and plant breeders argued that plants should be recognized as patentable inventions.

In the 1960s several European countries agreed to incorporate "variety" protection, a new type of intellectual property protection for plants, into their national laws, under a treaty known as the UPOV Treaty. The United States did not immediately sign the treaty, but did adopt variety protection, passing the PVPA in 1970.

Any seed-grown plant variety is potentially eligible for PVPA protection if the breeder files a proper application with the PVP Office and if the variety meets all of the prerequisites for protection. There are four major prerequisites: the variety must be new, distinct, uniform, and stable. "New" means that the variety has either not been commercialized at all before the PVP application filing date, or has been commercialized only within a specified time before the filing date and no earlier. "Distinct" means that the variety is clearly distinguishable from other known varieties. "Uniform" and "stable" mean that the variety's characteristics are predictable when the variety is reproduced.

If the PVP Office decides that an application meets all of the prerequisites, it issues a PVP certificate, which remains in force for twenty years for most varieties. The owner of a PVP certificate has the right to prevent others in the United States from reproducing the protected variety without authorization. However, there are many limitations on this general right. For example, reproducing a PVP-protected variety for noncommercial purposes or for bona fide plant breeding research is not prohibited. Another important limitation, the "saved seed" exemption, allows farmers who grow PVP-protected varieties to save some of the resulting seed to produce a subsequent crop for use on the farm, but does not allow the farmer to sell the saved seed to others for crop production.

The PVP Office has issued PVP certificates for many crop varieties, although PVP certificate owners have initiated very few court actions. In 1994 Congress amended the PVPA to clarify the "saved seed" exemption and to provide that PVP rights extended not only to the protected variety but also to varieties "essentially derived from" the protected variety. In 2001 the Supreme Court determined that the general U.S. patent law applies to seed-grown plants, so plant breeders today can seek both patent protection and protection under the PVPA for seed-grown plants.

In 2001 the Supreme Court determined that the general U.S. patent law applies to seed-grown plants, so plant breeders today can seek both patent protection and protection under the PVPA for seed-grown plants.

See also: Patent Acts.

BIBLIOGRAPHY

Janis, Mark D., and Jay P. Kesan. *Plant Variety Protection: Sound and Fury ... ?* 39 *Houston Law Review* 727 (2002).

INTERNET RESOURCE

Plant Variety Protection Office. U.S. Department of Agriculture. <http://www.ams.usda.gov/science/PVPO/PVPindex.htm>.

Posse Comitatus Act (1878)

Michael I. Spak and Donald F. Spak

common law: a system of laws developed in England—and later applied in the U.S.—based on judicial precedent rather than statutory laws passed by a legislative body

Posse comitatus means "the power or force of the county." The term refers to a doctrine of ancient English **common law** authorizing a sheriff to summon the assistance of the able-bodied male population above the age of 15. Appointed special deputies, these men would aid the sheriff in keeping the peace, executing writs, quelling riots, capturing felons, and otherwise enforcing the laws. Unlike the organized militia, a posse was usually gathered as needed. The practice continued in the United States, as the posse became a necessary American colonial and frontier tradition.

HISTORY LEADING UP TO THE ACT

Before 1878, it was common for the United States Army to enforce civilian laws. In frontier territories, the army was often the only source of law enforcement, supplemented by occasional U.S. Marshals. Over time, marshals and county sheriffs regularly called upon the army to assist in enforcing the laws. In 1854, for example, the U.S. attorney general wrote that the *posse comitatus* includes every male person above the age of 15, including the military:

Before 1878, it was common for the United States Army to enforce civilian laws.

> Whatever may be their occupation, whether civilian or not, and including the military of all denominations, militia, soldiers, marines, all of whom are alike bound to obey the commands of a sheriff or marshal. The fact that they are organized as military bodies, under the immediate command of their own officers, does not in any wise affect their legal character. They are still the posse comitatus.

Reconstruction: the political and economic reorganization of the South after the Civil War

Soldiers were called upon to assist in catching fugitive slaves, as well as to guard polling places in federal elections. During the **Reconstruction** period that followed the Civil War, the army, initially under the command of General Ulysses S. Grant (who was later elected president), occupied the South.

By the time of the 1876 presidential election, Southern states were reconstituted. Many Southerners opposed both Grant, the outgoing Republican president, and Rutherford B. Hayes, the Republican presidential candidate. Federal troops actively assisted U.S. Marshals in patrolling and monitoring polling places in the South, claiming to be enforcing the federal election laws and preventing former Confederate officers from voting (as was the law at that time). Following bitter election contests in four Southern states, Hayes won the presidency by one electoral vote. Many felt that the federal troops, which supported Hayes and the Reconstructionist Republican candidates for Congress, intimidated Southerners who would have voted for Samuel Tilden, the Democratic candidate.

The resulting Democratic Congress was at odds with the Republican President Hayes. In response to what was seen as undue influence over the 1876 election, Congress outlawed the practice of *posse comitatus* by enacting the Posse Comitatus Act (PCA) (as 20 Stat. 152) as a rider to the Army Appropriation Act for 1880. The act stated: "Whoever, except in cases and under circumstances expressly authorized by the Constitution or Act of Congress, willfully uses any part of the Army or the Air Force as a posse comitatus or otherwise to execute the laws shall be fined under this title or imprisoned not more than two years, or both."

Further legislative history indicates that the more immediate objective was to put an end to the use of federal troops to police elections in ex-Confederate states where civil power had been reestablished.

Congressional debates indicate that the PCA was intended to stop army troops from answering the call of a marshal to perform direct law enforcement duties and aid in execution of the law. Further legislative history indicates that the more immediate objective was to put an end to the use of federal troops to police elections in ex-Confederate states where civil power had been reestablished.

Significantly, President Hayes vetoed the act because it "makes a vital change in the election laws of the country, which is in no way connected to the use of the Army." Congress overrode the veto. Accordingly, the willful use of the army or air force as a *posse comitatus* or otherwise to execute the

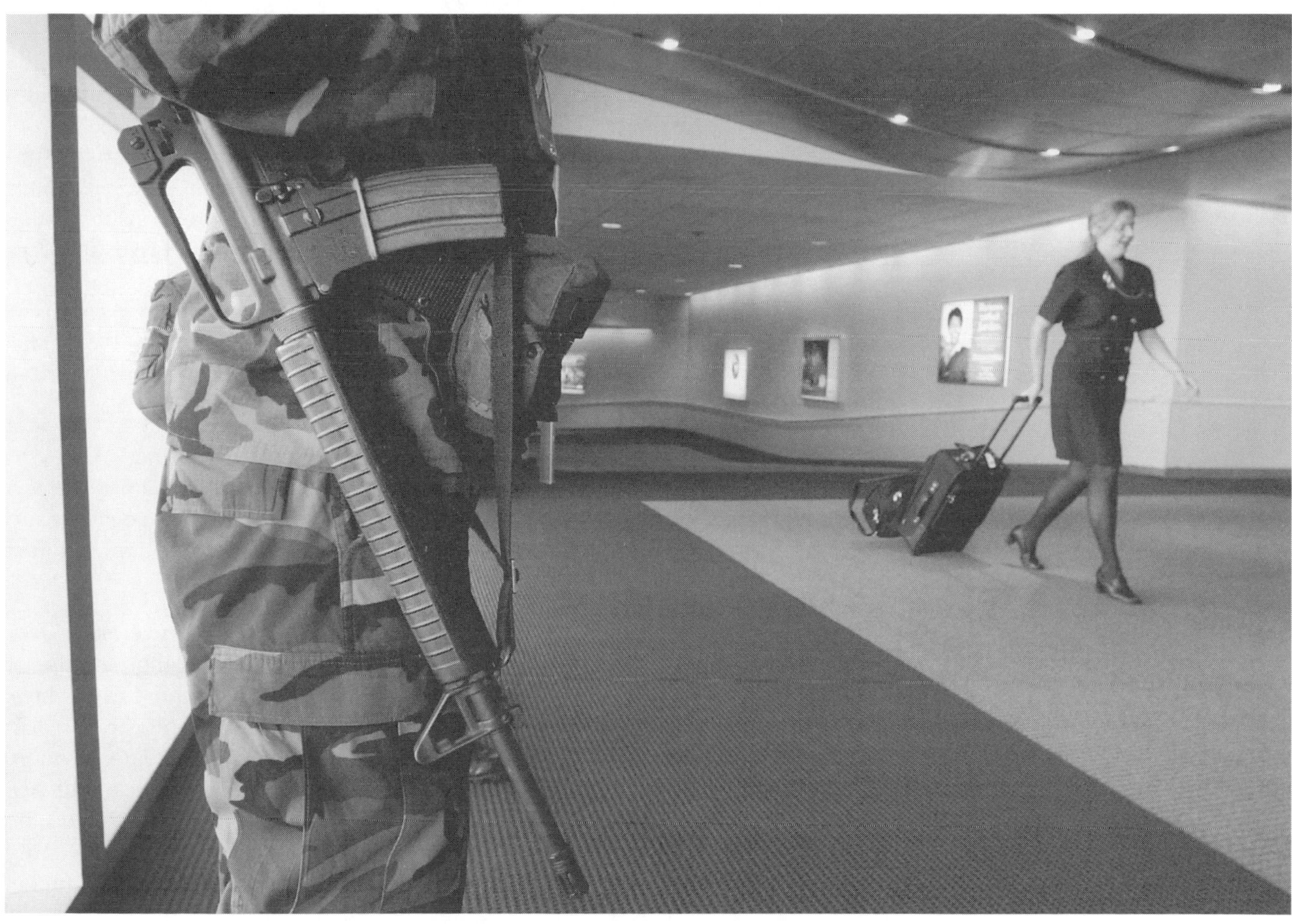

National Guardsmen, like this one on duty at LaGuardia airport in New York City, are not specifically mentioned in the Posse Comitatus Act. Unless called for federal service, the National Guard is under state control, and can be used by a state governor to enforce laws. (© AP/WIDE WORLD PHOTOS)

felony: a crime punished with a lengthy prison sentence (more than one year) or the death penalty

laws is a **felony**, unless the use is expressly authorized by the Constitution or an act of Congress.

UNITS AND ACTIONS COVERED BY THE ACT

The PCA directly applies only to the army and air force, without mentioning the navy, the Marine Corps, the Coast Guard, or the National Guard. The National Guard is subject to Article I, section 8 of the Constitution, "To provide for calling forth the Militia to execute the Laws of the Union, suppress Insurrections and repel Invasions." The National Guard is under state control until called into federal service, and is authorized to enforce the laws upon the request of a governor.

Because the Coast Guard has a law enforcement function and is not under the control of the Department of Defense, it is not subject to the PCA. Although the naval service is not mentioned in the PCA, Department of Defense regulations extend the PCA to the navy and Marine Corps.

Although the president has constitutional power to use the military to protect the nation in time of emergency and to repel invasions, in the Civil Disturbance Statutes Congress expressly authorized the president to use the armed forces under emergency circumstances. Where there is an insurrection in a state against its government, the president may, in addition to calling out the militia, "use such of the armed forces as he considers necessary to suppress the insurrection." Also, the president may use the armed forces to suppress a rebellion, insurrection, domestic violence, or unlawful conspiracy that obstructs the execution of the laws of the United States or deprives the people of the United States from their constitutional rights, privileges, and immunities. These statutes were relied on to authorize the use of federal troops to enforce federal court orders for school desegregation in Arkansas (1957), Mississippi (1962), and Alabama (1963), as well as to assist the National Guard in quelling urban riots.

Other statutory exceptions allow active use of the armed forces to remove persons wrongfully settling on Native American lands, and in emergency situations to actively enforce federal laws prohibiting the illegal possession and use of radioactive material. Other laws allow the president to direct the armed forces actively to enforce specific federal laws.

The PCA was originally intended to eliminate the direct active use of federal troops by law enforcement officers. The act does not prohibit the use of military supplies or equipment. To this end, Congress passed various laws expressly authorizing the use of military equipment and supplies by civilian law enforcement, with the accompanying use of military personnel to maintain and operate the equipment being used in civilian law enforcement. For example, military drug-sniffing dogs were designated as equipment, and military dog handlers operating the equipment have been lent to the Drug Enforcement Agency and other law enforcement agencies. Military equipment may be used for aerial reconnaissance, interception of aircraft and vessels, and in operations against terrorists, drug traffickers, prohibited narcotics and drugs, weapons of mass destruction, and components of weapons of mass destruction. Additionally, the military may share with civilian law enforcement "any information collected during the normal course of military training or operations that may be relevant to a violation of any federal or state law within the jurisdiction of such officials."

ONGOING DEBATE

Debate is ongoing as to whether the PCA should be repealed, moderated, or strengthened. Some argue that the act should be repealed because the federal government needs the full force of a flexible military to combat terrorism within the territorial United States. Others suggest the act is obsolete and should be repealed because numerous legislative exemptions have eroded the underlying policy and left the PCA a hollow shell. Others insist that although there are many exceptions, the act is essential to bar misuse of the military by civilian authorities and to prevent a military dictatorship from assuming control of the nation through use of the armed forces. Still others argue that the act means only that federal military forces may not be commandeered by civilian authorities for use in active and direct law enforcement as a *posse comitatus*. If local authorities need military personnel for specialized operations enforcing state laws, it is argued, they may call on the state governor for the assistance of the state National Guard.

Others insist that although there are many exceptions, the act is essential to bar misuse of the military by civilian authorities and to prevent a military dictatorship from assuming control of the nation through use of the armed forces.

See also: NATIONAL GUARD ACTS.

BIBLIOGRAPHY

Baker, Bonnie."The Origins of the Posse Comitatus." *Air and Space Power Chronicles* (1999). Online at <http://www.airpower.maxwell.af.mil/airchronicles>.

Hammond, Matthew Carlton. "The Posse Comitatus Act: A Principle in Need of Renewal." 75 *Washington University Law Quarterly* 953 (1997). Online at <http://law.wustl.edu/WULQ/75-2/752-10.html>.

Library Notes on Posse Comitatus (2002). Naval War College. <http://www.nwc.navy.mil/library>.

Quillen, Chris. "Posse Comitatus and Nuclear Terrorism, Spring 2002 Parameters." *U.S. Army War College Quarterly* 60 (2002). U.S Army. <http://carlisle-www.army.mil/usawc/Parameters/02spring/quillen.htm>.

Trebilcock, Major Craig T. "The Myth of Posse Comitatus." *Journal of Homeland Security* (2000). <http://homelandsecurity.org/journal>.

PREGNANCY DISCRIMINATION ACT (1978)

Ruth Colker

In 1978 Congress amended Title VII of the Civil Rights Act of 1964 to enact the Pregnancy Discrimination Act (PDA) (P.L. 95-555, 92 Stat. 2076). This act was passed to reverse the Supreme Court's decision in *General Electric Company v. Gilbert* (1976) in which the Supreme Court held that Title VII's prohibition against "sex" discrimination does not include a ban on pregnancy-based discrimination. Title VII generally bans sex discrimination in

Title VII generally bans sex discrimination in employment. By amending Title VII, Congress extended that prohibition to include pregnancy-based discrimination.

employment. By amending Title VII, Congress extended that prohibition to include pregnancy-based discrimination. In *Gilbert,* the Supreme Court held that General Electric's disability plan did not discriminate against women in violation of Title VII when it provided coverage for virtually all nonoccupational illnesses and accidents except pregnancy. Quoting analysis that it had used in a previous constitutional law decision, the Supreme Court explained that General Electric's plan did not constitute sex discrimination because "the program divides potential recipients into two groups—pregnant women and nonpregnant persons. While the first group is exclusively female, the second includes members of both sexes" (*Geduldig vs. Aiello* [1974]).

Congress passed the PDA to reverse the holding in *Gilbert,* but in doing so Congress went well beyond the fact pattern presented in the *Gilbert* case. It provided broad antidiscrimination protection to pregnant women, not simply disability-plan protection. The mechanism chosen by Congress to achieve this objective was to amend Title VII's definition of "sex" discrimination to include pregnancy-based discrimination. It defined the term "because of sex" to include discrimination "on the basis of pregnancy, childbirth or related medical conditions." It required that "women affected by pregnancy, childbirth, or related medical conditions shall be treated the same for all employment-related purposes, including receipt of benefits under fringe benefits programs, as other persons not so affected but similar in their ability or inability to work."

The Act provided broad antidiscrimination protection to pregnant women, not simply disability-plan protection.

Congress's intention to provide broad protection to women on the basis of pregnancy is reflected in the act's legislative history. Representative Augustus Hawkins, Democrat of California, introduced the act on the floor of the House, making it clear that the purpose of the act was to ban broadly discrimination on the basis of pregnancy. The Senate Committee on Human Resources and the House Committee on Education and Labor authored strong reports supporting a broad interpretation of the act. Despite the considerable support for the PDA within Congress, the courts were soon faced with difficult questions of interpretation under the act.

cause of action: reason or ground for initiating a proceeding in court

First, the courts had to determine whether men could bring a **cause of action** under the statute if pregnancy hospitalization benefits were not available to their spouses under the employer's health care policy (while all other conditions were covered). In a 7–2 decision, Justice John Paul Stevens wrote the Court's opinion in which he concluded that the act does provide a cause of action for male workers in that situation. Finding that Congress had disavowed the Court's earlier decision in *Gilbert,* the Supreme Court held that sex discrimination, as defined by Congress, did include pregnancy-based discrimination that creates economic harm for a male employee by providing him with a less favorable insurance policy than provided to employees without pregnant spouses. While the language of the act did not specifically address this problem, Justice Stevens concluded that coverage of that situation was wholly consistent with Congress's intentions when it enacted the PDA.

Second, the courts were faced with the question of whether the PDA created a cause of action to challenge a state statute that provided pregnant employees with *more favorable* disability protection than other employees. In

California Federal Savings & Loan Association vs. Guerra (1987), Justice Thurgood Marshall wrote a 6–3 majority opinion for the Court holding that the Pregnancy Discrimination Act does not bar employment practices favoring pregnant women.

The Supreme Court has continued to interpret the PDA broadly.

The Supreme Court has continued to interpret the PDA broadly. In 1991 it ruled in *UAW v. Johnson Controls* that an employer could not refuse to employ women who were of childbearing age because of potential hazards to a fetus that might result from exposure to chemicals in the workplace.

Although the PDA has been important in extending equality to pregnant women in the workplace, it does not require employers to provide any particular length of leave for pregnant workers. Congress took that important step in 1993 when it enacted the Family and Medical Leave Act (FMLA). Female employees who have worked for their employer for at least a year are now guaranteed six weeks of unpaid pregnancy leave upon the birth or adoption of a child.

The combination of the PDA and FMLA provides pregnant women with stronger job protection than at any time in our nation's history. Many women desire Congress to go further and guarantee *paid* leave to pregnant workers. Still others assert that they continue to face subtle forms of pregnancy-based discrimination that are difficult to prove in a court of law. Nonetheless, gone are the days when an employer may lawfully insist that a woman quit her job upon learning that she is pregnant, and because of the PDA and associated rulings, women do have legal redress available when overt acts of pregnancy-based discrimination occur.

Gone are the days when an employer may lawfully insist that a woman quit her job upon learning that she is pregnant, and because of the PDA and associated rulings, women do have legal redress available when overt acts of pregnancy-based discrimination occur.

See also: Civil Rights Act of 1964; Family and Medical Leave Act of 1993; Title IX, Education Amendments.

Privacy Act of 1974

John Cary Sims

The Privacy Act of 1974 (P.L. 93-579, 88 Stat. 1896) imposed an entirely new body of requirements on the federal government's handling of information concerning individuals. Although the statute incorporated a complex set of definitions and contained many exceptions, the Privacy Act reduced the unnecessary collection of private information by the federal government, prevented improper disclosure of such information, and gave individuals tools to determine what information the government held about them and how to correct errors in the records. The act also narrowed the range of circumstances under which any federal, state, or local government agency could deny an individual any right, benefit, or privilege for refusing to disclose his or her Social Security number.

Although the statute incorporated a complex set of definitions and contained many exceptions, the Privacy Act reduced the unnecessary collection of private information by the federal government, prevented improper disclosure of such information, and gave individuals tools to determine what information the government held about them and to how to correct errors in the records.

CONSTITUTIONAL BASIS

The Privacy Act principally imposes restrictions on the operation of the federal government itself, and there has not been extensive analysis of the constitutional basis for the legislation. Presumably, the ultimate authority for the act is in the powers underlying the federal activities to which the relevant information pertains. Congress may also be thought to have enacted a statute that is "necessary and proper" for carrying out those powers.

The agencies of the federal government collect, maintain, and use vast and varied quantities of information about individuals. This information is of critical importance to individuals seeking government benefits, licenses, or employment, yet often these records contain serious errors. Threats to personal privacy could further be exacerbated by the increasing sophistication of the computerized techniques available to collect and combine pieces of information. While there are many circumstances in which access to private information is essential to the efficient operation of the government, proponents have argued that there were too many situations in which the information was wrongly disclosed—either to persons with no proper need to receive it, or to others as retaliation against individuals who held unpopular or controversial views. Proponents argued that not only should information collection and retention by government agencies be narrowly confined to proper operational needs, but individuals should be given efficient means to determine this information and to force correction of inaccuracies.

As the legislation proceeded through the Senate and the House, two quite different approaches emerged. The Senate bill would have created a Federal Privacy Board with broad power to regulate the information practices of both public and private entities; the House bill provided access to records and a method of bringing about the correction of errors. Both the Senate and House bills were adopted by their respective bodies on November 21, 1974, but the substantial differences between the bills and the short time remaining in the session made it questionable whether there was time to follow the normal practice of appointing a Conference Committee to reconcile the conflicting versions of the legislation. Instead, the staffs of the relevant House and Senate committees worked with those members of Congress most directly involved to produce a compromise bill. The compromise package was then adopted by both houses of Congress.

POLITICAL CONTEXT

The Privacy Act was one of many statutes adopted in the immediate aftermath of Watergate, and the legislation (along with amendments to the Freedom of Information Act enacted the same year) responded to concerns about the potential for government misuse of private information and to calls for heightened government accountability to the public. The Ford Administration, however, raised a number of objections to the proposed legislation and in particular to the Senate bill. The compromise ultimately reached was much less sweeping than originally proposed, with the adopted legislation limited in applicability to the federal government, and a study commission on privacy replacing the proposed regulatory agency. A "routine use" exception to the restrictions on the transfer of

The Privacy Act was one of many statutes adopted in the immediate aftermath of Watergate, and the legislation (along with amendments to the Freedom of Information Act enacted the same year) responded to concerns about the potential for government misuse of private information and to calls for heightened government accountability to the public.

information between agencies was added to the bill as well. Taken together, the compromises removed the administration's objections to passage of the bill and paved the way for President Ford to sign the bill, which he did on December 31, 1974.

There has not been a sweeping interpretation of the Privacy Act by the Supreme Court; rather, there have been numerous decisions by lower federal courts interpreting and applying the statute's provisions. Many issues have arisen involving the relationship of the Privacy Act to other statutes or the precise meaning of the detailed definitions in the legislation. Since most aspects of the Privacy Act apply only if a "record" is "contained in a system of records," many cases have explored that threshold question; others have turned on whether an agency's use or disclosure of particular information was proper, and on whether one of the general or specific exemptions to the disclosure requirements of the act justified an agency's refusal to disclose its records to an individual requesting records about him or herself.

The Computer Matching and Privacy Protection Act of 1988 amended the Privacy Act by imposing safeguards designed to guard against unfair use of computer matching programs. There have also been a number of narrow amendments to specific provisions of the Privacy Act.

Federal employees who improperly disclose information about individuals may be prosecuted under certain circumstances, but the enforcement of the Privacy Act has principally been pursued through civil lawsuits authorized by the statute. Individuals may sue in federal district courts to obtain disclosure of records to which they are entitled under the statute, to obtain corrections of records, and to challenge the information practices followed by agencies. Successful plaintiffs may recover attorney fees and costs, and damage awards are also available if certain types of agency violations are "intentional or willful."

Excerpt from the Privacy Act of 1974

"No agency shall disclose any record which is contained in a system of records by any means of communication to any person, or to another agency, except pursuant to a written request by, or with the prior written consent of, the individual to whom the record pertains, unless disclosure of the record would be—(1) to those officers and employees of the agency which maintains the record who have a need for the record in the performance of their duties; (2) required under section 552 of this title [Freedom of Information Act]; (3) for a routine use ... (11) pursuant to the order of a court of competent jurisdiction..."

"Each agency that maintains a system of records shall—(1) maintain in its records only such information about an individual as is relevant and necessary to accomplish a purpose of the agency required to be accomplished by statute or by executive order of the President; (2) collect information to the greatest extent practicable directly from the subject individual when the information may result in adverse determinations about an individuals's rights, benefits, and privileges under Federal programs; ... (5) maintain all records which are used by the agency in making any determination about any individual with such accuracy, relevance, timeliness, and completeness as is reasonably necessary to assure fairness to the individual in the determination; ... (7) maintain no record describing how any individual exercises rights guaranteed by the First Amendment unless expressly authorized by statute or by the individual about whom the record is maintained or unless pertinent to and within the scope of an authorized law enforcement activity;.... "

The Privacy Act focused attention on the collection and possible misuse of information concerning individuals, and those issues have gained much greater prominence over the years since passage of the legislation.

The Privacy Act focused attention on the collection and possible misuse of information concerning individuals, and those issues have gained much greater prominence over the years since passage of the legislation. Congress considered taking a much broader approach, which would have regulated both private and governmental actors, but the final legislation was directed at federal agencies and hedged by many exceptions and limitations.

With the emergence of the Internet and the recognition that great quantities of information are readily available to private individuals, current debates about privacy rights and proposals for the protection of individual privacy tend not to be limited to information collection, handling, and dissemination conducted by federal agencies. Following the terrorist attacks of September 2001, there was considerable resistance to restricting information gathering, thought to make it more difficult to fight terrorism. Many aspects of the Privacy Act's application depend on other provisions of federal law, since under the terms of the act itself either release or disclosure records may ultimately be controlled by another statute. The Freedom of Information Act in particular deals with a number of closely related issues.

See also: FREEDOM OF INFORMATION ACT.

PROHIBITION OF THE SLAVE TRADE (1807)

Kevin Outterson

We tend to look back at slavery as though people took only two positions on it: pro or con. However, in the century prior to the Civil War, there was a middle position: regulation of slavery. For different reasons, both slave owners and their opponents agreed on measures to regulate slavery and the slave trade. The prohibition of the slave trade is a prime example of this uneasy compromise between slavery and freedom.

For different reasons, both slave owners and their opponents agreed on measures to regulate slavery and the slave trade. The prohibition of the slave trade is a prime example of this uneasy compromise between slavery and freedom.

The U.S. Constitution of 1789 includes a provision on the abolition of the slave trade. Article I, section 9 of the Constitution states:

> The Migration or Importation of such Persons as any of the States now existing shall think proper to admit, shall not be prohibited by the Congress prior to the Year one thousand eight hundred and eight, but a Tax or duty may be imposed on such Importation, not exceeding ten dollars for each Person.

This provision effectively gave Congress the power to prohibit the importation of slaves (exclusion power) and to impose an import tax on each slave, but delayed the exclusion power until 1808. The slave import tax was proposed several times but never adopted by the federal government. Congress exercised this Constitutional power in the Act to Prohibit the Importation of Slaves, passed on March 2, 1807 (2 Stat. 426). The Constitution required that the effective date be delayed until January 1, 1808.

EFFECTS ON THE SLAVE TRADE

This legislation was not particularly controversial and was not viewed as an **Abolitionist** measure. Before 1808 several slave states themselves banned the importation of foreign slaves and Congress had restricted slave importation to the slave states. In the decades prior to an effective cotton gin, the supply of slaves in the United States appeared to be adequate to meet domestic needs for slave crops. A ban on importation simply made the current slaves more valuable property for their masters and excluded slaves from rebellion-prone areas of the Caribbean sugar islands. The rise of cotton as a commercial crop outside of coastal areas fueled the spread of slavery throughout the Deep South. Demand for slaves was met primarily from within the United States, as slaves were increasingly sold and relocated from tobacco states such as Virginia, Maryland, and Kentucky to cotton states such as Georgia, Alabama, and Mississippi.

abolitionist: one favoring principles or measures fostering the end of slavery

Before 1808 several slave states themselves banned the importation of foreign slaves and Congress had restricted slave importation to the slave states.

The ban did nothing to hinder domestic sales of slaves between slave states, nor was enforcement particularly effective. Enforcement on the high seas was quite limited, and ships could avoid capture by the meager American squadron by flying a foreign flag, often falsely. The United States steadfastly refused to give the more substantial British Royal Navy the right to search and seize American slave ships. The United States also did not impose serious punishments against captains, officers, and owners of slave ships. Estimates of the number of slaves imported illegally after 1808 vary, but the number was substantial.

THE FATE OF CAPTURED SLAVES

One notable feature of the act concerned the fate of slaves captured while being illegally imported. Section 4 of the act of 1807 freed the slaves from the control of the importer but left their fates to the mercy of the state where the ship was brought, effectively condemning them to slavery:

> Neither the importer, nor any person or persons claiming from or under him, shall hold any right or title whatsoever to any negro, mulatto, or person of color, nor to the service or labor thereof, who may be imported or brought within the United States, or territories thereof, in violation of this law, but the same shall remain subject to any regulations not contravening the provisions of this act, which the Legislatures of the several States or Territories at any time hereafter may make, for disposing of any such negro, mulatto, or person of color.

Some slaves were seized by the state and sold on the auction block under this provision.

RELATIONS WITH GREAT BRITAIN

A few weeks after Congress's 1807 act, Great Britain also prohibited the slave trade in the Act for the Abolition of the Slave Trade, March 25, 1807. The British act, the culmination of decades of effort by British abolitionists, became effective in 1808. Great Britain freed its slaves in 1834 by paying compensation to slave owners. British enforcement efforts against slavery and the slave trade in the Atlantic were more vigorous and effective, including boarding apparently neutral vessels in violation of international law and strong-arming many nations into signing antislavery treaties. During the Civil War, the United States finally accepted an anti-slave trading treaty with Great Britain, signed in April 1862.

Slavery was legally abolished in the United States by the ratification of the Thirteenth Amendment to the Constitution in December 1865, although legal segregation and discrimination persisted for a century thereafter.

Slavery was legally abolished in the United States by the ratification of the Thirteenth Amendment to the Constitution in December 1865.

See also: FUGITIVE SLAVE ACTS; MISSOURI COMPROMISE; COMPROMISE OF 1850; NONINTERCOURSE ACT.

BIBLIOGRAPHY

Du Bois, W.E.B. *The Suppression of the African Slave-Trade To The United States of America, 1638–1870.* New York: Dover Publications, Inc. 1970 [1896].

Franklin, John Hope, and Alfred A. Moss, Jr. *From Slavery To Freedom: A History of African Americans,* 7th ed. New York: McGraw-Hill, Inc. 1994.

INTERNET RESOURCE

Historical documents on the slave trade. <http://www.yale.edu/lawweb/Avalon/slavery.htm>.

PUBLIC BROADCASTING ACT OF 1967

Corey Ditslear

Excerpt from the Public Broadcasting Act

The Congress hereby finds and declares that ... it is in the public interest to encourage the growth and development of public radio and television broadcasting, including the use of such media for instructional, educational, and cultural purposes; ... public television and radio stations and public telecommunications services constitute valuable local community resources for utilizing electronic media to address national concerns and solve local problems through community programs and outreach programs; ... a private corporation should be created to facilitate the development of public telecommunications and to afford maximum protection from extraneous interference and control.

With the growth in commercial radio and television throughout the 1950s and early 1960s, arts and education programming was being largely ignored by the major networks and radio broadcasters in favor of entertainment programming designed to lure advertisers. Locally run **nonprofit** television and radio stations attempted to fill the gap, but their smaller budgets made it difficult for them to produce the high-tech programming the public was coming to expect. In 1965 the Carnegie Corporation of New York, a nonprofit foundation, created a commission to study the problem and assist a legislative **lobbying** effort to provide public funding for what the commission dubbed *public broadcasting*. The commission's report, combined with efforts

nonprofit: an organization whose business is not conducted or maintained for the purpose of making a profit, but is usually aimed at providing services for the public good

lobby: to try to persuade the legislature to pass laws and regulations that are favorable to one's interests and to defeat laws that are unfavorable to those interests by the Ford Foundation and locally owned educational broadcasting stations around the country, led to the Public Broadcasting Act (P.L. 90-129, 81 Stat. 365), signed into law by President Lyndon B. Johnson on November 7, 1967, after efforts to convince the Federal Communications Commission (FCC) to use profits from nonprofit communications satellite systems were unsuccessful.

The act created the Corporation for Public Broadcasting (CPB) which was charged with using federal funds to help promote programming that involves creative risks the networks are unwilling to take, and provide educational and informative materials targeted primarily for audiences underrepresented in mainstream broadcasting, like children and minorities.

The act created the Corporation for Public Broadcasting (CPB) which was charged with using federal funds to help promote programming that involves creative risks the networks are unwilling to take, and to provide educational and informative materials targeted primarily for audiences underrepresented in mainstream broadcasting, like children and minorities. In order to fulfill its mission, the CPB formed the Public Broadcasting Service (PBS) in 1969 and National Public Radio (NPR) in 1970.

The CPB does not produce or distribute any radio and television programs, for that job remains with PBS and NPR and the locally operated PBS and NPR stations around the country. The CPB receives an annual appropriation from Congress that equals 12 percent of the annual revenues of public broadcasting. This money is used to help support privately owned PBS and NPR stations that receive a majority of their funds from a combination of state and local tax dollars; donations by private business; individual memberships of listeners and viewers; and operating budgets supplied by the state colleges and universities that run almost half of the approximately 1,100 public television and radio stations.

Many of today's adults have grown up on the product of public broadcasting. Without PBS and NPR, such shows as *Sesame Street, Mister Rogers' Neighborhood, The McNeil/Lehrer Report, Cosmos, Great Performances, A Prairie Home Companion,* and *All Things Considered* would not have been able to help educate America's children and information-hungry adults.

Without PBS and NPR, such shows as Sesame Street, Mister Rogers' Neighborhood, The McNeil/Lehrer Report, Cosmos, Great Performances, A Prairie Home Companion, *and* All Things Considered *would not have been able to help educate America's children and information-hungry adults.*

Federal funding of public broadcasting has not produced much controversy since its inception in 1967. However, the financial problems of NPR during the late 1980s, combined with the growth of cable television where arts, education, and news programming had been successfully commercialized, created a growing push to eliminate public funding of public broadcasting. This effort culminated in 1994 with the House of Representatives' new Republican majority's failed attempt to eliminate all funding for the CPB. With tight budgets and alternate sources of educational and informative programming, funding for the CPB will likely remain a focus of debate. But with at least three generations of Americans having grown up on *Sesame Street*, it would be difficult for any politician to stop paying for Big Bird and all of the other public broadcasting stalwarts.

See also: COMMUNICATIONS ACT OF 1934.

BIBLIOGRAPHY

Gibson, George H. *Public Broadcasting: The Role of the Federal Government, 1912–1976*. New York: Praeger, 1977.

Raboy, Marc, ed. *Public Broadcasting for the Twenty-First Century.* Luton, Bedfordshire, U.K.: University of Luton Press, 1995.

INTERNET RESOURCE

Corporation for Public Broadcasting. July 2003. <http://www.cpb.org>.

PUBLIC CONTRACTS ACT OF 1936

See WALSH-HEALEY ACT

PUBLIC DEBT ACTS

Edward J. McCaffery

This nation, conceived in debt, could hardly exist without the government's ability to borrow. Wars, beginning with the American Revolution, have until recent years been the main culprit in our national addiction to credit. The Founders, cognizant of the war debt after the revolution, gave Congress the express power in Article I, Section 8 of the Constitution "to borrow Money on the credit of the United States." This power was confirmed after the Civil War, in Section 4 of the Fourteenth Amendment: "The validity of the public debt of the United States, authorized by law, including debts incurred for payment of pensions and bounties for services in suppressing insurrection or rebellion, shall not be questioned." The constitutional power to issue debt requires specific congressional authorization to make it operative.

This nation, conceived in debt, could hardly exist without the government's ability to borrow.

The First and Second Liberty Loan Acts were each enacted in 1917 during World War I. These acts established different public debt limits for bonds, bills, certificates, and notes, and provided for full federal tax exemption for the interest on U.S. government obligations—an issue made important by the recently enacted federal income tax. The Liberty Loan Acts remained the basic public debt provisions until well into the Great Depression, after the advent of Keynesian economics (John Maynard Keynes, a celebrated British economist, argued that it was good for the government to borrow and spend under certain circumstances, giving intellectual support to **New Deal** spending programs), and right on the cusp of World War II. The initial Public Debt Act was passed in 1939, but it was the Public Debt Act of 1941 that fully set the modern stage for government debt finance. This 1941 Act not only raised the debt limit, it also eliminated the federal income tax exemption for future issues of U.S. debt, and consolidated virtually all federal borrowing into a unitary system run through the Department of the Treasury. The 1941 Act established the form—free of technical restrictions on the type of borrowing that might tie the Treasury's hands—for all subsequent public debt acts.

New Deal: the legislative and administrative program of President Franklin D. Roosevelt designed to promote economic recovery and social reform (1933–1939)

The Public Debt Act of 1941 raised the aggregate limit on all obligations to \$65 billion. Subsequent Public Debt Acts continued to amend the aggregate limit. The 1942, 1943, 1944, and 1945 acts raised the limit to \$125 billion, \$210 billion, \$260 billion, and \$300 billion respectively. In 1946, the Public Debt Act was amended, **mirabile dictu**, *to reduce the debt limit to \$275 billion.*

mirabile dictu: "wonderful to relate"

Until the Public Debt Act of 1941 the federal government treated all interest and gain on its own obligations as tax-exempt. The 1941 act changed this by making the difference between the purchase and redemption price for savings bonds taxable income. Section 4 of the act further provided: "Interest upon, and gain from the sale or other disposition of, obligations issued on or after the effective date of this Act by the United Sates or any agency or instrumentality thereof shall not have any exemption, as such, and loss from the sale or other disposition of such obligations shall not have any special treatment, as such, under Federal Tax Acts now or hereafter enacted."

Until the Public Debt Act of 1941 the federal government treated all interest and gain on its own obligations as tax-exempt.

The Treasury Department lobbied hard for this step—the only mildly controversial aspect of the bill at the time—in the interest of tax equity and possibly (and futilely) to effect the end of tax-exemption for state and local obligations. This change was not made retroactive. In addition, the Public Debt Act of 1941 consolidated virtually all federal borrowing under the Treasury's aegis. Any combination of notes, bills, and bonds up to the ceiling could be issued.

Neither the Public Debt Act in particular nor the more general congressional authority to borrow money has ever been seriously challenged in court. After some modest reductions in the debt limit following World War II, the federal debt stayed relatively constant, in real dollar terms, until the mid-1970s. Since then it has exploded. In the spring of 2003 Congress authorized an increase in the debt ceiling to $7.4 trillion, making a vote later in the same year on a further increase inevitable. The Public Debt Act of 1941 remains the essential venue for authorizing government debt and structuring debt ceiling increases.

The Public Debt Act of 1941 remains the essential venue for authorizing government debt and structuring debt ceiling increases.

See also: Balanced Budget and Emergency Deficit Control Act; Congressional Budget and Impoundment Control Act.

BIBLIOGRAPHY

Cooke, H.J., and M. Katzen. "The Public Debt Limit," In *Journal of Finance* vol. 9, no. 3 (September 1954): 298–303.

Lent, George E. "Major Trends in the Market for Tax-Exempt Securities," In *Journal of Finance* vol. 9, no. 2 (May 1954): 178–187.

INTERNET RESOURCE

Department of Treasury. Public Debt. <www.publicdebt.treas.gov>.

Public Utility Holding Company Act of 1935

James E. Hickey, Jr.

The Public Utility Holding Company Act of 1935 (PUHCA) (P.L. 74-333) reorganized the electric and gas industries and is one of the strongest congressional legislative responses to corporate abuse in American history. Congress declared in PUHCA its policy to "eliminate the evils" of interstate "public utility holding companies," to "compel" simplification of the pyramid

The Public Utility Holding Company Act of 1935 reorganized the electric and gas industries and is one of the strongest Congressional legislative responses to corporate abuse in American history.

system of public utility holding companies, and, with certain exceptions, to provide for "the elimination of public utility holding companies."

THE STRUCTURE OF EARLY HOLDING COMPANIES

In the 1920s and 1930s, electric and natural gas utilities increasingly consolidated their business operations into pyramid-like structures with a holding company at the top which owned or controlled a number of other subsidiary companies. This holding company structure helped utilities to reduce construction and operation costs by taking advantage of economies of scale. That structure helped to increase energy sales, lessen financing costs, lower costs of capital, and reduce costs of materials and equipment through bulk purchasing at discounted prices. For example, large central station electric power plants and interconnected electric service were made possible under the holding company structure. However, the holding company structure was not regulated as a public utility by the states or the federal government. The absence of either state or federal regulation led to holding company abuses like stock manipulation, excessive financial charges, promotion of price speculation, extraction of **exorbitant** profits and fees from subsidiaries, deceptive accounting, distorted earnings reports, and control by non-utilities like banks. By the early 1930s, just sixteen such holding companies controlled more than 75 percent of the electricity generated in the United States. In addition, during the **Great Depression** certain electric systems collapsed altogether. Those abuses and market failures provoked federal government intervention in the form of the PUHCA.

exorbitant: an amount that far exceeds what is fair or customary

Great Depression: the longest and most severe economic depression in American history (1929–1939); its effects were felt throughout the world

THE LEGISLATIVE RESPONSE TO MARKET PROBLEMS

The PUHCA requires public utility holding companies to register with the Securities and Exchange Commission (SEC). An interstate holding company, under PUHCA, is any company that holds ten percent or more of the voting stock of another company (public utility or holding company) or that has a controlling "influence" over another company's "management or policies." The SEC is given substantial and wide-ranging authority over public utility holding companies. If it is "necessary" and "in the public interest," the SEC may control new stock issues of a PUHCA-registered holding company, may prevent the buying and selling of holding company assets, and may, to a large extent, determine the terms of the acquisition of holding company property and stock. The SEC will approve holding company stock and property purchases if they are "economical and efficient" and protect consumers and investors. The SEC also is authorized under the PUHCA to regulate interstate holding company loans, the payment of dividends, utility service contracts, and accounting methods.

The SEC may order the breakup of holding companies to avoid financial abuses. The PUHCA, as implemented by the SEC, and with some exceptions, limits holding company operations to integrated, one system, one state (or at most its immediate neighboring state) operations and, for the most part, forbids holding companies from engaging in non-utility businesses. The PUHCA requires that all holding companies thrice removed or more from operating subsidiary companies

The PUHCA requires public utility holding companies to register with the Securities and Exchange Commission (SEC).

In this cartoon, published on January 15, 1935, the Bible story of David and Goliath is used as an analogy for the struggle between utility companies and rate-paying consumers. (LIBRARY OF CONGRESS, PRINTS AND PHOTOGRAPHS DIVISION)

must be abolished. Other holding companies that cannot comply with PUHCA also must be broken-up or restructured.

PUHCA'S EFFECTS AND PROPOSALS FOR REPEAL

The PUHCA resulted eventually in the reduction of public utility holding company influence. For example, holding company control of electricity generation was reduced from 75 percent of all generation to just 15 percent or so. The PUHCA, by effectively reorganizing the electric and gas industries, facilitated greater federal and state regulation of utility wholesale and retail prices and conditions of service.

For the past three decades, there have been calls to repeal PUHCA on grounds that it has successfully fulfilled its task and is no longer necessary. Among those that have supported the repeal of the PUHCA is the SEC itself. The reasons given for repeal include the desire to permit public utility holding companies to buy utilities in different parts of the country and to allow non-utilities to buy utility assets and property. Supporters of repeal argue that consolidation of utilities into holding company structures would provide economies of scale and thus lower utility rates to customers. To reduce the potential for holding company abuse, most advocates of repeal would increase the regulatory powers of the Federal Energy Regulatory Commission (FERC) and state public utility commissions that regulate electric prices and conditions of service to assure that non-utility business is not paid for by utility consumers. In 1992 PUHCA was amended by the Energy Policy Act to exempt from PUHCA's ownership restrictions firms engaged exclusively in wholesale sales of electricity. Even in this cycle of government deregulation, the PUHCA has withstood every attempt to repeal it. Perhaps, the persistence of PUHCA may be explained on several counts. First, regulation under PUHCA is of an *essential* public service, especially electric and gas service. Second, the availability of reliable and affordable energy is necessary for a healthy and growing American economy. Third, electric utilities are once again beginning to favor the formation of holding companies as they did in the pre-Depression days. Finally, notorius corporate scandals (fraud, mismanagement and the like) in energy companies and utilities like Enron and Worldcom remind many of the potential for precisely the sort of abuses PUHCA was enacted long ago to prevent.

Notorius corporate scandals (fraud, mismanagement and the like) in energy companies and utilities like Enron and Worldcom remind many of the potential for precisely the sort of abuses PUHCA was enacted long ago to prevent.

See also: SECURITIES EXCHANGE ACT OF 1934.

BIBLIOGRAPHY

Hawes, Douglas W. "Public Utility Holding Company, Act of 1935—Fossil or Foil?," *Vanderbilt Law Review* 30 (1977).

Hawes, Douglas W. *Utility Holding Companies.* New York: Clark Boardman Co. Ltd., 1984.

Phillips, Charles F. *The Regulation of Public Utilities: Theory and Practice.* Arlington, VA: Public Utilities Reports, 1993.

Pure Food and Drug Act (1906)

Daniel P. Carpenter

Excerpt from the Pure Food and Drug Act

An Act—

For preventing the manufacture, sale, or transportation of adulterated or misbranded or poisonous or deleterious foods, drugs, medicines, and liquors, and for regulating traffic therein, and for other purposes.

That the introduction into any State or Territory or the District of Columbia ... of any article of food or drugs which is adulterated or misbranded, within the meaning of this Act, is hereby prohibited?. [Section 2]

That the examinations of specimens of foods and drugs shall be made in the Bureau of Chemistry of the Department of Agriculture, or under the direction and supervision of such Bureau, for the purpose of determining from such examinations whether such articles are adulterated or misbranded within the meaning of this Act.... [Section 4]

It would not stretch matters to say that the Pure Food and Drug Act of 1906 (P.L. 59-384, 34 Stat. 768), also known as the Wiley Act, stands as the most consequential regulatory statute in the history of the United States. The act not only gave unprecedented new regulatory powers to the federal government, it also empowered a bureau that evolved into today's Food and Drug Administration (FDA). The legacy of the 1906 act includes federal regulatory authority over one-quarter of **gross domestic product**, and includes market gatekeeping power over human and animal drugs, foods and preservatives, medical devices, biologics and vaccines. Other statutes (such as the Interstate Commerce Act of 1887, the Sherman and Clayton antitrust laws, and the Federal Trade Commission Act of 1914) have received more study, but the Pure Food and Drug Act has had the longest-lasting and most widespread economic, political, and institutional impact.

gross domestic product: the total market value of goods and services produced within a nation in a given time period (usually one year)

BACKGROUND

The passage of regulatory legislation came only after two decades of wrangling and congressional opposition to federal regulation of food and drugs. Three political forces converged to force food and drug regulation onto the congressional agenda. First, consumer movements dominated by highly organized women activists put pressure on legislators to satisfy public wishes. The decades-long struggle for a law was actively supported by the General Federation of Women's Clubs (especially Alice Lakey) and the Women's Christian Temperance Union.

The act not only gave unprecedented new regulatory powers to the federal government, it also empowered a bureau that evolved into today's Food and Drug Administration (FDA).

A second force was the rise of journalism. In 1905 Upton Sinclair's *The Jungle,* which exposed practices in the Chicago meat-packing industry, sold 1 million copies in its first year after publication. Nearly as important were the articles of Samuel Collins Adams in *Collier's* magazine on patent medicines and

The 1906 act stands as one of the most daring demonstrations of bureaucratic autonomy in the history of the United States.

advertising fraud. These and other articles served to highlight the widespread adulteration of ethical drugs as well as of food.

The most important force behind the act was a single individual, Harvey Washington Wiley, and the agency he led, the Bureau of Chemistry in the U.S. Department of Agriculture (USDA). Wiley assumed leadership of this division of the USDA in 1883 and soon acquired legal and administrative power over the food, patent medicine, and pharmaceutical industries. Wiley experimented with small-scale programs in food regulation, built a multifaceted coalition behind food and drug regulation, and even helped Adams write his *Collier's* articles. Congress largely followed Wiley's lead, with opponents gradually giving way to Wiley's political machine. The 1906 act stands as one of the most daring demonstrations of bureaucratic autonomy in the history of the United States.

RELATIONSHIP WITH OTHER LAWS

The Pure Food and Drug Act was passed on the same day as the Meat Inspection Act of 1906. This act mandated examination of livestock before slaughter as well as analysis of carcasses, and required ongoing USDA

A food research laboratory in early-twentieth-century New York. (©CORBIS)

inspection of slaughterhouses and processing plants. The Pure Food and Drug Act and the Meat Inspection Act divided administration of food regulation into two bureaus. The Bureau of Chemistry, headed by Wiley, administered most provisions of the Pure Food and Drug Act. The Bureau of Animal Industry, led by Daniel Salmon, carried out federal meat inspections. This division of administrative oversight persists to this day. The USDA still inspects beef and poultry, whereas the FDA inspects most other foods.

The economic legacy of the act includes strong consumer safeguards, controls on pharmaceutical and medical device markets, regulatory intervention in the process of pharmaceutical development and advertising, and government oversight of food production and marketing.

At the time, the Pure Food and Drug Act of 1906 was the most daunting intrusion by federal authorities into interstate commerce. Although other federal agencies could regulate prices and occupational safety, the USDA was now engaged in the regulation of the very manufacture and sale of products, in addition to advertising. Two subsequent laws, the Food, Drug, and Cosmetic Act of 1938 and the 1962 Kefauver-Harris Amendments, strengthened the 1906 act's legacy of empowering the FDA. Today the FDA regulates one-quarter of gross domestic product, and not a week goes by without an FDA action making news headlines. The economic legacy of the act includes strong consumer safeguards, controls on pharmaceutical and medical device markets, regulatory intervention in the process of pharmaceutical development and advertising, and government oversight of food production and marketing.

See also: FEDERAL FOOD, DRUG, AND COSMETIC ACT; FOOD QUALITY PROTECTION ACT.

BIBLIOGRAPHY

Anderson, Oscar E. *The Health of a Nation: Harvey W. Wiley and the Fight for Pure Food.* Chicago: University of Chicago Press, 1958.

Bailey, Thomas A. "Congressional Opposition to Pure Food Legislation, 1879–1906." *American Journal of Sociology* 36 (July 1930): 52–64.

Carpenter, Daniel P. *The Forging of Bureaucratic Autonomy: Reputations, Networks and Policy Innovation in Executive Agencies, 1862–1928.* Princeton, NJ: Princeton University Press, 2001.

Young, James Harvey. *Pure Food: Securing the Pure Food and Drug Act of 1906.* Princeton, NJ: Princeton University Press, 1989.

R

Rail Passenger Service Act (1970)

Stephen C. Rogers

Congress enacted the Rail Passenger Service Act (RPSA) (P.L. 91-518, 84 Stat. 1327) in 1970 under the **commerce clause** of the U.S. Constitution to preserve intercity rail passenger service in the United States. For many years long-distance passenger trains were an essential mode of transportation in this country. By the second half of the twentieth century, however, competition from automobiles, buses, and airplanes had reduced passenger rail travel to a shadow of its former self and rendered the passenger rail business unprofitable.

Commerce Clause: the provision of the U.S. Constitution (Article I, section 8, clause 3) that gives Congress exclusive powers over interstate commerce—the buying, selling, or exchanging of goods between states

THE ORIGINS AND GOALS OF AMTRAK

In the RPSA, Congress declared that "modern, efficient, intercity railroad passenger service is a necessary part of a balanced transportation system" and could help end highway congestion and overcrowding of airways and airports. To preserve such service, the RPSA provided for the creation of the National Railroad Passenger Corp., commonly known as Amtrak, which was originally meant to be a for-profit corporation in the District of Columbia. Amtrak was to take over responsibility for operating intercity service from any railroad that desired to get out of the passenger business, as all railroads eventually did.

The RPSA required Amtrak to provide passenger service between points within an integrated "basic system" of routes designated by the U.S. Secretary of Transportation, with a view to eliminating the least necessary operations. Supporters of the RPSA expected that by operating a streamlined and cohesive national system, Amtrak would make rail passenger service profitable again, particularly using new equipment such as the Metroliner trains that had recently been introduced in the Northeast.

Amtrak was to take over responsibility for operating intercity service from any railroad that desired to get out of the passenger business, as all railroads eventually did.

Railroads transferring passenger service responsibilities to Amtrak were required to pay it an amount equal to only one-half of the railroads' financial losses from intercity passenger operations during a single year (1969). In addition, the RPSA authorized a $40 million federal appropriation and a $100 million loan guarantee program to assist Amtrak's start-up.

FINANCIAL TROUBLES AND FEDERAL SUPPORT

Amtrak has not succeeded in operating rail passenger service at a profit. In this respect, it is no different from any other national passenger rail system—all of them require government subsidies to sustain operations. Congress has amended the RPSA numerous times since 1970 in an effort to minimize Amtrak's need for federal financial support. Even so, a Senate committee found in 1997 that since 1971 Amtrak had received more than $20 billion in federal financial help but continued to struggle financially despite that assistance.

In 1997 Congress enacted the Amtrak Reform and Accountability Act of 1997 (ARAA), declaring its intention to terminate federal funding of Amtrak's operating losses after 2002. Congress also claimed the act would relieve Amtrak of legal constraints on its ability to improve its financial performance. The ARAA created an Amtrak Reform Council to monitor that performance. In November 2001 the council determined that Amtrak would be unable to function without federal operating subsidies after 2002. Despite its stated intention in the ARAA, Congress continued to fund Amtrak's operating losses after 2002 and renewed the debate over the future of Amtrak and of intercity rail passenger service in this country.

See also: STAGGERS RAIL ACT.

BIBLIOGRAPHY

Rogers, Stephen C. "Amtrak Chugs Along, for Now—'Reforms' Fall Short." *Legal Times,* April 27, 1998: S37.

Wilner, Frank N. *The Amtrak Story.* Omaha, NE: Simmons-Boardman Publishing, 1994.

RECONSTRUCTION ACTS

Daniel W. Hamilton

Well before the Civil War was over, even before a Union victory appeared imminent, politicians in the Union debated how to treat the defeated South after the war. Abraham Lincoln's dream of a ninety-day war dissolved into years of terrible bloodshed and total war. With every major battle and every passing year, a quick return to peace and a restoration of political ties between the North and the South became increasingly improbable, and for many northerners, undesirable. While leading Democrats wanted to restore the Union as it had been before the war, powerful voices within the Republican Party argued that not only must the rebellion be put down, the South itself must be fundamentally refashioned, or reconstructed. Republicans, especially those in the party's radical wing, argued that the leaders of the Confederacy must be forever kept out of political power in the states and the federal government. Southern states, they

Political cartoon depicting the struggle between President Andrew Johnson and Congress over Reconstruction, published in Frank Leslie's Budget of Fun, *November 1866. Johnson and Radical Republican leader Representative Thaddeus Stevens are pictured as drivers of locomotives that stand face to face on the same track. Johnson says in the caption, "Look here! One of us has got to go back," and Stevens replies, "Well, it ain't me that's going to do it—you bet!"* (Library of Congress, Prints and Photographs Division)

asserted, should not be allowed representation in Congress until they abolished slavery. As the war went on, Republicans began also to demand adoption of the Fourteenth Amendment and black male suffrage as a condition for reunion. Further, some radicals argued that the federal government must protect the civil and political rights of the millions of freed slaves in the South.

A great debate over reconstruction was underway. In response to those calling for fundamental change, President Lincoln offered a much milder program. Lincoln, who was very much involved in strategic decisions and day-to-day battle plans, was pained by the relentless bloodshed and became a forceful advocate for the quick resumption of political reunion without political upheaval. On December 8, 1863, Lincoln issued his Proclamation of Amnesty and Reconstruction and outlined his reconstruction program in his message to Congress. Lincoln offered a general amnesty to all southern whites, excluding certain high-ranking officials, who took an oath pledging loyalty to the United States and to support the Emancipation Proclamation and laws passed by the Congress that concerned slavery. Lincoln did not demand immediate, universal emancipation within a state as a condition for readmission, but instead provided that slaves freed during the war could not be enslaved again. Once 10 percent of the number of voters in the 1860 election had taken the oath, a state could establish a new government. Confederate political, judicial, and military officers could apply for individual pardons. Lincoln's reconstruction policy was part of his military strategy and he hoped that a lenient reconstruction program, adopted during the war, would prompt southern whites to reject the Confederacy.

As some southern states bean to reorganize according to Lincoln's plan, congressional opposition to the plan's leniency emerged. Ohio Senator Benjamin F. Wade and Henry Winter Davis in the House rejected Lincoln's plan and replaced it with a program detailed in a new bill. The Wade-Davis bill put the Confederate states under a military governor, and required a majority of a state's 1860 voters to pledge loyalty to the United States before they could form a new state government. The "iron clad oath" of the Wade-Davis bill was considerably more stringent than the one provided for by Lincoln. It was to be offered only to those who swore they had never voluntarily supported the Confederacy. The Wade-Davis bill required also that slavery be abolished in reconstructed states and barred Confederate officials from holding office. The bill drew widespread Radical Republican support and passed on July 2, 1863, a few days before adjournment. Lincoln pocket vetoed the bill by refusing to sign it after Congress adjourned.

Lincoln's pocket veto enraged the Congress, and Wade and Davis soon responded with a blistering Manifesto in August 1864, asserting that reconstruction policy was entirely within the authority of Congress. The fight over the Wade-Davis bill was the first battle in a decade-long war between Congress and the president over control of reconstruction. Reconstruction legislation, the central piece of the most dramatic and significant dispute between Congress and the president in American history, led to the near-removal of a president from office and plunged the South into political chaos.

This power struggle intensified with the assassination of Lincoln and the succession of Andrew Johnson to the presidency in April 1865. Johnson, a southerner from Tennessee, hated intensely the powerful planter aristocracy that, in his mind, had duped southern yeoman into war. Johnson rejected calls for reconstruction and soon declared his own plan of "restoration." He

U.S. Presidents

George Washington	1789–97
John Adams	1797–1801
Thomas Jefferson	1801–09
James Madison	1809–17
James Monroe	1817–25
John Adams	1825–29
Andrew Jackson	1829–37
Martin Van Buren	1837–41
William Henry Harrison	1841
John Tyler	1841–45
James Polk	1845–49
Zachary Taylor	1849–50
Millard Fillmore	1850–53
Franklin Pierce	1853–57
James Buchanan	1857–61
Abraham Lincoln	1861–65
Andrew Johnson	1865–69
Ulysses S. Grant	1869–77
Rutherford B. Hayes	1877–81
James Garfield	1881
Chester Arthur	1881–85
Grover Cleveland	1885–89
Benjamin Harrison	1889–93
Grover Cleveland	1893–97
William McKinley	1897–1901
Theodore Roosevelt	1901–09
William H. Taft	1909–13
Woodrow Wilson	1913–21
Warren Harding	1921–23
Calvin Coolidge	1923–29
Herbert Hoover	1929–33
Franklin D. Roosevelt	1933–45
Harry Truman	1945–53
Dwight Eisenhower	1953–61
John F. Kennedy	1961–63
Lyndon Johnson	1963–69
Richard Nixon	1969–74
Gerald Ford	1974–77
Jimmy Carter	1977–81
Ronald Reagan	1981–89
George H. W. Bush	1989–93
William J. Clinton	1993–2001
George W. Bush	2001+

Southern defiance of Reconstruction, depicted here by the three men—a thug with a club in his hand and bottle in his pocket; a Confederate soldier holding a dagger with the words "the lost cause" on it; and a wealthy man with "capital for votes" in his hand—standing over a black man, who appears to have been holding a U.S. flag. In the background a black orphanage and school burn. The caption reads, "'We regard the Reconstruction Acts (so called) of Congress as usurpations, and unconstitutional, revolutionary, and void.'—Democratic Platform." Published in Harper's Weekly, *September 5, 1868.* (LIBRARY OF CONGRESS, PRINTS AND PHOTOGRAPHS DIVISION)

offered a pardon to all those taking a loyalty oath, with the important exception that he would individually determine the status of those owning property valued more than $20,000. States seeking readmission also needed to abolish slavery, and each was required to repeal its ordinance of secession. This plan rejected the approach of the Wade-Davis bill and set the president and Congress on the road to another, more decisive, confrontation.

Events in the South dramatically affected debates over reconstruction. With the end of the war in April 1865, former Confederate states began to tightly restrict the freedoms afforded the millions of freed slaves. Several states soon passed "Black Codes," prohibiting blacks from, among other things, serving on juries, testifying against whites, or owning guns. The codes also created oppressive vagrancy laws that subjected those without work to arrest and prison. In 1865 the Ku Klux Klan formed in Tennessee as a secret society designed to terrorize blacks.

For many Republicans in Congress, the passage of the Black Codes and the reemergence of ex-Confederate leaders meant that the Union victory was being undermined. In December 1865 the thirty-ninth Congress convened for the first time after Lincoln's death. By that time, all of the Confederate states except Mississippi had met Johnson's requirements for readmission. In the House, Radical Republican leader Thaddeus Stevens successfully prevented recognition of the southern representatives during the roll call, effectively denying them admittance.

Republicans in the House and Senate created a Joint Committee on Reconstruction, consisting of nine representatives and six senators. Soon, Congress began to pass powerful new legislation directing the course of reconstruction, including the Freedmen's Bureau Bill and the Civil Rights Act of 1866, both designed to protect the rights and improve the conditions of blacks in the South. Johnson vetoed both measures, but Congress overrode both vetoes and the bills became law. Most importantly, in June 1866, Congress passed the Fourteenth Amendment, explicitly granting blacks state and federal citi-

In early 1866, Congress began to pass powerful new legislation directing the course of reconstruction, including the Freedmen's Bureau Bill and the Civil Rights Act of 1866, both designed to protect the rights and improve the conditions of blacks in the South.

Reconstruction Era

Alfred L. Brophy

As the Civil War drew to a close in the spring of 1865, President Abraham Lincoln began to lay plans for reuniting the American people. The United States military had already begun experimenting with plans for providing newly freed slaves with land and an opportunity for education. Lincoln's assassination in April 1865, however, led to a division within the government. The new president, Andrew Johnson, was sympathetic to the South and wanted to permit white southerners to be granted political rights quickly, while Republicans in Congress wanted to ensure that newly freed slaves' political rights were guaranteed and they were wary of granting voting rights to white southerners.

Congress and President Johnson sparred over how to restore the Union. The period from 1865 until 1877 is known as the "Reconstruction Era." The major legislation included the Freedman's Bureau Act, the Civil Rights Acts of 1866 and 1871, the Reconstruction Acts, the Force Act, and three constitutional amendments—the thirteenth, which outlawed slavery; the fourteenth, which ensures equal political rights regardless of race; and the fifteenth, which ensures equal voting rights regardless of race.

The Reconstruction Era ended with the Compromise of 1877, which settled the disputed presidential election of 1876. The Republicans agreed to withdraw federal troops from the southern states in return for allowing Rutherford B. Hayes, the Republican candidate, to become President.

Reconstruction legislation, the central piece of the most dramatic and significant dispute between Congress and the president in American history, led to the near-removal of a president from office and plunged the South into political chaos.

zenship, prohibiting any state from depriving "any person of life, liberty or property, without due process of law" and further prohibiting states from denying any person "the equal protection of the laws." In the election of 1866 Republicans campaigned largely on their support of the new amendment and increased their majority in Congress, forming anti-Johnson majorities in both the House and the Senate.

Congress soon took a decisive lead in directing the course of reconstruction. On March 2, 1867, on the last day of the session, Congress overrode Johnson's veto and passed the first of four Military Reconstruction Acts. The first act invalidated, but did not immediately disperse, the governments established under Johnson's plan. The ten Confederate states (all but Tennessee) that had refused to ratify the Fourteenth Amendment were divided into five military districts. Each military district was put under the direction of a military governor authorized to appoint and remove state officials. Voters were registered, and suffrage was extended to freedmen. State constitutional conventions were called, and elected delegates were charged with drafting new constitutional provisions providing for black suffrage. Finally, states were required to ratify the Fourteenth Amendment before readmission.

Congress passed the second Reconstruction Act over Johnson's veto in March 1867, directing military commanders to register voters, call conventions, and organize elections, rather than wait for state officials to act. In the face of recalcitrance from Johnson's executive branch and white southerners attempting to subvert the law, Congress in July 1867 passed a third Reconstruction Act, declaring the existing state governments in the South illegal and subject to military control and the U.S. Congress. In an attempt to delay the creation of new state governments, some southern whites turned to a provision of the first Reconstruction Act requiring that a majority of registered voters was necessary to ratify a new constitution and called for a boycott of the ratifying election. On March 11, 1868, Congress passed a fourth and final Reconstruction Act that allowed a majority of those voting to ratify a new constitution, regardless of the size of the turnout. President Johnson, as commander in chief, worked to delay and obstruct the army from enforcing these laws. Conflicts over the direction of reconstruction reached the boiling point in the spring of 1868, when the House of Representatives impeached Johnson. On May 26, 1868, the president escaped conviction by the Senate and removal from office by a single vote.

These acts have evoked intense scholarly controversy. To some important early historians of Reconstruction, they were emblematic of the Republican Party, captured by a radical wing, bent on taking vengeance against the South. More recent works take the opposite position, that these acts did not go nearly far enough—that their passage and implementation showed a Congress that ultimately abandoned any long-term, meaningful protection of freed slaves in the South. Still others argue that the Reconstruction Acts were the product of compromise within the Republican Party, reflecting the dominance of neither radicals nor conservatives, but all factions of the Republican Congress. Republicans, in this interpretation, seized control of reconstruction only after collaboration with President Johnson became impossible.

Reconstruction continues to be controversial because it remains, in the words of Eric Foner, "America's unfinished revolution."

Reconstruction continues to be controversial because it remains, in the words of Eric Foner, "America's unfinished revolution." In both the North and South, reconstruction ended not with racial equality, but rather with decades of discrimination—only haltingly reversed by the modern Civil Rights movement.

See also: Civil Rights Acts of 1866, 1871; Force Act of 1871; Freedmen's Bureau Act.

BIBLIOGRAPHY

Benedict, Michael Les. *A Compromise of Principle: Congressional Republicans and Reconstruction*. New York: Olympic Marketing Corporation, 1975.

Donald, David H., et al. *The Civil War and Reconstruction*. New York: Norton, 2001.

Foner, Eric. *Reconstruction: America's Unfinished Revolution, 1863–1877*. New York: HarperCollins, 1989.

Gienapp, William E. *Abraham Lincoln and Civil War America*. New York: Oxford University Press USA, 2002.

McPherson, James M. *Battle Cry of Freedom*. Reprint, New York: Ballentine Books, 1989.

Regulatory Flexibility Act (1980)

Jeffrey S. Lubbers

Excerpt from the Regulatory Flexibility Act

b. Each initial regulatory flexibility analysis ... shall contain—

(1) a description of the reasons why action by the agency is being considered;

(2) a succinct statement of the objectives of, and legal basis for, the proposed rule;

(3) a description of and, where feasible, an estimate of the number of small entities to which the proposed rule will apply;

(4) a description of the projected reporting, recordkeeping and other compliance requirements of the proposed rule ... ;

(5) an identification, to the extent practicable, of all relevant Federal rules which may duplicate, overlap or conflict with the proposed rule.

The Regulatory Flexibility Act (P.L. 96-354, 94 Stat. 1164-1170) requires agencies to consider the special needs and concerns of small entities (small businesses, organizations, and governmental jurisdictions) whenever they engage in rule making that is subject to the notice-and comment requirements of the Administrative Procedure Act (APA) or other laws. (Rule making is the process by which government agencies formulate and issue rules or statements designed to implement, interpret, or prescribe law or policy. Notice-and-comment requires that these rules be published in proposed form, giving the public an opportunity to comment on them.) The act also covers interpretive rules set forth by the Internal Revenue Service (IRS) that contain information collection requirements that affect small entities.

Federal Register: a newspaper published daily by the National Archives and Records Administration to notify the public of federal agency regulations, proposed rules and notices, executive orders, and other executive branch documents

GENERAL STRUCTURE OF THE ACT

Each time an agency publishes a notice-and-comment rule (or the IRS publishes an interpretive rule) in the ***Federal Register,*** it must prepare and publish an initial regulatory flexibility analysis (RFA) describing the impact of the proposed rule on small entities. An exception to this procedure is made when the agency head certifies that the proposed rule will not "have a significant economic impact on a substantial number of small entities."

The initial RFA is subject to public comment. The agency is encouraged to facilitate participation by small entities by providing actual notice of the proceeding to affected small entities, holding conferences and public hearings on the proposed rule as it affects small entities, and transmitting copies of its initial RFA to the Chief Counsel for Advocacy of the Small Business Administration (SBA).

Additional procedures are required to ensure participation by small entities in rule makings by either the Environmental Protection Agency (EPA) or the Occupational Safety and Health Administration (OSHA). Those two agencies must convene a regulatory review panel consisting of employees from that agency, the Office of Management and Budget, and the Chief Counsel for Advocacy of the Small Business Administration to review the rule and make recommendations to the agency from the perspective of small entities.

An agency's initial RFA must identify any "significant alternatives" to the proposed regulation that might achieve its goals while minimizing the impact on small entities. Approaches suggested in the act include modifying compliance or reporting timetables, simplifying compliance or reporting requirements, using performance rather than design standards, and exempting small entities from certain requirements. The final RFA must explain why any such significant alternatives to the rule were not adopted.

Agencies must also publish semiannual regulatory agendas identifying upcoming and current rule-making proposals that may affect small entities. In addition, the act directs agencies to apply regulatory flexibility analysis to their *existing* rules, initially evaluating them over a ten-year period, and reviewing them periodically.

CIRCUMSTANCES LEADING TO THE ADOPTION OF THE ACT

Congress's special concern for the problems of small business dates back to the passage of the Small Business Act in 1953. That act established the SBA and provided small businesses with assistance in receiving government grants and loans. In 1976, Congress established the Chief Counsel for Advocacy as an independent office within the SBA to protect the interests of small business. One of the chief counsel's tasks included measuring the costs of government regulation on small businesses and making proposals for eliminating excessive or unnecessary regulations of small businesses. The establishment of the office of chief council was followed by an influential White House Conference on Small Business that recommended the elimination or reduction of burdensome regulations and reporting requirements. That same year, President Jimmy Carter supported the passage of several new laws intended to aid small business, including the Regulatory Flexibility Act.

Congress's special concern for the problems of small business dates back to the passage of the Small Business Act in 1953.

EXPERIENCE UNDER THE ACT

As originally enacted, the act expressly prohibited judicial review of agency compliance with any of its requirements. Most courts limited review to a determination under the APA of the reasonableness of a final agency rule based on the record before it, which included the RFAs and any comments from small entities about the proposed rule.

In 1996, after noting that the requirements of the act were too often being ignored, Congress amended it. The amendments permitted judicial review of agency compliance with the act and allowed courts to send the rule back to the agency or defer its enforcement. These amendments, made by the Small Business Regulatory Enforcement Fairness Act, also (1) inserted the special provisions applying to EPA and OSHA (described above); (2) created a national small business ombudsman in the SBA to receive complaints relating to regulatory enforcement; (3) required that agencies produce compliance guides for small businesses; and (4) created a special regime for after-the-fact congressional review of agency rule making.

Since 1996, numerous cases have been brought challenging agency actions under the act. Most courts have held that the standard of review is one of reasonableness, meaning that the agency must have made a reasonable, good faith effort to carry out the requirements of the statute. Challenges to the adequacy of an agency certification or final RFA, claiming that the agency failed to consider the effects of the proposed rule on a particular entity, have been mostly unsuccessful. The Chief Counsel for Advocacy has, however, been very active in monitoring agency compliance with the act. The Office of Advocacy issues extensive annual reports on the implementation of the act as well as on the act's strengths and weaknesses as identified by that office. The General Accounting Office also provides regular reviews of the act's implementation, which it has characterized as a mixed success.

Most courts have held that the standard of review is one of reasonableness, meaning that the agency must have made a reasonable, good faith effort to carry out the requirements of the statute.

RELATIONSHIP WITH OTHER LAWS

The act is closely related to the Administrative Procedure Act because it supplements the APA's rule-making process, and, except for IRS rules, is applicable only to those rules that have to be issued after notice-and-comment procedures required by the APA or another statute. It also is linked to the legislation creating the SBA Office of Advocacy. Other related laws include such "small business relief" legislation as the Small Business Regulatory Enforcement Fairness Act and the Equal Access to Justice Act.

See also: ADMINISTRATIVE PROCEDURE ACT; SMALL BUSINESS ACT.

BIBLIOGRAPHY

Freedman, Doris S., Barney Singer, and Frank Swain. "The Regulatory Flexibility Act: Orienting Federal Regulation Toward Small Business." *Dickenson Law Review,* vol. 93 (1989): 439-464

Sargentich, Thomas O. "The Small Business Regulatory Enforcement Fairness Act." *Administrative Law Review,* vol. 49 (1997): 123-137

"Twenty Years of the Regulatory Flexibility Act: Rulemaking in a Dynamic Economy." Washington, DC: U.S. Small Business Administration, Office of Advocacy, 2000. Also available at <http://www.sba.gov/advo/laws/flex/00regflx.html>.

Verkuil, Paul R. "A Critical Guide to the Regulatory Flexibility Act." *Duke Law Journal,* vol. 213 (1982): 213-271

INTERNET RESOURCE

U.S. Small Business Administration. <http://www.sba.gov/regfair>.

RELIGIOUS FREEDOM RESTORATION ACT (1993)

Alan E. Brownstein and Melissa Rogers

Excerpt from the Religious Freedom Restoration Act

(a) In general. Government shall not substantially burden a person's exercise of religion even if the burden results from a rule of general applicability, except as provided in subsection (b).

(b) Exception. Government may substantially burden a person's exercise of religion only if it demonstrates that application of the burden to the person —- (1) is in furtherance of a compelling governmental interest; and (2) is the least restrictive means of furthering that compelling governmental interest.

(c) Judicial relief. A person whose religious exercise has been burdened in violation of this section may assert that violation as a claim or defense in a judicial proceeding and obtain appropriate relief against a government....

The purpose of the Religious Freedom Restoration Act (RFRA) (P.L. 103-141, 107 Stat. 1488) was to protect religious individuals and organizations against government interference with the practice of their faith. Under RFRA, people who claimed that laws or other governmental action substantially burdened their religious practice could bring a lawsuit against the federal, state, or local government alleged to be causing the problem. In this judicial proceeding, the government would have to demonstrate that its actions served a compelling interest and that there were no less restrictive ways to accomplish its goals. If the government failed to convince the court that its actions burdening religion met this rigorous standard, it would be found to have violated federal law.

Under RFRA, people who claimed that laws or other governmental action substantially burdened their religious practice could bring a lawsuit against the federal, state, or local government alleged to be causing the problem.

BACKGROUND

The constitutional basis for RFRA is the powers provided to Congress in section 5 of the Fourteenth Amendment to ensure that state and local governments do not interfere with the right to exercise one's religion as guaranteed by the free exercise clause of the First Amendment. Congress has enacted many important civil rights laws under its section 5 powers. But RFRA was unusual because it responded directly to a 1990 U.S. Supreme Court decision, *Employment Division v. Smith,* which sharply limited the scope of constitutional free exercise rights. In passing RFRA, Congress attempted to use a federal statute to restore rights that the Constitution itself had protected until the *Smith* decision reinterpreted the free exercise clause to withdraw that protection.

The *Smith* case involved a law prohibiting the possession of peyote, a hallucinogenic drug used by certain Native American groups during religious ceremonies. Because the law was not directed at the religious use of peyote, it could be described as a *neutral law of general applicability*—in other words, not specifically aimed at religion. But the effect of the law on Native American religions that used peyote was clear: it prohibited people from engaging in a religious ritual.

In two important cases prior to 1990, the Supreme Court had applied the free exercise clause to protect religious practices against neutral laws of general applicability. Most lower courts understood those decisions to mean that the free exercise clause provided some degree of protection to a person's ability to practice his religion against laws of this kind. This protection was not absolute. Often the government had a sufficiently strong reason for enforcing its law to justify interfering with religious practice. It was generally accepted, however, that the free exercise clause applied in such cases provided some protection for religious activities.

In *Smith,* the Supreme Court held that this commonly accepted understanding of the free exercise clause was incorrect. The Court stated that, except for two very limited exceptions, the free exercise clause provided no protection whatsoever to religious practices prohibited by neutral laws of general applicability. As long as a law did not single out religious activities for special restrictions (for example, a law that prohibited Catholics from attending Mass, or a law prohibiting anyone from using wine in a religious ceremony), the Constitution did not shield religious activities from the burden of the law. This was true, the Court said, even if the law made it illegal for people to obey the most important requirements of their faith.

A wide range of religious leaders, including Christians, Jews, Muslims, Sikhs, and Buddhists, greeted the *Smith* decision with great concern, as did civil rights activists and legal experts from across the political spectrum. When the Court declined requests to hear the case again, these leaders formed a coalition to work with a bipartisan group of lawmakers on Capitol Hill to draft RFRA.

RFRA IN CONGRESS

In a series of hearings, Congress heard evidence of the immediate impact of the *Smith* decision. This evidence included descriptions of court decisions applying the *Smith* rule.

A state government denied an Amish farmer's request to use silver reflector tape on his buggy rather than the bright orange triangle required by the government, which the farmer considered a "worldly," and thus religiously offensive, symbol. Even though the reflector tape was found to be equally effective in preventing traffic accidents, the court rejected his claim. This represented a reversal of an earlier ruling made prior to *Smith*.

Religious Land Use and Institutionalized Persons Act (2000)

Alan E. Brownstein and Melissa Rogers

The Religious Land Use and Institutionalized Persons Act (RLUIPA) (P.L. 106-274, 114 Stat. 803) gives religious institutions increased protection from state and local zoning and landmarking laws that substantially burden their religious practice. It also provides special protection for prisoners and others in governmental custody who wish to exercise their faith. In these contexts, RLUIPA requires the government to demonstrate that any substantial burden it places on religious practice is supported by a compelling interest and that there is no less restrictive way to advance that interest.

Initially a court had ruled that the First Amendment protected the rights of the Old Order Amish to be exempt from the state's requirement that the orange triangles be used. That court stated that the Amish must be allowed to use silver reflector tape or even lanterns, as those alternatives adequately met the state's compelling need for traffic safety while also protecting the Amish people's rights of conscience. In the post-*Smith* ruling that forced the use of the orange triangles, the court found that the Constitution no longer provided any relief in that situation. It should be noted, however, that the court did issue a new ruling in favor of the Amish under the state constitution.

In light of the *Smith* ruling, a court reversed its earlier ruling upholding Laotian Hmongs' religious objections to a government-mandated autopsy of a family member.

Another court decision after *Smith* upheld a zoning ordinance excluding churches from commercial zones while permitting secular (nonreligious) **nonprofit** organizations to be located in such areas.

nonprofit: an organization whose business is not conducted or maintained for the purpose of making a profit, but is usually aimed at providing services for the public good

While RFRA generally had wide support in Congress when it was proposed, some members were reluctant to enact it because they feared that the act might undermine security in state and federal prisons. Some religious practices that would routinely be protected outside of prison—such as holding services that were unsupervised—clearly presented a security risk inside prison, where such services would have to be supervised. RFRA supporters resolved this problem by including language in the legislative history of the law acknowledging that the need for prison administrators to preserve security and order had to be respected. With that issue resolved, RFRA passed Congress with little opposition and was signed into law in 1993.

While RFRA generally had wide support in Congress when it was proposed, some members were reluctant to enact it because they feared that the act might undermine security in state and federal prisons.

IMPLEMENTATION

Between 1993 and 1997 numerous RFRA lawsuits were brought in federal and state courts. Prisoners who argued that prison regulations prohibited them from practicing their religion brought many such suits. Several cases involved land-use regulations that made it more difficult to locate a house of worship in a community or regulated the kind of activities religious institutions might conduct in an area. In a particularly controversial group of cases, religious landlords argued that, because of RFRA, they did not have to obey certain civil rights laws that were inconsistent with their beliefs, such as laws that prohibited discrimination against unmarried couples seeking to rent housing.

CRITICS AND SUPPORTERS

Critics of RFRA raised several arguments against the substance and enforcement of the statute. Some claimed that it was never permissible to privilege religion by allowing religious people to ignore laws everyone else had to obey. Others argued that RFRA did not simply restore the old constitutional rule abandoned by the Supreme Court in the *Smith* case. Taken seriously, RFRA suggested that whenever government burdened religious practice, it must prove that its law serves a vital interest and that there is no alternative way to accomplish this goal other than to enforce the law without exemptions. The Supreme Court had applied this kind of strict scrutiny test in a few free exercise cases prior to the *Smith* decision, but in most cases it found some reason not to apply the test. In the great majority of free exercise cases brought to the Court, plaintiffs lost their claims. Most important, many state and local governments argued that RFRA was unconstitutional because it exceeded Congress's authority under the Fourteenth Amendment.

Supporters of RFRA responded that religious liberty was a fundamental right that fully deserved the protection provided by this statute. In this view, religion was not some minor interest to be sacrificed for trivial reasons. RFRA properly required states to have a strong justification before they interfered with citizens' religious freedom. Without a law like RFRA, state and local governments often ignored the interests of religious minorities. Under RFRA,

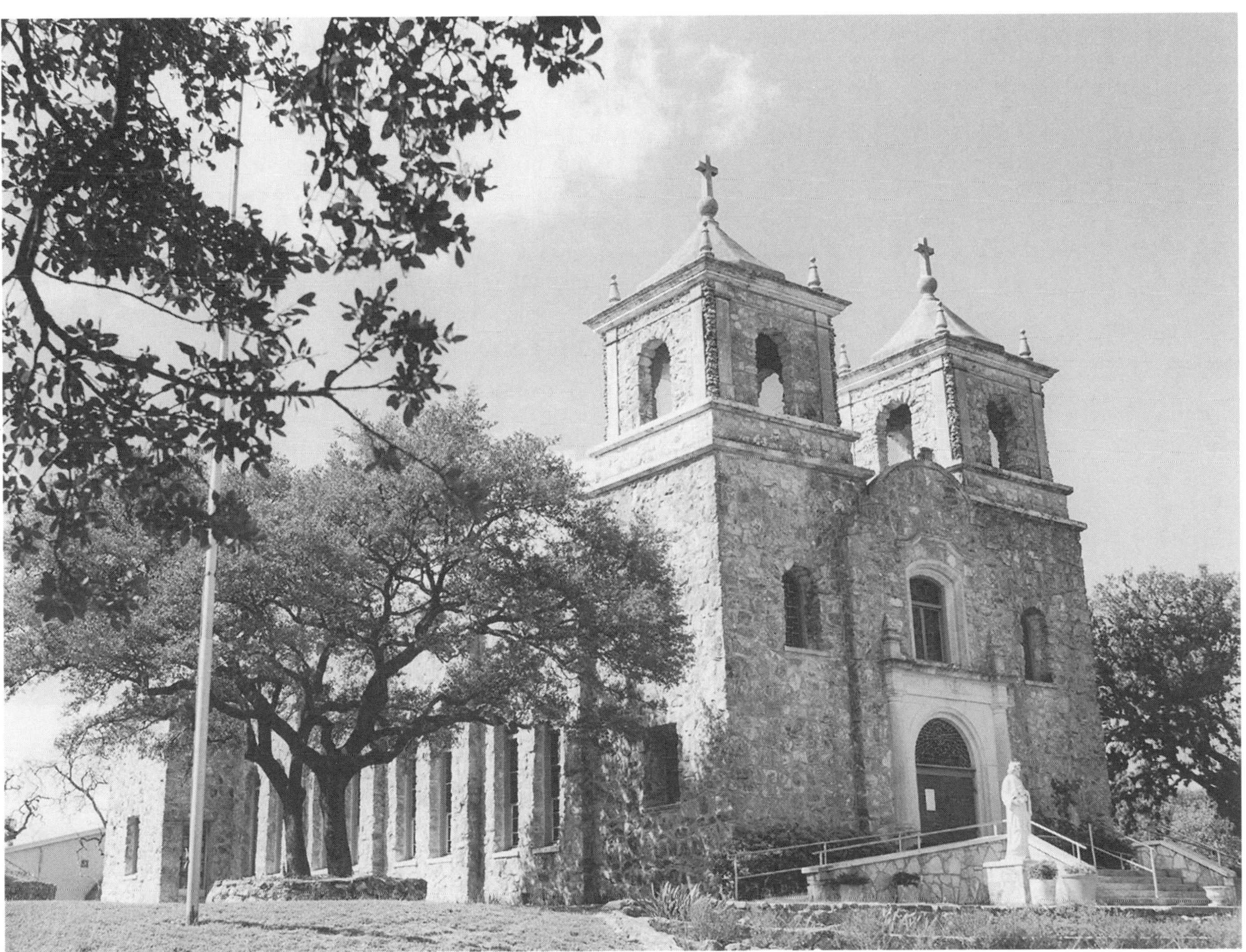

St. Peter Catholic Church in Boerne, Texas, claimed that the City of Boerne violated its right to religious freedom under the Religious Freedom Restoration Act (RFRA) when it blocked the church from building an addition under a local landmark-preservation law. The case went to the U.S. Supreme Court, where it was decided, in City of Boerne v. Flores *(June 25, 1997), that the RFRA was unconstitutional.* (© AP/Wide World Photos)

states would have to think carefully before denying an exemption from laws that substantially burdened religious practices. Moreover, supporters argued, although the compelling interest test was a rigorous standard of review, it did not prevent courts from carefully balancing the interests of state and local governments against the needs of religious practitioners. Indeed, plaintiffs lost most of the RFRA claims that were litigated in court. Although RFRA supporters acknowledged that RFRA extended beyond the limited free exercise protection the Constitution provided after *Smith,* they contended that the Supreme Court had never insisted that Congress could do no more than narrowly enforce the prohibitions of the Fourteenth Amendment.

UNCONSTITUTIONALITY OF RFRA

In 1997, the Supreme Court decided in *City of Boerne v. Flores* that RFRA exceeded Congress's power under the Fourteenth Amendment and was unconstitutional in its application to state or local governments. RFRA could protect the exercise of religion only against federal interference. The Court acknowledged that some state actions that did not technically violate the free exercise clause did, in fact, burden the exercise of religion. In a few such cases, Congress might prohibit those state activities through its power to prevent and remedy constitutional violations. However, according to the Court, RFRA extended far beyond Congress's limited discretion to prohibit state action that did not directly abridge constitutional rights. Furthermore, the Court believed that by subjecting *all* state laws substantially burdening religious practices to rigorous review, RFRA prevented the enforcement of many state laws that did not come close to violating the free exercise clause.

According to the Court, RFRA extended far beyond Congress' limited discretion to prohibit state action that did not directly abridge constitutional rights.

Even before the Court's decision in *Boerne,* a group called the RFRA Coalition had encouraged states to adopt their own laws to provide heightened protection for free exercise rights. The coalition was notable because its members—such as the Baptist Joint Committee, the American Muslim Council, People for the American Way, and the National Association of Evengelicals—normally had very different beliefs, and yet they all agreed that state laws were needed. The laws were known as state RFRAs. In the wake of the *Boerne* decision, the coalition launched a reinvigorated effort to pass state RFRAs. By 2003, more than ten such laws were enacted.

LATER LEGISLATION

After the *Boerne* case, the Coalition also urged the U.S. Congress to pass the Religious Liberty Protection Act (RLPA), which attempted once again to protect religion by enforcing the compelling interest standard through federal law. RLPA relied principally on two powers held by Congress: 1) its power to regulate many economic transactions that fall under the umbrella of interstate commerce (commerce between one state and another, or that crosses state lines); and 2) its power to offer financial grants to states on the condition that any state accepting those federal funds has to agree to obey certain regulatory conditions. RLPA passed the House of Representatives, but the Senate declined to vote on the legislation. Some civil rights and gay rights groups feared that RLPA would be interpreted to require governments to grant religiously based exemptions from state and local civil rights law prohibiting discrimination on the basis of sexual orientation. This controversy ultimately led to the enactment of more limited legislation, the Religious Land Use and Institutionalized Persons Act of 2000 (RLUIPA).

BIBLIOGRAPHY

Berg, Thomas C. "The New Attacks on Religious Freedom Legislation and Why They Are Wrong." 21 *Cardozo Law Review* 415 (1999).

Hamilton, Marci. "The Religious Freedom Restoration Act Is Unconstitutional, Period." 1 *University of Pennsylvania Journal of Constitutional Law* 1 (1998).

Laycock, Douglas. "The Remnants of Free Exercise." *1990 Supreme Court Review* 1.

Laycock, Douglas, and Oliver Thomas. "Interpreting the Religious Freedom Restoration Act." 62 *Texas Law Review* 210 (1994).

Marshall, William. "In Defense of *Smith* and Free Exercise Revisionism." 58 *University of Chicago Law Review* 308 (1991).

INTERNET RESOURCES

The Becket Fund for Religious Liberty on the Religious Land Use and Institutionalized Persons Protection Act. <http://www.rluipa.com/>.

The Pew Forum on Religion and Public Life. <http://www.pewforum.org/>.

RICHARD B. RUSSELL NATIONAL SCHOOL LUNCH ACT (1946)

James Walker

Throughout much of the nineteenth and early twentieth centuries, many state and local school districts provided food for their students to promote learning. The idea of whether the federal government ought to play a role in child nutrition was not raised until the Great Depression, when Congress began to appropriate federal dollars to assist states facing severe economic distress. In the 1930s the federal government began to distribute surplus food to states for use in local schools. Later, when food distribution became difficult during the war years, the government awarded cash grants enabling states to purchase food at local markets. Not only did these programs help states feed poor children, but they also created a market for farm goods, which worked to the benefit of the farmers.

By the 1940s, however, it was still painfully obvious that too many of America's youth, especially in the South, remained grossly undernourished. This lack of nourishment was especially problematic and notable when a number of young men failed armed forces physicals after being drafted for World War II.

> *By the 1940s, it was still painfully obvious that too many of America's youth, especially in the South, remained grossly undernourished.*

Richard B. Russell, a senator from Georgia, proposed a school lunch program in March 1944 to combat the problem of malnutrition. Senator Russell, although not personally touched by poverty, was well aware of the plight of many of his fellow Georgians, especially children. He also represented a rural

Richard B. Russell (1897–1971), Democratic senator from Georgia (1933–1971). LIBRARY OF CONGRESS

state, where farmers had suffered for years from chronically low prices for their goods. Russell proved well positioned to champion a federal program that could address both problems.

The school lunch proposal was very popular and its main opponent, Senator Robert Taft of Ohio, felt compelled to say that while providing school lunches to poor children was a good idea, it was not something in which the federal government should be involved. Taft, a traditional conservative, believed the federal government should have a very limited role in the lives of its citizens; the states, he believed, should provide the bulk of any services or assistance Americans needed. His view of American federalism allocated a very small role to the federal government, while Russell and others saw the federalist structure as essentially a cooperation between the two jurisdictions of state and federal government.

In passing the Richard B. Russell National School Lunch Act (79 P.L. 396, 60 Stat. 230), Congress relied on its constitutional power to tax and spend for the general welfare. The primary stated purpose of the act was to promote adequate nutrition among school-aged children, but a secondary purpose was to encourage domestic consumption of American agricultural products. The act did this by allocating surplus food and grants-in-aid to states so local school districts could provide lunches for children who might otherwise go hungry. In the legislation's words:

> It is hereby declared the policy of Congress, as a measure of national security, to safeguard the health and well-being of the Nation's children and to encourage the consumption of nutritious agricultural commodities and other food, by assisting the states, through grants-in-aid and other means, in providing an adequate supply of foods and other facilities for the establishment, maintenance, operation, and expansion of nonprofit school lunch programs.

Although litigants have not directly challenged the school lunch program, the issue of federal grants-in-aid to states with conditions attached has been litigated many times and has been firmly established as a constitutional power of the federal government. The U.S. Supreme Court held that the Constitution gives Congress broad powers to expend funds, as in *United States v. Butler* (1936), and to attach conditions to those expenditures, as in *Fullilove v. Klutznick* (1980).

Since its inception, the program has paid for hundreds of billions of meals to school children in every state and territory.

Over the years Congress has amended the act dozens of times to increase its scope and funding. The program that cost $70 million in 1947 grew to cost over $6.4 billion at the turn of the twenty-first century, when it provided lunches to twenty-five million students nationwide. Perhaps just as important, the school lunch program led directly to the Child Nutrition Act of 1966, an act that empowered the Department of Agriculture to expand nutrition programs. With this increased scope, the government also created the Special Supplemental Nutrition Program for Women, Infants, and Children in 1972. So what started out as a clever way to use surplus food, became a national commitment to nutrition for all American citizens.

See also: ELEMENTARY AND SECONDARY EDUCATION ACT.

BIBLIOGRAPHY

Fite, Gilbert C., and Richard B. Russell, Jr. *Senator From Georgia.* Chapel Hill: University of North Carolina Press, 1991.

Gay, James Thomas. "Richard B. Russell and the National School Lunch Program." In *Georgia Historical Quarterly* 80, no. 4, Winter (1996).

INTERNET RESOURCE

The School Lunch Program. <http://www.fns.usda.gov/cnd/Lunch>.

Rural Electrification Act (1936)

Andrew R. Klein

The Rural Electrification Act (49 Stat. 1363) was one of the most important pieces of legislation during the era of President Franklin D. Roosevelt's **New Deal**. It allowed the federal government to make low-cost loans to non-profit cooperatives (farmers who had banded together) for the purpose of bringing electricity to much of rural America for the first time.

New Deal: the legislative and administrative program of President Franklin D. Roosevelt designed to promote economic recovery and social reform (1933–1939)

President Roosevelt set the stage for the act's passage on May 11, 1935, when he issued an executive order that created the Rural Electrification Administration (REA). The REA was part of a relief package designed to stimulate an economy still in the grip of the **Great Depression**. On May 20, 1936, Congress passed the Rural Electrification Act, making the REA's promise of long-term funding for rural electricity a reality. In particular, the act permitted the president to appoint an administrator for the REA who was

Great Depression: the longest and most severe economic depression in American history (1929–1939); its effects were felt throughout the world

> authorized and empowered to make loans in the several States and Territories of the United States for rural electrification and the furnishing of electric energy to persons in rural areas who [were] not receiving central station service; ... to make or cause to be made, studies, investigations, and reports concerning the condition and progress of electrification of rural areas in the several States and Territories; and to publish and disseminate information with respect thereto.

The act addressed a serious need. When President Roosevelt created the REA, only 10 percent of rural Americans had electricity. This lack of power prevented farmers from modernizing their facilities. It also forced some people to live in unhealthful conditions. Many rural Americans, for example, lived in inadequately heated homes with poor sanitation. Most farmers had no running water and little means to store their food.

When President Roosevelt created the REA, only 10 percent of rural Americans had electricity.

Nevertheless, privately owned utility companies, which provided power to most of the country, were not eager to serve the rural population. These companies argued that supplying rural areas with electricity was not profitable. The lack of attention from private companies led farmers to form non-profit cooperatives to implement electrification even before the REA. But, without the government's assistance, these organizations lacked the technical and financial expertise they needed to succeed.

Creation of the REA changed the way that cooperatives worked. Most significantly, the government aided farmers by granting their cooperatives low-cost loans. Through these loans, the cooperatives could acquire the necessary generation and distribution facilities to supply their farms with electrical power. The REA also helped farmers develop assembly-line methods for electrical line construction with uniform procedures and standardized types of electrical hardware. The result was that more and more rural Americans could afford electricity. By 1950, 90 percent of American farms had electricity.

In addition to helping provide rural areas with electric and telephone service, the RUS took over the USDA's water and sewage programs and helped more than 20,000 rural communities obtain modern water systems.

On October 28, 1949, Congress made an important amendment to the Rural Electrification Act that permitted the further modernization of rural America. This amendment authorized the REA to make loans for the purpose of furnishing and improving rural telephone service.

The REA no longer exists in its original form. With the reorganization of the United States Department of Agriculture (USDA) in 1994, the REA became the Rural Utilities Service (RUS). In addition to helping provide rural areas with electric and telephone service, the RUS took over the USDA's water and sewage programs and helped more than 20,000 rural communities obtain modern water systems.

See also: FEDERAL POWERS ACTS; TENNESSEE VALLEY AUTHORITY ACT.

BIBLIOGRAPHY

Cuivre River Electric Cooperative, Inc. "America's Rural Electric Story." <http://www.cuivre.com/newpage12.htm>.

Depression America: Countryside and City, vol. 3. Danbury, CT: Grolier Educational, 2001.

Tennessee Valley Authority. "TVA: Electricity for All." <http://newdeal.feri.org/tva/>.

S

Safe Drinking Water Act (1974)

Kyle A. Loring

In 1974 Congress enacted the Safe Drinking Water Act (SDWA) (P.L. 93-523, 88 Stat. 1660) to protect the quality of both actual and potential drinking water in the United States. Congress had created the SDWA in response to a nationwide survey that revealed health risks from inadequate public water-supply facilities and operating procedures. To achieve its goal the SDWA provides water quality standards for drinking-water suppliers, protects underground drinking-water sources, and directs appropriate deep-well injection of wastes.

The SDWA requires the U.S. Environmental Protection Agency (EPA) to regulate all "public water systems," defined as systems that provide piped water for human consumption for at least sixty days a year to at least fifteen service connections or twenty-five people. The EPA does this through Primary Drinking Water Regulations, by which it first identifies contaminants that may pose a risk to human health and that occur in drinking water at potentially unsafe levels. Then the EPA specifies a Maximum Contaminant Level Goal (MCLG) for each contaminant, which is set at the level below which there is no predicted health risk. Finally the EPA creates a legally enforceable Maximum Contaminant Level (MCL), which is the greatest amount of contaminant that will be allowed in the public water supply. This MCL must be set as close as is feasible to the MCLG after taking into account the best technology, treatment techniques, and costs. Since the 1996 amendments discussed below, the EPA may instead require a Treatment Technique for removing the contaminant if there is neither an economically or technologically feasible MCL, nor an accurate way to measure the contaminant in water.

Congress had created the SDWA in response to a nationwide survey that revealed health risks from inadequate public water-supply facilities and operating procedures.

States generally obtain primary authority to implement the SDWA after proving to the EPA that they will adopt and enforce standards at least as stringent as the national standards. While the states may oversee the program, the public water systems themselves physically ensure the safety of the tap water through treatment, testing, and reporting. In addition to these "at the tap" protections, the SDWA requires states and public water suppliers to protect

Due to criticism that the original act was an inflexible, unfunded mandate with an unattainable regulatory schedule, the 104th Congress extensively amended the act in 1996.

initial water sources from contamination. In particular, the SDWA provides for an Underground Injection Control (UIC) program to prevent contamination of underground water sources by underground injection of contaminated fluids.

Due to criticism that the original act was an inflexible, unfunded mandate with an unattainable regulatory schedule, the 104th Congress extensively amended the act in 1996 (P.L. 104-182, 110 Stat. 1613). These amendments included new pollution prevention approaches, public information requirements, added flexibility to the regulatory process, and a Drinking Water State Revolving Fund. Pollution prevention took the form primarily of source-water quality assessment programs to determine the current health of water supplies and delineate the area to be protected. In addition, public water suppliers were required to inform their year-round customers about the source and quality of their tap water with an annual consumer confidence report.

The most important element of the amendments was the critically necessary funding mechanism added to the SDWA's stringent water quality requirements. This fund provided federal monetary aid to public water systems to repair and upgrade their facilities, focusing particularly on assisting small and disadvantaged communities that might otherwise find these repairs too expensive. The fund also gave priority to programs using pollution prevention to safeguard their drinking water supply.

See also: FEDERAL WATER POLLUTIOIN CONTROL ACT.

BIBLIOGRAPHY

Plater, Zygmunt J. B., Robert H. Abrams, et al. *Environmental Law and Policy: Nature, Law and Society,* 2nd ed. St. Paul, MN: West Publishing, 1998.

U.S. Environmental Protection Agency. "Safe Drinking Water Act Amendments of 1996" and "Understanding the Safe Drinking Water Act." July 2003. <http://www.epa.gov/>.

SECURITIES ACT OF 1933

Steven Ramirez

Excerpt from the Securities Act of 1933

(a) Unless a registration statement is in effect as to a security, it shall be unlawful for any person, directly or indirectly—

(1) to make use of any means or instruments of transportation or communication in interstate commerce or of the mails to sell such security through the use or medium of any prospectus or otherwise; or

(2) to carry or cause to be carried through the mails or in interstate commerce, by any means or instruments of transportation, any such security for the purpose of sale or for delivery after sale.

The Securities Act of 1933 (P.L. 73-22, 48 Stat. 74) was the first federal legislation specifically intended to regulate a company's sale of securities (i.e., stocks and bonds). The act required that all sales of securities be registered with the government unless there was a specific exemption to the contrary. The process of registration included the submission of a prospectus, a disclosure document that states all material facts relating to the securities and the company issuing them. The acts provided remedies for investors who are misled regarding the securities, or who purchase securities that should be registered but are not. The act also included civil and criminal penalties for violating its provisions.

interstate commerce: trade involving the transportation of goods from one state to another, or the transfer of property between a person in one state and a person in another

public offering: the making available of corporate stocks or bonds to the general public

The key operative provision of the act required that no securities be sold in **interstate commerce** without an effective registration statement in effect for the securities. There are exemptions provided for securities transactions that are not a **public offering**; certain specified small offerings; intrastate offerings; and transactions by other than the issuing company or underwriter. These exemptions, potentially very complicated in application, meant that ordinary transactions over a stock exchange were not covered by the Securities Act of 1933. The act was instead intended to regulate companies seeking to raise capital through a public offering.

The act required that all sales of securities be registered with the government unless there was a specific exemption to the contrary.

CONSTITUTIONAL BASIS

Congress promulgated the act pursuant to its authority to regulate interstate commerce, granted by Article II, Section 8 of the U.S. Constitution. The act therefore requires the use of an instrumentality of interstate communication or transportation before it applies. Courts have held that the use of mails or a telephone suffices to meet this requirement, even if the use is completely intrastate.

New Deal: the legislative and administrative program of President Franklin D. Roosevelt designed to promote economic recovery and social reform (1933–1939)

Great Depression: the longest and most sever economic depression in American history (1929–1939); its effects were felt throughout the world

CIRCUMSTANCES LEADING TO THE ADOPTION OF THE ACT

The Securities Act of 1933 was a key component of President Franklin D. Roosevelt's **New Deal**. The New Deal represented the first massive federal regulation of the economy. FDR intended the New Deal to help resolve the **Great Depression**, an unprecedented economic calamity that ultimately gave rise to an unemployment rate of 25 percent and a 33 percent contraction of the nation's economy. In the election of 1932, FDR promised to deliver economic reform, and the New Deal was an effort to fulfill this promise.

The regulation of securities was a natural starting place for the New Deal reforms, as the stock market crash of 1929 seemed to have triggered the deep economic malaise that became the Great Depression.

The regulation of securities was a natural starting place for the New Deal reforms, as the stock market crash of 1929 seemed to have triggered the deep economic malaise that became the Great Depression. Roosevelt sought to "bring back public confidence" in the securities markets and was convinced that a truth in securities act, at the federal level, was the right medicine. One-half of the $50 billion in new securities sold during the 1920s turned out to be worthless. Investor confidence was so devastated by the carnage that the issuance of new securities fell from $9.4 billion in 1929 to $380 million in 1933. By 1933 there was considerable economic and political pressure for regulation.

Nevertheless, the financial community opposed the act, adhering to a more **laissez-faire** approach that would have preserved the status quo. Some

laissez-faire: a doctrine opposing governmental interference in economic affairs beyond the minimum necessary for the maintenance of peace and property rights commentators worried that the bill would actually slow economic recovery by slowing the capital formation process and discouraging the flotation of new securities. Some even worried there would be a "capital strike," whereby financiers simply would not undertake any entrepreneurial activity. In the end, the forces arrayed against reform did not have a favorable political context, due in large part to continued macroeconomic distress, and the bill passed Congress. It was signed into law on May 27, 1933.

EXPERIENCE UNDER THE ACT

There was no capital strike and instead the nation's securities markets flourished, becoming a worldwide model. By the mid-1990s, for example, initial public offerings of securities by new firms grew from $43.6 billion in 1991 to $66.5 Billion in 1992, and to $112 billion in 1993. This flow of capital to new firms translated into a major competitive advantage for U.S. business. By 1995 experts widely viewed the American securities markets to be the strongest markets in the world.

Initially the courts were very receptive to the remedial and investor protection goals of the act.

Initially the courts were very receptive to the remedial and investor protection goals of the act. In *SEC v. Howey* (1946), the U.S. Supreme Court articulated a broad definition of securities that gave the act an extended reach. Similarly, in *Wilko v. Swan* (1953), the Supreme Court held that an arbitration agreement could not be raised as a defense to an action under the Securities Act. The Court refused to relegate investors to private arbitration proceedings, and instead affirmed investors could not waive the remedies under the act. This meant that investors would always retain the ability to vindicate their rights under the act in a court.

Still, as the decades passed and memories of the Great Depression faded, courts appeared to become far more skeptical of the act. In *Rodriguez v. Shearson* (1989), the Supreme Court overruled *Wilko* and held that an arbitration agreement barred a customer from suing in court under the Securities Act of 1933. In *Gustafson v. Alloyd* (1995), the Supreme Court severely limited the scope of remedies available under the act, holding that one of the most important remedial sections of the act only applied to initial public offerings made pursuant to a statutory prospectus, and not to exempt distributions or transactions on the secondary market. This was a surprise given that the plain meaning of the statute made no mention of any such requirement.

The impact of the Securities Act of 1933 on society has been controversial.

In addition to court rulings limiting the effect of the act, Congress has adopted certain additional limitations. Specifically, in 1995 Congress enacted (over a presidential veto) the Private Securities Litigation Reform Act, effectively limiting class actions under the act and shifting a large extent of the act's enforcement to the Securities and Exchange Commission. In 1998 Congress went an additional step, in the Securities Litigation Uniform Standards Act, preempting class actions based upon state law. The net effect of these two acts is to greatly undermine the efficacy of **private litigation** as a means of enforcement.

private litigation: a civil lawsuit (one brought to protect an individual right or redress a wrong), as distinct from criminal proceedings

The impact of the Securities Act of 1933 on society has been controversial. The laissez-faire enthusiasts who opposed the act, unsuccessfully, succeeded over the past few decades in raising questions about the efficacy of the act. They maintained, for example, that the quality of securities issued before the act was comparable to the quality of securities issued after the act. They further maintained that the market furnished sufficient incentives for the disclosure of information so no mandatory disclosure regime was needed. One commentator, Judge Richard Posner, who is a leading proponent of laissez faire efficiency, has argued that security regulations may be a waste of time.

Empirical studies to date have suggested that the act did not significantly raise investor returns, but Congress did not intend the act to accomplish such a goal. Congress intended to enhance the flow of information so investors could make intelligent investment decisions. On this point, every empirical study to date has shown that performance of new issues was less volatile after the act. This suggests that markets operated more efficiently after the act, as investors made decisions in a more intelligent manner.

The laws have been consistent with greater investor confidence, and this too was one of Congress's aims of the act. Economists increasingly believe that mandatory securities disclosure regimes, such as the Securities Act of 1933, are part of a sound regulatory infrastructure needed to facilitate the optimal performance of market-based economies.

George Stiglitz, 2001 Nobel laureate in economics, has specifically argued that the lack of adequate securities regulation is one of the reasons why the developing world has not achieved the promises of globalization. Other economists share this conclusion. Regardless of whether the securities laws have enhanced the efficient operation of markets by supporting more intelligent decision-making, it is clear that the act contributed to a stable macro economy and lowered the cost of capital by enhancing investor confidence. In the sixty years following its enactment, the economy suffered no shocks of the same magnitude of the Great Depression. On the other hand, shortly after significant dilution of the private enforcement of the act in 1995, and the judicial limitations imposed upon the act's reach, the United States experienced a severe crisis in investor confidence in the summer of 2002 that clearly increased the nation's cost of capital.

RELATIONSHIP WITH OTHER LAWS

There are a number of federal securities acts other than the Securities Act of 1933. The most important of these is the Securities Exchange Act of 1934. The Securities Exchange Act of 1934 does not generally regulate the initial distribution of securities like the Securities Act of 1933. Instead, the Securities Exchange Act of 1934 imposed continuing disclosure obligations on publicly held companies whether or not they were issuing securities. The 1934 Act also regulated the securities industry, including stock exchanges, broker-dealers and other securities professionals. Finally, it regulated certain aspects of publicly held companies like corporate governance, tender offers, and proxy solicitations.

As previously discussed, for over six decades the federal securities laws, including the Securities Act of 1933, provided investor remedies that were in addition to any remedies under state law. In 1998, however, Congress reversed this outcome and preempted all class actions under state "Blue Sky" laws, which generally extended investors more generous avenues of recovery than those remaining under the act after the Private Securities Litigation Reform Act of 1995.

See also: SECURITIES AND EXCHANGE ACT OF 1934.

BIBLIOGRAPHY

Davis, Kenneth S. *FDR: The New Deal Years*. New York: Random House, 1986.

Posner, Richard. *The Economic Analysis of Law*. New York: Aspen, 1998.

Ramirez, Steven. "The Law and Macroeconomics of the New Deal at 70." *Maryland Law Review* 62, no. 3 (2003).

Ramirez, Steven, "Fear and Social Capitalism." *Washburn Law Journal* 42, no. 1 (2002): 31–77.

Roosevelt, Franklin D. *The Public Papers and Addresses of Franklin D. Roosevelt*. New York: Random House, 1938.

Stiglitz, Joseph. *Globalization and its Discontents*. New York: W.W. Norton, 2002.

SECURITIES EXCHANGE ACT OF 1934

Steven Ramirez

Excerpt from the Securities Exchange Act of 1934

(3) Frequently the prices of securities on such exchanges and markets are susceptible to manipulation and control, and the dissemination of such prices gives rise to excessive speculation, resulting in sudden and unreasonable fluctuations in the prices of securities which (a) cause alternately unreasonable expansion and unreasonable contraction of the volume of credit available for trade, transportation, and industry in interstate commerce, (b) hinder the proper appraisal of the value of securities and thus prevent a fair calculation of taxes owing to the United States and to the several States by owners, buyers, and sellers of securities, and (c) prevent the fair valuation of collateral for bank loans and/or obstruct the effective operation of the national banking system and Federal Reserve System.

(4) National emergencies, which produce widespread unemployment and the dislocation of trade, transportation, and industry, and which burden interstate commerce and adversely affect the general welfare, are precipitated, intensified, and prolonged by manipulation and sudden and unreasonable fluctuations of security prices and by excessive speculation on such exchanges and markets, and to meet such emergencies the Federal Government is put to such great expense as to burden the national credit.

publicly held company: a corporation whose stock anyone can buy on a stock exchange

tender offer: a public offer to purchase shares of a specific corporation, usually at a price above what the market offers, in an attempt to accumulate enough shares to take control of the company

securities: stocks, bonds, and certain other instruments of investment

The Securities Exchange Act of 1934 (P.L. 73-291, 48 Stat. 881) was the first federal legislative initiative specifically intended to regulate stock exchanges and publicly held companies that have distributed securities (i.e., stocks and bonds) to the public. The act requires **publicly held companies** to make periodic public disclosures and disclosures in connection with proxy solicitations. The act also mandates certain disclosures in connection with **tender offers** for the shares of publicly held companies. Finally, the act regulates trading by certain company insiders and broadly prohibits all fraud in connection with the sale of **securities.**

With respect to stock exchanges including the National Association of Securities Dealers, which operates the NASDAQ market, or the New York Stock Exchange, the act requires registration and adherence to certain principles of self-regulation to ensure that exchanges operate transparently and fairly. Every securities broker and every securities dealer must be a member of a so-called self-regulatory organization. If either a securities firm or an individual affiliated with a securities firm violates the rules or regulations of the exchange, or the federal securities laws, or just and equitable principles of trade, the law permits the government to impose sanctions. These sanctions can range from fines to censures to permanent barring from the securities industry. The act also includes civil and criminal penalties against those who violate its provisions. The Securities and Exchange Commission (SEC) is the primary regulatory agency that enforces the federal securities laws, including the Securities Act of 1933, and the Securities Exchange Act of 1934.

The act requires registration and adherence to certain principles of self-regulation to ensure that exchanges operate transparently and fairly.

CONSTITUTIONAL BASIS

Congress promulgated the act under its authority to regulate interstate commerce, pursuant to Article II, section 8 of the U.S. Constitution. The act therefore requires the use of an instrumentality of interstate communication or transportation before it applies. The courts have held that the use of mails or a telephone suffices to meet this requirement, even if the use is completely intrastate.

CIRCUMSTANCES LEADING TO THE ADOPTION OF THE ACT

In the election of 1932, President Roosevelt promised to deliver economic reform in the effort to resolve the Great Depression, an unprecedented economic calamity that ultimately gave rise to an unemployment rate of 25 percent and to a 33 percent contraction of the nation's economy. The Securities Act of 1933 was the first piece of President Roosevelt's New Deal, and Congress enacted it during the first one hundred days of his administration. Nevertheless, President Roosevelt made it clear that more securities regulation was needed, specifically legislation "relating to better supervision of the purchase and sale of all [securities] dealt with on exchanges." The Securities Exchange Act of 1934 was this act, fulfilling the New Deal's promise for systematic securities reform. The New Deal represented the first massive federal regulation of the economy.

The regulation of securities was a natural starting place for the New Deal reforms, as the market crash of 1929 seemed to have triggered the deep economic malaise that became the Great Depression. Roosevelt sought to "bring back public confidence" in the securities markets and was convinced that truthful and full disclosure was essential to this goal. Congress joined in this conclusion, finding that full disclosure would give investors pause before falling prey to panic selling. Regulating the exchanges and publicly held companies is how lawmakers decided to achieve full disclosure, not just when a company first distributed securities, but on an ongoing basis. Congress was convinced that unregulated exchanges meant cycles of booms and terrible depressions when a company is a public traded company. The Great Depression was all the convincing most needed.

Roosevelt sought to "bring back public confidence" in the securities markets and was convinced that truthful and full disclosure was essential to this goal.

laissez-faire: a doctrine opposing governmental interference in economic affairs beyond the minimum necessary for the maintenance of peace and property rights

Nevertheless, the financial community opposed the act, preferring a more **laissez-faire** approach to preserve the status quo. One opponent testified to Congress that the act was a conspiracy to take the nation "down the road from democracy to communism." (Davis, 368). Business interests feared the act would lead to government supervision of much of the business sector, and stock exchanges fought hard to maintain their autonomy. Despite this opposition, the Securities Exchange Act passed both houses of Congress with overwhelming support and became law on June 6, 1934.

Relationship with Other Laws

Steven Ramirez

There are a number of federal securities acts other than the Securities Exchange Act of 1934. The most important of these is the Securities Act of 1933. The Securities Exchange Act of 1934 does not generally regulate the initial distribution of securities like the Securities Act of 1933. The Securities Act of 1933 imposes disclosure obligations upon companies when they are issuing securities.

As previously discussed, for over six decades the federal securities laws, including the Securities Exchange Act of 1934, provided investor remedies that were in addition to any remedies under state law. In 1998, however, Congress reversed this outcome and preempted all class actions under state "Blue Sky" laws, which generally extended investors more generous avenues of recovery than those remaining under the act after the Private Securities Litigation Reform Act of 1995.

EXPERIENCE UNDER THE ACT

By 1995 experts widely acknowledged that the American securities markets were the strongest in the world. A large part of this perception rested upon the effectiveness of the Securities Exchange Act of 1934. The act completed the work that Congress started with the Securities Act of 1933, by insuring traders had the ability to make intelligent investment decisions through full and truthful disclosure. The 1933 Act mandated disclosures when companies distributed securities, and the 1934 Act mandated disclosures when a company publicly traded its securities.

Initially the courts were very receptive to the remedial and investor protection goals of the act. In *J.I. Case v. Borak* (1964), the Supreme Court held that private investors could obtain remedies under the act's proxy disclosure rules. In *SEC v. Capital Gains Research* (1963), the Supreme Court decided that the terms fraud and deceit, as used in the act with respect to the regulation of securities professionals, must be construed broadly to reach all unjust and unfair practices used by brokers to abuse the trust of their clients. More recently, the Supreme Court held that trading on nonpublic inside information could amount to securities fraud even when the investor did not obtain the information from an officer or director of the issuer of the traded securities. This is known as the "misappropriation theory" of insider trading, adopted in *United States v. O'Hagan* (1998).

Still, as the decades passed and memories of the Great Depression faded, courts appeared to have become far more skeptical of the act. In *Lampf, Pleva, Lipkind, Purpis & Petigrow v. Gilbertson* (1991), the Supreme Court greatly restricted the time period for bringing securities fraud claims before they were barred by the statute of limitations. In *Central Bank of Denver v. First Interstate* (1994), the Supreme Court severely limited the potential liability of attorneys and accountants under the act. It is fair to say that the early twenty-first century Supreme Court is not positively inclined toward private enforcement of the act, although it appears to continue to strengthen government enforcement. In *SEC v. Zanford* (2002), the Supreme Court upheld the enforcement authority of the SEC against a miscreant broker.

Still, as the decades passed and memories of the Great Depression faded, courts appeared to have become far more skeptical of the act.

Recent legislative trimming of the act's operation mirrors this judicial pruning. Specifically, in 1995 Congress enacted (over a presidential veto) the Private Securities Litigation Reform Act, limiting class action lawsuits under the act and shifting most enforcement responsibility to the SEC. In 1998 Congress went an additional step, in the Securities Litigation Uniform Standards Act, and preempted class actions based upon state law. The net effect of these two acts was to greatly undermine the efficacy of **private litigation** as a means of enforcement.

private litigation: a civil lawsuit (one brought to protect an individual right or redress a wrong), as distinct from criminal proceedings

These legislative steps are particularly notable as Congress tends to chronically underfund the SEC, making it difficult for the agency to enforce the securities law. In addition, the SEC lacks one very important element—it has no authority to repay investors for their losses. Moreover, the SEC is certainly not immune from political pressure that may impact agency decisions and lead to a lax approach to law enforcement. Recently, former Chairman Arthur Levitt disclosed that political influence had undermined the SEC's ability to pursue a number of reform initiatives.

Moreover, the SEC is certainly not immune from political pressure that may impact agency decisions and lead to a lax approach to law enforcement.

The impact of the Securities Exchange Act of 1934 on society has been controversial. The laissez-faire enthusiasts that unsuccessfully opposed the act have succeeded over the past few decades in undercutting the act's efficacy. They maintain, for example, that the market furnishes sufficient incentives for the disclosure of information such that no mandatory disclosure regime is needed. One commentator, however, has recognized that the market did not seem to function in the way these laissez-faire enthusiasts predicted before 1934. This commentator recog-

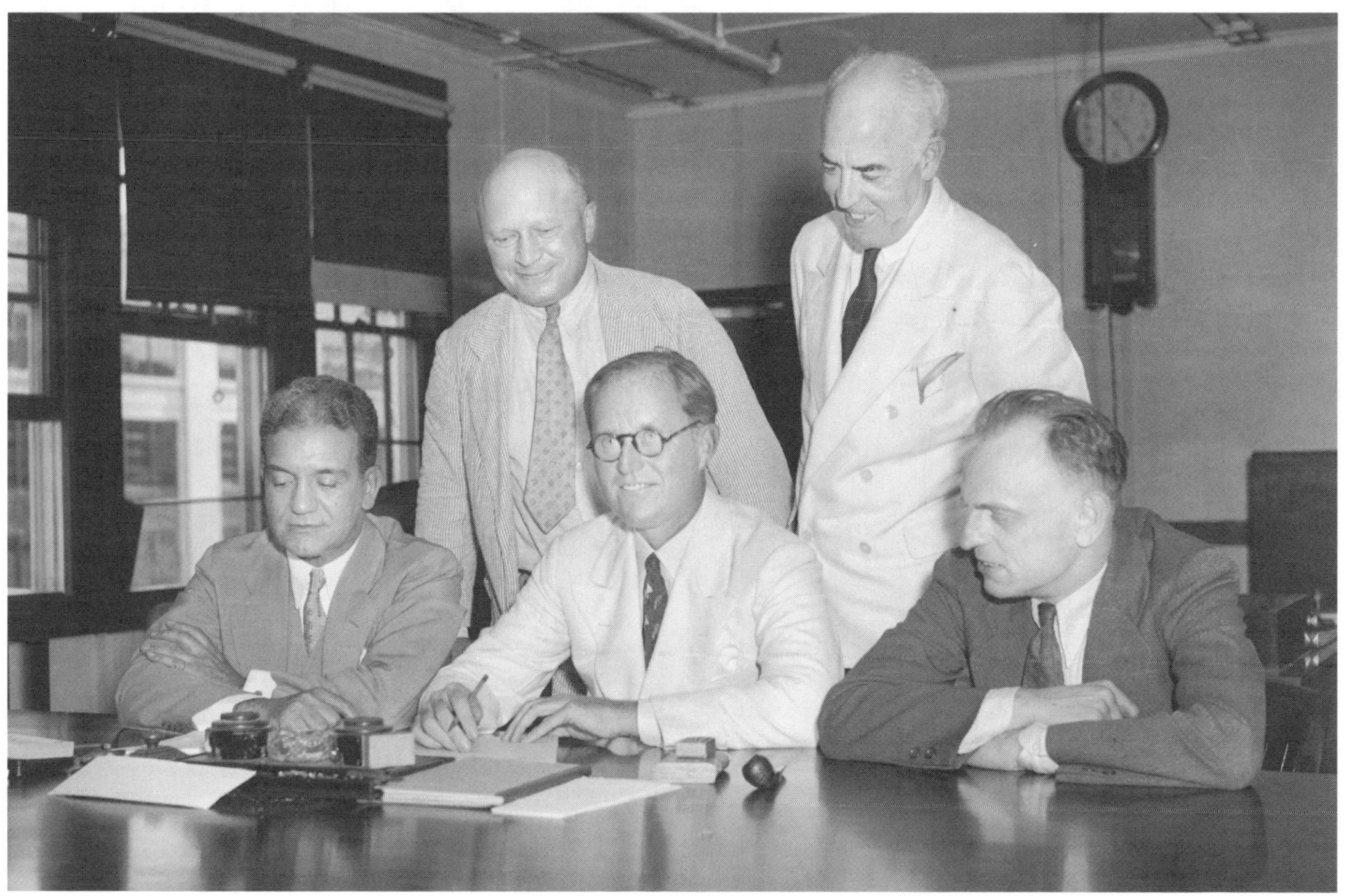

The new Securities and Exchange Commission (SEC), July 2, 1934. In the middle of those seated is Joseph P. Kennedy, whom President Roosevelt appointed to head the SEC. Seated to his left and right, respectively, are Ferdinand Pecora and James M. Landis. Standing are George C. Matthews, left, and Robert E. Healy. (©Bettmann/Corbis)

nized that "[p]ervasive systemic ignorance blanketed Wall Street like a perpetual North Atlantic fog before the New Deal." This suggests that regulation was needed to free up disclosure and to allow markets to operate more efficiently, as investors make more informed decisions. The act, together with the Securities Act of 1933, seems to have enhanced investor confidence as a result.

See also: Securities Act of 1933.

BIBLIOGRAPHY

Davis, Kenneth S. *FDR: The New Deal Years*. New York: Random House, 1986.

Posner, Richard. *The Economic Analysis of Law*. New York: Aspen, 1998.

Ramirez, Steven. "The Law and Macroeconomics of the New Deal at 70." *Maryland Law Review* 62, no. 3 (2003).

Ramirez, Steven. "Fear and Social Capitalism." *Washburn Law Journal* 42, no. 1 (2002): 31–77.

Ramirez, Steven. "The Professional Obligations of Securities Brokers Under Federal Law." *University of Cincinnati Law Review* 72, no. 2 (2002): 527–568.

Roosevelt, Franklin D. *The Public Papers and Addresses of Franklin D. Roosevelt*. New York: Random House, 1938.

Stiglitz, Joseph. *Globalization and its Discontents*. New York: W.W. Norton, 2002.

Sedition Act (1918)

See Espionage Act (1917) and Sedition Act (1918)

Selective Service Act of 1917

Adam P. Plant

The Selective Service Act of 1917 (P.L. 65-12, 40 Stat. 76) was the first act mandating American military service since the Civil War. In April 1917, before the act's passage, there were only 110,000 servicemen who could be deployed if America joined the war then raging in Europe. An army of this size would have been destroyed within months considering the brutal trench warfare employed during the Great War. All told, there were 116,516 American casualties in World War I—more than were in the service at the time war was declared.

President Woodrow Wilson, who had avoided American entry in the war for about three years, initially wanted to use only volunteers to augment the forces needed to fight and win the war. In his address before Congress calling for a declaration of war, Wilson stated:

All told, there were 116,516 American casualties in World War I—more than were in the service at the time war was declared.

> Our object now ... is to vindicate the principles of peace and justice in the life of the world as against selfish and autocratic power and to set up amongst the really free and self-governed

peoples of the world such a concert of purpose and of action as will henceforth insure the observance of those principles.

However, three weeks after war was declared, only 32,000 Americans had volunteered for service. Wilson realized that this was not enough military strength to win the war, so he called for a draft, which was decried by many members of his own party. Progressive Democrats, who usually sided with the president, asserted that a draft would destroy "democracy at home while fighting for it abroad." Republicans attacked Wilson on the draft issue to take political advantage of the Democrat's wartime leadership.

THE WORLD WAR I DRAFT

Wilson, however, would not lose on the issue of the draft. With the aid of Newton Baker, his secretary of war, Wilson brought about passage of the act, which allowed him to raise all branches of the armed forces to a level that could compete with the Axis powers of Germany, Austria-Hungary, and Turkey. All males aged twenty-one to thirty were required to register at local polling stations. The age limits were later changed to include all men from ages eighteen to forty-five. The drafts carried out during World War I led to the successful

With the aid of Newton Baker, his secretary of war, Wilson brought about passage of the act, which allowed him to raise all branches of the armed forces to a level that could compete with the Axis powers of Germany, Austria-Hungary, and Turkey.

Thomas R. Marshall, vice president to Woodrow Wilson, draws a World War I draft capsule, c. 1918. (LIBRARY OF CONGRESS, PRINTS AND PHOTOGRAPHS DIVISION)

Blacks were called on to defend the rights of Europeans while their own rights as America's citizen-soldiers were denied.

registration of almost 24 million American men. Because of a concerted effort to invoke a sense of patriotism in all Americans, the U.S. enlisted many to fight against the Axis powers. Less than 350,000 men "dodged" the World War I draft.

The 1917 act also contained a significant change from the Civil War draft: replacements could not be hired to fight in a person's place. Section 3 stated:

> No person liable to military service shall hereafter be permitted or allowed to furnish a substitute for such service; nor shall any substitute be received, enlisted, or enrolled in the military service of the United States; and no such person shall be permitted to escape such service or to be discharged

Fighting in France for Freedom!--Are YOU Helping at Home?
© International Film Service - N.Y.
NEW YORK STOP 61,000 MEN IN THEIR SEARCH FOR SLACKERS. PHOTO SHOWS A WAGON LOAD OF SUSPECTS.
As a result of a three days drive in New York special agents, soldiers and sailors "interviewed" over 61,000 men and made them produce registration cards and many were detained temporarily before they could be properly identified. About 1500 slackers were caught and sent to camps.
News Photo Poster No. 12
ISSUED FOR
Maine Committee On Public Safety
BLAINE MANSION, AUGUSTA, MAINE.
ILLUSTRATED CURRENT NEWS.
New Haven, Conn.
DON'T BE CAUGHT NAPPING.
Every man registered under the Selected Service Law must carry his registration card at all times.
Obey the law and save embarrassment.

A truck full of men detained for not carrying their registration cards are shown in this 1918 poster. The caption underneath the photo reads "As a result of a three days drive in New York special agents, soldiers and sailors 'interviewed' over 61,000 men and made them produce registration cards and many were detained temporarily before they could be properly identified. About 1500 slackers were caught and sent to camps." (LIBRARY OF CONGRESS, PRINTS AND PHOTOGRAPHS DIVISION)

> therefrom prior to the expiration of his term of service by the payment of money or any other valuable thing whatsoever as consideration for his release from military service or liability thereto.

This provision meant that wealthy people could not buy their way out of service. It was designed to ensure that all Americans fought in the war, not just the poor who could not buy their way out.

BLACK SERVICEMEN

Black Americans, of whom nearly 2.3 million were drafted, made a special sacrifice for the war effort. Conditions in America during the 1910s were in direct opposition to the ideals of the Republic: equality in voting rights, education, and use of public accommodations would not come for many black Americans for almost another half-century. Yet blacks were called on to defend the rights of Europeans while their own rights as America's citizen-soldiers were denied. This dichotomy was even the subject of a German propaganda campaign. However, many black Americans felt that their service would be rewarded with a concerted push for civil rights upon their return. W.E.B. DuBois, the famous black activist, spoke out in support of the war: "Let us, while the war lasts, forget our special grievances and close ranks shoulder to shoulder with our white fellow citizens ... fighting for democracy. We make no ordinary sacrifice, but we make it gladly and willingly."

Many black soldiers would not receive the honors they deserved back home, although some did in Europe. The French government awarded Croix de Guerre medals, high honors for bravery, to members of New York's 396th Infantry, nicknamed the Harlem Hellfighters. Sadly, though they made no ordinary sacrifice, many of the returning veterans were denied the basic opportunities and rights they fought for in Europe. Some were even subjected to lynching and mob brutality as they reentered the American workforce because white workers feared the black veterans would take their jobs.

SUCCESSFUL WAR EFFORT

American servicemen were supported by a patriotic push on the homefront. Wilson called for farmers, miners, housewives, and other domestic workers to keep the nation's armed forces well supplied by treating their everyday jobs as a part of the war effort. Because of the manpower the act brought into service, America and its allies emerged victorious from World War I.

See also: ENROLLMENT ACT.

BIBLIOGRAPHY

Evans, Harold. *The American Century*. New York: Knopf, 1998.

Mullen, R.W. *Blacks in America's Wars*. New York: Monad Press, 1975.

Wilson, Woodrow. "Joint Address to Congress Leading to a Declaration of War Against Germany (1917)." <http://www.history.com>.

Sentencing Reform Act (1984)

Barry L. Johnson

Excerpt from the Sentencing Reform Act

There is established as an independent commission in the judicial branch of the United States a United States Sentencing Commission which shall consist of seven voting members and one nonvoting member.... The purposes of the United States Sentencing Commission are to (1) establish sentencing policies and practices for the Federal criminal justice system that (A) assure the meeting of the purposes of sentencing ... (B) provide certainty and fairness in meeting the purposes of sentencing, avoiding unwarranted sentencing disparities among defendants with similar records that have been found guilty of similar criminal conduct ... and (C) reflect, to the extent practicable, advancement in knowledge of human behavior as it relates to the criminal justice process....

The Sentencing Reform Act of 1984 (P.L. No. 98-473, 98 Stat. 1987) marked a fundamental change in federal criminal sentencing policy and practice. Part of the broader Comprehensive Crime Control Act of 1984, the Sentencing Reform Act abolished parole in the federal system (although it did not affect the many state criminal justice systems that continued to use parole) and created the United States Sentencing Commission. This administrative body was given the task of crafting guidelines governing criminal sentencing in federal courts.

FEDERAL SENTENCING PRIOR TO THE SENTENCING REFORM ACT

Prior to the Sentencing Reform Act, federal judges had extremely broad discretion in sentencing.

Prior to the Sentencing Reform Act, federal judges had extremely broad discretion in sentencing. Most criminal statutes provided only broad maximum terms of imprisonment. Federal judges were free to impose any sentence, ranging from probation to the statutory maximum. No meaningful appeal of the sentence was available to the offender. Sentencing decisions therefore reflected each judge's individual notions of justice and views of the purposes of sentencing, and sentences for similar offenses varied dramatically depending on the identity of the sentencing judge. Moreover, discretion in the system was not limited to sentencing judges. The introduction of parole into the federal system in 1910 left each prisoner's release date to the discretion of parole officials, although most prisoners were ineligible for parole until one-third of their sentence was served.

THE DECLINE OF REHABILITATION AS AN IDEAL

The broad discretion of judges and parole officials and the indeterminate length of prison sentences prior to the Sentencing Reform Act stemmed from a concept known as offender rehabilitation. Prison-based rehabilitation programs were designed to reduce crime by helping offenders to function normally in society once their prison terms ended. As many experts in the field of criminal justice saw it, the rehabilitation of offenders required Congress give judges and parole officials sufficient discretion to permit "individualized sentencing." Under such sentencing, judges could tailor the length and nature of the sentence to the specific rehabilitative needs of the individual offender.

By the 1970s, however, studies questioning the effectiveness of prison-based rehabilitation programs in reducing crime led to a widespread loss of faith in the power of prisons to rehabilitate criminals. Many criminologists publicly questioned the effectiveness of prison-based rehabilitation while others challenged the legitimacy of the entire rehabilitation-based sentencing scheme. Theorists such as Andrew von Hirsch advocated a sentencing system that authorized punishment of offenders exclusively in proportion to the seriousness of their crimes. This theory was called "just desserts"—in simple terms, offenders would get the sentences they deserved. According to this view, the rehabilitative scheme was illegitimate, because it kept offenders who were not successfully rehabilitated in prison for time periods well in excess of the punishment deserved.

By the 1970s, studies questioning the effectiveness of prison-based rehabilitation programs in reducing crime led to a widespread loss of faith in the power of prisons to rehabilitate criminals.

As the rehabilitative ideal declined and the just desserts approach to sentencing gained ground, experts in the field became increasingly aware of the problems created by a sentencing system that gave discretion to judges. The chief problem was that judicial sentencing led to disparities, or inequalities, in sentences set for the same crimes. Judge Marvin Frankel's classic 1973 book, *Criminal Sentences: Law Without Order,* highlighted this problem. Judge Frankel, a sitting U.S. district judge, noted that "widely unequal sentences are imposed every day in great numbers for crimes and criminals not essentially distinguishable from each other." Judge Frankel explained that unequal treatment of offenders who had committed similar crimes was caused by the virtually unlimited discretion he and his colleagues on the federal bench enjoyed. He charged that this discretion was "terrifying and intolerable for a society that professes devotion to the rule of law." To address this problem, he urged the creation of an administrative agency, a Commission on Sentencing, that would be responsible for enacting rules to guide federal courts in the process of criminal sentencing.

PASSAGE OF THE SENTENCING REFORM ACT

The work of Judge Frankel and other critics of sentencing disparity prompted Senator Edward Kennedy, a Democrat from Massachusetts, to sponsor sentencing reform legislation in 1975. Although early reform efforts failed, Senator Kennedy continued to sponsor reform bills in succeeding terms of Congress.

By the early 1980s the political climate in Washington had changed considerably, as Ronald Reagan entered the White House and Republicans assumed control of Congress. This political shift did not, however, kill the sentencing reform movement. Conservative members of Congress, including Republican Senators Strom Thurmond of South Carolina and Orrin Hatch of Utah, joined forces with liberal sponsors of sentencing reform. This **bipartisan** support for guidelines-based sentencing reform eventually resulted in the attachment of the Sentencing Reform Act (as part of the Comprehensive Crime Control Act of 1984) to an **omnibus** funding bill. President Ronald Reagan signed the bill into law on October 12, 1984. With passage of the Sentencing Reform Act, the U.S. Sentencing Commission was born.

bipartisan: involving members of two parties, especially the two political parties

omnibus: including many things at once

THE COMMISSION AND THE GUIDELINES

Congress had two major purposes in enacting the Sentencing Reform Act: first, promoting "honesty in sentencing," and second, reducing "unjustifiably wide"

With passage of the Sentencing Reform Act, the United States Sentencing Commission was born.

sentencing disparity. Honesty in sentencing referred to the impact of parole. Under parole guidelines, it was not uncommon for an offender who was sentenced to fifteen years to be released on parole after serving only five. Congress addressed this issue by abolishing parole, and creating a system of "real-time" sentencing. In the wake of the Sentencing Reform Act, the sentence imposed by the judge is the sentence served by the offender, subject only to a minor adjustment for "good time" credits, administered by the Bureau of Prisons.

Congress addressed the problem of unwarranted sentencing disparity by creating the commission and instructing it to establish sentencing guidelines to limit and structure the sentencing discretion of federal judges. The commission consisted of seven members, appointed by the president and confirmed by the Senate. At least three members of the commission had to be federal judges, and no more than four commissioners could be affiliated with either major political party.

Although Congress left to the commission the task of crafting the specific guidelines, it did give the commission a number of specific directives. Among them, the Sentencing Reform Act specified that the guidelines were to be "neutral as to the race, sex, national origin, creed, and socioeconomic status of the offender," and that the guidelines should "reflect the general inappropriateness of considering the education, vocational skills, employment record, family ties and responsibilities, and community ties" of an offender in determining the nature or length of his sentence.

The commission worked from its appointment in October 1985 until April 1987 to create a set of guidelines consistent with congressional directives. The draft guidelines were submitted for public comment and congressional approval, and became effective on November 1, 1987.

THE REACTION TO THE GUIDELINES

Shortly after the guidelines took effect, criminal defendants began filing constitutional challenges to the Sentencing Reform Act. Many judges declared the Sentencing Reform Act unconstitutional, and by the summer of 1988 sentencing

Results of Sentencing Reform

After the Sentencing Reform Act of 1984, which provided guidelines for ensuring that similar crimes received similar punishments, Congress also enacted mandatory minimum sentences for certain crimes and drastically increased punishments for repeat offenders. Crime dropped steadily for more than a decade beginning in 1991, and while many people give these measures much of the credit, critics note that aspects of the current system are inherently unfair. For example, penalties for crack cocaine are one hundred times more stringent that penalties for powdered cocaine, because Congress considered the former a much larger threat at the time the law was enacted. Liberal critics have long maintained that the sentencing laws for nonviolent crimes are disproportionately cruel and take a particular toll on minorities and the poor. In addition, federal judges have become more and more frustrated by the lack of discretion they are allowed in evaluating the particulars of a case to hand down an appropriate sentence. Even as crime has dropped dramatically, the prison population has continued to grow, in part because of this strict sentencing, reaching a record of more than two million in 1999. The relationship between large numbers of inmates and the drop in crime is not clear. The drop during the 1990s can also be attributed to a booming economy, better tactics by police, and the end of a crack cocaine epidemic.

in the federal courts was in total disarray. The U.S. Supreme Court finally resolved the constitutional status of the guidelines in its 1989 decision in *Mistretta v. United States*, holding that the Sentencing Reform Act's creation of the commission and its delegation to the commission of the task of drafting guidelines were constitutionally permissible, clearing the way for the implementation of the guidelines in federal courts across the country.

The guidelines have been in place ever since. However, they remain controversial. Critics complain that they are excessively harsh, mechanical, and inflexible. Prominent judges and scholars have urged total reconsideration of the Sentencing Reform Act and a return to greater judicial discretion in sentencing. To this point, however, Congress has not been inclined to change the policies embodied in the Sentencing Reform Act.

The guidelines have been in place since 1987, but they remain controversial.

See also: Anti-Drug Abuse Act; Omnibus Crime Control and Safe Streets Act of 1968.

BIBLIOGRAPHY

Allen, Francis A. *The Decline of the Rehabilitative Ideal.* New Haven, CT: Yale University Press, 1981.

Committee Report on Sentencing Reform Act. S. Rep. No. 98-225 (1983), reprinted in U.S.C.C.A.N. 3182 (1984).

Frankel, Marvin E. *Criminal Sentences: Law Without Order.* New York: Hill and Wang, 1973.

Martinson, Robert. "What Works?—Question and Answers About Prison Reform." *The Public Interest* (Spring 1974): 22.

Nagel, Ilene H. "Structuring Sentencing Discretion: The New Federal Sentencing Guidelines." 80 *Journal of Criminal Law and Criminology* (1990): 883–943.

Stith, Kate, and Jose A. Cabranes. *Fear of Judging: Sentencing Guidelines in the Federal Courts.* Chicago: University of Chicago Press, 1998.

Stith, Kate, and Steve Y. Koh. "The Politics of Sentencing Reform: The Legislative History of the Federal Sentencing Guidelines." 28 *Wake Forest Law Review* 223 (1993).

Von Hirsch, Andrew. *Doing Justice: The Choice of Punishments.* New York: Hill and Wang, 1976.

Sherman Antitrust Act (1890)

Herbert Hovenkamp

In 1890 public hostility toward the **monopoly** actions of large corporations was at a feverish pitch. The Sherman Antitrust Act (26 Stat 209) was designed to limit monopolistic and other anticompetitive practices by large American corporations such as Standard Oil Company. The act, immensely popular when it was passed, was named after Senator John Sherman of Ohio, one of the senators who originally proposed such a law. Congress's main concern was that individual states were unable to deal effectively with large multistate corporations because state courts could control actions only within their own state. The control of corporations that did business in many states required a federal statute because federal power could reach across the entire United States.

monopoly: exclusive control of a market by one company, often marked by the controlling of prices and exclusion of competition

John Sherman (1823–1900), sponsor of the Sherman Antitrust Act. (Public Domain)

The theory of the Sherman Act is grounded in the basic capitalist idea that prices are lowest when multiple firms in a market are forced to compete with each other. Further, such competition is believed to produce the most innovation and to maximize the quality and variety of goods and services. Although the Sherman Act was not controversial when it was passed, there have always been disputes about its meaning. Its explicit goal was to protect the public from monopolies, but many critics have charged that more often it ended up protecting small, inefficient businesses from larger and more efficient firms. That debate has never fully been resolved.

The Sherman Act contains two main provisions. The act makes it unlawful (1) for a group of firms to enter into contracts or conspiracies "in restraint of trade" and (2) for a single firm to "monopolize" a particular market.

AGREEMENTS IN RESTRAINT OF TRADE

As section 1 of the act puts it, "Every contract, combination, ... or conspiracy in restraint of trade or commerce among the several States, or with foreign nations, is hereby declared to be illegal." The term "restraint of trade" is a very old one that had been used by British courts since before the seventeenth century. Today it describes actions that are unreasonably anticompetitive. The words "contract," "combination," and "conspiracy" all refer to types of agreements involving two or more persons or firms. A firm acting by itself cannot violate section 1 of the Sherman Act.

Horizontal Agreements Unlawful agreements in restraint of trade can be roughly grouped into two classifications, horizontal and vertical. An agreement is said to be horizontal if it involves two or more firms in competition with each other. The most common horizontal agreement in restraint of trade is *price fixing,* which occurs when two or more firms stop competing on price and agree that they will charge a specific price. In *United States v. Trans-Missouri Freight Association* (1897), the Supreme Court first held that price fixing was automatically unlawful under section 1 of the Sherman Act and a criminal violation. Price fixers could be sent to prison and also be fined.

boycott: to refuse to purchase goods or services from a specific company

The other horizontal agreements most frequently condemned as unreasonably anticompetitive are *market division agreements* and **boycotts**. A market division agreement occurs when competing firms "divide" the market by agreeing they will not sell in the same territory or to the same customers, or that they will not make products that can compete with each other. For example, two makers of a highly desired commercial cleanser might agree that one will sell only to retailers while the other will sell only to hospitals and professional offices. As a result, the two firms will not compete with each other for the same sales, and each can charge monopoly prices.

A boycott, or concerted refusal to deal, occurs when two or more actors agree with each other to keep some other set of actors out of the market. A common rationale for boycotts is exclusion of firms that might charge lower prices or offer more innovative products. A group of firms that are fixing prices might pressure a supplier to stop selling to a competitor who is charging lower prices. Many claimed boycotts resulted from activities such as efforts within a profession to set standards. Courts must then decide whether the exclusion is reasonable under the circumstances or unreasonably anticompetitive. For example, in *Wilk v. American Medical Association* (1990), a federal court concluded that it was anticompetitive for the AMA to pass an "accreditation rule" that forced hospitals to exclude chiropractors from access to medical facilities. The AMA claimed the exclusion was necessary because the chiropractors were not using proven methods of health care. However, the court decided that this choice should be made by consumers themselves and not through coerced exclusion of chiropractors from the market.

Vertical Agreements. A vertical agreement is one between a seller and a buyer. For example, if Goodyear sells tires to Ford, the tire-selling agreement between them would be described as vertical. Nearly all vertical agreements are lawful under the antitrust laws, but there are two exceptions. First, "resale price maintenance," or "vertical price fixing," occurs when a seller forces a buyer to charge a certain retail price. For example, Colgate might sell toothpaste to Osco Drugs with a contract requiring Osco to retail the toothpaste for $2.00 per tube. Such a practice is unlawful. Second, vertical "nonprice" restraints are agreements under which a manufacturer limits the locations or territories in which a retailer may sell or some other significant aspect of the retailer's business. In *Continental TV v. GTE Sylvania* (1977), however, the Supreme Court held that very few agreements of this nature are competitively harmful. Since then, almost none have been declared illegal.

Cartoon titled "The Bosses of the Senate," published in Puck, *January 23, 1889. The Senate is watched over by giants, representing various industry trusts, while the "People's Entrance," located on the balcony, is closed.* (Library of Congress, Prints and Photographs Division)

MONOPOLIZATION

Section 2 of the Sherman Act provides that "every person who shall monopolize, or attempt to monopolize ... any part of the trade or commerce among the several States, or with foreign nations shall be deemed guilty...." This section of the Sherman Act reaches "unilateral" practices by "dominant" firms—in other words, anticompetitive conduct by monopolists that increases their power. Typically a firm must control at least 70 percent of the market in which it operates to be considered a monopoly. Even then, the firm is not behaving unlawfully. To be considered guilty of monopolization, the firm must also engage in one or more "exclusionary practices."

An exclusionary practice is something that is "unreasonably anticompetitive," which generally means it causes more harm to rivals than by ordinary competitive processes. Monopolists generally use such practices to strengthen or prolong their monopoly positions, because a monopoly is usually very profitable. In *United States v. Standard Oil Co.* (1911), the Supreme Court held that Standard violated section 2 by using "predatory pricing" to drive rivals out of business. Standard allegedly charged very low prices in a town until competitors were forced to declare bankruptcy or to sell their plants to Standard at very low prices.

Other exclusionary practices involve misuse of patents or other intellectual property rights. For example, in *Walker Process Equip. v. Food Machinery Corp.* (1965), the Supreme Court held that it was unlawful for a monopoly firm to obtain a patent fraudulently (by lying on its patent application) and then use the patent to exclude other firms from making its product.

In *United States v. Microsoft Corp.* (2002), a federal court in Washington, D.C., held that it was unlawful for Microsoft to engage in a number of practices that tended to prolong Microsoft's monopoly of personal computer

Standard Oil Company

The Standard Oil Company was incorporated by John D. Rockefeller in Ohio in 1870. At the time, the refining business was highly competitive, and Standard Oil had more than 250 competitors. Rockefeller negotiated with the railroads to secure low shipping rates in return for regular business, and reduced costs still further through vertical integration, purchasing oil wells, pipelines, and retail outlets. With these advantages he began to drive competitors out of business, particularly as deteriorating market conditions increased competitive pressure on smaller firms. Rockefeller was then able to buy out independent refineries in Pennsylvania, New York, and New Jersey at very low prices. In 1882 Rockefeller formed the Standard Oil Trust as a holding agency for forty companies. This corporate structure, which was the first of its kind, gave authority to a board of trustees which governed on behalf of the member companies' shareholders, centralizing control while allowing Rockefeller to maneuver around state laws that might restrict his operations. The power wielded by Standard Oil and other monopolies engendered public opposition that led to the passage of the Sherman Antitrust Act in 1890. By the turn of the century, Standard Oil controlled more than 90 percent of the market for petroleum refining. Critics alleged that the company engaged in unfair practices, such as charging excessively high prices for products with no competition and using the profits to subsidize artificially low prices in contested markets, thereby driving competitors out of business. In 1906 Standard Oil was charged with violating the Sherman Act by conspiring "to restrain the trade and commerce in petroleum ... in refined oil, and in other products of petroleum," and was found guilty in 1909. The company appealed, and two years later the Supreme Court upheld the decision and ordered Standard Oil dismantled. The companies created in the dissolution included the future Exxon, Chevron, and Mobil.

operating systems. The practices generally limited the ability of rivals to produce competing operating systems that would have forced Microsoft to cut its prices. For example, the Netscape Internet browser and the Java programming language threatened to create an avenue through which computer users could run their programs on several different operating systems. Microsoft responded to the threat by "bundling" its own browser, Internet Explorer, into its Windows program and by developing an alternative version of Java that was incompatible with other operating systems. The result made it much more difficult for users of programs running on Windows to run them on other operating systems as well.

See also: Clayton Act of 1914; Federal Trade Commission Act.

BIBLIOGRAPHY

Chamberlain, John. *The Enterprising Americans: A Business History of the United States.* New York: Harper and Row, 1974.

Faulkner, Harold U. *American Economic History.* New York: Harper, 1960.

Hovenkamp, Herbert. *Federal Antitrust Policy: The Law of Competition and Its Practice,* 2d ed. St. Paul, MN: West Group, 1999.

Sklar, Martin J. *The Corporate Reconstruction of American Capitalism, 1890–1916.* Cambridge, U.K.: Cambridge University Press, 1988.

Thorelli, Hans B. *The Federal Antitrust Policy: Origination of an American Tradition.* Baltimore: Johns Hopkins University Press, 1955.

The Robinson-Patman Act of 1936

The Robinson-Patman Act—also known as the Federal Anti-Price Discrimination Act—was created to ensure that suppliers to independent businesses offered them the same prices they gave to chain stores. The legislation strengthened the provisions of the Clayton Act that prohibited price discrimination specifically when it lessened competition or created a monopoly. Robinson-Patman made discrimination illegal if its effect was "to injure, destroy, or prevent competition with any person who either grants or knowingly receives the benefit of such discrimination, or with customers of either of them." In other words, price discrimination would be illegal if it merely harmed a competitor, even without lessening competition or creating a monopoly. Discounts for bulk purchases were only allowed if they were directly attributable to cost savings resulting from the larger purchases.

Shipping Acts

Thomas Panebianco

Excerpt from the Controlled Carrier Act

(a) ... No controlled carrier subject to this section may maintain rates or charges in its tariffs or service contracts, or charge or assess rates, that are below a level that is just and reasonable, nor may any such carrier establish, maintain, or enforce unjust or unreasonable classifications, rules, or regulations in those tariffs or service contracts.... The Commission may, at any time after notice and hearing, prohibit the publication or use of any rates, charges, classifications, rules, or regulations that the controlled carrier has failed to demonstrate to be just and reasonable.

The shipping statutes include a number of laws affecting commercial ocean shipping in the international trades and the cruise industry. The primary statute is the Shipping Act of 1984, substantially amended in 1998 (P.L. 105-258, 112 Stat.1902), but with prior versions going back to 1916. Most of the general features of the 1916 statute, however, survive today. The federal agency that administers the Shipping Act is the Federal Maritime Commission (FMC).

SHIPPING ACT

The Shipping Act imposes obligations on both carriers (the shipping companies who own and operate cargo ships) and shippers (the importers and exporters whose cargo is carried by the carriers), and sets out basic rules for doing business. For example, shippers may not misrepresent to carriers what their cargo is or how much it weighs. They must accurately describe their cargo so the carrier can charge them the correct rate. Carriers may not unreasonably refuse to deal with any shipper, and are limited in the ways they may treat their shipper-customers differently from one another. The law also sets out how other entities, such as ports, terminal operators, and middlemen (often called "freight forwarders") may do business. The FMC has regulations providing more detailed rules for these businesses to follow.

A major and controversial feature of the Shipping Act is that it gives carriers the right to cooperate with one another in discussing and setting their rates.

A major and controversial feature of the Shipping Act is that it gives carriers the right to cooperate with one another in discussing and setting their rates. Ordinarily, this type of behavior would violate U.S. antitrust laws. Congress decided to give carriers limited immunity—that is, to excuse them—from the antitrust laws in 1916. Congress was concerned that if carriers were not permitted to cooperate with each other, "rate wars" would break out, as carriers could lower rates dramatically to drive their competitors out of a trade, and then raise them dramatically once a monopoly was achieved. Congress determined that it was important for both carriers and shippers to have stable rates, and thus allowed carriers to discuss and agree on certain rates and practices. This privilege, however, comes with responsibilities. The FMC reviews and monitors the results of such cooperation and can go to court to stop such arrangements (called "agreements" in the statute) if they are harmful. Many shippers dislike antitrust immunity and want the antitrust laws applied to the carriers. They believe immunity gives carriers an unfair advantage in dealing with their customers and keeps rates artificially high. Carriers point out that every major shipping nation has this feature as part of its laws and argue that the FMC's supervision of their agreements prevents them from abusing the privilege.

A feature of the original shipping act gradually being chipped away is the system of "common carriage": carriers had to provide service to shippers on equal terms, much as a taxi offers transportation to passengers on equal terms. It used to be that carriers had to charge their published rates to all their customers, with no special deals for anyone. Even today carriers must electronically publish"tariffs," that is, their schedules of rates and rules, under a system supervised by the FMC. In 1984 and in 1998, however, Congress increased the flexibility of carriers and shippers to create commercial relationships with each other. Shippers and carriers can now enter secret arrangements, called "service contracts," in which carriers offer special rates to shippers if they provide certain quantities of cargo for the carriers to transport.

Other Shipping-Related Acts

Thomas Panebianco

The Jones Act (41 Stat.988) is the common name for section 27 of the Merchant Marine Act of 1920. This law requires cargo in the domestic offshore trades—that is, ocean or coastwise trades within the United States—to be carried only on U.S.-built and U.S.-flagged ships with U.S. crews, and is designed to support the U.S. merchant fleet and U.S. labor interests. The Jones Act is administered by the U.S. Maritime Administration, which is part of the U.S. Department of Transportation. Many shippers, however, particularly farmers, protest that the Jones Act increases their transportation costs, because U.S. ships are more expensive to use than foreign ships. Shippers also argue that if they cannot choose a foreign carrier to ship their goods, this lack of choice results in higher payment for transportation.

CONTROLLED CARRIER ACT

The Controlled Carrier Act (1978) is an important law found in section 9 of the Shipping Act. A controlled carrier is one owned or controlled by a government, as opposed to by private parties. The FMC publishes a list of controlled carriers. Most of the major ones are Chinese companies. The Controlled Carrier Act gives the FMC power to ensure that controlled carriers' rates are not unfairly low, giving them an unfair advantage over privately owned companies.

MERCHANT MARINE ACT

The FMC has a powerful tool in the Merchant Marine Act of 1920; Section 19 gives the FMC the power to take action against the carriers of another nation if that nation has unfair shipping practices which harm the commercial interests of the United States. This law was invoked prominently against Japan in 1997. Sanctions were imposed on Japanese carriers as a way to force the government of Japan to reform port practices the FMC found were unfair to non-Japanese carriers in U.S.-Japan trade.

CRUISE INDUSTRY STATUTE

Public Law 89-777 (1966) addresses the cruise industry. This law makes cruise line operators who board passengers in U.S. ports prove to the FMC that they are financially responsible, usually by posting a bond or surety to cover some or all of the passenger fares that the cruise lines collect in advance of the voyage. If there is a casualty or nonperformance (such as if financial difficulties or weather cause the line to cancel a voyage), and if the line does not have the funds to reimburse passengers, the bond funds can be distributed to the injured or stranded passengers. This statute was enacted after a number of cruise lines went out of business in the 1960s, leaving passengers with useless tickets and no opportunity for refunds. (Information about passenger vessel bonds is available on the FMC web site.)

See also: MERCHANT MARINE ACT OF 1920.

INTERNET RESOURCES

Federal Maritime Commission. <http://www.fmc.gov>.

U.S. Maritime Administration. <http://www.marad.dot.gov>.

SMALL BUSINESS ACT (1953)

Ross Rosenfeld and Seth Rosenfeld

Passed in 1953, the Small Business Act (SBA) established the Small Business Administration to "encourage" and "develop" small business growth, and to aid minorities and other disadvantaged peoples in securing loans and learning management techniques. "The essence of the American economic system of private enterprise is free competition," the act reads, "Only through full and free competition can free markets, free entry into business, and opportunities for the expression and growth of personal initiative and individual judgment be assured. The preservation and expansion of such competition is basic not only to economic well-being but to the security of this Nation."

Congress adopted the act during the Eisenhower Administration, a time of economic expansion. Millions of G.I.'s returning from the army in 1945 and 1946 injected a renewed workforce into the economy, and factory jobs filled

Congress adopted the act during the Eisenhower Administration, a time of economic expansion.

up quickly. Factories were no longer producing for the war effort, and many of the returning G.I.'s, either unable or unwilling to find work in large industrial firms, sought out their own business ventures. With the help of families and personal loans, businesses such as camera stores, food services, and car dealerships sprang up across the country. Still, large firms had tremendous advantages over smaller start-ups, and Congress adopted the SBA to help even the playing field.

The act, a massive, verbose document, is at times very specific, and at other times is extremely vague. Currently, 99.7 percent of all employers could be considered small businesses under the SBA. The act sets the following guidelines for determining whether a business falls within its jurisdiction: manufacturing firms with more than 500 employees are small businesses, over 1,500 is not; retail firms with less than $3.5 million in annual sales are considered small businesses, more than $13.5 million are not; wholesale firms with under 500 employees or less are small businesses, over 500 employees are not; Service industries with less than $3.5 million earned are small businesses, more than $14.5 million are not; passenger transportation firms are small businesses with less than 1,500 employees and receipts total less than $3.5 million (except air travel). If a company's numbers fall within any of these prescribed ranges, the SBA can determine whether it merits assistance based on factors of competition and the disadvantages the company faces.

The act favors the disadvantaged, though it does not limit its assistance to members on the basis of race. By SBA standards, any individual unable to compete freely within the open market could be considered disadvantaged. The law views women, low-income individuals, and veterans to be disadvantaged and offers financial assistance for their business entities.

The law does not mention allotment standards. For the purposes of getting financial aid, the act suggests the SBA weigh the disadvantaged status of the applicant, along with the ability to find capital. How the SBA judges "need" can vary from person to person; if one lives in an economically disadvantaged urban area (a "hubzone"), chances of gaining an SBA-approved loan increase. Revitalizing downtrodden areas is one of the extended purposes of the Small Business Act.

Revitalizing downtrodden areas is one of the extended purposes of the Small Business Act.

The SBA does not make loans to individuals. Instead the SBA guarantees as much as 80 percent of the loan amount to an intermediary institution. With the significant risk reduction, the financial institution is more likely to grant the loan, typically running for six to ten years at about 2 percent below the market interest rate.

SBA guaranteed loans come in various forms. The "7a Loan Guaranty Program" insures 75 percent of loans up to $1 million. The one-page "Low-Doc Loan" can guarantee 80 percent of a loan up to $100,000. The "MicroLoan program" is for very small business owners, guaranteeing loans from under $100 to $25,000. The SBA can also guarantee performance contracts, enabling small business to competitively bid on larger projects. Lines of credit are available through the SBA as well.

Financing education is a big part of the SBA. Most small businesses do not have access to the same type of market research and strategists that are available to big business, and the SBA tries to counter this disadvantage by offering management counseling programs to small business owners. These programs teach buying, producing, and successful administrative methods. The Small Business Institute, founded in 1972, works with the small business community, the SBA, and about 500 colleges to offer training to small business owners and developers.

Many small business owners cannot afford to keep lawyers on their staff. Therefore the SBA works as a legal and political advocate as well. The SBA acts as a spokesperson for small business, representing the small business owner's interest to Congress and other organizations. In February 2003 the advocacy department of the SBA claimed to have saved small business owners $21 billion by working with federal agencies to offer alternatives to "overly burdensome federal regulations."

At the time of the Small Business Act, almost all major government contracts went to large industrial and agricultural firms. The act charged the SBA with procuring top government contracts for small businesses, contracts ranging from food to paper to defense equipment. Currently, about 20 percent of government spending is transacted through small businesses.

Currently, about 20 percent of government spending is transacted through small businesses.

When disaster strikes, the SBA is empowered to come to the rescue of small businesses with recovery loans. Since the SBA falls under the executive branch, the president wields control over when these funds are applied, and when the president offers disaster relief, the SBA is authorized to secure the necessary financial resources. By doing so, the SBA helps rebuild towns and cities and ensure overall economic tranquility. For example, within a month after the September 11, 2001, terrorist attacks, the SBA approved over $100 million to help restore businesses in downtown New York City.

The president appoints, with the consent of the Senate, an SBA administrator to run the agency. This administrator has general authority over every aspect of the SBA, from approving assistance loans to sanctioning employees who misappropriate funds. The administrator also chairs the loan policy board, on which the secretary of the treasury and the secretary of commerce sit upon as well. The board, however, is only advisory, and the administrator is not obligated to follow its recommendations.

The creation of the Small Business Administration increased the president's command over the economy. Presidents have used the SBA for various purposes. When U.S. Steel threatened to raise its prices after the negotiated end of a strike, President Kennedy threatened to go to small businesses and the existence of the SBA made the threat real. In the election year of 1972, Richard Nixon used the SBA to help shed his ultra-conservative image by expanding loans, especially to colleges and minorities.

There are over twenty-two million small businesses in the United States. The SBA estimates that more than half of all employees in the U.S. work for a small firm, and that small business employers provide approximately 44.5 percent of payroll in the private sector. Ninety-seven percent of all exporters are small business owners, comprising 29 percent of total exports. The most powerful statistic, however, is that 60 to 80 percent of all new jobs come from small businesses. This number fluctuates when some small businesses grow enough to become classified as large businesses, and when new small businesses are created. From 1999 to 2000, small businesses accounted for 75 percent of all new jobs created.

Immigrants, who make up a large portion of the small business workforce, are not excluded from the opportunities offered by the SBA. Many immigrants are unaware of these opportunities, and some have trouble getting through the legal forms. Still, the SBA views immigrants as vital to small business, and representation and support is available to them.

Since its creation, the SBA has become an integral part of the U.S. economy, guaranteeing approximately $2.8 billion in loans each year.

Altogether the SBA exercises control over a total of more than $45 billion. This includes loan guarantees, disaster relief loans, and business loans. It is the largest small business investment backer in the U.S., and the most powerful advocacy group for small business owners. Since its creation, the SBA has become an integral part of the U.S. economy, guaranteeing approximately $2.8 billion in loans each year.

BIBLIOGRAPHY

American Bar Association. *Legal Guide for Small Business.* New York: Three Rivers Press, 2000.

Attard, Janet. *The Home Office and Small Business Answer Book,* 2d ed. New York: Henry Holt and Company, 1993.

House of Representatives. *The Organization and Procedure of the Federal Regulatory Commissions and Agencies,* reprint ed. Washington, DC: U.S. Government Printing Office, 1979.

Parris, Addison W. *The Small Business Administration.* New York: Frederick A. Praeger, 1968.

Roberson, Cliff. *The Businessperson's Legal Advisor,* 2nd ed. New York: Liberty Hall Press, 1991.

INTERNET RESOURCE

Small Business Administration. <http://www.sba.gov>.

SMITH-HUGHES ACT

See VOCATIONAL EDUCATION ACT OF 1917

SMOOT-HAWLEY TARIFF ACT (1930)

Adam P. Plant

Many people reading this entry might know the following and no more about the Smoot-Hawley Tariff Act (P.L. 71-361, 46 Stat. 590):

> *Economics teacher:* In 1930, the Republican-controlled House of Representatives, in an effort to alleviate the effects of the ... Anyone? Anyone? ... the Great Depression, passed the ... Anyone? Anyone? The tariff bill? The Smoot-Hawley Tariff Act? Which, anyone? Raised or lowered? ... raised tariffs,

> in an effort to collect more revenue for the federal government. Did it work? Anyone? Anyone know the effects? It did not work, and the United States sank deeper into the Great Depression. Today we have a similar debate over this. Anyone know what this is? Class? Anyone? Anyone? Anyone seen this before? The Laffer Curve. Anyone know what this says? It says that at this point on the revenue curve, you will get exactly the same amount of revenue as at this point. This is very controversial. Does anyone know what Vice President [George H. W.] Bush called this in 1980? Anyone? Something-d-o-o economics. "Voodoo" economics.

Ah, yes, those lines delivered to a deeply disinterested high school class occur in one of the most memorable scenes in coming-of-age-film history. But what was not covered by actor Ben Stein—a speechwriter (under President Richard M. Nixon) turned comedian and actor—in that economics lecture? What else can this entry teach us about the economic climate surrounding the Smoot-Hawley Tariff Act that the film *Ferris Bueller's Day Off* (1986) did not? Anyone? Anyone? We will soon see.

The most important thing to know about the economic climate that spawned the Smoot-Hawley Tariff Act (and the other **tariff** bills that came before it) is this: in the days in which those acts were written, April 15 had much less significance than it does today. Federal income taxes, though authorized by the Sixteenth Amendment to the Constitution, were much lower and barely affected most Americans.

tariff: a tax imposed on goods when imported into a country

THE BASICS OF TARIFFS AND TRADE IN AMERICAN HISTORY

Tariffs had been a major topic of U.S. economic policy since 1789, when President George Washington's administration used a tariff to raise revenue to help fund the new national government. However, tariffs were used for other reasons as well. Sometimes the U.S. government placed tariffs on certain finished goods or raw materials to gain an economic advantage over foreign nations that sent a lot of goods to America. It also used these "protective tariffs" to keep foreign industries (for example, the English iron industry) from outselling and driving out of business comparable American industries (like the American iron and steel industry) because the foreign industry was either more established, had a better product, or sell their product at a cheaper price than could its American counterpart. The use of protective tariffs was a divisive issue to many Americans, such as those in the South, who sold agricultural goods or raw materials to overseas industries that would make the finished products. In fact, at times foreign nations who traded with America but were hurt by the use of these tariffs would enact their own tariffs on American goods sold in their country, therefore making the American goods more expensive abroad and less likely to be purchased.

Tariffs had been a major topic of U.S. economic policy since 1789, when President George Washington's administration used a tariff to raise revenue to help fund the new national government.

So, tariffs could either be for revenue, trade, or **protectionist** purposes. In the economic climate of the late 1800s and early 1900s, the tariff issue came to a head in American politics.

protectionist: advocating the use of tariffs to protect domestic industries from foreign competition

PREDECESSORS TO THE ACT

In the 1890s following the Civil War, the nation was in a period of rapid growth. It went from thirty-five states in 1867 to forty-eight states in 1912, and with the growing national government came the responsibility for funding

Representative Willis C. Hawley (R-Oreg.), left, and Senator Reed Smoot (R-Utah). (LIBRARY OF CONGRESS, PRINTS AND PHOTOGRAPHS DIVISION)

that government. America was just beginning to industrialize to a level where it could compete with other nations, however, it was not a leader in commercial production. The 1890s were still a period dominated by the United Kingdom and France. At the time, the British empire stretched over most of the world. The United States was still relatively young.

It was under these conditions that the McKinley Tariff was passed in 1890. In the presidential election of 1888, Republican Benjamin Harrison defeated Democrat Grover Cleveland, who had supported free trade (trade among nations without tariff restrictions). President Harrison's administration believed that American industries needed protection, so they wanted to pass protective tariffs. In fact, protectionist economic policies became the foundation of the Republican Party's economic outlook for the next two decades. The McKinley Tariff was the first in a string of tariff-raising bills that would set U.S. economic policy. It raised the tariff rate to a record high of 48 percent. It also set off a trend of American trading partners passing tariffs of their own in retaliation for the McKinley Tariff's passage.

The second major tariff passed during that era was the Payne-Aldrich Tariff. This bill, passed in 1909 by a Republican-controlled Congress, attempted to lower the average tariff rate paid on imported goods. However, the act caused little real change in the economic landscape of the United States. Politically, it angered progressive Democrats who had begun to gain some national prominence.

With Congress was so closely divided between the Democrats and Republicans, the Democrats were able to secure the proposal of the Sixteenth

Tax Freedom Day

"Tax Freedom Day" is the name given by the nonprofit Tax Foundation to the day that the average U.S. citizen has earned enough income to cover his or her taxes for the year. The Tax Foundation begins with government figures of all federal, state, and local taxes collected, including payroll taxes, sales taxes, property taxes, and corporate taxes (which are ultimately paid by the consumer). To calculate the average tax burden, this number is divided by the government's figures for total income earned in that year. Between 1990 and 2003, the average taxpayer worked between 109 and 120 days to pay taxes in any given year. In 2003, Tax Freedom Day was expected to fall on April 19th, or 109 days into the year.

Amendment to the U.S. Constitution on July 12, 1909, in exchange for the Payne-Aldrich bill's passing. The Sixteenth Amendment was ratified on February 3, 1913, and created the federal income tax, giving the U.S. government an alternative manner in which they could fund the federal government. The United States then became less reliant on the income tariffs produced. At last, the Democrats had gained a foothold in developing the economic policies of the United States.

The final important precursor to the Smoot-Hawley Act was the Underwood-Simmons Tariff, which was passed in 1913 shortly after the Sixteenth

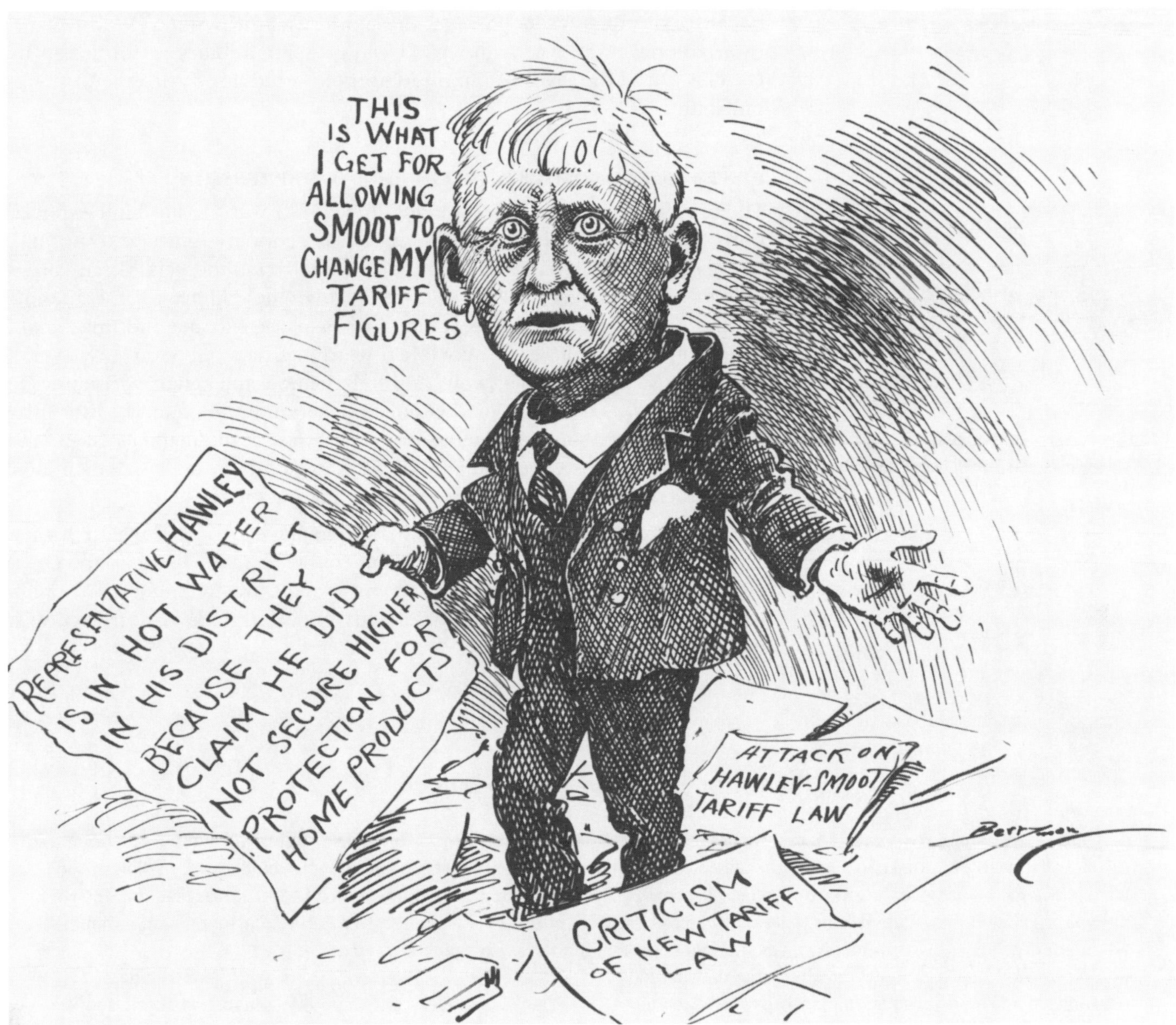

This cartoon, published in the Washington Evening Star, *October 25, 1930, depicts Willis C. Hawley sweating bullets over heavy criticism of the Smoot-Hawley Tariff. The tariff actually exacerbated the Great Depression by setting off a trade war (other countries responded to the tariff by shutting out U.S. goods), while failing to ease the fall in domestic prices and production. A Congressman since 1907, Hawley lost his seat in the House in the 1932 elections.* ©1932, 1935, 1941, 1947, (© THE WASHINGTON POST. REPRINTED WITH PERMISSION)

The Sixteenth Amendment was ratified on February 3, 1913, and created the federal income tax, giving the U.S. government an alternative manner in which they could fund the federal government.

Amendment was ratified. President Woodrow Wilson, who would lead the American people through World War I, was still in the early days of his first term. He appeared before a joint session of Congress, a rare occurrence, to make known his support for reforming U.S. tariff policies. Sponsored by Representative Oscar Underwood of Alabama in the House of Representatives and Senator F. M. Simmons of North Carolina in the Senate, the two legislators for whom the bill was named, this effort at tariff reduction eliminated tariffs on many goods, such as linens, iron, farm equipment, foods, and raw materials. Yet the effects of this legislation were largely unnoticed because, shortly after its passage, the world was thrown into World War I. International trade was hampered by aggressive military action taken by Germany, and the level of imported and exported goods dropped off significantly.

POSTWAR ECONOMICS AND THE GREAT DEPRESSION

The immediate economic boom right after World War I led to high expectations that were unrealized once the postwar economy returned to normal. Further, the policies passed during the 1920s reflected the Republican Party's belief that it was best to allow industry to drive the country as an economic engine. Congress passed bills setting low taxes on income and investment and establishing policies unfavorable toward international trade. However, a massive crisis unfolded that would severely hamper the nation's economy. In October of 1929 the stock market crashed, sending the country toward the **Great Depression**. Many major industries lost money in the market's crash, and workers at all levels were hurt either by the loss of their savings or their jobs. By 1932 almost one-quarter of Americans were unemployed.

Great Depression: the longest and most severe economic depression in American history (1929–1939); its effects were felt throughout the world

It was in the middle of this rapidly deteriorating economic situation that the Smoot-Hawley Tariff Act was passed. The country sank deeper into the Great Depression because of the poor economic climate created in the 1920s, high unemployment rates, and other nations that enacted their own protectionist trade measures in retribution.

The Laffer Curve and Voodoo Economics

At a party in the late 1970s—or so the story goes—economist Arthur Laffer used a cocktail napkin to sketch an upside-down U that became the basis for an entire movement in economic policy. The Laffer Curve, as the U came to be known, represented the theory that as taxes went down, government revenue would actually go up, as lower taxes would stimulate the economy and provide more receipts. Laffer's theory was adopted as part of Ronald Reagan's platform in his 1980 presidential campaign, and after he became president, Reagan pushed through the largest package of tax cuts in history. Counter to his expectations, the deficit mushroomed, and Laffer's theory was discredited. While most scholars agreed that a budget deficit would grow by slightly less than the full amount of a tax cut, because some economic growth would result, credible economists from across the political spectrum agreed that the net effect would be negative. During the 1980 presidential primaries, Reagan's opponent George H. W. Bush had ridiculed his theories as "voodoo economics." Twenty years later, Bush's son, President George W. Bush, promoted another package of enormous tax cuts, arguing that they would stimulate the economy, government receipts would increase, and the budget gap would be closed. Bush's detractors, who viewed the maneuver as blatant pandering to wealthy constituents, called it voodoo economics all over again.

See also: Tariff Act of 1789.

BIBLIOGRAPHY

Bartlett, Bruce. "The Truth About Trade in History."<http://www.freetrade.org>.

United States Information Agency. "An Outline of American History: Chapter Nine: War, Prosperity, and Depression."<http://www.usis.usemb.se/usis/history/chapter9.html>.

Social Security Act of 1935

Jerry W. Markham

Congress adopted the Social Security Act (P.L. 74-271, 49 Stat. 620) in 1935 for the purpose of providing retirement security for American workers. This legislation was a product of the **New Deal** legislation that spun out of the **Great Depression** of the 1930s.

New Deal: the legislative and administrative program of President Franklin D. Roosevelt designed to promote economic recovery and social reform (1933–1939)

Great Depression: the longest and most severe economic depression in American history (1929–1939); its effects were felt throughout the world

POPULIST PROPOSALS IN THE DEPRESSION ERA

Before Congress adopted the Social Security Act a number of individuals and leaders called for government payments to assist the poor and the elderly during this economically difficult period. Their programs promised wealth to everyone. The novelist Upton Sinclair, for example, ran for governor of California in 1934 on a platform that he called the End Poverty in California Plan (EPIC). One feature of the plan was a proposal for the state of California to tax corporations for purposes of getting the necessary revenue to feed the poor and to convert bankrupt factories and farms into cooperatives. Sinclair did not win the gubernatorial race, but his EPIC plan received much attention across the country. Dr. Francis Townsend, another **populist** with a large following, announced a plan that would entail monthly payments of $200 to nonworking elderly people to help relieve their hardships and difficulties. Over 7,000 "Townsend clubs" with 2.2 million members supported this program. Even Hollywood advertising executives formulated plans to assist the poor; two executives promoted a "Ham and Eggs" plan that would have given thirty dollars each Thursday to elderly people.

populist: someone who identifies with and believes in the rights and virtues of the common people (often as the foundation of a political philosophy)

"Kingfish" Huey Long, the **demagogue** , former governor and senator from Louisiana was promoting a "Share the Wealth" program, which would have made "every man a king" by providing pensions of thirty dollars per month to individuals over the age of sixty with annual incomes of less than $1,000 and no more than $10,000 in assets. Under Long's Share the Wealth program, every family in America was guaranteed a minimum annual income of $2,000, and each family was to be given $5,000 to buy a home, an automobile, and a radio. Long proposed to fund the plan by confiscating the assets of the wealthy.

demagogue: a leader who obtains power by means of impassioned appeals to the emotions and prejudices of the populace

While none of these plans succeeded, they were popular and placed considerable political pressure on President Franklin Roosevelt to propose a plan of his own. A public opinion poll suggested that if Huey Long challenged Franklin Roosevelt, for example, the challenge would split the Democratic voters and could result in the election of the Republican presidential challenger, Alf Landon. Accordingly, Marion Folsom, an executive with the Eastman Kodak Company, created an alternative program for the Roosevelt administration and this program eventually became the Social Security Act.

THE GROWTH OF THE SOCIAL SECURITY ACT

The Social Security Act created a federal pension system funded by taxes on employers and employees. Social Security was not "needs based"; rather, the theory was that workers would contribute to those already retired. These workers would in turn receive benefits upon their own retirement funded by the taxes paid by those still working and from new workers entering the marketplace. The amount of benefits was not limited by the retiree's assets or income from investment sources.

The Social Security Act created a federal pension system funded by taxes on employers and employees.

The Social Security program as Congress originally enacted it did not provide universal coverage for retirement benefits but provided benefits principally for industrial employees. The legislation initially excluded most workers, including farm laborers, the self-employed, educators, household servants, casual laborers, and the unemployed.

The government mailed the first Social Security check in 1940 to Ida May Fuller in Ludlow, Vermont, just as the Depression was ending. Ida May Fuller lived for thirty-five more years, until 1975, and by that date, Congress had expanded the Social Security system to cover nearly all workers. Coverage was also broadened to include dependents of workers and disabled employees. By the end of the twentieth century, almost 150 million Americans contributed to the system and more than forty million received benefits. The government paid about 7.5 million individuals survivor benefits, and six million received disability benefits.

SOCIAL SECURITY BENEFITS AND CONTRIBUTIONS

Social Security benefits are similar to an annuity concept in that the government pays them from the time of retirement until the beneficiary and certain dependents are no longer living. The government ties the level of benefits to the workers' annual contributions and number of years the workers made the contributions. Importantly, the law does not entitle all workers to benefits, but only those who satisfy the minimum qualification requirements associated with a certain number of years of contributions. The law caps maximum benefits at a level not far above a poverty level, but many people nonetheless believe the benefits are an important entitlement the government cannot reduce or eliminate. The Supreme Court, however, has held that Social Security contributions do not entitle individuals to some contractual amount on retirement. The Court held that contributions to Social Security are not accrued property rights and that benefits may be removed or changed by Congress. In the Court's words:

Importantly, the law does not entitle all workers to benefits, but only those who satisfy the minimum qualification requirements associated with a certain number of years of contributions.

> The "right" to Social Security benefits is in one sense "earned," for the entire scheme rests on the legislative judgment that those who in their productive years were functioning members of the economy may justly call upon that economy, in their later years, for protection from "the rigors of the poor house as well as from the haunting fear that such a lot awaits them when journey's end is near." ... But ... [t]o engraft upon the Social Security system a concept of "accrued property rights" would deprive it of the flexibility and boldness in adjustment to ever-changing conditions which it demands.

Congress increased Social Security benefits for the first time in 1950, but benefit levels were undercut by **inflation** in the 1960s. Congress increased benefits again in 1972, and then provided for automatic cost of living adjustments in subsequent years to ensure that the benefits payments kept up with inflationary pressures. This resulted in a mandate that workers pay more into the system before retirement and at the same time restricted access through increased eligibility ages for benefits. Originally, Social Security contributions were equal to a tax of three percent on salaries up to $3,000; both the employee and employer paid the tax into the Social Security fund. By 2000, the law required workers and their employers to contribute 6.2 percent (a total of 12.4 percent) on employees' salaries up to $76,200.

inflation: a general rise in the prices of goods and services

Congress originally intended Social Security benefits to be funded on a "pay-as-you-go" basis. This meant that the benefits paid out each year were to

President Franklin D. Roosevelt signs the Social Security Act, 1935. Standing immediately behind Roosevelt (left to right) are Representative Robert Doughton, Senator Robert Wagner, Secretary of Labor Frances Perkins, Senator Pat Harrison, and Representative David J. Lewis. (Library of Congress, Prints and Photographs Division)

An advertisement for Social Security, created by the Social Security Board, 1935.
(LIBRARY OF CONGRESS, PRINTS AND PHOTOGRAPHS DIVISION)

be funded from the annual contributions of workers and their employers. That plan later changed to reflect the fact that the aging "baby boomer" population placed demands on the system that workers could not meet. Congress changed the Social Security system from a pay-as-you-go to a partially funded system in 1977. This meant the law imposed taxes on existing workers that exceeded the amount needed for current payouts, but the government nevertheless collected the revenue and placed it in "trust" for future beneficiaries. This surplus was not actually placed in trust. Instead, the government used the money to pay down federal debt. When needed for Social Security, the funds will have to be reborrowed or taken from the surplus funds. In short, there is no "lockbox" where Social Security funds are being held secure for current and future recipients.

Congress originally intended Social Security benefits to be funded on a "pay-as-you-go" basis. This meant that the benefits paid out each year were to be funded from the annual contributions of workers and their employers.

PROBLEMS AND REFORM PROPOSALS

As noted above, Congress adopted a scheme of Social Security taxes largely to pay for benefits in retirement. Eighty percent of American households now pay more in Social Security taxes than they do in income taxes—and the taxes have become burdensome. At the same time, the Social Security benefits are largely insufficient for enabling a comfortable retirement without outside sources of income. Notwithstanding the high taxes and minimal benefits, the Social Security system faces bankruptcy down the road. The Social Security Administration, the agency Congress charged with administering the system, announced it will pay out more in benefits than it will collect in taxes by the year 2015. Sometime before the year 2040, Social Security contributions will enable the government to pay only 71 percent of the benefits it owes under the law to Social Security participants. This means Congress must also dramatically cut benefits or increase contributions or both to maintain the present system in some form. Of particular concern is the fact that the number of workers paying into the Social Security system is shrinking. At the time Social Security was adopted there were twenty-five workers for each retiree. In 2002 there were about 3.25 workers for each retiree. By the year 2030, this ratio will drop to two workers for each Social Security recipient.

Three-Legged Stool Model for Retirement

Jerry W. Markham

The combination of the growth of private pension plans and the low level of Social Security benefits has resulted in a three-legged stool model for retirement in America. This means that a combination of Social Security benefits, company pension plans, and savings in personal retirement accounts are needed to have a comfortable retirement.

The Social Security system has several flaws beyond its bankruptcy. Minority and low-income individuals have shorter life spans and receive less in Social Security benefits than longer-lived, more affluent individuals. In short, criticisms of the current law abound.

Various groups have begun to examine the problems facing the Social Security system and have generated a range of proposals, including privatization, a process through which the program would change from public to private control. In January 1997, a federal advisory council was divided over the issue of whether to allow private social security accounts, but seven of its thirteen members wanted to require compulsory saving through individual accounts. Another federal advisory committee unanimously recommended the use of private accounts to supplement Social Security. The 2000 presidential election focused further attention on the issue. Following his election, President George W. Bush appointed a **bipartisan** panel to make recommendations on how to privatize Social Security. That committee urged partial privatization.

Various groups have begun to examine the problems facing the Social Security system and have generated a range of proposals, including privatization.

bipartisan: involving members of two parties, especially the two political parties

Advocates of Social Security reform contend that private accounts would provide far more social security and retirement benefits than Social Security, and that private accounts would make more funds available for investment, strengthening the economy for the benefit of everyone. Reformists argue that private contributions compounding tax-free in a private account will not only enhance the retirement years of the workers but will create an estate for their descendants that will enhance their status in life. Opponents of reform claim privatization will result in a loss of the contributions already made into the system and that private accounts may incur investment losses that could devastate a pensioner. Although still controversial in many circles, the law has already effectuated privatization for the pension accounts of federal government employees. These employees may invest contributions in stocks and other securities, and the benefits received during retirement will depend on the success of those investments. State pension funds also allow employees to invest contributions in common stocks and other securities. Countries in Europe, South America, and in Australia are also privatizing some or all of their social security pensions.

See also: AID TO DEPENDENT CHILDREN; EMPLOYEE RETIREMENT INCOME SECURITY ACT OF 1974; MEDICAID ACT; MEDICARE ACT.

BIBLIOGRAPHY

Campana, Kristen V. "Paying Our Own Way: The Privatization of the Chilean Social Security System and Its Lessons for American Reform." *University of Pennsylvania Journal of International Economic Law* 20 (1999): 385–421.

Karmel, Roberta S. "Regulatory Implication of Individual Management of Pension Funds: The Challenge to Financial Regulators Posed by Social Security Privatization." *Brooklyn Law Review* 64 (1998): 1043–81.

Markham, Jerry W. "Privatizing Social Security." *San Diego Law Review* 38 (2001): 747–816.

INTERNET RESOURCE

Social Security Online. <http://www.ssa.gov/>.

SOIL CONSERVATION AND DOMESTIC ALLOTMENT ACT (1935)

Kyle A. Loring

On April 27, 1935, Congress responded to the dual threats of soil erosion and agricultural overproduction by passing the Soil Conservation and Domestic Allotment Act (P.L. 46-74, 49 Stat. 163), the nation's first national soil conservation program. Although geologists had first warned the White House about the dangers of soil erosion in 1908, the federal government did not begin to react to this hazard until Hugh Bennet, a soil scientist with the U.S. Department of Agriculture, published *Soil Erosion: A National Menace* in 1928. As a result, in 1929 Congress authorized soil conservation experiment stations and then in 1933 established the Soil Erosion Services (SES) to provide farmers with planning assistance and equipment, seeds, and seedlings. Then on May 12, 1934, the worst dust storm in the history of the United States grew out of the Dust Bowl, an area of the Great Plains known for its recurring droughts and dust storms. The 1934 dust storm worked its way to the Atlantic Ocean, obscuring the sun and leaving a dusty film in its wake. This catastrophe convinced Congress that the soil erosion caused by conditions in the Dust Bowl truly did pose a menace to the national welfare, and led directly to the enactment of the act.

The 1934 dust storm worked its way to the Atlantic Ocean, obscuring the sun and leaving a dusty film in its wake.

When it created the act, Congress "recognized that the wastage of soil and moisture resources on farm, grazing, and forest lands of the Nation, resulting from soil erosion, is a menace to the national welfare." The act stated that its ultimate goal was "to provide permanently for the control and prevention of soil erosion and thereby to preserve natural resources, control floods, prevent impairment of reservoirs, and maintain the navigability of rivers and harbors, protect public health, public lands and relieve unemployment." To do so, the act authorized the secretary of agriculture to survey and research soil erosion and methods for its prevention, to carry out preventive measures, to cooperate with state agencies or individuals, and to acquire any lands necessary to carry out the purpose of the act. To limit governmental interference in private actions, the act required landowner consent before the secretary could act on private land and prohibited actions that would interfere with the general production of food and fibers for ordinary domestic consumption.

The act established the Soil Conservation Services (SCS—now called the Natural Resources Conservation Service) as the successor to the SES and empowered it to conduct a national program of soil erosion prevention through technical and financial aid to farmers who agreed to implement soil conservation practices. The SCS did this first through demonstration projects with local farmers, where the cooperative effort employed contour plowing, strip cropping, erosion resistant crops, resting lands, and terracing. Then, in 1937, the SCS initiated the soil conservation district concept whereby the federal government would work through state-created conservation districts composed of local farmers.

Farmers approached the act's direct federal regulation with skepticism, worrying that the federal government would overregulate them and essentially take direct control of the farms. However, the conservation district approach eased their concerns. These conservation districts gave locally appointed directors, not federal officials, the authority to establish and manage local soil and water conservation. The federal government, in turn, cooperated by granting the districts equipment and technical assistance. This arrangement left local areas with the authority to shape conservation projects, but encouraged them to undertake such projects with federal funding. In 1937 Arkansas hosted the first such district, and now there are nearly 3,000, delivering conservation education, watershed protection, and technical assistance to the nation's farmers.

The act combated overproduction of crops by paying farmers to shift from production of "soil-depleting crops" to "soil-conserving crops." The act then defined soil-depleting crops to include surplus crops, even those such as wheat that had soil-conserving properties. Defining crops this way helped farmers who had to sell their crops at a low price because the market was flooded with them. Hence, the government indirectly paid farmers to reduce production of surplus crops to decrease overall overproduction.

The act combated overproduction of crops by paying farmers to shift from production of "soil-depleting crops" to "soil-conserving crops."

See also: Agricultural Adjustment Act; Farm Credit Act of 1933; National Industrial Recovery Act; Tennessee Valley Authority Act of 1933.

BIBLIOGRAPHY

Adler, Robert W. "Addressing Barriers to Watershed Protection." *Environmental Law* 25 (1995): 973–1106.

Lacy, Peter M. "Our Sedimentation Boxes Runneth Over: Public Lands Soil Law as the Missing Link in Holistic Natural Resource Protection." *Environmental Law* 31 (2001): 433–475.

INTERNET RESOURCE

"100 Years of Soil and Water Conservation." Soil and Water Conservation Society. <http://www.swcs.org/t_resources.htm>.

Solid Waste Disposal Act (1965)

Eugene H. Robinson, Jr.

The Solid Waste Disposal Act (SWDA) (P.L. 89-272, 79 Stat. 992) became law on October 20, 1965. In its original form, it was a broad attempt to address the solid waste problems confronting the nation through a series of research projects, investigations, experiments, training, demonstrations, surveys, and studies. The decade following its passage revealed that the SWDA was not sufficiently structured to resolve the growing mountain of waste disposal issues facing the country. As a result, significant amendments were made to the act with the passage of the Resource Conservation and Recovery Act of 1976 (RCRA), which became law on October 21, 1976. The SWDA as amended in 1976 is more commonly known as the RCRA.

In its original form, The Solid Waste Disposal Act was a broad attempt to address the solid waste problems confronting the nation through a series of research projects, investigations, experiments, training, demonstrations, surveys, and studies.

In the statute's findings, Congress indicated two reasons for the necessity of the SWDA: first, advancements in technology resulted in the creation of vastly more amounts and types of wastes than in the past; and second, rapid growth in the nation's metropolitan areas had caused these areas to experience significant financial, management, and technical problems associated with waste disposal. At the time SWDA was passed, there were ten other pending bills related to the subject of solid wastes and their potential impacts to public health. Besides totally revamping the SWDA's solid waste program in 1976, the RCRA also created a national "cradle to grave" hazardous waste management tracking program to deal with the nation's annual production of three to four billion tons of discarded material.

The SWDA was passed during the presidency of Lyndon B. Johnson. The Johnson Administration actively encouraged its passage and the president referred to the act several times in a speech made to Congress where he emphasized the need for legislation to address solid waste disposal. In addition, testimony in favor of the bill was received by Congressional committees from over twenty different entities, including associations, universities, cities, and states.

President Gerald Ford had the privilege of signing the RCRA into law. Though the RCRA was considered a major act of Congress and was passed relatively unopposed, its legislative history is fairly sparse compared to that of other federal legislation.

The most significant interpretation of the RCRA is the U.S. Supreme Court's decision in *Department of Energy v. Ohio* (1992). The Supreme Court ruled that the waiver of sovereign immunity in the RCRA and the Clean Water Act was not clear enough to allow states to impose civil penalties directly, but penalties could be allowed in situations where some type of court order had been issued and later violated.

Besides the RCRA, the SWDA has been significantly amended by the Hazardous and Solid Waste Amendments of 1984 (HSWA) and the Federal Facilities Compliance Act of 1992 (FFCA), of which the most significant feature was the federal sovereign immunity waiver with respect to federal, state, and local

Tires with "Keep Out" painted on them warn people to stay away from piles of chat—a waste material from mining lead and other minerals—in Webb City, Missouri. The Solid Waste Disposal Act was created to address waste disposal practices at open sites. The site pictured here, because it is inactive, will be handled as a Superfund site under the Comprehensive Environmental Response, Compensation, and Liability Act of 1980. (© AP/Wide World Photos)

Besides the RCRA, the SWDA has been significantly amended by the Hazardous and Solid Waste Amendments of 1984 (HSWA) and the Federal Facilities Compliance Act of 1992 (FFCA).

procedural and substantive requirements relating to the RCRA. This change was Congress's response to the Supreme Court ruling in *Doe v. Ohio* (1992), and required federal facilities to pay fines and penalties for violations of hazardous and solid waste requirements.

The Comprehensive Environmental Response, Compensation, and Liability Act (CERCLA, 1980) was not an amendment but did share a close relationship with the SWDA, as amended by the RCRA, in their common goals of protecting human health and the environment from the dangers posed by hazardous waste. Whereas the RCRA was enacted to address concerns at open disposal sites, CERCLA was passed to address past practices at inactive disposal sites.

See also: Comprehensive Environmental Response, Compensation, and Liability Act; Hazarrdous and Solid Waste Amendments of 1984.

BIBLIOGRAPHY

Hall, Ridgeway M. Jr., et al. *RCRA Hazardous Wastes Handbook,* 12th edition. Rockville, MD: Government Institutes, Inc., 2001.

Environment Protection Agency. "Twenty-Five Years of RCRA: Building on Our Past to Protect Our Future." <http://www.epa.gov/epaoswer/general>.

Southwest Ordinance (1790)

Daniel C. Wewers

The Southwest Ordinance (1 Stat. 123), approved on May 26, 1790, organized the "Territory of the United States, South of the River Ohio" into one political district and established provisions for its interim governance by Congress and expected transition to statehood. In effect, the Southwest Ordinance served the same purpose for the "Old Southwest" as the Northwest Ordinance of 1787 had for the "territory north-west of the Ohio." While the Southwest Territory comprised the former western districts of North Carolina, South Carolina, and possibly Georgia as far west as the Mississippi River, in practice its provisions for territorial government applied only to the future state of Tennessee.

While the Southwest Territory comprised the former western districts of North Carolina, South Carolina, and possibly Georgia as far west as the Mississippi River, in practice its provisions for territorial government applied only to the future state of Tennessee.

Modeled on the landmark Northwest Ordinance, the Southwest Ordinance granted "all the privileges, benefits and advantages" of its sister legislation and instituted a "similar" form of territorial government, except for certain stipulations set by North Carolina in its land cession of December 22, 1789. The principal among these was the preservation of slavery in the territory—in direct contrast to the prohibition of slavery in the Northwest Ordinance's famed Article VI. "*Provided always* that no regulations made or to be made by Congress shall tend to emancipate Slaves," the inhabitants of the Southwest Territory had guarantees of freedom of religion, the writ of **habeas corpus**, trial by jury, proportionate representation in the legislature, and judicial proceedings under common law. Some historians have argued that the defeat of the Ordinance of 1784, which had proposed to end slavery after 1800 in all the western territories, demonstrated Congress's tacit agreement to open the Southwest to slavery if the institution was prohibited in the Northwest.

habeas corpus: (Latin, "you should have the body") a written order to bring a prisoner in front of a judge, to determine whether his or her detention is lawful

Like its sister legislation, the Southwest Ordinance outlined a three-stage process for the transition from territorial status to statehood. In the first stage, Congress would appoint a governor, secretary, and three judges to administer the territory. Once the district reached a population of five thousand adult free males, the governor, an elected lower house, and an appointed legislative council would assume governing responsibility. When the district crossed the third-stage threshold of sixty thousand free inhabitants, it could adopt a "republican" state constitution and apply to Congress for full statehood.

The passage of the ordinance in 1790 brought order to a situation that had been highly chaotic in the 1780s. In the previous decade, the Old Southwest had experienced a failed attempt to organize the independent state of Franklin, controversy with Spanish agents over navigation rights on the Mississippi, the dissatisfaction of land speculators, and friction with Cherokee, Creek, Chickasaw, and Choctaw tribes. Territorial status paved the way for the nationalization of these problems. William Blount served as joint territorial governor and superintendent of Indian affairs for the entire six-year administrative history of the district. In 1795 the territory elected James White as its nonvoting representative to Congress, the first such member in Congressional history. A 1795 census in the district showed 66,650 free persons and 10,613 slaves, ample proof that slavery had taken root in the southwestern soil. On June 1, 1796, the Southwest Ordinance lost all official force with the admission of Tennessee to the United States as the second state (after Kentucky in 1792) created on the western frontier.

The passage of the ordinance in 1790 brought order to a situation that had been highly chaotic in the 1780s.

See also: COMPROMISE OF 1850; KANSAS NEBRASKA ACT OF 1854; MISSOURI COMPROMISE; NORTHWEST ORDINANCE.

BIBLIOGRAPHY

Carter, Clarence Edwin, ed. *The Territorial Papers of the United States. Vol. 4: The Territory South of the River Ohio, 1790–1796.* Washington, DC: U.S. Government Printing Office, 1936.

Durham, Walter T. *Before Tennessee: The Southwest Territory, 1790–1796.* Piney Flats, TN: Rocky Mount Historical Association, 1990.

STAGGERS RAIL ACT OF 1980

Christopher Zorn

Railroads were among the very first industries to be regulated in the United States. The Interstate Commerce Act of 1887, which regulated ship-

Railroads were among the very first industries to be regulated in the United States.

ping rates and prevented price discrimination by interstate carriers, was principally intended to prevent railroads from taking advantage of their near-monopoly over transportation. Over the next hundred years, with the development of oil pipelines, interstate highways, and effective air travel, the railroads' control over transportation of goods and people decreased. By the 1970s the combination of competition and close regulation of rail rates drove many railroads to the brink of bankruptcy.

In 1980 Congress passed sweeping reforms to railroad regulations. Named for Congressman Harley Staggers, Democrat of West Virginia, the Staggers Rail Act (P. L. 96-448) was signed into law by President Jimmy Carter on October 14, 1980. Among other things, the act removed most government controls over prices, instead allowing railroads to set their own rates according to what the market would allow. The act also allowed railroads to enter into contracts with shipping companies, and gave railroads greater freedom to adopt other cost-cutting measures such as abandoning unprofitable routes and merging with other companies.

The Staggers Rail Act was part of a larger move toward deregulation in the transportation industry which included the Airline Deregulation Act of 1978 and the Motor Carrier Act of 1980.

The Staggers Rail Act was part of a larger move toward deregulation in the transportation industry which included the Airline Deregulation Act of 1978 and the Motor Carrier Act of 1980. While there is disagreement over the precise magnitude of its effect, the Staggers Rail Act is generally credited with revitalizing the railroad industry, and with leading to lower rates for railroad shipping in general. However, the act also led to substantial decreases in employment in the railroad industry, as many railroads merged with their former competitors; between 1978 and 1994, the number of major railroad firms operating in the United States fell from forty-one to twelve. As a result, some companies (particularly shippers of such low-cost commodities as coal and grain) found rates to be higher under deregulation than they were prior to the act. These companies have continued to address market failures under deregulation.

See also: INTERSTATE COMMERCE ACT OF 1887; RAIL PASSENGER SERVICE ACT.

BIBLIOGRAPHY

American Association of Railroads. *Railroad Facts.* Washington, DC: Office of Information and Public Affairs, Association of American Railroads, various years.

Dooley, Frank J., and William E. Thoms. *Railroad Law a Decade after Deregulation.* Westport, CT: Greenwood, 1994.

SURFACE MINING CONTROL AND RECLAMATION ACT (1977)

Joseph P. Tomain

The Surface Mining Control and Reclamation Act (SMCRA) (P.L. 95-87, 91 Stat 445) is one of the most comprehensive federal regulations on land use. Congress passed the SMCRA, which was signed by President Jimmy Carter, to "assure that the coal supply essential to the Nation's energy requirements, and to its economic and social well-being, is provided and to strike a balance between protection of the environment and agricultural productivity and the Nation's need for coal as an essential source of energy." At the heart of the act is the "reclamation" provisions requiring mine operators to put land back in place after concluding mining operations.

At the heart of the Act is the "reclamation" provisions requiring mine operators to put land back in place after concluding mining operations.

Coal mining, particularly when using "surface" or "strip" mining techniques, has a significant detrimental impact on the land and environment, including water and soil pollution and erosion. Prior to 1977 individual state regulation had proved to be ineffective because state laws were underenforced. Congress believed that federal legislation was necessary to establish minimum nationwide standards, ensuring that competition among coal producers would not be used to induce states to lower environmental standards or fail to enforce existing laws. Before enacting the SMCRA, however, the legislature debated the issue for seven years, raising concerns over how well a uniform standard could be applied to varied regions.

KEY REGULATIONS

The effect the SMCRA would have on various agricultural and environmental interests were among the chief concerns of Congress. The act contained four key regulations to protect these interests:

(1) It required potential miners to submit a permit and detailed application before commencing surface coal mining.
(2) It required coal companies to post a bond to ensure that the costs of reclamation would be covered.
(3) Miners would have to satisfy highly detailed standards for reclamation.
(4) The act delegated regulatory enforcement to the secretary of the interior and individual state regulatory agencies.

In general, the act required mining companies to restore to the mined land its approximate contour and use capacity, to stabilize the soil and redistribute the topsoil, and to restore plant life to the site.

CONSTITUTIONALITY

The SMCRA was enacted under the **commerce clause** powers found in Article I, section 8 of the Constitution, allowing Congress to regulate activities that have an effect on interstate commerce. In *Hodel v. Virginia Surface Mining and Reclamation Association, Inc.* (Hodel No. 1) and *Hodel v. Indiana* (Hodel No. 2), the U.S. Supreme Court upheld the constitutionality of the SMCRA and its regulations as intended to protect interstate commerce.

Commerce Clause: the provision of the U.S. Constitution (Article I, section 8, clause 3) that gives Congress exclusive powers over interstate commerce—the buying, selling, or exchanging of goods between states

EXPERIENCE UNDER THE ACT

Although the SMCRA met with considerable resistance—mine owners rejected the added costs and states did not want additional federal intervention—the act allows for a great deal of state autonomy in the implementation of its provisions. The SMCRA is administered through a system of permits, inspec-

Once a state develops a plan of reclamation that is approved by the Interior Department, state agencies are in charge of the administration, and state courts have jurisdiction over any disputes.

tions, and fines. Once a state develops a plan of reclamation that is approved by the Interior Department, state agencies are in charge of the administration, and state courts have jurisdiction over any disputes. Although no significant amendments have been made since 1977, the specific regulations and final rules have been subject to continued adjustment by the courts and various administrations. Tension between the relative powers of federal and state agencies still exist. In addition, questions are often raised about the economic effectiveness of the regulations, as the sums required to restore mined land to agricultural use often exceed the sums such use of the land will yield.

See also: MINERAL LEASING ACT OF 1920; SOIL CONSERVATION AND DOMESTIC ALLOTMENT ACT.

BIBLIOGRAPHY

Bosselman, Fred, Jim Rossi, and Jacqueline Lang Weaver. *Energy, Economics and the Environment*. New York: Foundation Press, 2000.

Fox, William F., Jr. *Federal Regulation of Energy*. Colorado Springs, CO: Shepard's/McGraw-Hill, 1983.

Mansfield, Marla E. "Coal." In *Energy Law and Policy for the 21st Century,* ed. Energy Law Group. Denver, CO: Rocky Mountain Mineral Law Foundation, 2000.

Muchow, David J., and William A. Mogel. *Energy Law and Transactions*. Newark, NJ: Lexis Nexis, 2002.

T

TAFT-HARTLEY ACT (1947)

Holly A. Reese

Excerpt from the Taft-Hartley Act

It is the purpose and policy of this Act, in order to promote the full flow of commerce, to prescribe the legitimate rights of both employees and employers in their relations affecting commerce, to provide orderly and peaceful procedures for preventing the interference by either with the legitimate rights of the other, to protect the rights of individual employees in their relations with labor organizations whose activities affect commerce, to define and proscribe practices on the part of labor and management which affect commerce and are inimical to the general welfare, and to protect the rights of the public in connection with labor disputes affecting commerce.

The Taft-Hartley Act (61 Stat. 136), also known as the Labor Management Relations Act of 1947, was created after a great number of large-scale strikes had nearly disabled the automobile, steel, and packing industries, among others. These work stoppages had caused a ripple effect through the economy, leading to public panic. The Taft-Hartley Act, an amendment to the Wagner Act of 1935, was designed to benefit all parties to a labor agreement—the employer, employees, and the labor union. Whereas the Wagner Act had spoken only of the right to participate in union activities, the new act included the right to refrain from union activities. It was clear that this new act was designed to level the unfair playing field formerly tipped in favor of labor unions.

The Taft-Hartley Act, an amendment to the Wagner Act of 1935, was designed to benefit all parties to a labor agreement—the employer, employees, and the labor union.The Taft-Hartley Act, an amendment to the Wagner Act of 1935, was designed to benefit all parties to a labor agreement—the employer, employees, and the labor union.

FEATURES OF THE ACT

To reach that result, the act placed restrictions on unions that were already imposed on the employer. For example, the act made it illegal to restrain or coerce employees wishing to exercise their rights to self-organization. Also made illegal were secondary strikes, secondary boycotts, and sympathy strikes, which were designed to influence employers other than those with whom the union had a contract. Many union leaders and supporters were unhappy with these new laws, and would seek repeal or revision on many different occasions.

The act gave the employer a First Amendment right to free speech that had been severely limited by the former laws. This change allowed the employer to speak out against unionization as long as the speech did not contain threats or promises to employees. The act also limited the liability of employers based on acts of managers or supervisors to those who would be considered part of these supervisors' official duty. Therefore an employer could not be held liable for a supervisor who was harassing union members for reasons unrelated to the supervisor's actual job duties.

In addition, the Taft-Hartley Act allowed states to enact right-to-work laws, which made it illegal to set union membership as a condition for employment. Many states did choose to enact such laws. Other changes included removing supervisors from the bargaining unit so as to avoid the possibility of conflicting interests, and placing guards in a separate bargaining unit without any rank-and-file members. There were also special rules for professional workers allowing them to choose whether or not they wished to be part of a separate bargaining unit.

Finally, the act required a both sides of a labor contract to bargain in good faith, which means they must meet at regular times and try to reach an agreement on a range of issues related to the employment contract. The parties must also create a written contract that includes any agreed-upon provisions. Additionally, the act created the Federal Mediation and Conciliation Service (FMCS) to assist in the settlement of labor disputes and increased the number of National Labor Relations Board (NLRB) members from three to five.

CIRCUMSTANCES LEADING TO ENACTMENT

During World War II labor organizations had increased their membership at a record pace. The government relied on the labor unions during the war and

The Wagner Act

The Taft-Hartley Act was an amendment to an earlier piece of legislation known as the Wagner Act, or the National Labor Relations Act. Passed in 1935, the law was named for Robert F. Wagner, a champion of the poor, minorities, and organized labor who served as a New York State senator, a New York State Supreme Court justice, and a U.S. senator from New York. Throughout his career Wagner was a major advocate of pro-Labor legislation, establishing public works programs, promoting industrial safety, and sponsoring numerous bills, including the Social Security Act. The legislation bearing his name contained three principal elements: First, it guaranteed American workers the right to join the labor union of their choice and to engage in collective bargaining; second, it prohibited companies from interfering with labor unions or punishing union members; and third, it established the National Labor Relations Board (NLRB). The NLRB oversaw union elections, in which workers voted whether to be represented by a union, and if so, which one. The NLRB also heard grievances from workers who felt they had been treated improperly and was empowered to issue "cease and desist" orders to employers found to be violating the law. Extremely radical in its time, the Wagner Act is considered a cornerstone of American labor law.

Three powerful labor leaders—John L. Lewis, Walter Reuther, and George Meany—ride a horse, whose head is an axe, toward the Taft-Hartley Act, which put restrictions on organized labor. Published in the Buffalo Courier-Express, *February 24, 1953, this cartoon reflects the demands of labor to amend, if not repeal, the act.* (COURTESY OF E. H. BUTLER LIBRARY, BUFFALO STATE COLLEGE, BUFFALO COURIER-EXPRESS COLLECTION/LIBRARY OF CONGRESS)

even made agreements with them to prevent strikes and keep production from slowing down or grinding to a halt. During this postwar period there were concerns that labor unions had grown too powerful, as evidenced by the impact that the large-scale strikes had had on the nation.

Whether in times of war or peace, the relationship between employer and employee can have an enormous impact on commerce. Because labor disputes can interrupt commerce, it is of great importance to the federal government to maintain open communication between labor unions and employers. The Constitution's commerce clause, which allows the federal government to regulate interstate commerce, was the constitutional basis for the act.

National Labor Relations Board v. Jones & Laughlin Steel Corporation (1937)

Immediately after it was established in 1935, the National Labor Relations Board was the object of a wave of lawsuits and injunctions initiated by businesses and anti-labor organizations seeking to challenge its legality and prevent it from operating as outlined in the Wagner Act. In 1937, in the case of the *National Labor Relations Board v. Jones & Laughlin Steel Corporation*, the Supreme Court upheld the constitutionality of the Wagner Act and ensured the continued operation of the NLRB. The majority opinion, written by Chief Justice Charles Evans Hughes, hinged on the idea that labor unrest could disrupt interstate commerce, so Congress was indeed within its rights to provide a mechanism such as the NLRB to help prevent strikes. At the same time, the ruling described relationships between employers and employees as being inherently unequal and maintained that collective bargaining was an appropriate tool to redress the inequality. The Court prohibited employers from blacklisting union members, employing spies to report on union activities, and other unfair practices.

PUBLIC AND LEGISLATIVE DEBATE

Proponents of the act mostly fell into two categories. The first group included those who were opposed to all collective bargaining of any kind. The second group consisted of people who were generally not opposed to collective bargaining but who felt the labor unions had gained too much power during the war. Both groups thought the government should put limitations on the unions that would coincide with the limitations already in place for employers. Still others felt that labor organizations had become a cover for racketeering (fraudulent business schemes involving intimidation) and other unsavory activities.

Prior to the Taft-Hartley Act, courts had gone back and forth on the issue of supervisors and their role in bargaining activities. Legislative debate over the act focused much attention on the exclusion of supervisors from the bargaining unit. Legislators in favor of the act believed that a firm exclusionary rule was necessary, and it was ultimately included in the final version of the act. Another debated topic was the exclusion of members of the Communist Party from union leadership. Many feared labor unions were predominantly controlled by communists, although that was most likely an overstatement. The act did contain such an exclusion, but it was later repealed.

POLITICAL CONTEXT

On the political front, President Harry S. Truman was calling for changes to the Wagner Act, while cautioning against legislation that could be considered punitive against the unions. The 1946 election brought a Republican majority to both houses of Congress for the first time in sixteen years. That majority wanted more changes than Truman had suggested and set about writing a new bill, which ultimately became the Taft-Hartley Act. Representative Fred A. Hartley, Jr., the chair of the House Committee on Education and Labor, sponsored the bill in the House of Representatives. Senator Robert A. Taft, the chair of the Senate Labor and Public Welfare Committee, sponsored the bill in the Senate. The bill passed both houses, although the vote was much closer in the Senate than in the House.

President Truman then vetoed the bill on June 20, 1947. He felt that the proposed bill gave the government too much involvement in labor management relations. He also said that the reporting requirements for unions were overly burdensome and the bill would not have the effect desired by Congress. The House disagreed with Truman and quickly overrode the presidential veto. Two days of debate later, the Senate followed suit and the Taft-Hartley Act became law.

ENFORCEMENT AND JUDICIAL REVIEW

Enforcement of the Taft-Hartley Act comes in large part from the NLRB. With the advice and consent of the Senate, the president appoints the general counsel, who is responsible for conducting hearings in front of the NLRB. When one party wants to file unfair labor practice charges against the other party, that party may also do so in any federal court with proper jurisdiction.

The Supreme Court considered a part of the act in *United States v. Brown* (1965). The Court ruled that the laws preventing members or former members of the Communist Party from holding office in a labor union to be unconstitutional. Courts have gone on to define and shape various portions of the act while maintaining its congressional intent and integrity.

AMENDMENTS

The Taft-Hartley Act has been amended many times over the years, with the majority of amendments occurring in the 1950s. For example, in 1951 the act was amended to allow union shops to be formed without the formality of an authorization election. Later, in 1974, the act was amended to include corporations or associations that operate nonprofit hospitals and healthcare facilities.

The Labor Management Reporting and Disclosure Act of 1959 (LMRDA) was an extension of the Taft-Hartley Act and its reporting requirements. It established what is considered a bill of rights for union members. It also requires full, fair, and participatory elections, as well as disclosure of union financial statements and expenditures. It follows the Taft-Hartley Act's intent to protect employers and employees while providing adequate means of dispute resolution.

EFFECTIVENESS

The Taft-Hartley Act remains a powerful tool for labor-management relations. From its narrow adoption, and despite its many opponents, the 1947 act continues to provide valuable protection to employees, employers, and labor unions. Although labor strikes are still a very real consequence of failed labor negotiations, the rules of the Taft-Hartley Act have reduced the severity and frequency of such strikes.

From its narrow adoption, and despite its many opponents, the 1947 act continues to provide valuable protection to employees, employers, and labor unions.

See also: National Labor Relations Act; Norris-LaGuardia Act.

BIBLIOGRAPHY

Cox, Archibald, Derek Curtis Bok, Robert A. Gorman, et al. *Labor Law: Cases and Materials,* 13th ed. New York: Foundation Press, 2001.

Iserman, Theodore R. *Changes to Make in Taft-Hartley*. New York: Dealer's Digest Publishing, 1953.

Jasper, Margaret C. *Oceana's Law for the Layperson: Labor Law*. New York: Oceana Publications, 1998.

Raza, M. Ali, and A. Janell Anderson. *Labor Relations and the Law*. Upper Saddle River, NJ: Prentice-Hall, 1996.

INTERNET RESOURCE

National Labor Relations Board. <http://www.nlrb.gov>.

Tariff Act of 1789

Michael P. Malloy

The Tariff Act of 1789 (1 Stat. 24), signed into law by President George Washington on July 4, 1789, was the first substantive legislation passed by the first Congress. This act, together with the Collection Act of 1789, operated as a device both to protect trade and to raise revenues for the federal government. The constitutional authority for the act is found in the powers given to Congress "to lay and collect Taxes, Duties, Imports and Excises" and "to regulate Commerce with foreign Nations." Among other things, the act established the first schedule of import duties and created an additional duty of 10 percent on imports carried on vessels "not of the United States."

This act, together with the Collection Act of 1789, operated as a device both to protect trade and to raise revenues for the federal government.

U.S. TRADE POLICY

The specific provisions of the act are of little interest (by 1799 it had been superseded by subsequent, more detailed legislation). However, the act remains significant for setting the basics of U.S. trade policy. In supporting its enactment, Alexander Hamilton argued that **tariffs** would encourage domestic industry. Other nations offered their industries significant subsidies, or money given by a government to support a private business. Hamilton contended that a tariff would protect U.S. industry from the effects of these subsidies. (Concerns over "dumping"—imported goods sold at less than their fair value to gain unfair advantage over domestic goods—would also be addressed in the Tariff Act of 1816.) Another argument in favor of tariffs is now easy to forget. Before the income tax was authorized by the Sixteenth Amendment in 1913, the tariff was a key source of federal revenue. Thus, for over a century import duties (along with domestic excise taxes) were the major source of government revenue, with sugar duties alone accounting for approximately 20 percent of all import duties.

tariff: a tax imposed on goods when imported into a country

CONSTITUTIONAL CRISIS

The politics of tariffs soon became intertwined with disputes between legislators from the North and South. For example, a Northern manufacturer of cloth would benefit from a tariff on cloth imported from England, which would make English cloth less competitive. However, a Southern planter who sold cotton to an English cloth manufacturer would benefit if there were no tariff on imports of English cloth, which would keep English cloth (made from U.S. cotton) cheaper and more competitive on the U.S. market. Thus Northern manufacturers favored high tariffs, whereas Southern planters, dependent on exports, favored free trade. However, the North wanted tariffs without public expenditures for a costly upgraded transporta-

The politics of tariffs soon became intertwined with disputes between legislators from the North and South.

tion system that would be paid for by tariff revenues, and the South was opposed to any tariff supporting the price of manufactured goods because the tariffs would make it harder for the South to export its agricultural products to nations affected by the tariffs. A high tariff did pass Congress as the Tariff Act of 1828. Legislators from Southern states called this the "Tariff of Abominations," and it nearly brought about a constitutional crisis.

In December 1828 South Carolina endorsed the South Carolina Exposition, a document asserting that the tariff was unconstitutional and thus could be nullified by individual states. It was an open secret that the document had been drafted by Vice President John C. Calhoun, acting more as a Southern partisan than a national leader. By February 1829 five Southern state legislatures had protested the tariff as unfair. In 1832 a South Carolina state convention passed an ordinance (a law or order issued by a local government) to nullify the act, but President Andrew Jackson responded with a proclamation that acts of nullification were themselves unconstitutional and **treasonous**. One great effort at political compromise based on tariffs was Senator Henry Clay's "American Plan." Under Clay's proposal, the manufacturers of the North would be protected by relatively high tariffs and would become a large market for agricultural products of the West and the South. Revenue from the tariffs would support the construction of the transportation system needed to make internal trade feasible. In a compromise, Congress enacted the Force Act, authorizing the president to use armed force to enforce the tariff, but also amended the act to substantially reduce the tariff rates. The crisis was defused when South Carolina finally accepted the lowered rates.

treason: the offense of attempting to overthrow the government of one's own state

In a compromise, Congress enacted the Force Act, authorizing the president to use armed force to enforce the tariff, but also amended the act to reduce the tariff rates substantially.

A series of judicial decisions later upheld the constitutional authority of the Congress and the president to regulate international trade. These decisions imply that the Southern states' attack on the Tariff of Abominations was unconstitutional. For example, in *United States v. Curtiss-Wright Export Corp.* (1936) the Supreme Court ruled that Congress could delegate authority to the president to impose an arms **embargo** because the president holds authority over foreign affairs. In *United States v. Yoshida International, Inc.* (1975) the Court of Customs and Patent Appeals upheld the president's power under the Trading with the Enemy Act (1917) to impose an import duty surcharge (an extra fee) of 10 percent to counteract a balance of payments crisis.

embargo: a prohibition on commerce with a particular country for political or economic reasons

TARIFF ADJUSTMENTS

After the Civil War, domestic policies continued to favor high tariffs, strengthened perhaps by the fact that industry was spreading through more of the nation. By the 1890s Congress had added an important innovation to the legislation: a delegation of power to the executive branch to adjust tariffs in specific circumstances. An early example was what are now called "countervailing duties." These were tariffs the executive branch would order to counteract foreign subsidies on products exported to the United States. The executive branch, without further action by Congress, could measure the foreign subsidy and determine the duty to countervail, or compensate for, that duty. This became one of a large number of such adjustment devices.

Another such device was the antidumping duty, designed to prevent foreign exporters from outselling competing U.S. products by underpricing their goods. Also, the "peril point" or "escape clause" measure was designed to protect an industry suffering serious injury from competition by imports. The United States Tariff Commission, an administrative agency created in 1916 and renamed the United States International Trade Commission (ITC) in 1974, played an important role in these tariff adjustments.

EFFECTS OF THE SMOOT-HAWLEY TARIFF

President Woodrow Wilson, an ardent supporter of free trade, sought to reform tariffs. He argued against a "tariff which cuts us off from our proper part in the commerce of the world, violates the just principles of taxation, and makes the government a facile instrument in the hands of private interests." His efforts were eventually repudiated by the Tariff Act of 1930, known as the Smoot-Hawley Act. This act increased duties on more than a thousand items. By the end of 1931, twenty-six foreign nations had retaliated by raising their tariffs against the United States. The resulting harm to international trade undoubtedly contributed to the severity of the **Great Depression.** The economic misery of the 1930s eventually led to a change in tariff law that reflected free-trade principles.

Great Depression: the longest and most severe economic depression in American history (1929–1939); its effects were felt throughout the world

This new approach was called the "reciprocal trade agreement" concept and was based on the idea that nations trading with each other might agree to reduce their tariffs in a mutually corresponding way. Each nation's increase in exports would lead to a larger number of jobs (because more workers would be needed to make more goods for sale to other nations). If that increase in jobs was greater than the number of jobs lost to increased imports, such an agreement might be politically beneficial and would almost certainly be economically desirable. Franklin D. Roosevelt's secretary of state, Cordell Hull, obtained from Congress the delegation of authority needed to facilitate this process. The Reciprocal Trade Agreements Act, passed in 1934, contributed to major reductions in tariffs through negotiations with other nations. By 1940 twenty-eight agreements had been concluded under the Trade Agreements Program.

The economic misery of the 1930s eventually led to a change in tariff law that reflected free-trade principles.

See also: NORTH AMERICAN FREE TADE AGREEMENT IMPLEMENTATION ACT; SMOOT-HAWLEY TARRIFFS; TRADE ACT OF 1974.

BIBLIOGRAPHY

Bess, H. David, and Martin T. Farris. *U.S. Maritime Policy.* New York: Praeger, 1981.

Condliffe, J. B. *The Commerce of Nations.* London: Allen and Unwin, 1950.

Metzger, S. *Trade Agreements and the Kennedy Round.* Fairfax, VA: Coiner Publications, 1964.

Stanwood, E. *American Tariff Controversies in the Nineteenth Century.* New York: Russell and Russell, 1903.

Tarbell, I. *The Tariff in Our Times.* New York: Macmillan, 1911.

Tax Reform Act of 1986

Richard A. Westin

Before and after the Tax Reform Act of 1986, the income tax law relied on the concept of taxing only the income that taxpayers realized during the taxable year (usually in the form of cash).

The Tax Reform Act of 1986 (P.L. 99-514, 100 Stat. 2085) implemented a tax code that at once swept away and reenacted its predecessor, the Internal Revenue Code of 1954. As a result, the tax code is now formally known as the Internal Revenue Code of 1986. Although the 1986 act reenacted the great bulk of the 1954 code, the fact that Congress renamed the Internal Revenue Code indicates the importance of the changes put in place by the 1986 act.

The new law did not affect the bedrock concepts of federal taxation. Before and after the Tax Reform Act of 1986, the income tax law relied on the concept of taxing only the income taxpayers realized during the taxable year (usually in the form of cash). The new law did not initiate radical variations of taxation, such as a sales or value-added tax base. Nor did the 1986 act have any meaningful impact on other components of the existing Internal Revenue Code, including:

- Excise taxes, such as taxes on gasoline, cigarettes, and alcohol
- Estate taxes, meaning taxes imposed on the taxable value of the estate of a dead person
- Social Security taxes

The heart of the 1986 changes in the federal income tax act consist of the following six features:

(1) The act equalized the rate of taxation on **long-term capital gains** paid by individual taxpayers with the top rate of federal income taxation imposed on individuals. This was a dramatic change, because up to that point, capital gains enjoyed lower rates of taxation than did ordinary income from labor and investments, such as wages and **dividends**. Prior to 1986, these lower rates of taxation on capital gains led wealthy taxpayers to spend time and energy structuring their finances to maximize the portion of their incomes earned in the form of long-term capital gains. Consequently, the 1986 tax reform seemed to close a tax loophole . Later amendments to the Internal Revenue Code of 1986, however, reinstated the divergence in tax rates between capital gains and ordinary income this reform-minded element was eliminated, and the loophole continues to exist.

(2) The act decreased the use of **tax shelters**, devices taxpayers used to generate **deductions** and **tax credits** Congress accomplished this goal by enacting Section 469 of the Internal Revenue Code, known to tax experts as the "passive loss rules." The heart of the passive loss rules is that losses from passive tax shelters and losses from operating rental real estate can only be used as a deduction, or credit, against profits from other passive tax shelters and real estate. For example, a doctor could not deduct losses from real estate holdings against the income she earned in her medical practice. This largely put an end to taxpayers' use of tax shelters, which had, up until 1986, dramatically reduced federal revenues. Section 469 has a number of exceptions and limits, the most important of which are the following: (a) the rules do not apply to widely held corporations; and (b) passive losses are available in full only when a taxpayer disposes of the entire investment in a taxable sale or exchange. The new rules reportedly resulted in significant declines in the values of real estate.

long-term capital gains: profit made on the sale or exchange of a capital asset (usually stock or real estate) that has been owned for more than twelve months

dividend: a payment made by a company, based on its earnings, to its shareholders

tax shelter: a strategy or method that allows one to legally reduce or avoid tax liabilities

deduction: an amount subtracted from the amount of income that is used to calculate income tax due

tax credit: a reduction in the amount an individual or corporation owes in taxes

(3) The act dropped the top rate of federal income taxation of individuals from 50 percent to 28 percent. After Congress reduced the tax rate to 28 percent, however, it increased the rate to almost 40 percent, but is on its way to reducing it again. The 28 percent rate applied equally to capital gains, discussed above, and all forms of other income. In addition, Congress reduced the top rate of taxation on corporations from 46 percent to 34 percent.

interest expense: the money a corporation or individual pays out in interest on loans

personal consumption goods: goods purchased for personal use

individual retirement account (IRA): an account into which a person can deposit up to a certain amount of money annually without being taxed until either retirement or early withdrawal (withdrawal when the person is under a certain age)

(4) The act eliminated deductions for **interest expenses** associated with buying **personal consumption goods**. (The sole exception is interest payments on home loans.) The prior law allowing interest expense deductions for borrowing money to buy consumer goods has always been questionable because it encouraged personal consumption. The repeal of the deduction eliminated this incentive. This part of the 1986 act has withstood the test of time and remains an important feature of American tax law.

(5) The act repealed the universal **individual retirement account (IRA)** deduction in favor of restricting the deduction to people who did not have pension coverage through other avenues, such as their employer. Before repeal, everyone, no matter how wealthy or how much they benefited from other pension arrangements, could take a deduction for contributions made to an IRA. Now, only certain taxpayers are permitted to do so. The universal IRA deduction was appropriately considered an unjustifiable source of revenue losses. The 1986 act is applauded for this change.

inflation: a general rise in the prices of goods and services

(6) The act eliminated federal income tax liability for those below the poverty line. This restored the laws as they existed in the late 1970s, when poor people were excluded from the obligation to pay taxes. This particular reform was made necessary by the effects of **inflation**: inflation increases people's nominal income and therefore their income taxes, even though in real economic terms they live in poverty.

HISTORY OF THE 1986 ACT

The first inkling of the 1986 act appeared in 1984 in President Ronald Reagan's State of the Union address. Reagan announced that he was asking the secretary of the treasury to develop and present a comprehensive plan to simplify the tax code by the year 1984. Reagan was reacting to Republican concerns that Senator Walter Mondale, Democrat of Minnesota, might propose radical simplifications of the Internal Revenue Code and thus gain political popularity—popularity Reagan and his Republican Party hoped to enjoy. Reagan proposed that the new law be simple, fair, and broad-based. Specifically, it had to contain these features:

Reagan proposed that the new law be simple, fair, and broad-based.

- It had to be revenue-neutral, that is, neither adding to nor subtracting from federal revenues. Instead, the focus was on broadening the tax base and reducing rates.
- It had to be distributionally neutral, that is, not favor one economic group over another.
- It had to close major tax loopholes, such as the tax shelters described above. Reagan hoped that by closing loopholes, more taxes would be paid into the government, which would, in turn, allow an overall reduction in the tax rates (like the reduction in tax rates from 50 percent to 28 percent described above).

These proposals sat well with the powerful head of the House Ways and Means Committee, Representative Dan Rostenkowski of Illinois. Rostenkowski, a traditional populist Democrat, wanted to reduce the burden of taxation on working people and was capable of imposing his will on his committee. Without his cooperation, the proposals would have been doomed. On the opposite side of the aisle, Senator Robert Packwood, Republican of Oregon, played a less significant but nevertheless important role in working for passage of the act.

The act itself was capable of passage only because it had features that were attractive to both conservative and liberal politicians. To fiscal conservatives, dropping tax rates represented an opportunity to impose supply-side economics (a theory of economics that assumes lower taxes will generate more government revenue in the long run). Liberal tax theorists were attracted to broadening the tax base by closing loopholes, arguably taken advantage of by wealthy taxpayers and paid for by the poor through higher tax rates. Both conservatives and liberals believed the act promised higher levels of compliance by the taxpaying public.

Both conservatives and liberals believed that the act promised higher levels of compliance by the taxpaying public.

Since passage of the Tax Reform Act of 1986, Congress has tinkered with the tax code almost every year, generally adding to the code's complexity and length.

See also: CORPORATE INCOME TAX ACT OF 1909; FEDERAL INCOME TAX ACT OF 1913; INTERNAL REVENUE ACT OF 1954.

BIBLIOGRAPHY

Birnbaum, Jeffrey, and Alan Murray. *Showdown at Gucci Gulch: Lawmakers, Lobbyists and the Unlikely Triumph of Tax Reform*. New York: Vintage Books, 1987.

Graetz, Michael. "Paint-by-Numbers Lawmaking." 95 *Columbia Law Review* 609 (1995).

Steuerle, C. Eugene. *The Tax Decade*. Washington, DC: Urban Institute Press, distributed by National Book Network, Lanham, MD, 1992.

TAXPAYER BILL OF RIGHTS III (1998)

Richard Gershon

The IRS Restructuring and Reform Act of 1998 (P.L. 105-206), which Con gress signed into law on July 22, 1998, contains the Taxpayer Bill of Rights 3 (T3). By enacting the T3 Congress sought to address criticisms of the Internal Revenue Service and its dealings with taxpayers. In creating this legislation, it was important for Congress to balance taxpayers' rights with the Internal Revenue Service's obligation to administer the tax laws efficiently. The Taxpayer Bill of Rights 3 modifies the Taxpayer Bill of Rights 2 by expanding taxpayer rights in several areas. Specifically, the T3 expanded or created the following rights for taxpayers:

In creating this legislation, it was important for Congress to balance taxpayers' rights with the Internal Revenue Service's obligation to administer the tax laws efficiently.

Attorney-Client Confidentiality Expanded to Certain Non-Attorneys Prior to the enactment of T3, confidentiality protection was only provided between taxpayers and their attorney representatives. Accordingly, the IRS could question non-attorney representatives about their thoughts, impressions, opinions, or analysis. T3 expands the traditional attorney-client privilege to taxpayer representatives authorized to practice before the IRS (enrolled agents and Certified Public Accountants) with respect to their thoughts, impressions, opinions, or analysis during a noncriminal administrative proceeding. This newly created privilege does not apply to civil or criminal court trials.

Shifting the Burden of Proof to the IRS Under the prior law, the taxpayer had the burden of proof in an action by the IRS against that taxpayer. T3 provides that the burden of proof will shift to the government in some cases. To shift the burden, taxpayers must have "fully cooperated" with IRS at the administrative level by providing all witnesses, information, and documentation reasonably requested, possibly including confidential communications between taxpayers and their representatives.

PROVISIONS RELATING TO SPOUSES

Joint Returns When spouses file a joint tax return, they are treated as a single unit; therefore, each is individually responsible for all tax liabilities, penalties and interest, even if the liability was caused by the other spouse. While filing a joint return usually provides a small tax benefit, each spouse becomes personally liable for all additional taxes the other spouse may have accrued. Many taxpayers hoped that T3 would relieve taxpayers of joint return liability. Instead, Congress opted to require the IRS to explain this potential unlimited liability in its publications.

Innocent Spouse Relief Even though Congress retained joint liability in T3, the legislation provides relief for innocent spouses who sign a joint return. An innocent spouse is one who establishes that when the return was signed, he or she did not know, and had no reason to know, there was an understatement of taxes by the other spouse. Further, the innocent spouse must prove that under the circumstances, it would be inequitable to hold the innocent spouse liable for any liability arising from the other spouse's conduct in failing to report income in an accurate manner. T3 also provides for apportionment of relief if the spouse was innocent as to some items, but not others.

Offers in Compromise T3 changes the law regarding Offers in Compromise involving spouses. Under the prior law, if one spouse's actions caused the termination of the offer, the offer was terminated for both spouses. Under T3, if the offer is terminated due to the actions of one spouse, the offer will continue for the spouse (or former spouse) who remains in compliance.

SMALL TAX CASE LIMITATIONS

T3 raised the maximum amount in controversy for a small tax case (an informal proceeding similar to small claims court) from $10,000 to $25,000.

STATUTORY REFUND PERIOD TOLLED

The prior law barred a taxpayer's claim for a refund if the claim was not filed within two years. T3 allows for the period to be extended if the taxpayer proves a medical disability during this period that prevented filing for the refund.

DAMAGES FOR NEGLIGENT COLLECTION ACTION

T3 provides that a taxpayer may recover a maximum of $100,000 for negligent collection actions by the IRS.

RESTRICTIONS ON ECONOMIC REALITY AUDITS

T3 restricts the use of "economic reality" audits to those situations where the IRS believes there is a reasonable likelihood of unreported income. Economic reality audits focus on a taxpayer's assets and lifestyle, rather than the income and expenses claimed on the tax return.

See also: Federal Income Tax Act of 1913; Internal Revenue Act of 1954; Tax Reform Act of 1986.

BIBLIOGRAPHY

Your Rights As a Taxpayer. IRS Publication 1.

Tennessee Valley Authority Act (1933)

Kyle A. Loring

On May 18, 1933, President Franklin D. Roosevelt signed the Tennessee Valley Authority Act (TVAA) (P.L. 73-17, 48 Stat. 58) as part of his **New Deal** legislation to invigorate the economy of the Tennessee Valley in particular, and the United States generally. Congress defined the act's purpose as "maintaining and operating properties now owned by the United States in the vicinity of Muscle Shoals, Alabama, in the interest of national defense and for agricultural and industrial development, and to improve navigation in the Tennessee River and to control the destructive flood waters in the Tennessee River and Mississippi River basins."

New Deal: the legislative and administrative program of President Franklin D. Roosevelt designed to promote economic recovery and social reform (1933–1939)

To do so, the act established the Tennessee Valley Authority (TVA), a unique federal corporation that erected massive dams and gained world renown for its engineering achievements. The TVA has since constructed over sixty-five dams and expanded to producing other forms of electricity, providing agricultural assistance to farmers, and promoting environmental stewardship.

The TVA has since constructed over sixty-five dams and expanded to producing other forms of electricity, providing agricultural assistance to farmers, and promoting environmental stewardship.

In 1916, the federal government purchased Alabama's Muscle Shoals region of the Tennessee River to build a dam to enable passage by ship and harness electricity from the thirty mile long, 40-foot drop in elevation. When World War I (1914–1919) ended, so did the need for this electricity. During the 1920s, however, Nebraska Senator George Norris continued to press for development of the Tennessee River Valley,

George William Norris (1861–1944), known as the "father of the TVA." Pictured here, Senator Norris inspects the Norris Dam. (TENNESSEE VALLEY AUTHORITY)

introducing six bills in Congress to provide economic growth in the area. Finally, with the advent of the Great Depression and a public citizenry clamoring for large-scale government intervention, Senator Norris gained President Roosevelt's support. The Tennessee Valley Authority Act created the TVA with a mission to improve "the economic and social well-being of the people living in said river basin." (TVAA, Section 23).

The TVA is a federal corporation that blends government authority with a private enterprise problem-solving approach, and it has become the largest public power system in the United States. This power system currently includes three nuclear power plants, eleven coal-fired plants, twenty-nine hydroelectric dams, five combustion-turbine plants, and about 17,000 miles of transmission lines. TVA electricity produced in these facilities now reaches over eight million residents of the Tennessee Valley.

The TVA is a federal corporation that blends government authority with a private enterprise problem-solving approach, and it has become the largest public power system in the United States.

The Tennessee Valley runs through seven Southern states: Tennessee, Kentucky, Virginia, North Carolina, Georgia, Alabama, and Mississippi. At the time of the TVA's creation, electricity was available to fewer than three percent of the region's households, the average Tennessee Valley farmer earned about one-third the national average, and education expenditures reached only about one-third of the national average. During the eight years that followed passage of the act, household electricity use grew from six thousand houses to nearly five hundred thousand. The TVA also instructed local farmers on demonstration farms on the use of improved fertilizers, increasing agricultural production. In addition, the newly abundant electricity attracted industries to the Tennessee Valley, especially aluminum producers during World War II (1939–1945).

At the time of the TVA's creation, electricity was available to fewer than three percent of the region's households, the average Tennessee Valley farmer earned about one-third the national average, and education expenditures reached only about one-third of the national average.

Early in its existence, the TVA gained fame primarily for its dambuilding expertise and its construction of some of the world's largest structures. In its first twenty years, the TVA erected twenty multipurpose dams to support flood control while generating electricity. By 1950 the TVA had attracted many international admirers and its chairman, David Lilienthal, wrote *TVA: Democracy on the March,* which was later translated into fourteen languages. China consulted with the TVA because of its international reputation soon after World War II, when China began to plan the Three Gorges Dam to control the flow of the Yangtze River.

Throughout its existence, the TVA has met with strong opposition from both electric companies and environmentalists. Soon after Congress created the TVA, electric companies grew wary of the business threat of inexpensive federal electricity, and they filed lawsuits claiming the federal govern-

Senators on an inspection tour of a Tennessee Valley Authority project, June 27, 1959. (TENNESSEE VALLEY AUTHORITY)

The TVA met its greatest resistance in 1978 in TVA v. Hill, *when a law school professor filed a lawsuit on behalf of a small fish, the snail darter.*

ment exceeded its constitutional authority by entering into the electric utility business. In 1935 John Battle, executive secretary of the National Coal Association, expressed industry sentiments in congressional testimony when he stated that "we are willing to be put out of business it if can be done in a plain straightforward business–like manner, but we do object to our Government putting us out of business." In 1936, in *Ashwander v. TVA*, the United States Supreme Court upheld both the constitutionality of the act and the TVA's electricity sales and distribution.

The TVA met its greatest resistance in 1978 in *TVA v. Hill*, when a law school professor filed a lawsuit on behalf of a small fish, the snail darter. In 1959, Aubrey "Red" Wagner, the TVA's general manager, had planned a new initiative that would begin with Tellico Dam, a structure that would trap the last thirty-three free-flowing miles of the Little Tennessee River. Prior to this initiative, the TVA had fallen into low morale. It had constructed more than sixty-five dams and slowed 2,500 linear miles of river, exhausting nearly all of the possible locations for dams. Although the TVA had shifted much of its energy production to coal and nuclear-powered plants, it could not easily relinquish its mission to build dams. Wagner planned a new series of developments to reinvigorate the TVA, including Tellico Dam, which would serve as the focal point of a model industrial city on the shores of the new reservoir. The high cost/benefit ratio and adverse environmental impact of the proposal led to an outcry from both local farmers and the fledgling environmental movement.

The opposition gained a legal tool to combat the construction of Tellico Dam in 1973, when Congress enacted the Endangered Species Act (ESA). The act contained stringent safeguards to ensure the continued existence of endangered or threatened species. Section 7 of the ESA prohibited government action leading to the destruction of habitats critical to such species. As a result, a lawsuit was filed against the TVA alleging that the construction of the Tellico Dam would destroy the habitat critical to the snail darter's continued survival. The Supreme Court initially upheld this challenge and halted the Tellico Dam project. In 1979, however, a small rider snuck into the large Energy and Water Development bill that protected Tellico Dam from the prohibition on its completion. The TVA completed it in mid-1979.

See also: FEDERAL POWERS ACTS; RURAL ELECTRIFICATION ACT.

BIBLIOGRAPHY

Tennessee Valley Authority. "A Short History of the Tennessee Valley Authority History." <http://www.tva.gov/abouttva/history.htm>.

Freeman, Marsha. "The World Needs the TVA, Not the IMF." *Executive Intelligence Review,* (June 12, 1998).

Lilienthal, David E. *TVA: Democracy on the March*. New York: Harper & Brothers, 1944.

Plater, Zygmunt J.B. "Environmental Law in the Political Ecosystem—Coping with the —Reality of Politics." *Pace Environmental Law Revue* 19 (2002): 423–88.

"TVA: Electricity for All." <http://newdeal.feri.org/tva/index.htm#2>.

Title IX, Education Amendments (1972)

Julie A. Davies

Title IX was enacted as part of the Education Amendments of 1972 (P.L. No. 92-318, 86 Stat. 373). This amendment prohibits sex discrimination in education by programs that receive federal financial assistance. It was patterned after Title VI of the Civil Rights Act of 1964, which prohibits discrimination on the grounds of race, color, or national origin in any program or activity receiving federal financial assistance. Unlike Title VI, however, Title IX prohibits discrimination only in education: "no person in the United States shall, on the basis of sex, be excluded from participation in, be denied the benefits of, or be subjected to discrimination under any education program or activity receiving federal financial assistance." This provision covers programs such as admissions, recruitment, financial aid, academic programs, physical education, athletics, grading, discipline, housing, and employment in school districts, colleges, and universities, and for-profit schools that receive federal money.

This amendment prohibits sex discrimination in education by programs that receive federal financial assistance.

The basic idea behind statutes such as Title VI and Title IX is that federal tax money should not be used to support programs that discriminate on certain bases. The U.S. Constitution gives Congress the power to decide how federal money is spent, and Congress has chosen to condition grants of federal funds on the recipients' promise not to discriminate on the grounds of race or sex. The statute contains certain exemptions, including social fraternities or sororities, father-son or mother-daughter activities, and educational programs in religious organizations whose beliefs are contrary to the statute.

HISTORY AND POLITICAL CLIMATE SURROUNDING ENACTMENT

Titles VI and VII of the Civil Rights Act of 1964 paved the way for Title IX's passage eight years later. In Title VI, Congress utilized the threat of withholding federal money to help overcome massive resistance to desegregation that followed the Supreme Court's decision in *Brown v. Board of Education of Topeka, Kansas*. However, Title VI did not include a prohibition on sex discrimination; the concept of equality between the sexes was only beginning to emerge. Title VII included protection from sex discrimination in employment, although this was added by amendment as an afterthought. Title IX was notable because it combined the elements of restrictions on federal funding and protection from sex discrimination and applied them for the first time to education.

Title IX was notable because it combined the elements of restrictions on federal funding and protection from sex discrimination and applied them for the first time to education.

In 1972 girls and women faced numerous barriers in education. Nationwide, awareness of societal discrimination against women was growing. Representative Patsy Takemoto Mink (Hawaii), Title IX's author and co-sponsor, had experienced educational barriers firsthand when, despite strong undergraduate preparation, she could not gain admission to medical school. Mink and co-sponsor Representative Edith Green of Oregon introduced Title IX in the House of Representatives. The bill's chief advocate in the Senate was Birch Bayh of Indiana.

Has Title IX Helped?

- In 1972, women earned 9 percent of medical degrees. In 1994, women earned 38 percent.
- In 1972, women earned 7 percent of law degrees. In 1994, women earned 43 percent.
- In 1972, women earned 25 percent of doctoral degrees. In 1994, women earned 44 percent.
- In 1971, 18 percent of women had completed four years of college, compared to 26 percent of men. In 1994, 27 percent of both men and women had earned a bachelor's degree.
- In 1972, women comprised 15 percent of college student athletes. In 1995, women comprised 37 percent.
- In 1971, 300,000 high school girls participated in athletics. In 1996, there were 2.4 million.

During the Congressional hearings, witnesses presented evidence of rampant discrimination in education. Some colleges offered admission only to those women who were "especially well qualified" but placed no such restriction on men. Schools commonly spent money on athletic programs devoted to boys while offering little, if any, opportunity to girls. Boys were much more likely to be recruited and to receive athletic scholarships. Curricula often perpetuated long-standing stereotypes, channeling girls into sewing and cooking classes and boys into "shop" (which taught such skills as woodworking). Boys were viewed as more capable in math and science and encouraged to take advanced courses. Professional career options such as law, medicine, and accounting were overwhelmingly male.

ENFORCEMENT

Originally, Title IX was to be enforced by the Office of Education in the Department of Health, Education and Welfare. Later, after the creation of the Department of Education, enforcement of Title IX, along with Title VI and other statutes, was transferred to that department's Office for Civil Rights (OCR). OCR's duties include making and implementing policy, investigating complaints of discrimination, and initiating enforcement actions against entities that refuse to comply. Although in theory the remedy for noncompliance is a cutoff of funding, in practice this has not occurred, no doubt because of the devastating impact of such a cutoff on students. Instead OCR has typically worked to obtain an agreement from the funded program that it will comply. OCR is also permitted to refer cases to the U.S. Department of Justice.

After Title IX had been in effect for a number of years, critical analysis of its impact suggested that federal enforcement was not as effective as it could have been. In addition, critics thought it troubling that the victims of discrimination could neither enforce the statute through litigation nor obtain any remedy for discrimination. In response, the Supreme Court, in *Franklin v. Gwinnett County Public Schools* (1992), recognized the right of a private individual injured by discrimination to sue the federally funded entity for damages. Recognition of this private right of action (and the availability of attorneys' fees under the Civil Rights Attorneys' Fees Awards Act of 1976) gave people who suffer sex discrimination in education a powerful additional enforcement tool.

IMPORTANT TITLE IX ISSUES

In the decades since the enactment of Title IX, the most intolerable barriers to women's advancement in education have fallen. Some issues, however, remain at the forefront of public attention. One controversial issue concerns Title IX's impact on the funding of men's and women's sports, particularly at the collegiate level. Title IX detractors claim the OCR's interpretation of Title IX policy has forced the elimination of some men's sports by requiring schools to spend proportionate amounts on both women's and men's sports. Title IX advocates argue that proportionality in spending is only one indicator of compliance, with the other factors not based

In the decades since the enactment of Title IX, the most intolerable barriers to women's advancement in education have fallen.

on numbers. They claim that by offering men extremely costly programs, such as football, colleges and universities have created the need to cut lesser sports.

Another important issue, unrecognized at the time of Title IX's adoption, is sexual harassment in education. The Supreme Court, following the development of the concept of sexual harassment in employment law, has held that entities violate Title IX when they know of teacher-to-student and student-to-student harassment and respond with deliberate indifference, and harassment deprives the student of equal educational opportunity. A 1993 survey by the American Association of University Women called *Hostile Hallways* found sexual harassment to be common in schools and saw little evidence that educational entities were doing anything to address it. A survey ten years later still found harassment to be common, but concluded that federally funded entities were much more likely to be aware of the issue and to have a sexual harassment policy.

Another subject of debate is whether Title IX's regulations allow sufficient flexibility for educators to establish single-sex classes and schools at the elementary and secondary levels. Title IX does permit such classes, but only

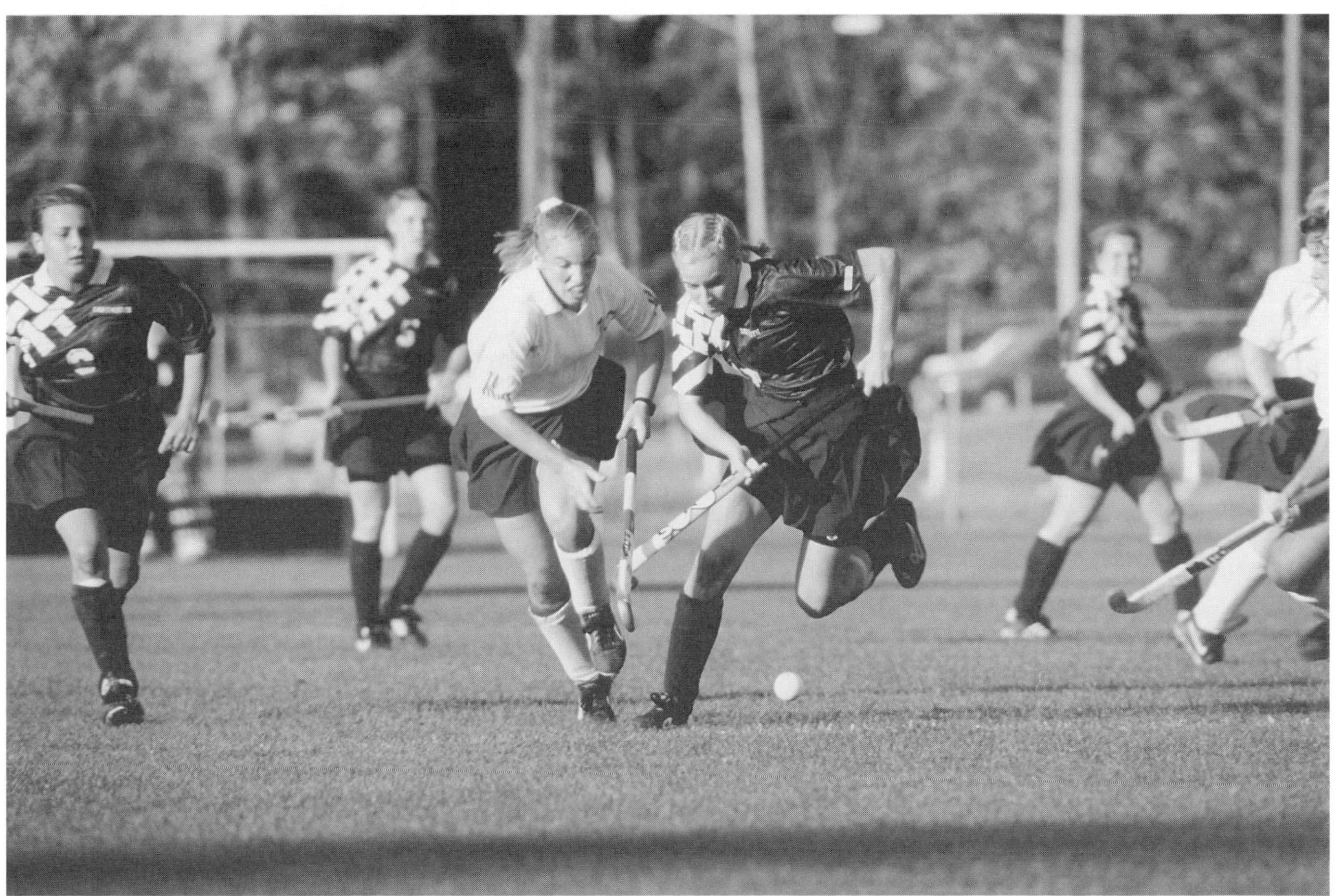

A women's field hockey match, Dartmouth College vs. University of Massachusetts, Amherst, October 1995. Athletics is one of the many educational programs and activities covered under Title IX. (©PHIL SCHERMEISTER/CORBIS)

when the classes are designed to remedy a sex-based disadvantage. Some argue this option should be made more freely available.

STATUS OF TITLE IX AND ITS IMPACT

To the modern student, the educational obstacles that faced females in 1972 may seem unbelievable. The degree of equity between the sexes in all aspects of federally funded educational programs is a testament to Title IX's success. Title IX's advocates believe there is much more to be done, as evidenced by the continued underrepresentation of women in science and technology, disparities between numbers of men and women receiving athletic scholarships, and the prevalence of sexual harassment in education. Others claim that Title IX is too restrictive and call for reform, particularly in the areas of athletic equity and single-sex education.

The degree of equity between the sexes in all aspects of federally funded educational programs is a testament to Title IX's success.

See also: Civil Rights Act of 1964; Equal Pay Act of 1963; Individuals with Disabilities Education Act.

BIBLIOGRAPHY

American Association of University Women. *Hostile Hallways: The AAUW Survey on Sexual Harassment in America's Schools.* Washington DC: American Association of University Women Educational Foundation, 1993.

American Association of University Women. *Hostile Hallways: Bullying, Teasing and Sexual Harassment in School.* Washington, DC: American Association of University Women Educational Foundation, 2001.

American Association of University Women. *A License for Bias, Sex Discrimination, Schools and Title IX.* Washington, DC: American Association of University Women Legal Advocacy Fund, 2000.

Spring, Joel. *The Sorting Machine: National Educational Policy Since 1945.* New York: David McKay, 1976.

Stein, Nan. *Classrooms and Courtrooms: Facing Sexual Harassment in K-12 Schools.* New York: Teacher's College Press, 1999.

United States Commission on Civil Rights. *Equal Opportunity Project Series,* Vol. 1. Washington, DC, 1996.

Yuracko, Kimberly, "One for You and One for Me: Is Title IX's Sex-Based Proportionality Requirement for College Varsity Athletic Positions Defensible?" *Northwestern University Law Review* 97 (2003).

INTERNET RESOURCES

American Association of University Women. <http://www.aauw.org>.

Office for Civil Rights. <http://www.ed.gov/offices/OCR>.

National Coalition for Women and Girls in Education. "Title IX at 30, Report Card on Gender Equity." <http://www.ncwge.org/title9at30-6-11.pdf>.

U.S. Department of Education. "Title IX, 25 Years of Progress."<http://www.ed.gov/pubs/TitleIX>.

U.S. Department of Education. "Open to All: Title IX at 30." <http://www.ed.gov.pubs/title9_report.pdf>.

Women's Educational Equity Act Resource Center. "Title IX and Education Policy." <http://www.edc.org/WomensEquity/resource/title9/index.htm>.

Toxic Substances Control Act (1976)

William V. Luneburg

Excerpt from the Toxic Substances Control Act

It is the policy of the United States that ... adequate authority should exist to regulate chemical substances and mixtures which present an unreasonable risk of injury to health or the environment, and to take action with respect to chemical substances and mixtures which are imminent hazards.

Prior to 1970, federal regulation of harmful chemical substances was not extensive. The Federal Insecticide, Fungicide and Rodenticide Act (FIFRA), for example, was limited in its health and environmental focus, and federal legislation that protected against environmental contamination and the health hazards caused thereby was similarly of modest ambition. However, with increasing evidence of an "environmental" crisis and of the risks posed by industrial pollution and exposure to modern chemicals, and with state governments unable or unwilling to aggressively come to grips with the perceived threats, Congress had no choice but to fill the regulatory vacuum. In quick succession, it passed the Clean Air Act (1970), the Clean Water Act (1972), and the Federal Environmental Pesticide Control Act (FEPCA, 1972), to name a few of the statutory responses.

Prior to 1970, federal regulation of harmful chemical substances was not extensive.

Characteristic of many of these regulatory schemes was 1) a concentration on one medium (for example, air or water) through which harmful contaminants might reach the environment, thereby leaving other media for harm to be regulated by other statutes or entirely unregulated; 2) a focus less on directly changing manufacturing processes and more on controlling the quantity and quality of waste streams produced; 3) to accept the installation of the best pollution control technology as adequate even if that technology did not eliminate adverse impacts on the environment; and finally, 4) to intervene at the point where environmental harm was already occurring. Two of the prominent gaps in regulatory coverage were illustrated by polychlorinated biphenyls (PCBs) found in river sediment that could contaminate fish, and chlorofluorocarbons (CFCs) used as spray-can propellants and refrigerants that were destroying the stratospheric ozone layer, which protects against harmful ultraviolet radiation.

While FEPCA focused on the pre-marketing review of chemicals to avoid unreasonable environmental effects before they could occur, it dealt with only a small part of the universe of chemicals, that is, those that were used as pesticides. And that universe is a large one indeed: at least five million chemicals are known, with 250,000 new chemical compounds produced each year, thousands of which enter the commercial marketplace over the space of a few years.

At least five million chemicals are known, with 250,000 new chemical compounds produced each year, thousands of which enter the commercial marketplace over the space of a few years.

PROVISIONS OF THE TOXIC SUBSTANCES CONTROL ACT

When it enacted the Toxic Substances Control Act (TSCA) (P.L. 94-469, 90 Stat. 2003) in 1976, Congress intended that the statute fill significant regulatory gaps that threatened not only public health but the natural environment. The TSCA could be utilized as the ideal pollution prevention statute. After all, review of a chemical or compound before it reaches the market and before it is used in manufacturing and elsewhere could, theoretically, insure that the health and environmental risks presented by it are both understood before harm can be inflicted and minimized throughout the lifecycle of the chemical as it is manufactured, used, and disposed of.

The touchstone of TSCA is its focus on identifying and eliminating "unreasonable risk[s] of injury to health or the environment." In other words, this is not a statute that demands a total elimination of all adverse effects. Rather, Congress intended that the U.S. Environmental Protection Agency (EPA), the agency responsible for TSCA implementation, balance the risks created by a chemical or compound against its potential benefits. For example, a particular chemical used in a manufacturing process might, if released into a river along with the rest of the manufacturer's waste stream, induce nausea in some swimmers ingesting the water even several miles downstream of the plant. But the chemical might also be the only one that could produce a particular type of drug proven effective in slowing the development of liver cancer. In these circumstances, TSCA might allow marketing of the chemical without significant restrictions on the basis that benefits of the chemical outweighed its costs.

RISK ASSESSMENT AND TSCA

Essential to the implementation of TSCA is what is called risk assessment. Such assessment poses a number of questions. Is there a scientific basis to conclude a particular substance causes or contributes to an adverse health effect (*e.g.,* cancer)? At what level of exposure to the substance will these effects occur? And what is the extent of actual exposure of humans to the substance? The endpoint of analysis is a description of the nature and magnitude of human risk, including an estimate of the uncertainty that accompanies that conclusion. Such an assessment is crucial not only to TSCA decision-making, but also to regulatory action under other important statutory schemes for the protection of public health and the environment.

In order to carry out its purposes in enacting TSCA, Congress required the manufacturer of a new chemical or an existing chemical proposed for a new use give the EPA ninety days notice of intent to produce the substance in order for the EPA to determine whether or not the substance will create an unreasonable risk of injury. The EPA compiles a list of existing chemicals; if not on the list, a substance is considered a new chemical.

In order to determine if a new chemical proposed for manufacture creates unreasonable risks or if such risks are presented by a chemical currently being manufactured and used, the EPA may order companies that manufacture or propose to manufacture the substance test it for the adverse effects which might be produced. If the EPA believes there is a "reasonable basis to conclude that the manufacture, processing, distribution in commerce, use, or disposal of a chemical substance or mixture...presents or will present an unreasonable risk of injury to health or the environment," the agency may impose one or more requirements that vary in stringency from outright banning of the manufacture and use, to simple public notification of the risks involved. The EPA is directed to apply the "least burdensome requirements" that are "necessary to protect adequately against" the risk.

For a variety of reasons, despite what appear to be the ambitious goals and ample regulatory authority of TSCA, it has never achieved its potential.

For a variety of reasons, despite what appear to be the ambitious goals and ample regulatory authority of the TSCA, it has never achieved its potential. For example, the EPA was sued and its action in regulating PCBs was overturned by a court on the basis that the agency did not regulate the chemicals stringently enough (*Environmental Defense Fund, Inc. v. EPA,* 1980). On the other hand, the agency's ban on the use of asbestos, the most **draconian** regulatory option available, was struck down for a variety of reasons, including inadequate and unreasonable cost/benefit analysis (*Corrosion Proof Fittings v. EPA,* 1991). Attempting to regulate thousands of chemicals and chemical compounds, which often present uncertain and difficult-to-identify risks, with neither too much nor too little stringency imposes huge costs on the EPA, whose resources for TSCA implementation have been limited. Given these circumstances, the relatively minor role the TSCA has filled to date in protecting public health and the environment should not come as a surprise, as disap-

draconian: severe, harsh

Three thousand or so drums of hazardous industrial waste stored near Ville Platte, Louisiana—certainly an environmental concern and potential hazard to human health. (US National Archives and Records Administration)

pointing as it may be to those who held high hopes for the statute when enacted.

See also: COMPREHENSIVE ENVIRONMENTAL RESPONSE, COMPENSATION, AND LIABILITY ACT; HAZARDOUS AND SOLID WASTE AMENDMENTS OF 1984.

BIBLIOGRAPHY

Breyer, Stephen G. *Breaking the Vicious Circle: Toward Effective Risk Regulation.* Cambridge, MA: Harvard University Press, 1993.

Lave, Lester B., and Arthur C. Upton, eds. *Toxic Chemicals, Health, and the Environment.* Baltimore, MD: Johns Hopkins University Press, 1987.

Ricci, Pacolo F., and Lawrence S. Molton. "Risk and Benefit in Environmental Law." *Science* 214 (1981): 1096–1100.

INTERNET RESOURCE

U.S. Environmental Protection Agency. <http://www.epa.gov/>.

TRADE ACT OF 1974

W. Eric McElwain

Excerpt from the Trade Act of 1974

If the United States Trade Representative determines ... that ... (B) an act, policy, or practice of a foreign country—(i) violates ... the provisions of, or otherwise denies benefits to the United States under, any trade agreement, or (ii) is unjustifiable and burdens or restricts United States commerce; the Trade Representative shall take action authorized in subsection (c) of this section subject to the specific direction, if any, of the President..., and shall take all other appropriate and feasible action ... that the President may direct the Trade Representative to take ... to obtain the elimination of such act, policy, or practice.

The Trade Act of 1974 (P.L. 93-618, 88 Stat. 1978) is the centerpiece of a series of acts passed by Congress with the intent of promoting worldwide reductions in economic barriers to trade, while at the same time protecting and promoting the interests of American-owned businesses. United States trade law is not contained in any one law but in a series of laws, from the Tariff Act of 1930 to the Agreement Establishing the World Trade Organization (WTO) in 1994. The Trade Act of 1974 gave the president authority to negotiate trade agreements with other countries, particularly with regard to multilateral trade negotiations under the General Agreement on Tariffs and Trade (GATT), which led to today's WTO. The act's primary importance, however, lies in Title II, Section 201, which gives the president

The Trade Act of 1974 is the centerpiece of a series of acts passed by Congress with the intent of promoting worldwide reductions in economic barriers to trade, while at the same time protecting and promoting the interests of American-owned businesses.

authority to take actions to protect U.S. businesses from injury caused by increased quantities of imports, even though the increase in imports violates no ban on unfair trade practices; and Title III, Section 301, which allows retaliatory measures to be taken against imports from countries that injure U.S. economic interests by using unfair trade practices. Other provisions governed trade relations with nonmarket-economy countries, a reference to countries that were then under communist rule, and created the general system of preferences, which allows the president to favor products from specific developing countries in order to aid their development and to discourage them from engaging in protective trade practices.

CONSTITUTIONAL BASIS FOR THE ACT

Article II of the U.S. Constitution has been interpreted to vest authority to conduct foreign policy in the president, but Article 8, Section 1 gives Congress the power to lay and collect duties and the power to regulate foreign commerce. Therefore the power to regulate trade with other nations must be delegated by Congress to the president. While the Trade Act of 1974 granted the president authority to engage in trade negotiations, Congress limited the president's authority by requiring a determination that any agreement will not endanger national security and will promote the purposes of the act.

POLITICAL BACKGROUND OF THE ACT

The Trade Act of 1974 was a response to changes that had occurred in the international economic framework under which U.S. trade laws had been created. **Tariffs** had lessened as a barrier to trade, but there had been growth in the use by other nations of nontariff trade barriers, such as special subsidies to protect local industries by allowing goods to be sold abroad at lower cost. Also, developing countries had become a major force in international markets, and a need was perceived for a legal response to such actions as the oil embargo imposed by the OPEC nations in 1973. Dissatisfied with the time-consuming procedures for resolving disputes under the GATT, Congress wanted the president to use executive power more proactively to influence trade practices and policy worldwide. Congress deliberated on a new trade bill for twenty months before the Trade Act was ultimately passed on December 20, 1974. The act delegated significant power to the president to invoke measures to protect American industries from increased imports from other nations, whether or not injury was being caused by unfair trade practices.

tariff: a tax imposed on goods when imported into a country

The Trade Act of 1974 was a response to changes that had occurred in the international economic framework under which U.S. trade laws had been created.

SUBSTANCE OF THE ACT

Section 201, known as the "Escape Clause," creates a mechanism for the president to grant relief measures to industries, workers, firms, and communities injured by increased imports from foreign industries producing competing products. Any industry can ask the U.S. International Trade Commission (ITC) to recommend that measures be taken to protect it from competing imports, even though those goods are being imported legally. If the ITC recommends invoking the Section 201 Escape Clause to protect the affected industry, the president may deny the request only on grounds of the "national economic interest" (Trade

protectionist: advocating the use of tariffs to protect domestic industries from foreign competition

Act, Section 202[a][1][A]). Because of the **protectionist** nature of Section 201, only a handful of requests for action have resulted in protective measures being imposed by the president. Since the "escape clause" does not require a finding of any unfair trade practices by the exporting nation, that nation can then freely retaliate against measures imposed by the United States. Therefore, it is often not in the "national economic interest" to pursue such measures.

Section 301 expanded presidential authority to retaliate against trade practices by other nations that unfairly burden or restrict U.S. commerce, whether through high tariffs or through nontariff trade barriers. The president may suspend trade concessions, impose new higher tariff rates on a selective basis, or take other retaliatory actions. Such actions include the imposition of antidumping duties (special assessments against imports sold in the United States at less than fair value, thereby harming a U.S. industry); countervailing duties, which are assessments against imported goods receiving subsidies from their governments so that they can be sold in the U.S. at an unfairly low price, thereby injuring a U.S. industry; and cease and desist orders (demanding that the unfair practice be stopped) or exclusion orders (that bar a product from being imported into the United States), which can be imposed directly by the International Trade Commission, subject to presidential veto.

Primarily because of Section 301, the Trade Act has been used more to open foreign markets to U.S. exports and investments than to protect American industries from unfair competition.

United States Trade Representative (USTR): a cabinet-level official appointed by the president who has primary responsibility for directing U.S. trade policy and trade negotiations

Section 301 was strengthened in the Trade Agreements Act of 1979 by the imposition of time limits for investigation by the **United States Trade Representative (USTR)** of complaints filed by private parties and for action by the president on such complaints. The Omnibus Trade and Competitiveness Act of 1988 transferred decision making power from the president to the USTR, and it made retaliatory action mandatory whenever illegal trade practices were identified. It also created the so-called "Super 301" procedure, which requires the USTR to undertake actions against certain countries deemed to be blocking access to imports of critical American goods (for example, Japanese restrictions that existed on American supercomputers and space satellites).

IMPACT OF THE ACT

unilateral: undertaken by one person, party, or entity

multilateral: undertaken by multiple persons, parties, or entities, in conjunction with one another

Primarily because of Section 301, the Trade Act has been used more to open foreign markets to U.S. exports and investments than to protect American industries from unfair competition. Section 301 is a **unilateral** provision in U.S. law that can be invoked irrespective of any remedies available under the **multilateral** GATT or WTO. Although the United States has generally upheld its treaty obligations under the GATT, Section 301 actions or threats of action, despite at times creating resentment from U.S. trading partners, have been highly effective tools in negotiating trade concessions.

See also: North American Free Trade Agreement Implementation Act; Smoot-Hawley Tariff Act; Tariff Act of 1789.

BIBLIOGRAPHY

Barton, John H., and Bart S. Fisher. *International Trade and Investment: Regulating International Business.* Boston, MA: Little Brown, 1986.

Folsom, Ralph H.; Michael Wallace Gordon; and John A. Spanogle. *International Trade and Investment in a Nutshell,* 2d ed. St. Paul, MN: West Group, 2000.

Low, Patrick. *Trading Free: The GATT and U.S. Trade Policy*. New York: Twentieth Century Fund Press, 1993.

Nanda, Ved. P. *The Law of Transnational Business Transactions*. Deerfield, IL: Clark Boardman, 2002.

Trading with the Enemy Act (1917)

Michael P. Malloy

Excerpt from the Trading with the Enemy Act

During the time of war [or during any other period of national emergency declared by the President,] the President may...

(B) investigate, regulate, direct and compel, nullify, void, prevent or prohibit, any acquisition, holding, withholding, use, transfer, withdrawal, transportation, importation or exportation of, or dealing in, or exercising any right, power, or privilege with respect to, or transactions involving, any property in which any foreign country or a national thereof has any interest by any person, or with respect to any property, subject to the jurisdiction of the United States.

The Trading with the Enemy Act (TWEA) (1917, ch. 106, 40 Stat. 411), which authorized the use of economic sanctions against foreign nations, citizens and nationals of foreign countries, or other persons aiding a foreign country, is the oldest such statute still in use by the United States. Most U.S. sanctions programs (like those against Iran, Libya, terrorists, and, before the 2003 war, Iraq) contain the same basic features. Although authorized by more recent statutes, these programs follow an approach to sanctions that has been in use under the TWEA from 1917 to 1975. The constitutionality of the TWEA, based on the foreign affairs powers of the United States, has been consistently recognized by the courts in such cases as *Propper v. Clark* (1949), *Zittman v. McGrath* (1951), and *Freedom to Travel Campaign v. Newcomb* (1996). Because it is important that the foreign affairs of the nation be conducted in a consistent and coherent manner, the courts have tended to give great respect to the president's judgment and discretion. As a result, presidential actions taken under TWEA are rarely challenged successfully in litigation.

The key provision of the TWEA is section 5(b), which delegates to the president powers of economic warfare during a time of war or any other period of national emergency. Since 1977, when the International Emergency Economic Powers Act was enacted, the use of section 5(b) has been limited to periods of declared war. The exception is programs, such as the U.S. trade and financial embargo against Cuba, that were in existence before the 1977 change in section 5(b).

Because it is important that the foreign affairs of the nation be conducted in a consistent and coherent manner, the courts have tended to give great respect to the president's judgment and discretion.

TWEA IN U.S. HISTORY

Congress enacted the TWEA in anticipation of U.S. involvement in World War I. The original act was intended to grant the president broad discretion and authority to regulate foreign currency transactions, transactions in gold or silver, and transfers of credit or evidences of indebtedness or property during a time of war "between the United States and any foreign country, whether enemy, ally of enemy or otherwise, or between residents of one or more foreign countries." In creating the TWEA Congress sought to establish a set of restraints on international commerce, based on traditional **common law** and international legal principles that made commerce with declared enemy states and their nationals illegal. During the two world wars, the TWEA was used against states that were declared enemies of the United States. From 1933 to 1977, it was also used in situations not involving declared war (like the Korean conflict of 1950 to 1953) against states pursuing policies considered hostile to U.S. interests.

common law: a system of laws developed in England—and later applied in the U.S.—based on judicial precedent rather than statutory laws passed by a legislative body

In March 1933 Congress amended the TWEA with virtually no debate to apply not only during periods of declared war but also "during any other period of national emergency declared by the President." Over time, the active involvement of the United States in World War II and a series of international crises (primarily those resulting from the Cold War between the United States and the Soviet Union during the second half of the twentieth century) broadened the perceived purpose of the TWEA. The act came to be seen as an overall weapon of economic warfare, whether or not the United States was formally at war.

On April 10, 1940, twenty months before U.S. entry into World War II, President Franklin D. Roosevelt used section 5(b) to impose prohibitions on transfers of property in which Norway or Denmark or any citizen or national of those countries or any other person aiding those countries had any interest, unless the transactions were licensed by the Department of the Treasury. The president took this step in response to the invasion of the two countries by Nazi Germany. He hoped to prevent extortion of property subject to U.S. jurisdiction from its rightful owners in the occupied countries. The president repeatedly expanded the April 1940 Executive Order to cover other countries occupied by the Axis powers of Germany, Italy, and Japan, and eventually to cover the Axis powers themselves.

This broader purpose of "economic warfare" was carried over into the World War II sanctions program. It was also the basic purpose of the post-World War II sanctions programs enforced principally by the Treasury and Commerce Departments. For example, President Harry S Truman declared a state of national emergency on December 16, 1950, invoking the TWEA as the legal basis for imposing financial and trade restrictions against the People's Republic of China and North Korea during the Korean conflict. Truman's declaration was the legal basis for the postwar TWEA controls that remain in effect to this day.

MAJOR AMENDMENT

A major legislative change occurred in 1977 with the return of TWEA to its status as a legal authority to be used only in wartime.

A major legislative change occurred in 1977 with the return of the TWEA to its status as a legal authority to be used only in wartime. Congress was concerned that presidents had invoked "national emergency" powers too easily from 1933 through the 1970s. Despite these congressional concerns, however, the existing uses of the TWEA were continued until September 14, 1978. Under the amended statute, these uses could be extended for successive one-year periods by presidential determination and in fact have been routinely extended on a yearly basis. As a result, two "national emergency" sanctions programs continue to operate under the TWEA: (1) the Treasury Department's Foreign Assets Control Regulations, originally established in 1950, which imposed full economic sanctions on North Korea and nationals thereof until June 2000 and continues to impose significant, though selective, sanctions against North Korea; and (2) the Treasury Department's Cuban Assets Control Regulations, originally established in July 1963, which continues to impose full economic sanctions on Cuba and its nationals.

EFFECTIVENESS

Despite the continuing use of the TWEA and other, later statutes as the legal basis for economic sanctions, legislators and other policy makers, as well as scholars, have frequently questioned whether economic sanctions are effective in achieving their various goals. For example, despite the Cuban sanctions, the Communist regime of Fidel Castro remains in power. On the other hand, unilateral U.S. sanctions imposed on Iran during the hostage crisis of 1979–1981 appear to have been significant in obtaining the release of U.S. embassy personnel held hostage in Teheran by the Islamic Republic of Iran. Likewise, in the early 1990s internationally supported U.S. sanctions against Iraq significantly contributed to ending Iraq's occupation of Kuwait and containing the threat that Iraq posed to its other neighbors at that time.

Each sanctions episode tends to exhibit unique features, making it difficult to reach hard and fast conclusions about the effectiveness of sanctions as a general rule. As a result, the national and international debate over the effectiveness of sanctions will undoubtedly continue.

See also: United Nations Participation Act.

BIBLIOGRAPHY

Carter, Barry E. *International Economic Sanctions.* Cambridge, U.K.: Cambridge University Press, 1988.

Hufbauer, Gary C., and Jeffrey J. Schott. *Economic Sanctions Reconsidered.* Washington, DC: Institute for International Economics, 1985.

Malloy, Michael P. *United States Economic Sanctions: Theory and Practice.* The Hague, Netherlands: Kluwer Law International, 2001.

U.S. Senate Special Committee on the Termination of the National Emergency. *Emergency Powers Statutes: Provisions of Federal Law Now in Effect Delegating to the Executive Extraordinary Authority in Time of National Emergency.* 93d Cong., 1st Sess. 1-6 (Comm. Print 1973).

Truth in Lending Act (1969)

Richard Slottee

The Truth in Lending Act (TILA) (P.L. 90-321, 82 Stat.146) is a federal statute which Congress enacted in 1969 and amended and expanded on numerous occasions after that date. In adopting TILA, the legislature declared:

> The Congress finds that economic stabilization would be enhanced and the competition among the various financial institutions and other firms engaged in the extension of consumer credit would be strengthened by the informed use of credit. The informed use of credit results from the awareness of the cost thereof by consumers. It is the purpose of this subchapter to assure the meaningful disclosure of credit terms so that the consumer will be able to compare more readily the various credit terms available to him and avoid the uninformed use of credit, and to protect the consumer against inaccurate and unfair credit billing and credit card practices.

TILA generally applies to creditors who regularly extend consumer credit that is primarily used for personal, family, or household purposes. The lender must extend the credit to a natural person, and the loan must be repayable with either a finance charge or by written agreement in more than four installments. TILA does not apply to (1) credit transactions in which the total amount financed exceeds $25,000 and which are not secured by real property or personal property used as a dwelling, or (2) loans made pursuant to a student loan program under the Higher Education Act of 1965. To effectuate TILA's goals and policies, the Federal Reserve Board promulgated "Regulation Z," which is found in the Code of Federal Regulation. Contained in the appendices to Regulation Z are a number of model forms for use in lending contracts, and creditors who properly use the forms are deemed to be in compliance with TILA. The United States Supreme Court has held both TILA and Regulation Z constitutional (*Mourning v. Family Publications Service, Inc.,* [1973]).

Congress' primary purpose in adopting TILA was to provide disclosure of credit terms to consumers, and consequently it devoted much of the act to financial disclosure issues. It requires sellers and lenders to inform consumers of terms in a manner that clarifies their meaning and promotes understanding. This enables consumers to easily compare compare the credit terms of various sellers and lenders, which in turn enables them to shop for a contract that most suits their needs.

In addition to credit term disclosure requirements, TILA and Regulation Z also contain provisions governing credit card issuance, **liability** for unauthorized credit card use, credit card billing error resolution procedures, **notice and disclosure requirements** for credit card solicitations, disclosure requirements for high-rate mortgages and reverse mortgages, and **rescission provisions** for various types of transactions in which a security interest is retained in a consumer's principal residence.

liability: an obligation, responsibility, or duty that one is bound by law to perform

notice and disclosure requirements: in contracts and other transactions, the law requires that key provisions and penalties be disclosed in plain English so a consumer can make an informed decision

rescission provisions: provisions in a contract which, if they occur or fail to occur, allow the contract to be rescinded

THE DEFINITION OF "CREDITOR"

TILA applies only to "creditors," a term defined to include natural persons, business organizations, estates, trusts, and governmental units who *regularly extend* consumer credit and to whom the obligation is initially payable on its face. A person regularly extends consumer credit and so is subject to TILA only if the person extended credit more than twenty-five times in the calendar year immediately preceding the transaction that was subject to TILA and was not secured by the consumer's principal dwelling (*unsecured credit*). A person may also become a creditor by extending consumer credit secured by the consumer's principal dwelling (*secured credit*) more than five times in the preceding calendar year. Persons who satisfy either standard are creditors, for both types of transactions. Once a person becomes a creditor in a calendar year, that person is a creditor for all credit transactions in the next calendar year, regardless of the number of transactions that take place. But for the subsequent year, the counting test again comes into play, and a person will not be a creditor until the requisite number of transactions takes place.

Finally, the legislation and accompanying regulations consider the person to whom the obligation is initially payable a creditor subject to TILA. If the creditor assigns the contract to another person, however, that person (called the *assignee*) is subject to liability for violations of the act if the assignment was voluntary and if the violations are apparent on the face of the instrument assigned. A violation is considered "apparent" if it involves a disclosure which can be determined to be incomplete or inaccurate from the face of the disclosure statement or other documents, or a disclosure which does not use the terms required by the act.

Reverse Mortgages

A reverse mortgage is a type of loan used by older homeowners to tap the equity they have in their homes. Borrowers can receive three types of payments: a lump sum, a line of credit to be used as need arises, or a monthly payment for a fixed amount of time or as long as the homeowner lives. The borrower continues to hold the title to the home, and the loan does not have to be repaid until he or she moves out or dies—in the latter case, the borrower's heirs usually sell or refinance the home to pay off the debt. There are only two requirements for eligibility: the borrower must own his or her own home and be at least sixty-two years old. There are no restrictions on how the payments may be used.

DISCLOSURE REQUIREMENT

Regarding the disclosure provisions, the TILA applies to both open-end and closed-end extensions of credit. Open-end credit is typified by the conventional credit card plan, and all other types of consumer credit are closed-end transactions. For open-end credit transactions TILA's disclosure requirements include:

(1) general disclosure requirements;
(2) credit and charge card applications and solicitations;
(3) home equity plans;
(4) initial disclosure statements for charge cards; and
(5) periodic billing statements for credit cards.

For purposes of closed-end transactions required disclosures include:

(1) the name of the creditor;
(2) the amount financed;
(3) the payment schedule;
(4) the total of payments;
(5) the total sale price; and
(6) the existence of any security interest.

The two most important disclosures are the finance charge and the annual percentage rate. The finance charge is the term used to reflect the cost of credit as a dollar amount and includes any charge, such as interest, imposed by the creditor as a condition of the extension of credit. The annual percentage rate is the term used to reflect the finance charge as a percentage of the total annual payments made on the debt. Both terms have to be disclosed more conspicuously than any other terms. Sellers and lenders in closed-end transactions must disclose information clearly, conspicuously and in writing and must provide a copy to the consumer. The disclosures must be grouped together, segregated from everything else, and must contain only information directly related to the required disclosures. This requirement has resulted in use of what is commonly called the "Federal Box," a place on the document where all TILA disclosures are grouped together, separating them from all other information.

LEGAL DISPUTES UNDER TILA

TILA prohibits a card issuer from issuing unsolicited credit cards to either businesses or consumers. It also allows a consumer to assert against the card issuer any claims or defenses that the consumer has against a seller, provided the dispute involved a sale of more than fifty dollars and occurred either in the same state as the consumer's residence address or within 100 miles of the address. Finally, consumers may dispute any errors which appear on a credit card statement, and TILA requires the card issuer to promptly investigate the dispute and correct any errors.

If a creditor takes a security interest in the consumer's principal dwelling as part of a transaction, TILA allows the consumer three business days to rescind, or cancel, the transaction. The creditor must provide the consumer with a notice of this rescission right when the contract is consummated, and cannot loan any money or provide any services until the expiration of the three business days. If the creditor fails to make the appropriate disclosure of the rescission right or certain other material disclosures, the right of rescission continues until three years after the contract is signed, the transfer of all of the consumer's interest in the property, or the sale of the property, whichever occurs first.

A violation of TILA renders the creditor liable for actual damages, and statutory damages of twice the amount of the finance charge, with a minimum recovery of $100 and a maximum recovery of $1,000. If the violation involves a transaction with a security interest in the consumer's principal dwelling, the creditor may be liable for minimum damages of $200 and maximum damages of $2,000.

A creditor may avoid TILA liability for a violation if within sixty days of discovery of the disclosure error, and prior to the litigation or receipt of written notice of the error, the creditor notifies the consumer of the error and makes the necessary adjustments to ensure that the consumer will not pay a charge in excess of the annual percentage rate actually disclosed. A creditor may also avoid liability if it shows by a preponderance of evidence that the violation was not intentional and resulted from a bona fide error notwithstanding the maintenance of procedures reasonably adapted to avoid the error. Examples of a bona fide error include clerical, calculation, computer malfunction and printing errors. An error in legal judgment in regard to the, requirements of TILA is not a bona fide error, even if made in good faith.

A consumer may file an action under the TILA in any United States District Court, regardless of the amount in controversy, or in any state court of competent jurisdiction. In an affirmative action for damages, the litigation must commence within one year of the date of the violation, and because disclosures must be made at the time the parties consummate the transaction, the date of the violation is the date of the transaction.

BIBLIOGRAPHY

Clontz, Ralph, Jr. *Truth-in-Lending Manual,* 6th ed. 1995.

Fonesca, J. *Consumer Credit Compliance Manual,* 2nd ed. 1984.

U

United Nations Participation Act (1945)

Michael P. Malloy

The United Nations Participation Act (UNPA) (59 Stat. 619) provides the basic authority for U.S. participation as a member of the United Nations Organization. In particular, it is the authority for the president to apply economic and other sanctions against a target country or its nationals pursuant to mandatory decisions by the United Nations Security Council under Article 41 of the United Nations Charter. Until recently, this statutory authority was rarely invoked, but in current practice it has become a significant basis for U.S. economic sanctions.

The United Nations Participation Act is the authority for the president to apply economic and other sanctions against a target country or its nationals pursuant to mandatory decisions by the United Nations Security Council under Article 41 of the United Nations Charter.

The UNPA emerged from Congress with considerable optimism and with relative swiftness. According to the House report accompanying the bill, it was intended to "prescribe the domestic, internal arrangements within [the U.S.] Government for giving effect to [U.S.] participation in [the United Nations] and [to] set up the machinery whereby [U.S.] national authorities can comply with certain of the major international commitments" assumed by the United States upon its ratification of the U.N. Charter. These commitments included the requirement that U.N. members comply in good faith with any Security Council decision under Article 41 to apply specified measures short of the use of armed force to implement Security Council decisions.

Such measures might include a complete or partial interruption of economic relations with a target country, prohibition of communication, or severance of diplomatic relations. Section 5 of the UNPA created domestic authority to comply with this obligation, authorizing the president, to the extent necessary, to apply measures decided upon by the U.N. Security Council pursuant to Article 41 to "investigate, regulate, or prohibit, in whole or in part, economic relations or rail, sea, air, postal, telegraphic, radio, and other means of communication between any foreign country or any national thereof or any person therein and the United States or any person subject to the jurisdiction thereof, or involving any property subject to the jurisdiction of the United States."

At least in terms of its potential effect on economic relations, this authority is quite broad. It is comparable to the statutory authority extended to the president for economic sanctions in such enactments as Section 5(b) of the Trading With the Enemy Act (TWEA, 1917) and its nonwartime successor, 1977's International Emergency Economic Powers Act (IEEPA). One obvious difference, however, is that presidential discretion to shape a program of sanctions under the UNPA is guided by the mandatory call for specified sanctions in the triggering Security Council resolution, rather than by specific statutory conditions contained in the TWEA and IEEPA.

Presidential discretion to shape a program of sanctions under the UNPA is guided by the mandatory call for specified sanctions in the triggering Security Council resolution, rather than by specific statutory conditions contained in the TWEA and IEEPA.

The UNPA's broad authorization permitting presidential prohibition of international communications arguably would raise constitutional concerns under the freedom of speech provision of the First Amendment if the UNPA were a purely domestic legislative provision. Nevertheless, case law suggests that the UNPA authorization is reinforced by the international obligations of the United States as a U.N. member to comply with a Security Council mandate for such prohibitions on communications with a target country. The legislative history surrounding the enactment of the act in 1945 appears to argue that such authority is constitutionally permissible. This is reinforced by such Supreme Court cases as *Missouri v. Holland* (1920), holding that a treaty obligation may empower the federal government to regulate in an area otherwise beyond its domestic power under the Constitution.

Section 5 also provides for penalties for willful violations, evasions, or attempts to violate or evade any order, rule, or regulation issued by the president pursuant to the section. These are criminal sanctions, providing for a fine of not more than $10,000 or for natural persons, imprisonment of not more than ten years, or both. Knowing participation by an officer, director, or agent of a corporation in such a violation carries the same penalties. The Section also provides for forfeiture of property concerned in any such violation. According to the Federal District Court in *United States v. Eight Rhodesian Stone Statues* (1978), due process protections (such as written notice of forfeiture and an opportunity to file a petition for return of forfeited property) apply to such forfeiture proceedings.

In 1971 the Strategic and Critical Materials Stockpiling Act of 1939 was amended to authorize the importation of Rhodesian chrome ore, ferrochrome, and nickel, despite a U.N. embargo against Southern Rhodesia. These products were important economic resources of the illegal regime in Southern Rhodesia, and so prohibiting trade in these products placed significant pressure on the regime. However, access to these products was of strategic importance to U.S. national security. The amendment placed the United States in noncompliance with its obligations under the U.N. Charter, resulting in a conflict between U.S. foreign policy with respect to compliance with U.N. obligations and U.S. national security policy. Repeated efforts in Congress to repeal the amendment and to reimpose a total U.S. embargo on imports of Rhodesian origin were unsuccessful until 1977. The UNPA's Section 5 itself was amended in 1977 to authorize the president to reinstitute the embargo on imports of chrome ore, ferrochrome, nickel, and other materials from Southern Rhodesia. The 1977 amendment also established a certi-

President Harry Truman signs a document ratifying the United Nations Charter, with Secretary of State James F. Byrnes by his side. The United Nations Participation Act gives the president authority to impose sanctions on a country as mandated by the U.N. Security Council, pursuant to Article 41 of the U.N. Charter. (©CORBIS)

fication procedure to prevent indirect importation of Rhodesian chrome through the importation of third-country specialty steel products. With the eventual resolution of the Rhodesian situation (and the emergence of the new state of Zimbabwe) in December 1979, the president revoked the Rhodesian sanctions.

After the Rhodesian sanctions, U.S. government interest in the UNPA as a statutory source of economic sanctions authority was in decline until 1990, with administrative attention shifting decisively to the unilateral authority of the IEEPA. With the withering away of the Soviet Union and the emergence of a more cooperative relationship between Washington and Moscow, the stage was set for a resurgence of U.S. government interest in the mandatory authority of the Security Council under Article 41. In more recent years, the UNPA has been invoked regularly to implement Security Council resolutions under Article 41, for example, in response to the Iraqi invasion of Kuwait in 1990 (terminated in 2003); to ban overflight, takeoff, and landing of aircraft flying to or from Libya; to impose sanctions against the Federal Republic of Yugoslavia (since suspended); to impose sanctions against Haiti (terminated); to implement a 1993 arms embargo against Angola and the insurgent group, the National Union for the Total Independence of Angola (known by its acronym, "UNITA") (terminated); a 1994 arms embargo against Rwanda; and to impose a broad range of sanctions against terrorist organizations and states supporting or facilitating terrorism after the attacks on the United States in September 2001.

See also: FOREIGN SERVICE ACT OF 1946; TRADING WITH THE ENEMY ACT

BIBLIOGRAPHY

Carter, Barry E. *International Economic Sanctions.* Cambridge, UK: Cambridge University Press, 1988.

Hufbauer, Gary C., and Schott, Jeffrey J. *Economic Sanctions Reconsidered.* Washington, DC: Institute for International Economics, 1985.

Malloy, Michael P. *United States Economic Sanctions: Theory and Practice.* The Hague, Netherlands: Kluwer Law International, 2001.

UNITED STATES HOUSING ACT OF 1937

Charles E. Daye

Excerpt from the United States Housing Act of 1937

It is the policy of the United States (1) to promote the general welfare of the Nation by employing the funds and credit of the Nation...(A) to assist States and political subdivisions of States to remedy the unsafe housing conditions and the acute shortage of decent and safe dwellings for low-income families; [and] (B) to assist States and political subdivisions of States to address the shortage of housing affordable to low-income families....

The United States Housing Act of 1937 (P.L. 75-412, 50 Stat. 888) created the public housing program. The act is also known as the Wagner-Steagall Housing Act (after Representative Henry B. Steagall, Democrat of Alabama, and Senate Robert F. Wagner, Democrat of New York) and the Low-Rent Housing Act. Under the program, the federal government, through the Department of Housing and Urban Development (HUD), provides subsidies to local public housing agencies (PHAs) that rent housing to low-income families.

The financial structure of the program rests on three subsidies: (1) one subsidy covers the cost to build the units, (2) another subsidy goes to investors who buy federally guaranteed bonds that the PHAs issue to raise money to build the units (but the investors do not pay taxes on the interest the bonds pay them), (3) a subsidy added in 1969 pays some of the PHAs' operating expenses.

PHAs are independent entities with limited accountability to local governments. However, local governments determine where public housing may be located. In addition, local governments charge for certain services such as water and sewers. Instead of collecting taxes to pay for police and fire protection, local governments charge the PHAs 10 percent of their rental collections for those services. The low-income tenants who live in the public housing pay rent equal to just 30 percent of their income. At the start of the twenty-first century, over three million residents lived in roughly 1.3 million units of public housing throughout the nation.

At the start of the twenty-first century, over three million residents live in roughly 1.3 million units of public housing throughout the nation.

PROPONENTS AND OPPONENTS OF THE ACT

The public housing program has always been controversial. The act, based on Congress' power, under Article I, section 8 of the United States Constitution, to provide for the general welfare, was a late part of President Franklin Roosevelt's Depression-era legislation. Proponents included social reformers who wanted to remedy "unsafe and insanitary" housing for poor people. Some argued that bad housing contributed to other problems, including poor health, political corruption, crime, and even immorality. Others argued that housing assistance should be provided to the "submerged middle class" that was temporarily out of work because of the Depression. Labor unions and political leaders supported housing subsidies as aids to recovery from the Depression because building housing would create jobs and stimulate the construction industry.

Opponents objected that providing housing subsidies was inappropriate for the federal government on three grounds. They believed subsidies would 1) undermine the private housing market, 2) diminish homeownership incentives, and 3) be a form of **socialism.** Opponents included chambers of commerce, business organizations, and real estate interests, such as associations of home builders. To meet opponents' objections, President Roosevelt accepted the limitation that only the "poorest and lowliest people" would qualify to live in public housing. This provision would ensure that a government program would neither interfere with the **private sector** nor diminish personal incentives for those the private sector could serve.

socialism: any of various economic and political theories advocating collective or governmental ownership and administration of the means of production and distribution of goods

private sector: the part of the economy that is not controlled by the government

Under the act, assistance would go through the states to local entities that would provide and operate the subsidized housing. The policy assured that local government would share in the responsibility and public housing would not be forced upon communities that did not want it.

EXPERIENCE UNDER THE ACT

Whether public housing has been partly successful or mostly a failure depends on the individual observer's perspective. The federal law enables many low-income families to gain access to housing that may otherwise be unavailable. Yet serious financial, social, and safety problems have plagued the low-income housing program.

Whether public housing has been partly successful or mostly a failure depends on the individual observer's perspective.

Problems Created by Restricted Rents The original concept of the act was for federal subsidies that would cover the costs to build the housing, and rent from tenants would cover the PHAs' operating costs. Although some tenants paid rents that required a large share of their income, the PHAs sometimes suffered from deficits because restricted rent payments did not cover operating costs. In 1969 Congress enacted the Brooke Amendments, named for Senator Edward Brooke, a Republican from Massachusetts and the third African American elected to the U.S. Senate since the reconstruction period of the 1870s. Brooke sponsored an amendment limiting the rent that tenants could be charged to 25 percent of their income (later raised to 30 percent during

President Ronald Reagan's term in 1980). Another Brooke amendment authorized operating subsidies to cover the PHAs' deficits. Congress never appropriated sufficient funds to cover all deficits, and HUD, which had opposed operating subsidies, did not use all the funds that Congress provided.

The Problem of Changing Tenant Demographics By 1937 the Depression had thrown masses of people out of work. Many in government assumed that when prosperity and jobs returned, tenants would move out of public housing. Some "wealthier" tenants did in fact leave public housing as the economy improved, but they were replaced by tenants with dim economic prospects. The people in this new demographic were poorer and not just temporarily out of work: they were welfare recipients, elderly persons, the chronically unem-

The shacks in this photograph (Atlanta, Georgia, c. 1940) would be replaced by Capitol Homes, a public housing project completed under the public housing program of the United States Housing Act of 1937. Capitol Homes, a 694-unit apartment complex one block from the State Capitol building, was redeveloped under the Department of Housing and Urban Development's Hope VI program in the early years of the twenty-first century. (FRANKLIN D. ROOSEVELT LIBRARY)

ployed, people with disabilities, female-headed households, and families with multiple economic and social needs. Moreover, public housing developments started out and stayed racially segregated. White tenants left at a faster rate than did black tenants. In many metropolitan areas, the view of public housing was that only very poor members of racial minorities lived in it.

Policy Problems. Some policies adopted by Congress or imposed by HUD added to public housing's problems. Building sites were chosen that reinforced racial and economic segregation. Some sites were unsuitable environmentally or were in undesirable locations. Local zoning caused "over-concentration" of public housing in distinct parts of municipalities. Construction was sometimes shoddy because of scandalous mismanagement and lack of HUD oversight. The buildings were frequently high rises located in high-density developments that proved to be unsuitable for families with young children. As a result of these powerful social, economic, and political forces, many associated public housing with problems in older, deteriorating urban centers of our nation.

ATTEMPTS TO IMPROVE PUBLIC HOUSING

Congress has enacted many amendments to try to solve some of public housing problems. One program, called HOPE VI, derived from a related series of programs under the name "Homeownership and Opportunity for People Everywhere," was enacted in 1992. HOPE VI funds may be used to offer homeownership opportunities, demolish deteriorated units, and rebuild low-density developments. The HOPE VI program is funded by a process in which PHAs apply to and compete for funding from HUD. At the beginning of the twenty-first century, the success of HOPE VI programs was not yet clear.

Drugs and crime in public housing present a difficult and controversial problem. Many tenants support stringent measures to rid public housing of drugs and crime. Congress enacted the Anti-Drug Abuse Act to provide for evictions of entire families if any family member is involved with drugs or crime, even when the other family members are innocent. These evictions are known as "one-strike" (one strike and you're out) and "no fault." The U.S. Supreme Court upheld the provisions in 2002. **Civil libertarians** objected that tenants in public housing were being denied basic civil liberties that included privacy, due process, and fairness.

civil libertarian: one who is actively concerned with the protection of the fundamental freedoms guaranteed to the individual by the Bill of Rights

INTERACTION WITH OTHER LAWS

The act is the precursor of all subsequent housing legislation. Indeed, many housing programs are named for the section number of the Housing Act of 1937 in which they were placed (for example, the Section 8 program).

The act is the precursor of all subsequent housing legislation.

- The Housing Act of 1949 announced a goal of a "decent home and suitable living environment for every American family" and funded "slum clearance" activities.
- The Housing Act of 1954 enacted the urban renewal program.
- The Department of Housing and Urban Development Act of 1965 created HUD to consolidate federal agencies that dealt with urban housing, including, the Public Housing Administration, the Federal Housing Administration, and Federal National Mortgage Association (popularly

know as Fannie Mae), which operates extensive insurance and mortgage-buying operations from banks and selected other lenders.

- The Housing Act of 1965 created a rent supplement program for use in privately owned housing.
- The Housing and Urban Development Act of 1968 enacted a series of assisted programs for private housing that continued the shift to using federal subsidies for privately owned housing and away from publicly owned housing.
- The Housing and Community Development Act of 1974 consolidated community development programs into **block grants** and created the Section 8 housing assistance program.
- The Civil Rights Act of 1964 prohibited certain forms of racial discrimination in federally assisted programs.
- The Civil Rights Act of 1968 enacted the Fair Housing Act, which prohibits racial discrimination, with a 1974 amendment prohibiting sex discrimination, and a 1988 amendment prohibiting discrimination against families with children or handicapped persons.

block grant: an unrestricted grant of federal money to state and local governments to support social welfare programs

See also: HOUSING AND URBAN DEVELOPMENT ACT OF 1965; NATIONAL HOUSING ACT.

BIBLIOGRAPHY

Bratt, Rachel G. *Rebuilding a Low-Income Housing Policy.* Philadelphia: Temple University Press, 1989.

Freedman, Lawrence M. *Government and Slum Housing.* Chicago: Rand McNally, 1968.

Keith, Nathaniel S. *Politics of the Housing Crisis Since 1930.* New York: Universe Books, 1973.

Mandelker, Daniel R. *Housing Subsidies in the United States and England.* Indianapolis, IN: Bobbs-Merrill, 1973.

McDonnell, Timothy L. *The Wagner Housing Act.* Chicago: Loyola University Press, 1957.

UNITED STATES INFORMATION AND EDUCATIONAL EXCHANGE ACT (1948)

Shala F. Maghzi

The United States Information and Educational Exchange Act of 1948 (IEEA) (P. L. 80-402, 62 Stat. 6) is an educational exchange initiative established to "promote better understanding of the United States among the peoples of the world and to strengthen cooperative international relations." Prior to the act's passage, exchange programs in the United States were conducted infrequently in a few select countries. In 1940, for example, Nelson Rockefeller, the Coordinator of Commercial and Cultural Affairs for the American Republics, initiated the exchange of persons program with Latin America, inviting 130 Latin American journalists to the United States. The scope of the exchange activities soon broadened to include a wider array of countries.

The United States Information and Educational Exchange Act of 1948 (IEEA) is an educational exchange initiative established to "promote better understanding of the United States among the peoples of the world and to strengthen cooperative international relations."

In 1948, following World War II, Representative Karl E. Mundt (South Dakota) and Senator H. Alexander Smith (New Jersey) introduced the Smith-Mundt bill in Congress. This act, later known as the United States Information and Educational Exchange Act, was passed on January 27, 1948. According to the Bureau of Educational and Cultural Affairs, the act established an information agency for the first time in a period of peace with a mission to "promote a better understanding of the United States in other countries, and to increase mutual understanding" between Americans and foreigners. The act recognized the importance of educational and cultural exchanges sponsored by the government and the need to build up a corps of well informed intellectuals and opinion leaders in the political and social infrastructure. Section 2 of the act lists several "objectives" to be used in achieving its goals:

(1) an information service to disseminate abroad information about the United States, its people, and policies promulgated by Congress, the president, the secretary of sstate and other responsible officials of government having to do with matters affecting foreign affairs; and
(2) an educational exchange service to cooperate with other nations in the interchange of persons, knowledge, and skills; the rendering of technical and other services; and the interchange of developments in the field of education, the arts, and sciences.

Following its passage, the IEEA went through a series of modifications and amendments. In 1953 President Eisenhower submitted Reorganization Plan Number 8 to Congress which established the United States Information Agency (USIA) to consolidate information functions administered by the State Department and other agencies. In 1961 the Fulbright-Hays Act reaffirmed the objective of increasing mutual understanding between Americans and the people of other nations.

Among the provisions of the 1948 Act was "the creation of an information service to disseminate abroad information about the United States, its people, and policies." A major vehicle to achieve this objective was the development of the international broadcasting station, the Voice of America (VOA). Prior to the passage of the act the VOA was transmitted in 1942 by a network of fourteen private shortwave transmitters. According to the Bureau of Educational and Cultural Affairs, following the act in 1948 the VOA grew to include transmission in twenty-four of the world's languages. That same year, sixty-seven information centers and libraries stocked books, displayed exhibits, and showed films about the United States through a network of seventy-six branches in the world.

The IEEA made a significant contribution to the exchange of students and professionals from all parts of the world, and it has served to increase understanding between the United States and other nations.

The IEEA made a significant contribution to the exchange of students and professionals from all parts of the world, and it has served to increase understanding between the United States and other nations. By 2003, according to Patricia S. Harrison, Assistant Secretary of State for Educational and Cultural Affairs (ECA), among the activities carried out under the auspices of the act included teacher training programs, HIV/AIDS educational exchange with teachers in Africa, and exchange between Kazakh religious leaders and American leaders through an International Visitor program. According to Assistant Secretary Harrison, the activities carried out under the act "are working for—democracy, peace, prosperity, and the non-negotiable demands of human dignity, engaging today with a new generation who will be part of the partnership for the future."

See also: FOREIGN SERVICE ACT OF 1946.

BIBLIOGRAPHY

Bureau of Educational and Cultural Affairs. "International Visitor Program History." <http://exchanges.state.gov/education/ivp/history.htm>.

"Message from Assistant Secretary of State for Educational and Cultural Affairs, Patricia S. Harrison." In *Bureau of Educational and Cultural Affairs: The Exchange* Vol. 2 (March/April 2003). <http://exchanges.state.gov/education/newsletter>.

UNITED STATES PATRIOT ACT

See USA PATRIOT ACT

URBAN MASS TRANSPORTATION ACTS

William S. Morrow, Jr.

The Urban Mass Transportation Act of 1964 (referred to here as the Act) (P. L. 88-365, 78 Stat. 302) ushered in the modern era of financing mass transportation research, planning, and operations in the United States principally through federal grants and loans. President Lyndon B. Johnson signed the Act into law in 1964 as part of his **Great Society** programs. However, it was a speech to Congress in 1962 by President John F. Kennedy that provided the impetus for federal participation in local transportation funding. In that speech President Kennedy articulated the need for federal financial assistance in fostering urban development and renewal through the planning and implementation of regional mass transportation systems across the country.

Great Society: broad term for the domestic programs of President Lyndon B. Johnson, in which he called for "an end to poverty and racial injustice"

NATURE OF THE ACT

The act authorized grants and loans to assist states and local public bodies and agencies in financing mass transportation capital project costs, specifically including "the acquisition, construction, reconstruction, and improvement of facilities and equipment for use ... in mass transportation service in urban areas and in coordinating such service with highway and other transportation in such areas." The act authorized $375 million for a three–year period, fiscal year (FY) 1965 through FY1967. By 1998 total authorizations had increased to $41 billion for the six years, FY1998 through FY2003, with $36 billion guaranteed (Federal Transit Act of 1998).

The act authorized grants and loans to assist states and local public bodies and agencies in financing mass transportation capital project costs, specifically including "the acquisition, construction, reconstruction, and improvement of facilities and equipment for use ... in mass transportation service in urban areas and in coordinating such service with highway and other transportation in such areas."

Individual grants were limited to two-thirds of a project's net cost, defined as that portion of a project's total cost the administrator estimated could not be reasonably financed from project revenues. The individual limit was later raised to 80 percent of net project cost by the Federal-Aid Highway Act of 1973.

Section 13(c) of the act required state and local governments to make arrangements to preserve transit workers exercising collective-bargaining rights as a condition of receiving federal assistance in acquiring a privately owned transit company. The Supreme Court later held that this part of the act did not create a federal **cause of action**. Rather, Congress intended that collective-bargaining agreements between federal aid recipients and transit unions would be governed by state law applied in state courts (*Jackson Transit Auth. v. Local Div. 1285, Amalgamated Transit Union,* 1982).

cause of action: reason or ground for initiating a proceeding in court

Primary responsibility for administering the act was transferred to the secretary of transportation in 1968 according to a plan of reorganization. This plan created the Urban Mass Transportation Administration (UMTA) within the Department of Transportation and authorized the secretary to delegate his responsibilities under the act to the UMTA administrator (Reorganization Plan No. 2, 82 Stat. 1369, 1968).

RELATED ACTS

The Urban Mass Transportation Assistance Act of 1970 (UMTAA) added acquisition of real property to the list of qualified uses of federal funds and authorized the secretary to incur obligations on behalf of the United States to finance grants and loans made under the act. UMTAA also mandated that planners prepare environmental impact analyses, hold public hearings, and make "special efforts" to accommodate the elderly and handicapped.

The National Mass Transportation Assistance Act of 1974 added a provision requiring transit systems to charge elderly and handicapped persons half-fares during off-peak hours. It also authorized states and localities to use up to one-half of funds received under the act to defray transit system operating expenses.

The Federal Public Transportation Act of 1978 expanded the authorized uses of funds received under the act to include capital and operating assistance for fixed rail projects, empowered the secretary to convert preexisting loans into grants, and established the creation of "metropolitan planning organizations" (MPOs).

The Reagan Administration sent tremors through the public transit industry in 1982 when it proposed eliminating financial assistance for transit system operating expenses. President Reagan ultimately approved legislation in early 1983 authorizing assistance for both operating expenses and capital expenditures through a program of block grants. However, the percentage of funds available for spending on operating expenses was capped at 80 to 95 percent of preexisting funding levels, depending on the size of the population served by the project (Federal Public Transportation Act of 1982).

Congress later increased the cap on financial assistance for operating expenses by 32.2 percent for urban areas with populations of less than 200,000, over the veto of President Reagan (Federal Mass Transportation Act of 1987 [FMTA]). The FMTA also included a provision authorizing future increases in the cap for such areas based on changes in the Consumer Price Index and, for all urban areas, excluded from the calculation of net project cost advertising and concession revenue in excess of 1985 levels.

The name of the agency was changed to the Federal Transit Administration in 1991, and references to the "Urban Mass Transportation Act" were

President John F. Kennedy:

To conserve and enhance values in existing urban areas is essential. But at least as important are steps to promote economic efficiency and livability in areas of future development. Our national welfare therefore requires the provision of good urban transportation, with the properly balanced use of private vehicles and modern mass transport to help shape as well as serve urban growth.

changed to the "Federal Transit Act" (Federal Transit Act Amendments of 1991). MPOs were given more authority but also more responsibility in project planning. Each MPO was now required to develop and periodically update a long-range plan taking into account project finances, land use, air quality, traffic congestion, and other related factors, as well a Transportation Improvement Program (TIP) containing a prioritized list of projects.

The Federal Transit Act Amendments of 1998 introduced a clean fuel grant program. This program encourages the purchasing or leasing of clean-fuel buses and facilities. Permissible uses of federal funds were expanded to include spending on preventive maintenance, nonfixed route (or door-to-door) paratransit service (for passengers with some physical or mental disability), equipment and facilities leases, safety equipment and facilities, and community facilities such as daycare and healthcare. However, urban areas with populations of 200,000 or more were no longer permitted to use federal dollars to help defray operating expenses. The operating expense spending limitations were lifted, on the other hand, for urban areas with populations of less than 200,000.

The Urban Mass Transportation Act of 1964 is one of the few Great Society programs of President Johnson to enjoy broad bipartisan support over the years. It is emblematic of the spending programs Americans have come to expect from the federal government. Public transit has its share of problems, but without the massive federal assistance these transportation systems receive every year, those problems would be magnified beyond recognition. The country's transportation systems would scarcely resemble those in existence today, and in some areas of the country might not even exist.

BIBLIOGRAPHY

Federal Transit Authority. "Mass Transportation: A Bibliography for Students." <http://www.fta.dot.gov/transcity/sch/bibliography.html>.

"Transportation Equity Act for the 21st Century: A Summary." Washington, DC: U.S. Department of Transportation, 1998. Available online at <http://www.fhwa.dot.gov/tea21/sumcov.htm>.

Weiner, Edward. "Urban Transportation Planning in the United States: An Historical Overview," 5th ed. Westport, CT: Praeger, 1999. Available online at <http://tmip.fhwa.dot.gov/clearinghouse/docs/utp>.

USA PATRIOT ACT (2001)

Lynne K. Zusman and Neil S. Helfand

History illustrates that in times of war or threat to our country's national security, our government will tend to relax restrictions on its incursions on American civil liberties.

History illustrates that in times of war or threat to our country's national security, our government will tend to relax restrictions on its incursions of American civil liberties. If the government exercises too much self-restraint in the surveillance and apprehension of persons presenting a potential threat to the security of the United States, it is believed, our national security will be jeopardized. After the terrorist attacks of September 11, 2001, the U.S. government immediately responded to the perceived need for broader governmental powers in detecting and preventing future terrorist attacks by enacting the USA Patriot Act (USAPA) on October 26, 2001.

Congress introduced the USA Patriot Act with the principal aim of preventing and punishing terrorist acts in the United States and around the world, as well as enhancing law enforcement investigative tools. Given the perceived need for prompt and immediate action in the wake of September 11th, the USA Patriot Act was approved by Congress and the president without the normal procedural review processes of intensive debate and hearings. The USAPA is a lengthy piece of legislation making broad and fundamental changes to the previous law governing the executive branch's powers in law enforcement and intelligence. In enacting the USAPA, Congress and the president was sought to promptly provide the legal tools necessary to deal with the current terrorist threats.

MAIN PROVISIONS OF THE USAPA

The USAPA calls for:

- The enhancement of domestic security against terrorism.
- The enhancement of surveillance procedures.
- The abatement of money laundering and terrorism financing.
- The protection of the northern border.
- The removal of obstacles to the investigation of terrorism.
- The provision of aid and assistance to victims of terrorism, public safety officers, and their families.
- Increased information sharing between federal, local, and state governments.
- The strengthening of criminal laws against terrorism.
- The improvement of intelligence capabilities.

Although the USAPA's intent is to address the security needs of the United States in the wake of the terrorist attacks of September 11th, the act makes special provision for the preservation of the civil rights and civil liberties of all Americans, including Arab Americans, Muslim Americans, and Americans from South Asia, and states that every effort must be taken to preserve their safety. The USAPA also condemns discrimination against Arab and Muslim Americans and demands acts of violence against those individuals be punished to the full extent of the law.

FEDERAL GOVERNMENT SEARCH AND SEIZURE CAPABILITIES

Profound enhancements of the government's power of search and seizure now permit expanded government search capabilities with less judicial oversight. The USAPA also greatly expands the authority to intercept wire, oral, and electronic communications relating to terrorism, and to investigate computer fraud and abuse offenses. In addition to enhancing the abilities of the federal government to engage in domestic surveillance of individuals, the act calls upon citizens to report the suspicious activity of persons and businesses, thereby making the American public the eyes and ears of the government. This last provision is intended to overcome limitations in the

Profound enhancements of the government's power of search and seizure now permit expanded government search capabilities with less judicial oversight.

government's resources and ability to monitor and detect potential terrorist threats and other crimes.

Under the USAPA the government also benefits from increased powers of record examination. The government can view educational, library, medical and financial records without demonstrating evidence of commission of a crime. The government is also now able to employ its newly acquired surveillance capabilities to review personal internet use.

RELATIONSHIP BETWEEN LAW ENFORCEMENT AND INTELLIGENCE AGENCIES

The USAPA aims to remove hindrances to the detection and prevention of terrorist threats. To that end, in addition to enhancing the federal government's surveillance capabilities, the USAPA makes sweeping changes in the relationship between law enforcement and intelligence agencies, by breaking down traditional barriers to their coordination and cooperation. The USAPA provides for the expanded sharing of information gathered as part of criminal investigations with intelligence agencies and the expanded use of foreign intelligence surveillance tools and information in criminal investigations.

In addition to enhancing the federal government's surveillance capabilities, the USAPA makes sweeping changes in the relationship between law enforcement and intelligence agencies, by breaking down traditional barriers to their coordination and cooperation.

EXECUTIVE BRANCH ABUSES OF POWER

In the mid-1970s, Congressional investigations revealed extensive domestic surveillance and intelligence abuses by the executive branch of the government. Lawmakers had expressed concern about the potential for civil liberties violations by domestic law enforcement and intelligence agencies. For instance, the National Security Act of 1947, which established the Central Intelligence Agency, states that the CIA "shall have no police, subpoena, or law enforcement powers or internal security functions." Although limitations already existed on executive branch abuses in this area, Congress endeavored to create a greater system of checks and balances against such abuses.

As a result of these Congressional investigations, the Foreign Intelligence Surveillance Act of 1978 (FISA) was enacted, requiring court orders for national security electronic surveillance in the United States. The intended aim of FISA was to restrain the power of the federal government, in particular law enforcement agencies of the executive branch, from engaging in unfettered domestic surveillance of individuals.

Prior to the enactment of the USAPA, however, attempts were made to broaden and expand the government's surveillance authority. In May 1995, Senator Joseph Lieberman proposed an amendment to the bill that became the Antiterrorism and Effective Death Penalty Act of 1996 which would have expanded the government's authority to conduct emergency wiretaps in cases of domestic or international terrorism. However, Congress's reluctance to expand wiretap laws any further led to the defeat of Senator Lieberman's amendment.

These previous prohibitions and checks on the executive branch's domestic surveillance and information sharing abuses are largely undone by the new law created by the USAPA.

These previous prohibitions and checks on the executive branch's domestic surveillance and information sharing abuses have been largely undone by the new law created by the USAPA. It permits, for instance, the wider sharing of information from grand juries, domestic law enforcement wiretaps, and criminal investigations, and it also requires federal law enforcement agencies to share this information with intelligence agencies through the Director of Central Intelligence. In addition, law enforcement and intelligence agencies may now share information obtained by means of the government's enhanced surveillance capabilities.

OVERSIGHT OF IMPLEMENTATION OF POWERS GRATED BY THE USAPA

While these enhanced governmental powers of search and seizure serve the purpose of security, history has shown that such powers, absent effective oversight of their use, may lead to profound abuses. Critics of the act voice their deep concerns regarding the likelihood of the government's undue infringement upon civil liberties and rights of privacy.

In recognizing these concerns, Congress incorporated a so-called "sunset provision" that causes certain USAPA provisions to end on December 31, 2005. This is also acknowledgment on Congress' part that certain elements of the USAPA run counter to America's traditional democratic principles, and that although current circumstances warrant such a deviation from traditional norms, such changes should not become a permanent piece of the U.S. government's framework. However, the sunset provision only applies to certain enumerated provisions of the law.

Although the act significantly curtails judicial oversight of law enforcement and intelligence activities, the act does provide for congressional oversight of the executive branch's expanded powers. In particular, the Senate Judiciary Committee is charged with establishing and maintaining an oversight panel responsible for examining how these newly granted powers are exercised.

LONG–TERM RAMIFICATIONS OF USAPA

The justification for expanding the executive branch's authority in the short term is clear. Passed less than two months after the September 11th attacks, the law's intended purpose of preventing and detecting future attacks was the preeminent concern of lawmakers. However, the hasty manner in which the law passed through Congressional lawmaking processes causes opponents to argue that lawmakers gave disproportionate consideration to the law enforcement and intelligence community's viewpoint in drafting the provisions.

It is anticipated that in the future the law will face challenges in the American court system.

It is anticipated that in the future the law will face challenges in the American court system. Although the security concerns of the United States may temporarily override these challenges, in the long-term, it is possible that certain controversial provisions of the law may not withstand judicial challenges.

See also: Antiterrorism and Effective Death Penalty Act; Department of Homeland Security Act; Espionage Act (1917) and Sedition Act (1918); Foreign Intelligence Surveillance Act; National Security Act of 1947

BIBLIOGRAPHY

"FFC Analysis of the Provisions of the USA Patriot Act that Relate to Online Activities." October 31, 2001. <http://www.eff.org/Privacy/Surveillance/Terrorism>.

Harrison, Ann. "Behind the USA Patriot Act," November 5, 2001. <http://www.alternet.org/story.html?StoryID–11854>.

Testimony of Senator Patrick Leahy before the Senate, October 25, 2001.

V

Veterans' Preference Act of 1944

John P. Stimson

The U.S. Government is our nation's largest employer, and throughout history Congress has used the power of an employer to shape or express public policy. One such policy is the recognition that our society owes a debt to those who face the horrors of combat in defense of American freedom and values. To repay this debt, the government tries to make the veterans' return from military service to civilian life an easier transition. It does so by offering veterans preferential treatment in federal employment. Congress adopted the first of such preferences in the Civil War era, and they have continued to evolve over the years. World War II was the occasion for a major milestone with passage of the Veterans' Preference Act of 1944 (P.L. 78-359, 58 Stat. 387).

It does so by offering veterans preferential treatment in federal employment.

ORIGINS OF VETERANS PREFERENCES

Congressional concern for veterans' postwar employment opportunities dates to 1865. That year the Senate and House of Representatives issued a joint resolution urging that disabled veterans "be preferred for appointments to civil offices." (Confederate soldiers were not considered veterans until they were pardoned in 1958, at which point few were still alive.) Congress supplemented the 1865 hiring preference in 1876 with a retention preference for honorably discharged veterans, or their widows or orphans, faced with any reduction-in-force. This meant that an honorably discharged veteran who might be laid off because of a lack of work, lack of funds, reorganization, or other factors would have a better chance of retaining his job. The retention preference served as a tiebreaker among equally qualified federal employees, and did not depend on whether the veteran had served in wartime or was disabled.

A 1912 law, as implemented and expanded through a series of presidential executive orders and Civil Service Commission regulations, granted an absolute retention preference to any honorably discharged service member with good performance ratings. This meant that the veteran was preferred for job retention even over nonveteran federal employees with more seniority or higher performance ratings.

Section 8 of the Selective Training and Service Act of 1940 added reemployment rights to the list of veterans' preferences. Any nontemporary federal employee called for military training and service was guaranteed the right to return to a federal position previously held, or an equivalent one, without loss of seniority or benefits. Such an employee could not be discharged within a year of reemployment, unless the employer had good cause such as misconduct.

The network of federal veterans' preference laws and regulations was substantial by 1944, including hiring, retention, and reemployment preferences. Many states had their own laws for similar preferences in hiring in state and municipal government. The World War II Congress, however, believed further action was appropriate.

The American effort in World War II required an unprecedented mobilization, with millions of citizens placing their private lives on hold to join bloody battles in faraway places.

THE 1944 ACT: CODIFY, EXPAND, IMPROVE

The American effort in World War II required an unprecedented mobilization, with millions of citizens placing their private lives on hold to join bloody battles in faraway places. Congress anticipated that returning war veterans would have particularly acute needs for employment assistance. Lawmakers believed that the federal government should enhance veteran hiring preferences as a display of gratitude and as an example for other employers. As Representative Thomas D'Alesandro put it during committee hearings: "[T]his nation has trained 12,000,000 fighting men to destroy and kill. They have been taken away from schools, colleges, and jobs. Their home life has been broken up, and they have turned into tough soldiers and sailors.... The millions of men and women returning from the war fronts and camps will need jobs, money, training, hospitalization, and other assistance. They expect stability and security, so that they can start rebuilding their private lives. We must give them all that. It is the least we can do for them" (90 *Congressional Record* 3506 [1944]).

The 1944 law, unlike some earlier veterans' preference laws, covered only veterans with disabilities as a result of wartime service, along with their wives or widows, and other veterans who served during war. Peacetime veterans who already enjoyed preferences under previous laws and regulations did not forfeit those benefits, but those preferences did not extend to peacetime veterans discharged after 1944.

The new set of preferences covered hiring, reemployment, retention during a reduction-in-force, and the right to appeal decisions based on rules of employee discipline. Veterans after World War II could qualify for federal jobs without meeting age, height, and weight requirements. Education requirements were eliminated from all federal positions except for certain scientific, technical, and professional positions as considered necessary by the Civil Service Commission. Veterans also received, in certain cases, credit for military service in meeting the experience requirements of a position. Once found qualified for a federal position, veteran applicants enjoyed a leg-up in competition for the job.

A World War II veteran takes an aptitude test at a Philadelphia office where veterans applied for employment, 1944. ©BETTMAN/CORBIS

Federal hiring for most positions was based on competitive examinations. The 1944 law added ten points to the test scores of disabled veterans or their widows or wives, and added five points to the test scores of other war veterans. This often served to elevate veterans to the top of the hiring list. Federal agencies had to hire from the top three names on the list, and could not pass by a veteran for a nonveteran without justification.

Reemployment and retention preferences did not depart dramatically from those already in effect, but Congress considered it important to "give legislative sanction" to benefits that had been created by executive branch rules and regulations. Reemployed veterans could not be terminated within a year of their return to duty. Eligible veteran employees with good performance ratings could not be laid off before a nonveteran in a reduction-in-force, regardless of seniority.

The Veterans' Preference Act of 1944 bestowed on war veterans certain notice and appeal rights in matters of employee discipline. A veteran could not be fired, suspended, demoted, or reduced in pay without good cause and without first receiving written notice of the allegations, an opportunity to respond, and thirty days' notice. The veteran then could appeal the termination to the Civil Service Commission. Veterans were the first group of federal employees to enjoy these rights. Nonveterans did not acquire them until President Kennedy's Executive Order 10987 in 1962.

THE CONSTITUTIONAL LEGITIMACY OF VETERANS' PREFERENCES

A preference, by definition, comes at the expense of those who are not preferred. Yet the 1944 act has withstood constitutional challenges by nonveterans. One such case was *White v. Gates, Secretary of the Navy* (1958). The U.S. Court of Appeals for the District of Columbia Circuit held that Congress, by restricting the ability of the executive branch to hire and fire relatively low-level employees, did not unconstitutionally infringe on the powers of the president. In another case, *Colemere v. Hampton, Chairman, U.S. Civil Service Commission* (1973), the U.S. District Court in Utah held that veterans' preferences in federal employment do not violate the Constitution's equal protection requirements because there was a rational basis for distinguishing between veterans and nonveterans, and because there is no fundamental right to work for the government.

The Supreme Court ruled in *Arnett v. Kennedy* (1974) that federal employees have a property interest in their job, and the Fifth Amendment of the U.S. Constitution requires due process when the government takes away a property interest. The Court found that the review rights prescribed by the Veterans' Preference Act of 1944 and Executive Order 10987 were central to the constitutionality of the civil service system.

CONTINUED RELEVANCE OF VETERANS' PREFERENCES

Congress has taken many opportunities to adjust veterans' preferences since 1944, but the basic program remains in place. The Vietnam Era Veterans Readjustment Act requires private employers to take affirmative action to hire disabled veterans and Vietnam era veterans for work on federal contracts. The right to notice and review of employee discipline formed the foundation for due process rights in the Civil Service Reform Act of 1978. The Uniformed Services Employment and Reemployment Rights Act of 1994 bolstered reemployment rights of veterans and reservists in federal, state, and private employment. Disabled veterans still receive a ten-point preference, war veterans still receive a five-point preference, and veterans' retention preferences still trump nonveterans in a reduction-in-force. U.S. lawmakers, in short, continue to recognize a debt and express gratitude to the veterans of American wars.

Congress has taken many opportunities to adjust veterans' preferences since 1944, but the basic program remains in place.

BIBLIOGRAPHY

Hoogenboom, Ari. *Outlawing the Spoils: A History of the Civil Service Reform Movement, 1865–1883*. Urbana, IL: University of Illinois Press, 1961.

VIOLENCE AGAINST WOMEN ACT OF 1994

Elizabeth M. Schneider

The Violence Against Women Act of 1994 (VAWA) (P.L. 103-322, 108 Stat. 1902) was introduced in Congress in 1990 and enacted as part of the Violent Crime Control and Law Enforcement Act of 1994 to address the widespread problems of domestic violence, sexual assault, and other forms of violence against women. VAWA is a comprehensive law that includes measures to reduce the frequency of violence against women, provide services to victims of gender-based violence, and hold perpetrators accountable.

FEATURES OF VAWA

The act effected the following changes:

- the creation of a national domestic violence hotline
- increased funding for battered women's shelters
- new criminal penalties for domestic violence committed across state lines and interstate violations of protection orders
- required states to enforce orders of protection issued by other states
- increased prison sentences for certain federal sex crimes, with perpetrators required to make restitution to victims
- the creation of a mechanism enabling battered immigrant women to obtain lawful immigration status without relying on the assistance of an abusive citizen husband
- provided funding for increased education on sexual assault and domestic violence and for studies of gender bias in federal courts
- the creation of a civil rights remedy for victims of gender motivated violence, which would allow victims of such violence to bring suits in federal court against perpetrators for violation of the victims' civil rights—a remedy later deemed unconstitutional by the Supreme Court

PROPONENTS OF THE ACT

Support for VAWA came from a broad range of organizations, and much of the organizing around this legislation occurred at the **grassroots** level. Proponents of VAWA argued that violence against women is a form of discrimination based on sex. Because a climate of fear prevents women from participating equally in society, gender-based violence has the effect of turning women and girls into second-class citizens. Proponents argued that violence against women is a pervasive problem that keeps women from fully participating as citizens in their homes, workplaces, and in society in general. Existing state and federal laws, they claimed, were inadequate to address this problem.

grassroots: originating or operating at the basic level of society

Congress heard testimony from a wide variety of witnesses, who presented the following information in support of VAWA:

Proponents of VAWA argued that violence against women is a form of discrimination based on sex.

- three out of four American women will be victims of violent crimes sometime during their life
- as many as 50 percent of homeless women and children are fleeing domestic violence
- an estimated four million women are battered each year by their husbands or partners
- the incidence of rape rose four times as fast as the total national crime rate
- an individual who commits rape has only about 4 chances in 100 of being arrested, prosecuted, and found guilty of any offense
- less than 1 percent of rape victims has collected damages

- almost one-quarter of all convicted rapists never go to prison and another quarter received sentences in local jails where the average sentence is eleven months
- almost 50 percent of rape victims lose their jobs or are forced to quit because of the crime's severity

After intensive lobbying by supporters, VAWA gained wide bipartisan support in Congress for most of its provisions. The civil rights remedy created by the VAWA was by far the most controversial element of the legislation. Opponents argued that the civil rights remedy would bring before the federal courts issues traditionally and more properly dealt with by the state courts, such as domestic relations and other family and crimincal law matters. Proponents maintained that existing state laws provided inadequate and ineffective remedies to victims of gender-based violence.

SUPREME COURT CHALLENGE AND SUBSEQUENT LEGISLATION

In 2000 the Supreme Court considered a challenge to the civil rights remedy created by VAWA in *United States v. Morrison*. The Court held that Congress did not have the power to enact this provision and deemed it unconstitutional. The act's other provisions were unaffected.

The Clothesline Project, on the Mall in Washington, D.C., April 8, 1995. The Clothesline Project was created in 1990 to address the issue of violence against women. Each shirt tells a woman's story with her own artwork and words; the shirts are color coded to show the form of abuse and whether or not the victim survived the experience. (© AP/WIDE WORLD PHOTOS)

The same year Congress passed VAWA 2000, which reauthorized the original VAWA provisions and created a number of new provisions. One of these provisions made it easier for battered immigrant women to obtain lawful permanent resident status by cooperating in the prosecution of their batterers. VAWA 2000 also made money available to develop policies and training programs to address the needs of older women and women with disabilities.

VAWA directed a great deal of public attention to the issue of violence against women. As a result of this legislation, a federal office was created to administer VAWA grant programs, conduct studies, and provide information to the public on to gender-based violence.

Statistics on Violence against Women

From the Urban Institute, a nonprofit organization for economic and social policy research:

- More than half of sexual assaults are committed by partners, friends, or acquaintances of the victim.
- Approximately two million women per year are severely assaulted by male partners in the United States.
- Domestic violence occurs in more than twenty-five percent of marriages. Severe, repeated violence occurs in one of every fourteen marriages.
- In 1994, twenty-eight percent of female murder victims were killed by their husbands or boyfriends.
- One-fifth of all medical visits by women, and one-third of all emergency room visits by women, are due to battering.

BIBLIOGRAPHY

Frazee, David, et al., eds. *Violence Against Women, Law and Litigation.* Deerfield, N.Y.: Clark Boardman Callaghan, 1997.

Schneider, Elizabeth M. *Battered Women and Feminist Lawmaking.* New Haven, CT: Yale University Press, 2002.

Schneider, Elizabeth M., and Clare Dalton. *Battered Women and the Law.* New York: Foundation Press, 2001.

VIOLENT CRIME CONTROL AND LAW ENFORCEMENT ACT OF 1994

Norman Abrams

The bills that eventually became the Violent Crime Control and Law Enforcement Act of 1994 (VCCLEA) were originally proposed as amendments to the Omnibus Crime Control and Safe Streets Act of 1968. The VCCLEA is directly linked to its historical predecessor, the 1968 legislation that was the first in a series of **omnibus** legislative packages whose provisions were aimed at street and violent crime. With the 1968 enactment, President Lyndon Johnson moved the subject of violent local crime onto the front burner of national politics, where it has remained ever since. In the intervening thirty-five years Congress enacted a number of lengthy legislative packages, each containing a potpourri of provisions dealing with crime, law enforcement, and crime prevention subjects. Between 1984 and 1990, for example, four such omnibus bills were enacted; the VCCLEA continued that tradition.

omnibus: including many things at once

Described by President Bill Clinton as "the toughest, largest and smartest federal attack on crime in the history of...[the country]," the VCCLEA contained both provisions supported by liberals and attacked by conservatives (e.g., gun control) and provisions where the liberal-conservative perspectives were reversed (e.g. death penalty). It also contained provisions dealing with such varied subjects as violence against women, drug courts, marketing scams that victimized the elderly, crimes against children, and criminal street gangs. Among its most controversial and/or widely noted provisions were those establishing a ban on assault weapons; a federal mandatory life term three-strikes law; a federal grant program to fund more police at the local level and to help build more prisons; and additions to the Federal Rules of Evidence dealing with the admissibility of evidence in sexual assault and child molestation cases.

The congressional and lobbying infighting that preceded the final enactment of the act was classic in its Byzantine complexity. During the first President George Bush's administration, different versions of a comprehensive bill were passed by the two Houses of Congress, but died because of their inability to bridge the liberal-conservative divide on some key issues, such as **habeas corpus** and exclusionary rule reform. Early in his administration, President Clinton set forth the elements of a crime bill he would support, including a ban on assault weapons, federal grants for more police, and habeas corpus reform. Putting more police on the street at the local level became the centerpiece of his anticrime program.

habeas corpus: (Latin, "you should have the body") a written order to bring a prisoner in front of a judge, to determine whether his or her detention is lawful

Later, after a series of notorious violent crimes in different parts of the country, the State of Washington enacted a three strikes-mandatory life provision, and soon other states began introducing similar legislation. Three strikes, which had originally been a Republican proposal, was soon endorsed by the President and added to his priorities for the Violent Crime bill.

The House version of the crime bill also contained a "Racial Justice Act" which would have allowed individuals sentenced to death to challenge their sentence based on a statistical showing that race had affected the imposition of death sentences in the jurisdiction. Strongly supported by the Congressional Black Caucus and Democrats and opposed with equal fervor by Republicans who believed it would effectively block the use of the death penalty, it was dropped in conference. Similarly, habeas corpus reform did not make it into the final bill.

The most hotly contested issue in this legislation, however, involved the ban on assault weapons. Because the chairman of the House Judiciary Committee was a strong opponent of gun control, the Senate initially became the main arena for including an assault weapons ban in the crime bill. Eventually, compromise provisions were crafted. The conference bill (the product of a second conference) was almost immediately approved by a close vote in the House. After a short-lived Republican filibuster in the Senate was broken by a cloture vote, the crime bill was approved and subsequently signed into law by President Clinton on September 13, 1994.

The main elements of the assault weapons provisions were a listing of named banned weapons, a ban on copies of the listed banned weapons, a ban on weapons that fell within a definition containing specific criteria, and a ban on large capacity ammunition magazines. The legislation also contained a ten-year sunset provision and a listing of 670 hunting and sport weapons exempted from the prohibition.

EFFECT OF THE LEGISLATION

What has been the effect of the VCCLEA? Has it had an impact on crime? Through grants made under its COPS (Community Oriented Policing Services) program the act had as one of its goals putting 100,000 additional police on the streets during a five year period through hiring and redeployment. Reportedly, the total number of sworn officers grew during that period by about 87,000, but historic rates of growth might have significantly increased the number of officers, possibly by an almost similar number, so it is difficult to determine how much difference the program made.

Other grant programs have also been implemented: For example, by the year 2000, the Justice Department made grants of more than $700 million through its Violence Against Women office, to support programs for computer tracking, mandatory training for police, and the creation of community coalitions. In 1998 the General Accounting Office did a study to determine the impact of the grant program in support of "truth-in-sentencing" (TIS) laws that provided incentive grants to states with laws requiring violent offenders to serve at least 85 percent of their imposed sentences. A survey showed that twenty-seven states had TIS laws; in twelve of these states, the availability of the federal grant was not a factor contributing to the enactment of the TIS law and in eleven other states, it was only a partial factor; only in four states was the cause-effect relationship clear.

The provisions banning assault weapons had some impact but also proved fairly easy for gun manufacturers to evade. In the year 2002 for example, the person charged as the Washington D.C. area sniper, John Allen Muhammad, allegedly used an assault weapon the manufacturer had modified by removing two military-type components, thus escaping the ban.

Five years and more after enactment of the legislation, President Clinton still viewed the VCCLEA as "landmark legislation...[that] put thousands of new police officers into America's communities,...[gave] crime victims a greater voice in the criminal justice process...and protected women and children from violence and abuse in their homes and communities..." Further, it "helped reduce the violent crime rate in the United States to its lowest level in nearly a quarter century." The Violent Crime Control and Law Enforcement Act of 1994 undoubtedly did some of these things and more, and did have some impact on the crime rate; precisely how much is indeterminable.

Vocational Education Act of 1917

Pamela L. Gray

Excerpt from the Vocational Education Act

An Act to provide for the promotion of vocational education; to provide for cooperation with the states in the promotion of such education in agriculture and the trades and industries; to provide for cooperation with the states in the preparation of teachers of vocational subjects; and to appropriate money and regulate its expenditures.

The Vocational Education Act of 1917 (P.L. 65-347), also known as the Smith-Hughes Act, was designed to provide federal assistance to states to promote vocational education. The act marked the first time that state and local public institutions formed a partnership to provide vocational training in the areas of agriculture, home economics, and trade and industrial education. Legislators and business leaders, recognizing the need for a technically trained workforce (as well as efficiently run households), felt that federal assistance was needed to help the states achieve this goal.

The act required the states to establish a board to develop and administer vocational programs. Some states used existing boards of education, whereas others created separate entities. A major interpretation of the Smith-Hughes Act, which became known as the 50-25-25 Rule, required 50 percent of students' time in school to be spent in shop work, 25 percent in classes related to vocational study, and 25 percent in academic courses.

HISTORICAL BACKGROUND

Before the Industrial Revolution in the mid-nineteenth century, workers became skilled at various tasks by means of apprenticeships. After the 1880s, elementary schools used a program of manual training to prepare future factory workers. The first public vocational high school, with a comprehensive training program in agriculture, was established at the University of Minnesota in 1888.

Also in the late nineteenth century, many educators believed that home management was an important skill that could be taught through scientific principles. The development of home economics began with experimental stations and courses established in the 1870s. Annie Dewey, Maria Daniell (a specialist in institutional management), and Ellen Swallow Richards were pioneers in the profession and training of students in what was called domestic sciences. This group organized meetings in Lake Placid, New York, from 1899 through 1909, developing training standards and an overall agenda for the field.

PUSHING FOR PASSAGE OF THE ACT

The Morrill Acts of 1862 and 1890, the first federal legislation in the vocational area, required state proceeds from federally donated land to be utilized for creation and maintenance of at least one college dedicated to instruction in agriculture and mechanical arts. The Morrill Acts were precursors to the Vocational Act of 1917. Several legislators were highly influential in the passage of the 1917 act. Dudley M. Hughes, Democratic congressman from Georgia, was a longtime advocate of agricultural clubs and secondary school agricultural education. Carroll Page, Republican senator from Vermont, upheld the Vermont tradition begun by former Senator Justin Morrill (for whom the Morrill Acts were named). Other important figures were Dr. Charles Prosser, an educator and first executive secretary and lobbyist for the National Society for the Promotion of Industrial Education (NSPIE), and Hoke Smith, former governor of Georgia and Democratic senator, who wrote several important pieces of legislation and helped to create the political coalition that would secure passage of the 1917 act.

Page and Prosser formed an alliance in 1911 to advance the goals of vocational study. President Woodrow Wilson, an advocate for vocational education, appointed Dudley M. Hughes to the Commission on National Aid to Vocational Education in 1914. The passage of the Smith-Lever Act of 1914 established the Cooperative Extension Service (programs of practical applications of research knowledge including public instruction and demonstration), and Smith, Page, Hughes, and Prosser were appointed as members. World War I also helped to focus national attention on the need for a technically trained workforce for the war effort.

However, political maneuvering, personality differences, and the health problems and deaths of key supporters delayed the passage of a comprehensive vocational education act until 1917. The major topics of debate were the division of funds among the areas of study and the degree of federal involvement in education. Legislators recognized that the Constitution left the matter of education to the states and local governments. Ultimately, a coalition of political parties, industry, education leaders, and **lobbyists** brought about passage of the act.

lobby: to try to persuade the legislature to pass laws and regulations that are favorable to one's interests and to defeat laws that are unfavorable to those interests

LATER LEGISLATION

Later legislation extended the Smith-Hughes Act by expanding federal assistance in specific areas, including teacher education and new building construction. The most significant changes to the act came with the adoption of the Carl D. Perkins Vocational and Applied Technology Act of 1984 (P.L. 98-524), which was expanded in 1990 and again in 1997. The Smith-Hughes/Vocational Education Act of 1917 was officially repealed by the Carl D. Perkins Act of 1997 (also known as Perkins III). The new direction of vocational education then shifted to encourage integration of academic and vocational content.

See also: MORRILL LAND GRANT ACT OF 1862.

BIBLIOGRAPHY

Evans, Rupert N. *The Foundations of Vocational Education.* Upper Saddle River, NJ: Pearson Higher Education, 1971.

Krug, Edward A. *The Shaping of the American High School, 1880–1960,* 2 vols. New York: Harper and Row, 1972.

Lazerson, Marvin, and W. Norton Grubbs, eds. *American Education and Vocationalism: A Documentary History, 1870–1970.* New York: Teachers College Press, 1974.

VOLSTEAD ACT

See NATIONAL PROHIBITION ACT

VOTING RIGHTS ACT OF 1965

William D. Araiza

Excerpt from the Voting Rights Act of 1965

Section 2: No voting qualification or prerequisite to voting, or ... procedure shall be imposed ... to deny or abridge the right of any citizen of the United States to vote on account of race or color.

Section 5: **Whenever a [covered] State ... shall enact ... any voting qualification ... different from that in force ... on November 1, 1964, such State ... may institute an action ... for a declaratory judgment that such qualification ... does not have the purpose and will not have the effect of...denying or abridging the right to vote on account of race or color ... *Provided* ... that such qualification ... may be enforced ... if [it] has been submitted ... to the Attorney General and the Attorney General has not interposed an objection within sixty days.**

The Voting Rights Act of 1965 (VRA) (P. L. 89-110, 79 Stat. 437) was designed to protect and ensure the right to vote that is guaranteed by the Fifteenth Amendment to the United States Constitution. The Fifteenth Amendment, which prohibited racial discrimination in voting, was enacted in the immediate post-Civil War period. Yet as late as the early 1960s the country witnessed systematic efforts to deny the right to vote to racial and ethnic minorities, especially blacks in the South. Southern politicians attempted to prevent blacks from voting by using a variety of devices, including literacy and good character tests that were easily manipulated by poll officials. As a result, blacks participated in voting and political activity in very low numbers in the areas where such devices were employed. The VRA was designed to eliminate the use of these devices as a means of preventing blacks from exercising their right to vote.

The Voting Rights Act of 1965 (VRA) was designed to protect and ensure the right to vote that is guaranteed by the Fifteenth Amendment to the United States Constitution.

FEATURES OF THE ACT

The most important provisions of the VRA are contained in sections 2 and 5. Section 2 prohibits states from establishing voting qualifications or standards in a way that results in a denial of the right to vote on account of race. Section 5 requires states and other jurisdictions with a history of race discrimination in voting to obtain the approval of the United States Department of Justice before changing any law with regard to voting. This provision has become known as the "preclearance" provision because it requires states to obtain the clearance of the Justice Department before changing its voting laws.

The preclearance provision has a wide scope. It includes, for example, the redrawing of electoral districts that occurs after every national census (a population count conducted every ten years), voter qualification rules, and changes in government structure. (Such changes include the decision to change some offices from elective to appointive, or to change a city council from one in which one representative is elected from each district to one in which all representatives run city-wide.) All of these changes have the potential to weaken, or, in the words of the statute, "dilute" the strength of minority voting. To prevent such dilution, the statute requires Justice Department clearance before such changes can be put into effect. If a state concludes that the Justice Department's disapproval of a desired change is unwarranted, the matter is decided by a federal court. The Supreme Court may review these federal court decisions if it so chooses. In its review of several decisions, the Court has interpreted section 2 to prohibit a broad array of government conduct.

Sections 2 and 5 are similar, in that they both seek to combat government practices making it difficult for minorities either to vote or, more generally, to participate effectively in government. Section 5 differs from section 2, though, in that it puts the burden on state and local governments with a history of discrimination to obtain approval for any changes that might possibly have these effects. Section 2, which applies throughout the nation, does not include such a preclearance requirement.

Other important sections of the act forbid the use of literacy and good character tests to determine eligibility for voting and provide for federal officials to register voters and observe elections in certain circumstances.

Other important sections of the act forbid the use of literacy and good character tests to determine eligibility for voting and provide for federal officials to register voters and observe elections in certain circumstances.

CONSTITUTIONALITY

The constitutional basis for the VRA is Congress' power under section 2 of the Fifteenth Amendment. Section 1 of that Amendment states that "the right

President Lyndon B. Johnson gives Dr. Martin Luther King one of the pens used to sign the Voting Rights Act of 1965. Also in the picture are Representative Claude Pepper (D-Fla.) (center, glasses) and Reverend Ralph Abernathy (to King's right). (LIBRARY OF CONGRESS, PRINTS AND PHOTOGRAPHS DIVISION)

of citizens of the United States to vote shall not be denied or abridged by the United States or by any State on account of race, color, or previous condition of servitude." Section 2 states that "the Congress shall have the power to enforce [the Amendment] by appropriate legislation." In debating the VRA, Congress uncovered a large number of examples of states violating the Fifteenth Amendment, and determined that guaranteeing (or, in the words of section 2, "enforcing") the rights granted in that amendment justified enactment of the VRA.

CIRCUMSTANCES LEADING TO ADOPTION OF THE ACT

Civil Rights movement: the movement to win political, economic, and social equality for African Americans

In the late 1950s and early 1960s leaders of the **Civil Rights movement** realized that race-based voting restrictions severely impeded the political, economic, and social progress of black Americans. Civil rights activists initiated voter registration drives and educational campaigns in the early 1960s to encourage greater black political participation. In the summer of 1964, for example, white college students traveled to the South to assist in voter registration and educational efforts, and civil rights organizations such as the National Association for the Advancement of Colored People (NAACP) and the Southern Christian Leadership Conference (SCLC) spearheaded similar drives. Some whites responded to these campaigns with violence, both against the civil rights leadership, the workers in the civil rights campaigns, and local blacks who expressed sympathy or support for them. This violence, and pressure from the civil rights community, prompted Congress to take action.

Great Society: broad term for the domestic programs of President Lyndon B. Johnson, in which he called for "an end to poverty and racial injustice"

President Lyndon B. Johnson, who had become president after the assassination of John F. Kennedy in 1963, made completion of his predecessor's civil rights agenda one of his top priorities and one of the foundations of his **Great Society** program. Dr. Martin Luther King Jr., the acknowledged leader of the Civil Rights movement, was also a major supporter of the VRA. The civil rights agenda was not limited to the VRA. It also included the Civil Rights Act of 1964, which provided broad guarantees against racial and other discrimination in private employment and federally sponsored activities, and the Fair Housing Act of 1968, which prohibited racial discrimination in the housing market.

LEGISLATIVE DEBATE

The legislative debate leading to the act focused on the seriousness and breadth of states' deprivations of the right to vote. The debate also concerned the appropriateness of federal legislation overseeing states' conduct of their elections. Under the Constitution, the conduct of elections is a matter for state regulation. Opponents of the VRA argued that the VRA was an inappropriate federal interference in state affairs. On the other side, proponents noted that the right to vote was enshrined in the U.S. Constitution, and argued, ultimately successfully, that it was appropriate for the federal government to take steps to safeguard that right.

The legislative debate leading to the act focused on the seriousness and breadth of states' deprivations of the right to vote.

The debate on the VRA was heavily influenced by current events. The Civil Rights movement was in full swing by the mid-1960s. Southern opposition to that movement, in particular acts of violence and intimidation led both by private parties and by government officials, were national news. Pictures of police using dogs and water cannons on nonviolent protesters appeared prominently on national television, and reports of mob violence against civil rights activists appeared on the front pages of newspapers. All of this persuaded many Americans who had previously been uninformed or apathetic about civil rights issues that strong federal action was necessary.

IMPORTANT COURT INTERPRETATIONS

The constitutionality of the VRA was established in an important 1966 case, *South Carolina v. Katzenbach*. In that case the Supreme Court held that the VRA was an appropriate use by Congress of its power to "enforce" the Fifteenth Amendment. *South Carolina* is notable because it inaugurated a period during which the Supreme Court gave a more permissive interpretation to Congress' power to enforce the Fifteenth Amendment. Also in 1966, the Court gave a similarly broad reading to Congress' power to enforce the Fourteenth Amendment in *Katzenbach v. Morgan*.

Most of these African-American voters were able to vote for the first time after the passage of the Voting Rights Act of 1965. Here, in Wilcox County, Alabama, voters line up in front a polling station at The Sugar Shack, a local general store, May 3, 1966
(©BETTMANN/CORBIS)

In other important cases the Supreme Court interpreted provisions of the VRA itself. For example, in *Allen v. State Board of Elections* (1969), the Court interpreted section 5's preclearance requirements to apply to any change that had the effect of diluting the voting strength of minorities, rather than merely to changes in laws dealing with the act of voting itself. Vote dilution occurs when a government entity, such as a city government, changes its structure in a way that reduces minority voting strength. In *Perkins v. Matthews* (1971), for example, the Court held that a city's annexations of surrounding areas had to be precleared under section 5. If the annexed area was primarily occupied by whites, then such annexations might dilute minority voting strength. The result would be a new, larger city with a larger percentage of whites than before, thus weakening minority political power.

Another important electoral practice involves redistricting. States redraw their legislative districts every ten years to take account of population changes reflected in the census. Depending on how those districts are drawn, minority voting strength might be diluted. For example, a black neighborhood might be split up into several districts rather than concentrated in one, with the result that in no one district would black voting power be decisive. In *Georgia v. United States* (1973), the Court held that state legislative redistricting would also have to be precleared. Today both state legislative and congressional district lines must be precleared in the states subject to section 5.

At other times, the Court has adopted narrower interpretations of the VRA. For example, in *Mobile v. Bolden* (1980), the Court held that section 2's prohibitions on voter qualification tests that are racially discriminatory included only those tests specifically motivated by a desire to discriminate on the

The Great Society

Alfred L. Brophy

In May 1964, President Lyndon B. Johnson delivered a graduation speech at the University of Michigan, which established the idea that the United States should strive for "abundance and liberty for all." He told the graduating students that "Your imagination, your initiative, and your indignation will determine whether we build a society where progress is the servant of our needs, or a society where old values and new visions are buried under unbridled growth. For in your time we have the opportunity to move not only toward the rich society and the powerful society, but upward to the Great Society." The two key elements of that "Great Society" were "an end to poverty and racial injustice."

Johnson focused on equal opportunity and assisting racial minorities and the poor of any race. The Civil Rights Act of 1964 and the Economic Opportunity Act were important early Great Society legislation. They were followed in January 1965, after Johnson's landslide victory in the November 1964 presidential election against Republican Barry Goldwater, with legislation to establish Medicare (for elderly Americans) and Medicaid (for poor Americans), the Voting Rights Act of 1965, and the Immigration Act of 1965. Other legislation included the Housing and Urban Development Act, the Motor Vehicle Traffic Safety Act, the National Endowment for the Humanities, and the Elementary Secondary Education Act, the Higher Education Act, and the Fair Housing Act of 1968.

In the closing months of Johnson's presidency, the war in Vietnam and increasing domestic violence—like the long, hot summer of 1968 and the assassination of Robert Kennedy and Martin Luther King—signaled the unraveling of Johnson's programs. They also signaled the end of the optimism, born of America's triumphs in World War II and the New Deal, in government. The era of Great Society legislation ended in 1968 with the election of President Richard Nixon, although many of its accomplishments continue to this day.

basis of race. The VRA does not apply, the Court said, to those requirements that merely affect blacks and other minorities differently than they affect whites. Two years later, Congress amended the VRA to make clear that it intended to prohibit actions with discriminatory results, not just actions that were intentionally discriminatory.

The VRA was originally written to expire in five years. In 1970 Congress renewed the act for another five years, and in 1975 and subsequent years it was renewed again. Each time, Congress has renewed the act for only a limited period, with the idea that it would reconsider whether the federal intrusions on state electoral processes were still necessary, or even needed strengthening. In each case Congress decided to renew the act. In renewing the act in 1970, Congress indicated its approval of the broad interpretations the Supreme Court gave to the act in cases like *Allen*.

Each time, Congress has renewed the act for only a limited period, with the idea that it would reconsider whether the federal intrusions on state electoral processes were still necessary, or even needed strengthening.

THE VRA AND EQUAL PROTECTION

In the 1990s the Justice Department's use of the VRA to prevent minority vote dilution came under attack in the Supreme Court. The Justice Department has sometimes insisted that compliance with section 5 requires maximizing minority voter strength. This in turn would require taking race significantly into account when states redraw their legislative and congressional districts. Some legal scholars and political leaders have claimed that the practice of placing voters in particular districts based on their race violates the equal protection clause of the Fourteenth Amendment. This clause prevents states from denying to individuals "the equal protection of the laws" and has long been understood as prohibiting government from classifying individuals on the basis of their race. In *Shaw v. Reno* (1993) and *Miller v. Johnson* (1995), the Court suggested that such use of race might violate the equal protection clause if race was the predominant motivating factor in the state's redistricting plan. The Court's suggestion raises questions about how stringently the VRA may be used in the districting context. So far, the Court has not squarely faced those questions.

Georgia v. Ashcroft

Before 2003, the sections of the Voting Rights Act dealing with "dilution" of the minority vote were interpreted to mean that any reduction in the percentage of minority voters in a legislative district would result in a reduction of minority voting rights, and so could not be permitted. In the South, this concentration of black voters in particular districts came to result in more black candidates being elected, but fewer Democrats overall winning office, because black voters (who tended to vote Democratic) were excluded from districts with white majorities. In *Georgia v. Ashcroft* (2003), however, the Supreme Court refined the previous interpretation, ruling that states may consider the overall influence of minority voters, not just their relative percentages of the population, when redrawing district lines. In effect, the reasoning went, minority voters might have more power if they were able to have an influence in many districts. Justice Sandra Day O'Connor, who wrote the majority opinion, stated that it was necessary to take into consideration districts in which minority voters could join coalitions to elect representatives supportive of minority interests, even if minorities did not hold enough votes to elect a minority candidate. "The state may choose," she wrote, "that it is better to risk having fewer minority representatives in order to achieve greater overall representation of a minority group by increasing the number of representatives sympathetic to the interests of minority voters."

EFFECTIVENESS

Section 2 of the VRA has gone a long way toward ending the discriminatory use of voter qualifications tests. Before the VRA these tests were used to deprive blacks and other minorities of their rights to vote. Today it is rare, though still not unknown, for government officials to seek to deprive minority voters of their rights through obvious means such as voter qualification tests. Dilution claims, however, are far more common, given how broadly "voter dilution" is defined. In fact, this loose understanding of the term has the potential to affect almost any structural or electoral change a government may make.

Section 5 has also become extraordinarily important. Congressional district boundaries are redrawn every ten years to correspond with population changes as reflected in the census. In the states subject to section 5 of the VRA, the U.S. Justice Department heavily influences the redrawing of those lines, a practice normally performed by state legislatures. Under section 5, the Justice Department must approve those district lines before they can go into effect to become the new congressional and state legislative boundaries. Redistricting is a hotly contested political issue, because the shape of legislative districts influences how heavily Democratic or Republican the district will be. Thus Justice Department involvement in redistricting has often led to lengthy legal and political conflicts.

Redistricting is a hotly contested political issue, because the shape of legislative districts influences how heavily Democratic or Republican the district will be.

See also: Civil Rights Acts of 1866, 1875, 1957, 1964; Fair Housing Act of 1968; Force Act of 1871; Ku Klux Klan Act.

BIBLIOGRAPHY

Branch, Taylor. *Pillar of Fire: America in the King Years 1963–1965.* New York: Simon & Schuster, 1998.

Garrow, David J. *Protest at Selma: Martin Luther King, Jr., and the Voting Rights Act of 1965.* New Haven, CT: Yale University Press, 1978.

Thernstrom, Abigail. *Whose Votes Count? Affirmative Action and Minority Voting Rights.* Cambridge, MA: Harvard University Press, 1987.

U.S. Commission on Civil Rights. *A Citizen's Guide to the Voting Rights Act.* Washington, DC: The Commission, 1984.

Williams, Juan. *Eyes on the Prize: America's Civil Rights Years 1954–1965.* New York: Viking, 1987.

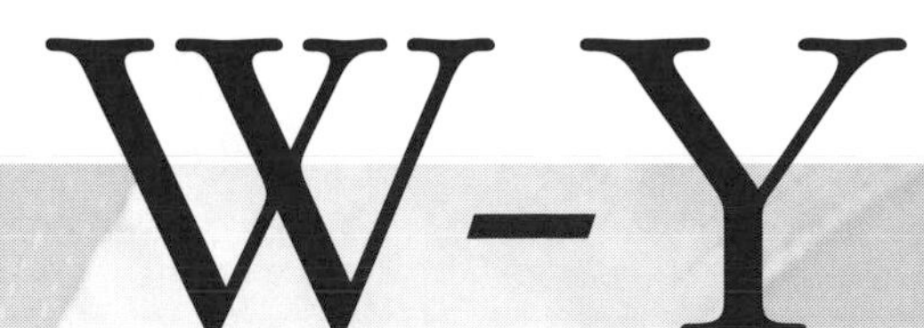

Wagner-Steagall Housing Act

See United States Housing Act

Walsh-Healey Public Contracts Act (1936)

Hether C. Macfarlane

On May 27, 1935 the U.S. Supreme Court declared the National Industrial Recovery Act (NIRA) unconstitutional. The Court's decision ended the first effort of the administration of Franklin D. Roosevelt to address the unemployment of nearly thirteen million American men and women caused by the Great Depression. Within a month, the Senate began considering a bill proposed by Secretary of Labor Frances Perkins to address the same problems on a much less sweeping scale, a proposal that became the Walsh-Healey Public Contracts Act (P.L. 74-846, 49 Stat. 2036).

The Walsh-Healey Act required that all contracts with any part of the U.S. government for goods or supplies worth at least $10,000 must state that:

1) the supplier was a manufacturer or regular dealer in the supplies;
2) all people employed in making or furnishing the supplies would be paid no less than what the Secretary of Labor had previously determined to be the "prevailing minimum wages for persons employed on similar work or in the particular or similar industries or groups of industries currently operating in the locality" where the supplies were made or furnished;
3) no one employed in making or furnishing the supplies would work more than eight hours a day or forty hours a week;
4) the business would not employ boys under sixteen, girls under eighteen, or prisoners; and
5) none of the work for the contract would be done under hazardous or unsanitary working conditions.

The act's provisions—the use of regular manufacturers or dealers rather than "bid brokers" who subcontracted to sweatshops; a minimum wage; the

The act's provisions—the use of regular manufacturers or dealers rather than "bid brokers" who subcontracted to sweatshops; a minimum wage; the eight-hour day and forty-hour week; the elimination of child labor;, and health and safety standards—were measures reformers had advocated for much of the twentieth century to address conditions created by industrialization.

eight-hour day and forty-hour week; the elimination of child labor; and health and safety standards—were measures reformers had advocated for much of the twentieth century to address conditions created by industrialization. The wage and hour provisions were promoted as a means of decreasing unemployment and increasing the purchasing power of American workers.

The act's supporters believed employers would have to hire additional workers to keep their businesses working the same number of hours a week, thereby reducing the ranks of the unemployed. They also argued that requiring employers to pay the prevailing minimum wage would raise wages, allowing workers to purchase more goods from American businesses. The child and convict labor provisions similarly were designed to free those jobs for unemployed adults, as well as to protect children from exploitation.

Proponents of the bill argued that, because the federal government was required to accept the lowest bid for all its contracts, government agencies were often forced to contract with suppliers who paid insufficient wages, or who required workers to give "kickbacks" to cover employer expenses, or who required forty-four to sixty hours of work a week. Opponents noted that the bill defined neither "locality" nor "prevailing" and argued the bill was simply an attempt to reinstate the NIRA and again have the government, rather than the market, set wages. The proponents responded that the Walsh-Healey Act was different from the NIRA because the secretary of labor would not "set" wages but would instead determine the "prevailing" minimum wage that already existed in the industry and locality.

Frances Perkins (1880–1965)

Hether C. Macfarlane

Frances Perkins was the nation's fourth secretary of labor and the first woman in the United States to serve as a Cabinet officer. Born in Boston in 1880, Ms. Perkins graduated in 1903 from Mount Holyoke College in Massachusetts. Visits to local textile and paper mills during a college history course showed her the difficult and dangerous conditions under which men, women, and children worked in the early twentieth century, which led her to a career in social work and public service. As a result of her efforts and those of other reformers, between 1911 and 1915 the New York state assembly rewrote the state's Industrial Code and passed thirty-six new laws that provided for increased worker safety, limited hours worked by women and children, and established financial compensation for workers injured on the job. Governor Al Smith appointed Ms. Perkins to the state's Industrial Board in 1926, and the next governor, Franklin Roosevelt, appointed her as Industrial Commissioner of New York in 1928.

When Roosevelt was elected president, he offered Ms. Perkins the Cabinet post of secretary of labor. She accepted, but only after she got the president-elect's agreement to her list of goals. The list included much of what became the New Deal's important social legislation: Social Security, minimum wage and overtime laws, child labor laws, federal aid to states for unemployment relief, public works projects, and unemployment insurance. She also reorganized the Department of Labor to make it a more effective agency. Ms. Perkins served as secretary of labor from 1933 until President Roosevelt's death in 1945. From 1946 until 1952, she served on the Civil Service Commission. Frances Perkins died in 1965. The headquarters of the Department of Labor in Washington, D.C. is today named the Frances Perkins Building.

The constitutionality of the wage provision of the act was upheld by the Supreme Court in 1940 in *Perkins v. Lukens Steel Company*. The secretary of labor's power to determine the "locality" of the prevailing wage as either a regional or a national locality has also been upheld, although the locality determinations for numerous industries have been contested by business. The most significant amendment to the act since 1936 occurred in 1985 when the eight-hour limit was deleted, leaving suppliers free to pay employees for longer hours in a single day, so long as the total number of hours worked in a week remained at forty.

The most significant amendment to the act since 1936 occurred in 1985 when the eight-hour limit was deleted, leaving suppliers free to pay employees for longer hours in a single day, so long as the total number of hours worked in a week remained at forty.

Despite the passage of the Fair Labor Standards Act in 1937, which mandated minimum wage and maximum hour standards for workers throughout the United States, the Walsh-Healey Public Contracts Act remains in force.

See also: Contract Disputes Act; National Industrial Recovery Act; Fair Labor Standards Act; Occupational Safety & Health Act

BIBLIOGRAPHY

Brandeis, Elizabeth, "Organized Labor and Protective Labor Legislation." In *Labor and the New Deal*. Derber, Milton, and Edwin Young, eds. Madison, WI: University of Wisconsin Press, 1957.

Leuchtenberg, William E. *Franklin D. Roosevelt and the New Deal 1932–1940*. New York: Harper and Row, 1963.

Paulsen, George E. *A Living Wage for the Forgotten Man: The Quest for Fair Labor Standards, 1933–1941*. Cranbury, NJ, London, and Mississauga, Ontario: Associated University Presses, Inc. 1996.

Reilly, Gerard D. "Madam Secretary." In *The Making of the New Deal: The Insiders Speak*. Louchheim, Katie, eds. Cambridge, MA: Harvard University Press, 1983.

War Powers Resolution (1973)

Louis Fisher

Excerpt from the War Powers Resolution

Sec. 2. (a) It is the purpose of this joint resolution to fulfill the intent of the framers of the Constitution of the United States and insure that the collective judgment of both the Congress and the president will apply to the introduction of United States Armed Forces into hostilities, or into situations where imminent involvement in hostilities is clearly indicated by the circumstances, and to the continued use of such forces in hostilities or in such situations.

(b) Under article I, section 8, of the Constitution, it is specifically provided that the Congress shall have the power to make all laws necessary and proper for carrying into execution, not only its own powers but also all other powers vested by the Constitution in the Government of the United States, or in any department or officer thereof.

(c) The constitutional powers of the president as Commander-in-Chief to introduce United States Armed Forces into hostilities, or into situations where imminent involve-

ment in hostilities is clearly indicated by the circumstances, are exercised only pursuant to (1) a declaration of war, (2) specific statutory authorization, or (3) a national emergency created by attack upon the United States, its territories or possessions, or its armed forces.

After World War II, Congress watched its institutional powers decline. President Harry Truman's military initiatives in Korea in 1950 and the escalation of the Vietnam War by President Lyndon B. Johnson beginning in 1965 both contributed to this reduced role for Congress. In an effort to restore its prerogatives and limit presidential wars, Congress passed the War Powers Resolution in 1973 (P.L. 93-148, 87 Stat. 555). However, in many instances the statute contradicts itself, reflecting major differences between the House and the Senate. Despite passage of the act, in the years since 1973 presidents have continued to dominate decisions concerning military operations.

Despite passage of the act, in the years since 1973 presidents have continued to dominate decisions concerning military operations.

DRAFTING THE BILL

In 1970 the House of Representatives passed by a vote of 289 to 39 a bill recognizing that the president "in certain extraordinary and emergency circumstances has the authority to defend the United States and its citizens without specific prior authorization by the Congress." Instead of trying to define the precise conditions under which presidents may use military force, the House preferred to rely on procedural safeguards. The bill required the president, "whenever feasible," to consult with Congress before sending American forces into armed conflict. He was also to report (1) the circumstances necessitating the action; (2) the constitutional, legislative, and treaty provisions authorizing the action, together with his reasons for not seeking specific prior congressional authorization; and (3) the estimated scope of activities. The Senate did not act on this measure.

Later, both houses of Congress passed legislation that went beyond mere reporting requirements. Following its earlier model, the House of Representatives did not try to define or codify presidential war powers. It directed the president "in every possible instance" to consult with Congress before sending forces into hostilities or situations where hostilities might be imminent. If unable to do so, he was to report to Congress within seventy-two hours, setting forth the circumstances and details of his action. Unless Congress declared war within 120 days or specifically authorized the use of force, the president had to terminate the commitment and remove the troops. Congress could also direct disengagement at any time during the 120-day period by passing a concurrent resolution, which must pass both houses but is not presented to the president for his signature or **veto.**

veto: when the president returns a bill to Congress with a statement of objections

Senators, regarding the House bill as too favorable to presidential power, decided to spell out the conditions under which presidents could act alone without Congress. Armed force could be used in three situations:

(1) To repel an armed attack on the United States, or its territories and possessions, to retaliate in the event of such an attack, and to prevent the direct and imminent threat of such an attack.

President Richard Nixon visits troops at their headquarters, twelve miles north of Saigon, July 1969. Congress largely acquiesced to presidential policy during the early years of the Vietnam War. Later in the war—especially during Nixon's second term as president—Congress played a more active role in Vietnam policy decisions.(© AP/WIDE WORLD PHOTOS)

(2) To repel an armed attack against U.S. armed forces located outside the United States, or its territories and possessions, and prevent the direct and imminent threat of such an attack.
(3) To rescue endangered American citizens and nationals in foreign countries or at sea.

The Senate bill also required the president to cease military action unless Congress, within thirty days, specifically authorized the president to continue. A separate provision allowed him to act militarily beyond the thirty-day limit if he determined that "unavoidable military necessity respecting the safety" of the armed forces required their continued use for purposes of "bringing about a prompt disengagement." Efforts to legislate presidential war powers carried a number of risks. Presidents and officials of the executive branch could broadly interpret such terms as "necessary and appropriate retaliatory actions," "imminent threat," and "endangered citizens."

THE FINAL BILL

The two houses settled on a compromise measure. Instead of the 120-day House limit and the thirty-day Senate limit, the final bill allowed the president to use military force for up to sixty days, with an additional thirty days to permit disengagement. The bill directed the president "in every possible instance" to consult with lawmakers, and required the president to report to Congress within forty-eight hours. At any time during military operations, Congress could pass a concurrent resolution directing that U.S. troops be removed.

As the bill emerged from Congress, a number of lawmakers who had initially offered support now spoke out in opposition. Senator Thomas Eagleton, a Democrat from Missouri and one of the original sponsors, denounced the conference product as a "total, complete distortion of the war powers concept." Instead of the three exceptions specified in the Senate bill and the thirty-day limit, the conference version gave the president carte blanche authority to use military force anywhere, for any reason, for up to ninety days. Eagleton confessed to being "dumbfounded." With memories so fresh about presidential extension of the war in Vietnam, he argued, "how can we give unbridled, unlimited total authority to the president to commit us to war?" In his view, the bill, after being nobly conceived, had "been horribly bastardized to the point of being a menace."

President Nixon vetoed the bill primarily because he regarded it as impractical and dangerous to establish in a statute the procedure by which the president and Congress should share the war power. He also believed that the legislation encroached on the president's constitutional responsibilities as Commander in Chief. Both Houses mustered a two-thirds majority to **override** the veto: the House narrowly (284 to 135), the Senate by a more comfortable margin (75 to 18).

override: if the President vetoes a bill passed by Congress, the bill can still become law if two-thirds of each house of Congress votes to override the veto

Some of the congressional support for the override reflected party politics and a willingness to settle for symbolic value over substance. Fifteen members of the House, after voting against the House bill and the conference version because they surrendered too much power to the president, now voted for the override. To be consistent, they should have sustained the veto to prevent the bill from becoming law. Some of the fifteen voted for the override because they feared that a vote to sustain might lend credence to the views advanced in Nixon's veto message. Others among the fifteen believed that a vote to override would help propel the House to impeach Nixon. Democratic Representative Bella Abzug of New York voted against the House bill and the conference version because they expanded presidential war power. Yet she strongly supported a veto override: "This could be a turning point in the struggle to control an administration that has run amuck. It could accelerate the demand for the impeachment of the President."

Fifteen members of the House, after voting against the House bill and the conference version because they surrendered too much power to the president, now voted for the override.

ANALYZING THE STATUTE

According to section 2(a) of the War Powers Resolution, it was the purpose of Congress

> to fulfill the intent of the framers of the Constitution of the United States and insure that the collective judgment of both the Congress and the president will apply to the introduction of United States Armed Forces into hostilities, or into situations where imminent involvement in hostilities is clearly indicated by the circumstances, and to the continued use of such forces in hostilities or in such situations.

The statute falls short on both goals. Allowing the president to initiate war for up to ninety days does not fulfill the intent of the framers, and nothing in the statute insures the collective judgment of both branches in the use of military force.

The framers placed in Congress not only the sole authority to declare war, but to initiate any kind of offensive operations, big and small. They limited the president's initiative to defensive war for the purpose of repelling sudden attacks. Deliberations at the Constitutional Convention and the ratifying conventions demonstrate that the framers embraced three notions: (1) the principle of collective decision making, (2) the concept of shared power in foreign affairs, and (3) the democratic ideal that war power is placed with the legislative branch, which is the branch closest to the people. At the Pennsylvania ratifying convention, James Wilson expressed the prevailing sentiment that the system of **checks and balances** "will not hurry us into war; it is calculated to guard against it. It will not be in the power of a single man, or a single body of men, to involve us in such distress; for the important power of declaring war is vested in the legislature at large." The War Pow-

checks and balances: the limiting powers that each branch of government has over the other two. (The government is divided into three branches: legislative, executive, and judicial, each with distinct powers.)

A U.S. Army soldier watches helicopters as they prepare to land troops in a rice field eight miles from Bien Hoa, Vietnam, May 29, 1965. Congress granted President Lyndon B. Johnson broad authority to use military force in Vietnam with the passage of the Gulf of Tonkin Resolution in August 1964. (©CORBIS)

Military initiatives from presidents in the years following the War Powers Resolution reveal a glaring deficiency in the statute.

ers Resolution replaces that value with a trust in, or acceptance of, presidential wars.

Military initiatives from presidents in the years following the War Powers Resolution reveal a glaring deficiency in the statute. The resolution is written in such a way that the sixty- to ninety-day clock begins ticking only if the president reports under a very specific section: not section 4, not section 4(a), but only section 4(a)(1). Not surprisingly, presidents do not report under 4(a)(1). They report, for the most part, "consistent with the War Powers Resolution." The only president to report under 4(a)(1) was Gerald Ford in the capture of the *Mayaguez* ship in Cambodia. But even in that case, his report had no substantive importance because it was issued only after the military operation had been completed.

Finally, the use of a concurrent resolution to control the president is of questionable potency because of the Supreme Court's decision in *INS v. Chadha* (1983). This ruling struck down the legislative veto—one-house or two-house—as unconstitutional. The Court said that whenever Congress wants to control the executive branch it has to act not merely by both houses but in a bill or joint resolution that is presented to the president. In response to *Chadha,* Congress considered amending the War Powers Resolution to replace the concurrent resolution with a joint resolution. Instead, the 1983 amendment was enacted as a freestanding statute, providing expedited procedures that can be used to force the president to withdraw troops.

JUDICIAL INVOLVEMENT

On four occasions during the 1980s, members of Congress went to court to charge that President Ronald Reagan had violated the War Powers Resolution. The first case, *Crockett v. Reagan* (1982), involved his sending military advisers to El Salvador. A district court refused to do the fact-finding that would have been necessary to determine whether hostilities or imminent hostilities existed in El Salvador. The judge pointed out that Congress had failed to act legislatively to restrain Reagan. A similar case was *Conyers v. Reagan* (1984). Eleven members of Congress brought action against President Reagan for his invasion of

Presidential Perspective

Throughout U.S. history, presidents have routinely deployed military forces without the consent of Congress. While these actions have not always been popular, serious opposition to the practice did not arise until Presidents Lyndon Johnson and Richard Nixon conducted the conflict in Vietnam without a declaration of war or the authorization of Congress. The movement to pass the War Powers Resolution grew out of increasing frustration with the deadly, costly, and seemingly unwinnable conflict, and out of personal antagonism toward Nixon himself. (As Senator Gaylord Nelson of Wisconsin memorably stated, "I love the Constitution, but I hate Nixon more.") Nixon vetoed the resolution on the grounds that it was both unconstitutional and dangerous. He argued that the sixty-day limit on presidential authority could "prolong or intensify a crisis" by discouraging an adversary from serious negotiations before the sixty days were up or escalating hostilities to achieve particular objectives, in hopes that Congress would then force the president to withdraw. Congress passed the resolution over Nixon's veto. Since then, presidents have consistently taken Nixon's perspective, and have reverted to tradition by continuing to deploy military forces on their own authority. Every U.S. president since Nixon has been accused of violating the War Powers resolution.

Grenada in 1983. The district court declined to exercise its jurisdiction because lawmakers had failed to use available powers within their own institution. Two other cases, involving President Reagan's activities in Nicaragua and his use of military force in the Persian Gulf, were avoided by the courts on similar grounds (*Sanchez-Espinoza v. Reagan,* [1983], *Sanchez-Espinoza v. Reagan,* [1985], *Lowry v. Reagan,* [1987]). The judicial advice was consistent: if Congress fails to defend its prerogatives, it cannot expect to be bailed out by the courts.

Later cases struck the same note. In 1990, when President George H. W. Bush sent troops to Saudi Arabia and neighboring countries to prepare for war against Iraq, a federal court turned aside a lawsuit brought by members of Congress who charged that he had acted without legal authority. The court concluded that only if Congress confronted the president as an institution, acting through both houses, would the case be ready for the courts (*Dellums v. Bush,* [1990]). Essentially the same result occurred when Representative Tom Campbell, a Republican of California, went to court with twenty-five other House colleagues to seek a declaration that President Bill Clinton had violated the Constitution and the War Powers Resolution by conducting an air offensive in Yugoslavia without congressional authorization. A district court held that Campbell lacked standing to bring the suit. Congress had never, as an institution, directed Clinton to cease military operations. That decision was upheld on appeal (*Campbell v. Clinton,* 1999).

Congress has been unwilling to confront the president with legislative restrictions, and the courts decline to reach the merits of these cases unless lawmakers have exercised powers available to them. As a result, presidents may initiate and conduct wars whenever and wherever they like. In this fundamental respect, the framers' model of a system of checks and balances, with each branch able and willing to fight off encroachments from other branches, and with the power to initiate war securely vested in Congress, has failed.

Congress has been unwilling to confront the president with legislative restrictions, and the courts decline to reach the merits of these cases unless lawmakers exercise powers available to them.

See also: National Security Act of 1947.

BIBLIOGRAPHY

Adler, David Gray. "The Constitution and Presidential Warmaking: The Enduring Debate." *Political Science Quarterly* 103 (1988): 1–36.

Adler, David Gray, and Larry N. George, eds. *The Constitution and the Conduct of American Foreign Policy*. Lawrence, KS: University Press of Kansas, 1996.

Eagleton, Thomas F. *War and Presidential Power: A Chronicle of Congressional Surrender.* New York: Liveright, 1974.

Ely, John Hart. *War and Responsibility: Constitutional Lessons of Vietnam and Its Aftermath*. Princeton, NJ: Princeton University Press, 1993.

Fisher, Louis. *Presidential War Power,* 2d ed. Lawrence, KS: University Press of Kansas, 2004.

Fisher, Louis, and David Gray Adler. "The War Powers Resolution: Time to Say Goodbye." *Political Science Quarterly* 113 (1998): 1–20.

Hess, Gary R. *Presidential Decisions for War: Korea, Vietnam, and the Persian Gulf.* Baltimore, MD: Johns Hopkins Press, 2001.

Javits, Jacob K. *Who Makes War: The President Versus Congress*. New York: Morrow, 1973.

Powell, H. Jefferson. *The President's Authority Over Foreign Affairs: An Essay in Constitutional Interpretation*. Durham, NC: Duke University Press, 2002.

Weissman, Stephen R. *A Culture of Deference: Congress's Failure of Leadership in Foreign Policy*. New York: Basic Books, 1996.

Wormuth, Francis D., and Edwin B. Firmage. *To Chain the Dog of War: The War Power of Congress in History and Law,* 2d ed. Urbana, IL: University of Illinois Press, 1989.

WATER POLLUTION PREVENTION AND CONTROL ACT

See FEDERAL WATER POLLUTION CONTROL ACT

WEAPONS OF MASS DESTRUCTION CONTROL ACT (1992)

David A. Koplow

With the Weapons of Mass Destruction Control Act (P.L. 102-484, 106 Stat. 2569), Congress expressed its strong fear that, in a post–Cold War world, the greatest dangers to U.S. national security and global stability came from the threatened proliferation of advanced and extraordinarily lethal weapons. The act reflects the belief that American policy and funding ought to put a higher priority on efforts to impede those developments.

The act addresses several categories of modern armaments. The term "weapons of mass destruction" (WMD) includes nuclear weapons first and foremost. But it also includes chemical and biological weapons (which might prove cheaper and more accessible for poor countries and terrorist groups). The act also highlights missile systems that could be used to deliver WMD or other arms with great speed and precision while evading many countries' defensive systems for detecting and intercepting aircraft. Together, these weapons of extraordinary lethality threaten to undermine peace and stability because they could give an aggressor country a substantial advantage in a surprise first strike. Such a strike could deliver a devastating blow to an unsuspecting target country, deciding the outcome of a war in the opening moments.

Through this law, Congress sought to take greater advantage of the "unique expertise" of the U.S. Departments of Defense and Energy in international nonproliferation activities, including "(A) to detect and monitor proliferation, (B) to respond to terrorism, theft, and accidents involving weapons of mass destruction, and (C) to assist with interdiction and destruction of weapons of mass destruction and related weapons material." Although the statute declares it to be "the sense of Congress" that U.S. policy ought to "seek to limit both the supply of and demand for" WMD, most of the statute's provisions are aimed at limiting a country's access to, rather than its demand for, such arms.

The law has two key aspects of operation. The first requires a wide-ranging report to Congress from the secretaries of defense and energy

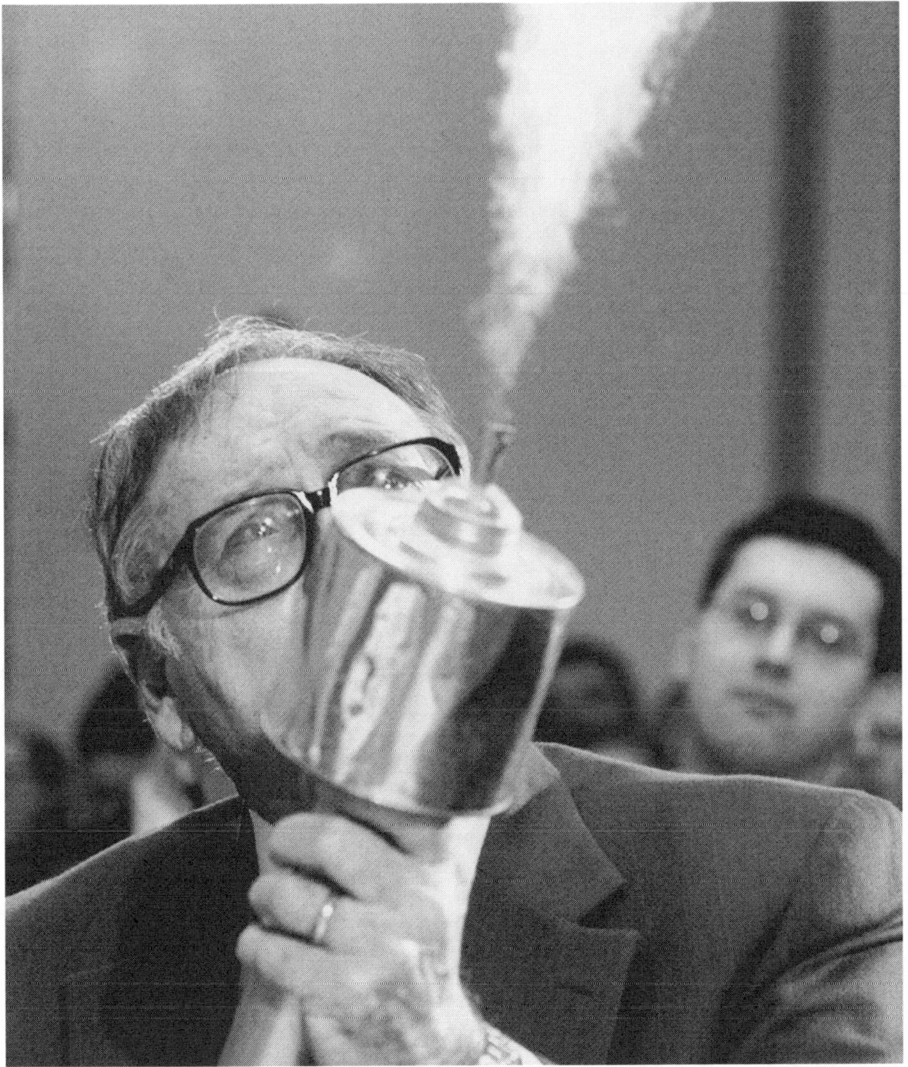

Dr. William Patrick, the former chief of U.S. offensive biological weapons, shows the House Select Committee on Intelligence how easy it is to launch biological agents, March 3, 1999. (© AP/Wide World Photos)

regarding U.S. nonproliferation policy and activities. Congress specified that the report should address topics such as how the two departments coordinate their intelligence, military capabilities, and emergency response capacities, and how this integration could be improved. The statute also sought additional information about existing and planned departmental capabilities "to (A) detect and monitor clandestine weapons of mass destruction programs, (B) respond to terrorism or accidents involving such weapons and to theft of related weapons materials, and (C) assist with interdiction and destruction of weapons of mass destruction and related weapons materials."

The other key aspect concerns increased funding for a variety of activities in the category of the "nonproliferation technology initiative." Congress here authorized additional support for research, testing, and procurement of systems to sense chemical and biological weapons, to accomplish seismic monitoring of nuclear explosions, and to detect concealed nuclear materials. It also permitted further assistance to international nonproliferation activities, such as providing international organizations with money, supplies, equipment, personnel, and training to support security, counterterrorism, and related efforts. One example of such activity authorized by the act is the assistance the Department of Defense gave to the United Nations Special Commission (UNSCOM) for its inspections in Iraq. The Defense Department provided U-2 surveillance flights and other intelligence and logistics support at a cost of $15 million per year. The U.S. support to UNSCOM was suspended after the December 15, 1998 UNSCOM pullout from Iraq.

See also: Arms Control and Disarmament Act and Amendments; Nuclear Non-Proliferation Act.

Whistleblower Protection Laws (1989)

Robert G. Vaughn

The whistleblower provision of the Civil Service Reform Act of 1978, known as the Reform Act (P.L. 95-454, 92 Stat. 111) is the major piece of legislation protecting federal employees who disclose information (blow the whistle) on government misconduct or waste. In his presidential campaign, Jimmy Carter had promised to push for legislation to protect federal employee whistleblowers from retaliation. Carter made good on his campaign promise, and the provision he proposed received bipartisan support in Congress. In 1989 the Whistleblower Protection Act, known as the WPA (P.L. 101-12, 103 Stat. 16), strengthened the protections provided in the Reform Act.

These whistleblower protection laws prohibit reprisal against federal employees who "reasonably" believe that their disclosures show "a violation of law, rule, or regulation, gross mismanagement, a gross waste of funds, an abuse of authority, or a specific and substantial danger to public health and safety." Disclosures can be made to any person, and internal disclosure (within the government agency) is not required. Disclosures are only protected if "not specifically prohibited by law and if such information is not specifically required by an Executive Order to be kept secret in the interest of national defense or the conduct of foreign affairs." These prohibited disclosures, however, can be made to the inspector generals of government agencies or to the Office of Special Counsel, an office created in part to represent the interests of whistleblowers.

Disclosures are only protected if "not specifically prohibited by law and if such information is not specifically required by an Executive Order to be kept secret in the interest of national defense or the conduct of foreign affairs."

ENFORCEMENT

These laws create a structure of administrative enforcement. Whistleblowers who have been subjected to certain personnel actions, such as removal, suspension, transfer, reassignment, or other similar actions taken as punishment, can raise whistleblowing as a defense before the United States Merit Systems Protection Board, a type of administrative court. Whistleblowers who were subject to personnel actions not appealable to the board have to rely either on the Office of Special Counsel to bring their claims before the board or may commence an independent right of action before the board. This independent right of action allows the board to address only employees' whistleblower claims. The decisions of the board are reviewed by the United States Court of Appeals for the Federal Circuit.

Whistleblowers are entitled to a number of remedies, including back pay and compensatory damages. These laws permit the Office of Special Counsel to commence disciplinary actions against federal officials who have retaliated against whistleblowers. Under this authority, a number of individual federal officials have been dismissed or suspended. In addition, the Special Counsel may require the head of an agency to respond to the allegations made by a whistleblower.

Protecting Whistleblowers

According to the nonprofit group the National Whistleblower Center, about half the whistleblowers who responded to a 2002 survey reported that they had been fired after reporting misconduct. Most of those who remained on the job reported harassment or discipline. The Office of Special Counsel, a government agency that protects government whistleblowers, reports that they handle nearly 700 complaints per year about employer retaliation. While more than a dozen federal laws protect whistleblowers in particular circumstances, there are still many complainants who do not receive government protection, including those who report election fraud, campaign finance abuse, and obstruction of justice.

INCREASED PROTECTION

The WPA strengthened whistleblower protection. Perhaps the most important change eases the burden on federal employees of proving they have been subjected to a reprisal. Employees need only show that protected disclosures were a "contributing factor" to the personnel action alleged to have been taken in reprisal. If an employee can demonstrate this connection, the agency must show by "clear and convincing evidence" that it would have taken the same action had the employee not made a disclosure protected by law. The WPA also rejects a number of decisions of the U.S. Court of Appeals for the Federal Circuit that Congress believed were unduly restrictive interpretations of the law.

WHISTLEBLOWING AS CIVIC DUTY

One of the most important effects of these whistleblower laws has been to legitimize whistleblowing. Whistleblowing is no longer seen as an act of disloyalty but as the fulfillment of civic responsibility. Whistleblowers protect society not only from misconduct and waste but also from unsafe and dangerous conditions.

Whistleblowing is no longer seen as an act of disloyalty but as the fulfillment of civic responsibility.

At the time of the passage of the Reform Act, whistleblowing was a scorned activity often officially punished. Today, Congress approves of whistleblowing in the strongest terms and has acted often to protect whistleblowers from reprisal. Dozens of state statutes, many modeled after the Reform Act or the WPA, protect whistleblowers in both the **public sector** and **private sector.**

public sector: the part of the economy concerned with providing basic government services such as the police, military, public roads, public transit, primary education and healthcare for the poor

private sector: the part of the economy that is not controlled by the government

PROTECTION IN THE PRIVATE SECTOR

Federal legislation protects whistleblowers who work in the private sector and who report violations of a variety of federal health, safety, and environmental laws. Also, in response to fraud and misconduct by large corporations and the accountants and attorneys representing them, Congress included whistleblower protection in the Sarbanes-Oxley Act of 2002 (P.L. 107-204, 116

Stat. 802), a law addressing this misconduct. Federal whistleblower protections now cover millions of private sector employees.

The private sector provisions are administrated by the United States Department of Labor. The whistleblower provision of the Sarbanes-Oxley Act permits private-sector whistleblowers to bring an action in federal district court if the Department of Labor does not resolve their claims of reprisal in a timely manner. In those district court actions, whistleblowers are entitled to receive a trial by jury.

Like public sector whistleblowers, those in the private sector also support the public's right to know about the operations of government. The disclosures by private-sector whistleblowers often concern the misconduct of government officials as well as their employers. Disclosures concerning health or safety or the environment, likewise, may identify weaknesses in government administration or regulation. In these ways, protections of private-sector whistleblowers support the freedom of expression and the right to know as do the protections of public employees.

EXPOSING CORRUPTION AND FRAUD

Public and private sector employees are important sources of information about the corruption of government officials and fraud regarding public funds.

Public and private sector employees are important sources of information about the corruption of government officials and fraud regarding public funds. The federal False Claims Act, after amendments in 1986 (P.L. 99-562, 100 Stat. 3153), has encouraged disclosures by both private and public employees that have led to the recovery of billions of dollars fraudulently obtained from the government. The False Claims Act contains its own whistleblower provision to protect those employees who seek to use the act to challenge fraud and misconduct. The act encourages whistleblowing not only through whistleblower protection but also by permitting them in some circumstances to receive a percentage of the funds recovered on behalf of the government.

INTERNATIONAL PROTECTIONS

More recently there has been a growing international consensus for whistleblower protection. Many countries in Europe, Asia, Africa, and South America have adopted provisions applying whistleblower protection to large segments of society. Several international instruments, including multinational treaties, regulations of international institutions, and codes of conduct now include protections of whistleblowers.

Whistleblower protection, like freedom of information laws and other open government provisions, supports the right of freedom of expression. This right is the foundation of democratic accountability and of democratic government.

See also: Civil Service Reform Act; Freedom of Information Act.

BIBLIOGRAPHY

Devine, Thomas. "The Whistleblower Protection Act of 1989: Foundation for the Modern Law of Employment Dissent." *Administrative Law Review* 35 (1999): 531–579.

Vaughn, Robert G. "Statutory Protection of Whistleblowers in the Federal Executive Branch." *University of Illinois Law Review* (1982): 615–667.

White Slave Traffic Act

See Mann Act

Wiley Act

See Pure Food and Drug Act

Wiretap Act

See Electronic Communications Privacy Act

World War Adjusted Compensation Act

See Bonus Bill

Yellowstone National Park Act (1872)

Brian E. Gray

On March 1, 1872, President Ulysses S. Grant signed into law the Yellowstone National Park Act (17 Stat. 32), which withdrew from settlement, occupancy, and sale a vast expanse of public land along the continental divide where the states of Wyoming, Montana, and Idaho intersected. The act "dedicated and set aside" the land "as a public park or pleasuring ground for the benefit and enjoyment of the people." Congress placed the land and resources of the park "under the exclusive control of the Secretary of the Interior" and directed the secretary to set forth rules and regulations "to provide for the preservation ... of all timber, mineral deposits, natural curiosities, or wonders within said park, and their retention in their natural condition." It also declared that the secretary "shall provide against the wanton destruction of the fish and game found within said park, and against their capture or destruction for the purposes of merchandise or profit." As one historian put it, the "reservation of this large tract of over 2 million acres of land—larger than a couple of the smallest states—with its wealth of timber, game, grass, water power, and possible minerals barred from all private use, was so dramatic a departure from the general public land policy of Congress that it seems almost a miracle" (Ise 1961, p. 17).

In 1864 Congress had set aside the lands and resources of Yosemite Valley and the Mariposa Grove of Sequoia Redwoods for "public use, resort, and recreation." But it gave title (ownership) and management responsibility for

While the Yellowstone Act was not the earliest reservation of park land, Yellowstone became the first national park to be administered by the United States for the preservation and enjoyment of its scenic wonders.

the Yosemite Park to the State of California. While the Yellowstone Act was not the earliest reservation of park land, Yellowstone became the first national park to be administered by the United States for the preservation and enjoyment of its scenic wonders.

Congress' principal purpose in creating Yellowstone National Park was to preserve the geysers and hot springs of the region and to protect the herds of bison, elk, and other wildlife that inhabited the park. They did so by closing the land to entry under the Homestead Act, mining laws, and other public lands statutes. With little knowledge of the geography and hydrogeology (the study of the geological formation and the movement of ground water) of the area and only sketchy maps, the sponsors of the legislation simply drew a square that would encompass the most important natural features—Old Faithful, Mammoth Hot Springs, the Norris and Mid-

Tourists and guides picnicking in Yellowstone National Park, 1903. (LIBRARY OF CONGRESS, PRINTS AND PHOTOGRAPHS DIVISION)

way Geyser Basins, Yellowstone Falls and the Grand Canyon of the Yellowstone River, the meadows of the great central plateau, Yellowstone Lake, the Absaroka Range, and the headwaters of the Missouri and Snake River systems.

Its alpine meadows—alive with bison, elk, antelope, deer, grizzly bear, peregrine falcon, bald eagles, kingfishers, pelicans, trumpeter swans, cutthroat trout, graylings, and an occasional cougar and wolf—make Yellowstone the nation's greatest wildlife haven.

Yet the park stands at the top of a much larger ecosystem that has been divided into seven national forests and three wildlife refuges. It includes Grand Teton National Park to the south and a mixture of state and private lands that abut Yellowstone's boundaries on the north, west, and east. As an island resting at the pinnacle of the Greater Yellowstone Ecosystem, Yellowstone National Park has been a testing ground for contemporary park policy. Oil and natural gas drilling in the Targhee National Forest to the west, and geothermal (heat generated from the Earth's core) exploration on private lands to the north, have threatened the groundwater basin that supplies the geysers and hot springs of the park. Clear-cutting in the national forests on all sides of the park has disrupted grizzly bear habitat and mating. Bison that stray across park borders in search of winter pasture have been slaughtered by hunters licensed under state law. Snowmobiles have so fouled the air that rangers at park entrances are forced to wear gas masks. With more than 3 million visitors annually, Yellowstone's roads, campgrounds, and most popular tourist destinations are overcrowded and overused. The great fires of 1988, and former Secretary of the Interior Bruce Babbitt's decision to reintroduce wolves to the park in 1995, sparked bitter debates over the National Park Service's resource management policies.

As an island resting at the pinnacle of the Greater Yellowstone Ecosystem, Yellowstone National Park has been a testing ground for contemporary park policy.

For all of its controversies, Yellowstone remains the keystone of our national park system. Its mountains form the spine of the continent. Its geysers, hot springs, lakes, rivers, and waterfalls are the font of our greatest waterways. Its alpine meadows—alive with bison,

Yellowstone's Precarious Early Years

When Yellowstone National Park was established in 1872, it was the first preserve of its kind in the United States, and no blueprint existed for its maintenance. There was no funding for the park, no salary for its first superintendent, and no means to enforce protection of its wildlife. With the arrival of the Northern Pacific Railroad at the north entrance to the park, tourism exploded from 300 visitors in 1872 to approximately 5,000 in 1873; however, by 1876, the park was in grave danger, with poachers slaughtering wildlife, squatters living in the woods, souvenir vendors destroying geological formations, and delicate thermal springs being used as wishing wells or collecting garbage. The secretary of the interior requested help from the secretary of war, and the U.S. Cavalry was deployed to restore order. While the troops strictly enforced park regulations, they had little ability to control poachers, as their authority was limited to confiscating a poacher's belongings and escorting him from the park—whereupon most snuck right back in. Poachers in Yellowstone freely hunted the last remaining herd of free-ranging bison in the United States, with devastating results, until an article in the magazine *Forest and Stream* publicized the situation. The resulting public outrage inspired Congress to pass the National Park Protection Act, which permitted the prosecution of poachers, and the tide was turned. By 1914 there were thirty national parks and monuments in the United States, two years later the National Park Service was formed to manage them, and in 1918 the cavalry turned over protection of the park to this new service. Today the flat-brimmed hats of the National Park Service rangers still pay tribute to the cavalry's role in safeguarding Yellowstone during its early years.

elk, antelope, deer, grizzly bear, peregrine falcon, bald eagles, kingfishers, pelicans, trumpeter swans, cutthroat trout, graylings, and an occasional cougar and wolf—make Yellowstone the nation's greatest wildlife haven.

See also: NATIONAL HISTORIC PRESERVATION ACT; NATIONAL PARK SERVICE ACT.

BIBLIOGRAPHY

Chase, Alston. *Playing God in Yellowstone: The Destruction of America's First National Park.* Boston, MA: Atlantic Monthly Press, 1986.

Chittenden, Hiram Martin. *The Yellowstone National Park.* Norman, OK: University of Oklahoma Press, 1964.

Ise, John. *Our National Parks Policy: A Critical History.* Washington, DC: Resources for the Future, 1961.

Keiter, Robert B., and Mark S. Boyce. *The Greater Yellowstone Ecosystem: Refining America's Wilderness Heritage.* New Haven, CT: Yale University Press, 1991.

Runte, Alfred. *National Parks: The American Experience,* 3d ed. Lincoln, NB: University of Nebraska Press, 1992.

APPENDICES

Constitution of the Unites States of America

We the People of the United States, in Order to form a more perfect Union, establish Justice, insure domestic Tranquility, provide for the common defense, promote the general Welfare, and secure the Blessings of Liberty to ourselves and our Posterity, do ordain and establish this Constitution for the United States of America.

ARTICLE I

Items in italic have since been amended or superseded. A portion of Article I, Section 2, was modified by Section 2 of the Fourteenth Amendment; Article I, Section 3, was modified by the Seventeenth Amendment; Article I, Section 4, was modified by Section 2 of the Twentieth Amendment; and Article I, Section 9, was modified by the Sixteenth Amendment.

Section 1: All legislative Powers herein granted shall be vested in a Congress of the United States, which shall consist of a Senate and House of Representatives.

Section 2: The House of Representatives shall be composed of Members chosen every second Year by the People of the several States, and the Electors in each State shall have the Qualifications requisite for Electors of the most numerous Branch of the State Legislature.

No Person shall be a Representative who shall not have attained to the Age of twenty five Years, and been seven Years a Citizen of the United States, and who shall not, when elected, be an Inhabitant of that State in which he shall be chosen.

Representatives and direct Taxes shall be apportioned among the several States which may be included within this Union, according to their respective Numbers, which shall be determined by adding to the whole Number of free Persons, including those bound to Service for a Term of Years, and excluding Indians not taxed, three fifths of all other Persons. The actual Enumeration shall be made within three Years after the first Meeting of the Congress of the United States, and within every subsequent Term of ten Years, in such Manner as they shall by Law direct. The Number of Representatives shall not exceed one for every thirty Thousand, but each State shall have at Least one Representative; and until such enumeration shall be made, the State of New Hampshire shall be entitled to chuse three, Massachusetts eight, Rhode-Island

and Providence Plantations one, Connecticut five, New-York six, New Jersey four, Pennsylvania eight, Delaware one, Maryland six, Virginia ten, North Carolina five, South Carolina five, and Georgia three.

When vacancies happen in the Representation from any State, the Executive Authority thereof shall issue Writs of Election to fill such Vacancies.

The House of Representatives shall chuse their Speaker and other Officers; and shall have the sole Power of Impeachment.

Section 3: The Senate of the United States shall be composed of two Senators from each State, *chosen by the Legislature thereof* for six Years; and each Senator shall have one Vote.

Immediately after they shall be assembled in Consequence of the first Election, they shall be divided as equally as may be into three Classes. The Seats of the Senators of the first Class shall be vacated at the Expiration of the second Year, of the second Class at the Expiration of the fourth Year, and of the third Class at the Expiration of the sixth Year, so that one third may be chosen every second Year; *and if Vacancies happen by Resignation, or otherwise, during the Recess of the Legislature of any State, the Executive thereof may make temporary Appointments until the next Meeting of the Legislature, which shall then fill such Vacancies.*

No Person shall be a Senator who shall not have attained to the Age of thirty Years, and been nine Years a Citizen of the United States, and who shall not, when elected, be an Inhabitant of that State for which he shall be chosen.

The Vice President of the United States shall be President of the Senate, but shall have no Vote, unless they be equally divided.

The Senate shall chuse their other Officers, and also a President pro tempore, in the Absence of the Vice President, or when he shall exercise the Office of President of the United States.

The Senate shall have the sole Power to try all Impeachments. When sitting for that Purpose, they shall be on Oath or Affirmation. When the President of the United States is tried, the Chief Justice shall preside: And no Person shall be convicted without the Concurrence of two thirds of the Members present.

Judgment in Cases of Impeachment shall not extend further than to removal from Office, and disqualification to hold and enjoy any Office of honor, Trust or Profit under the United States: but the Party convicted shall nevertheless be liable and subject to Indictment, Trial, Judgment and Punishment, according to Law.

Section 4: The Times, Places and Manner of holding Elections for Senators and Representatives, shall be prescribed in each State by the Legislature thereof; but the Congress may at any time by Law make or alter such Regulations, except as to the Places of chusing Senators.

The Congress shall assemble at least once in every Year, and such Meeting shall *be on the first Monday in December,* unless they shall by Law appoint a different Day.

Section 5: Each House shall be the Judge of the Elections, Returns and Qualifications of its own Members, and a Majority of each shall constitute a Quorum to do Business; but a smaller Number may adjourn from day to day, and may be authorized to compel the Attendance of absent Members, in such Manner, and under such Penalties as each House may provide.

Each House may determine the Rules of its Proceedings, punish its Members for disorderly Behaviour, and, with the Concurrence of two thirds, expel a Member.

Each House shall keep a Journal of its Proceedings, and from time to time publish the same, excepting such Parts as may in their Judgment require Secrecy; and the Yeas and Nays of the Members of either House on any question shall, at the Desire of one fifth of those Present, be entered on the Journal.

Neither House, during the Session of Congress, shall, without the Consent of the other, adjourn for more than three days, nor to any other Place than that in which the two Houses shall be sitting.

Section 6: The Senators and Representatives shall receive a Compensation for their Services, to be ascertained by Law, and paid out of the Treasury of the United States. They shall in all Cases, except Treason, Felony and Breach of the Peace, be privileged from Arrest during their Attendance at the Session of their respective Houses, and in going to and returning from the same; and for any Speech or Debate in either House, they shall not be questioned in any other Place.

No Senator or Representative shall, during the Time for which he was elected, be appointed to any civil Office under the Authority of the United States, which shall have been created, or the Emoluments whereof shall have been encreased during such time; and no Person holding any Office under the United States, shall be a Member of either House during his Continuance in Office.

Section 7: All Bills for raising Revenue shall originate in the House of Representatives; but the Senate may propose or concur with Amendments as on other Bills.

Every Bill which shall have passed the House of Representatives and the Senate, shall, before it become a Law, be presented to the President of the United States: If he approve he shall sign it, but if not he shall return it, with his Objections to that House in which it shall have originated, who shall enter the Objections at large on their Journal, and proceed to reconsider it. If after such Reconsideration two thirds of that House shall agree to pass the Bill, it shall be sent, together with the Objections, to the other House, by which it shall likewise be reconsidered, and if approved by two thirds of that House, it shall become a Law. But in all such Cases the Votes of both Houses shall be determined by yeas and Nays, and the Names of the Persons voting for and against the Bill shall be entered on the Journal of each House respectively. If any Bill shall not be returned by the President within ten Days (Sundays excepted) after it shall have been presented to him, the Same shall be a Law, in like Manner as if he had signed it, unless the Congress by their Adjournment prevent its Return, in which Case it shall not be a Law.

Every Order, Resolution, or Vote to which the Concurrence of the Senate and House of Representatives may be necessary (except on a question of

Adjournment) shall be presented to the President of the United States; and before the Same shall take Effect, shall be approved by him, or being disapproved by him, shall be repassed by two thirds of the Senate and House of Representatives, according to the Rules and Limitations prescribed in the Case of a Bill.

Section 8: The Congress shall have Power To lay and collect Taxes, Duties, Imposts and Excises, to pay the Debts and provide for the common Defence and general Welfare of the United States; but all Duties, Imposts and Excises shall be uniform throughout the United States;

To borrow Money on the credit of the United States;

To regulate Commerce with foreign Nations, and among the several States, and with the Indian Tribes;

To establish an uniform Rule of Naturalization, and uniform Laws on the subject of Bankruptcies throughout the United States;

To coin Money, regulate the Value thereof, and of foreign Coin, and fix the Standard of Weights and Measures;

To provide for the Punishment of counterfeiting the Securities and current Coin of the United States;

To establish Post Offices and post Roads;

To promote the Progress of Science and useful Arts, by securing for limited Times to Authors and Inventors the exclusive Right to their respective Writings and Discoveries;

To constitute Tribunals inferior to the supreme Court;

To define and punish Piracies and Felonies committed on the high Seas, and Offences against the Law of Nations;

To declare War, grant Letters of Marque and Reprisal, and make Rules concerning Captures on Land and Water;

To raise and support Armies, but no Appropriation of Money to that Use shall be for a longer Term than two Years;

To provide and maintain a Navy;

To make Rules for the Government and Regulation of the land and naval Forces;

To provide for calling forth the Militia to execute the Laws of the Union, suppress Insurrections and repel Invasions;

To provide for organizing, arming, and disciplining, the Militia, and for governing such Part of them as may be employed in the Service of the United States, reserving to the States respectively, the Appointment of the Officers, and the Authority of training the Militia according to the discipline prescribed by Congress;

To exercise exclusive Legislation in all Cases whatsoever, over such District (not exceeding ten Miles square) as may, by Cession of particular States, and the Acceptance of Congress, become the Seat of the Government of the United States, and to exercise like Authority over all Places purchased by the

Consent of the Legislature of the State in which the Same shall be, for the Erection of Forts, Magazines, Arsenals, dock-Yards, and other needful Buildings;—And

To make all Laws which shall be necessary and proper for carrying into Execution the foregoing Powers, and all other Powers vested by this Constitution in the Government of the United States, or in any Department or Officer thereof.

Section 9: The Migration or Importation of such Persons as any of the States now existing shall think proper to admit, shall not be prohibited by the Congress prior to the Year one thousand eight hundred and eight, but a Tax or duty may be imposed on such Importation, not exceeding ten dollars for each Person.

The Privilege of the Writ of Habeas Corpus shall not be suspended, unless when in Cases of Rebellion or Invasion the public Safety may require it.

No Bill of Attainder or ex post facto Law shall be passed.

No Capitation, or other direct, Tax shall be laid, *unless in Proportion to the Census or enumeration herein before directed to be taken*.

No Tax or Duty shall be laid on Articles exported from any State.

No Preference shall be given by any Regulation of Commerce or Revenue to the Ports of one State over those of another; nor shall Vessels bound to, or from, one State, be obliged to enter, clear, or pay Duties in another.

No Money shall be drawn from the Treasury, but in Consequence of Appropriations made by Law; and a regular Statement and Account of the Receipts and Expenditures of all public Money shall be published from time to time.

No Title of Nobility shall be granted by the United States: And no Person holding any Office of Profit or Trust under them, shall, without the Consent of the Congress, accept of any present, Emolument, Office, or Title, of any kind whatever, from any King, Prince, or foreign State.

Section 10: No State shall enter into any Treaty, Alliance, or Confederation; grant Letters of Marque and Reprisal; coin Money; emit Bills of Credit; make any Thing but gold and silver Coin a Tender in Payment of Debts; pass any Bill of Attainder, ex post facto Law, or Law impairing the Obligation of Contracts, or grant any Title of Nobility.

No State shall, without the Consent of the Congress, lay any Imposts or Duties on Imports or Exports, except what may be absolutely necessary for executing it's inspection Laws: and the net Produce of all Duties and Imposts, laid by any State on Imports or Exports, shall be for the Use of the Treasury of the United States; and all such Laws shall be subject to the Revision and Controul of the Congress.

No State shall, without the Consent of Congress, lay any Duty of Tonnage, keep Troops, or Ships of War in time of Peace, enter into any Agreement or Compact with another State, or with a foreign Power, or engage in War, unless actually invaded, or in such imminent Danger as will not admit of delay.

ARTICLE II

Article II, Section 1, was superseded by the Twelfth Amendment; Article II, Section 1, was modified by the Twenty-fifth Amendment.

Section 1: The executive Power shall be vested in a President of the United States of America. He shall hold his Office during the Term of four Years, and, together with the Vice President, chosen for the same Term, be elected, as follows:

Each State shall appoint, in such Manner as the Legislature thereof may direct, a Number of Electors, equal to the whole Number of Senators and Representatives to which the State may be entitled in the Congress: but no Senator or Representative, or Person holding an Office of Trust or Profit under the United States, shall be appointed an Elector.

The Electors shall meet in their respective States, and vote by Ballot for two Persons, of whom one at least shall not be an Inhabitant of the same State with themselves. And they shall make a List of all the Persons voted for, and of the Number of Votes for each; which List they shall sign and certify, and transmit sealed to the Seat of the Government of the United States, directed to the President of the Senate. The President of the Senate shall, in the Presence of the Senate and House of Representatives, open all the Certificates, and the Votes shall then be counted. The Person having the greatest Number of Votes shall be the President, if such Number be a Majority of the whole Number of Electors appointed; and if there be more than one who have such Majority, and have an equal Number of Votes, then the House of Representatives shall immediately chuse by Ballot one of them for President; and if no Person have a Majority, then from the five highest on the List the said House shall in like Manner chuse the President. But in chusing the President, the Votes shall be taken by States, the Representation from each State having one Vote; A quorum for this purpose shall consist of a Member or Members from two thirds of the States, and a Majority of all the States shall be necessary to a Choice. In every Case, after the Choice of the President, the Person having the greatest Number of Votes of the Electors shall be the Vice President. But if there should remain two or more who have equal Votes, the Senate shall chuse from them by Ballot the Vice President.

The Congress may determine the Time of chusing the Electors, and the Day on which they shall give their Votes; which Day shall be the same throughout the United States.

No Person except a natural born Citizen, or a Citizen of the United States, at the time of the Adoption of this Constitution, shall be eligible to the Office of President; neither shall any Person be eligible to that Office who shall not have attained to the Age of thirty five Years, and been fourteen Years a Resident within the United States.

In Case of the Removal of the President from Office, or of his Death, Resignation, or Inability to discharge the Powers and Duties of the said Office, the Same shall devolve on the Vice President, and the Congress may by Law provide for the Case of Removal, Death, Resignation or Inability, both of the President and Vice President, declaring what Officer shall then act as President, and such Officer shall act accordingly, until the Disability be removed, or a President shall be elected.

The President shall, at stated Times, receive for his Services, a Compensation, which shall neither be increased nor diminished during the Period for which he shall have been elected, and he shall not receive within that Period any other Emolument from the United States, or any of them.

Before he enter on the Execution of his Office, he shall take the following Oath or Affirmation:—"I do solemnly swear (or affirm) that I will faithfully execute the Office of President of the United States, and will to the best of my Ability, preserve, protect and defend the Constitution of the United States."

Section 2: The President shall be Commander in Chief of the Army and Navy of the United States, and of the Militia of the several States, when called into the actual Service of the United States; he may require the Opinion, in writing, of the principal Officer in each of the executive Departments, upon any Subject relating to the Duties of their respective Offices, and he shall have Power to grant Reprieves and Pardons for Offences against the United States, except in Cases of Impeachment. He shall have Power, by and with the Advice and Consent of the Senate, to make Treaties, provided two thirds of the Senators present concur; and he shall nominate, and by and with the Advice and Consent of the Senate, shall appoint Ambassadors, other public Ministers and Consuls, Judges of the supreme Court, and all other Officers of the United States, whose Appointments are not herein otherwise provided for, and which shall be established by Law: but the Congress may by Law vest the Appointment of such inferior Officers, as they think proper, in the President alone, in the Courts of Law, or in the Heads of Departments.

The President shall have Power to fill up all Vacancies that may happen during the Recess of the Senate, by granting Commissions which shall expire at the End of their next Session.

Section 3: He shall from time to time give to the Congress Information of the State of the Union, and recommend to their Consideration such Measures as he shall judge necessary and expedient; he may, on extraordinary Occasions, convene both Houses, or either of them, and in Case of Disagreement between them, with Respect to the Time of Adjournment, he may adjourn them to such Time as he shall think proper; he shall receive Ambassadors and other public Ministers; he shall take Care that the Laws be faithfully executed, and shall Commission all the Officers of the United States.

Section 4. The President, Vice President and all civil Officers of the United States, shall be removed from Office on Impeachment for, and Conviction of, Treason, Bribery, or other high Crimes and Misdemeanors.

ARTICLE III

A portion of Section 2 was modified by the Eleventh Amendment

Section 1: The judicial Power of the United States shall be vested in one supreme Court, and in such inferior Courts as the Congress may from time to time ordain and establish. The Judges, both of the supreme and inferior Courts, shall hold their Offices during good Behaviour, and shall, at stated Times, receive for their Services a Compensation, which shall not be diminished during their Continuance in Office.

Section 2: The judicial Power shall extend to all Cases, in Law and Equity, arising under this Constitution, the Laws of the United States, and Treaties made, or which shall be made, under their Authority;—to all Cases affecting Ambassadors, other public Ministers and Consuls;—to all Cases of admiralty and maritime Jurisdiction;—to Controversies to which the United States shall be a Party; to Controversies between two or more States;—*between a State and Citizens of another State;*—between Citizens of different States; between Citizens of the same State claiming Lands under Grants of different States, and between a State, or the Citizens thereof, and foreign States, Citizens or Subjects.

In all Cases affecting Ambassadors, other public Ministers and Consuls, and those in which a State shall be Party, the supreme Court shall have original Jurisdiction. In all the other Cases before mentioned, the supreme Court shall have appellate Jurisdiction, both as to Law and Fact, with such Exceptions, and under such Regulations as the Congress shall make.

The Trial of all Crimes, except in Cases of Impeachment, shall be by Jury; and such Trial shall be held in the State where the said Crimes shall have been committed; but when not committed within any State, the Trial shall be at such Place or Places as the Congress may by Law have directed.

Section 3: Treason against the United States, shall consist only in levying War against them, or in adhering to their Enemies, giving them Aid and Comfort. No Person shall be convicted of Treason unless on the Testimony of two Witnesses to the same overt Act, or on Confession in open Court.

The Congress shall have Power to declare the Punishment of Treason, but no Attainder of Treason shall work Corruption of Blood, or Forfeiture except during the Life of the Person attainted.

ARTICLE IV

A portion of Section 2 was superseded by the Thirteenth Amendment.

Section 1: Full Faith and Credit shall be given in each State to the public Acts, Records, and judicial Proceedings of every other State. And the Congress may by general Laws prescribe the Manner in which such Acts, Records and Proceedings shall be proved, and the Effect thereof.

Section 2: The Citizens of each State shall be entitled to all Privileges and Immunities of Citizens in the several States.

A Person charged in any State with Treason, Felony, or other Crime, who shall flee from Justice, and be found in another State, shall on Demand of the executive Authority of the State from which he fled, be delivered up, to be removed to the State having Jurisdiction of the Crime.

No Person held to Service or Labour in one State, under the Laws thereof, escaping into another, shall, in Consequence of any Law or Regulation therein, be discharged from such Service or Labour, but shall be delivered up on Claim of the Party to whom such Service or Labour may be due.

Section 3: New States may be admitted by the Congress into this Union; but no new State shall be formed or erected within the Jurisdiction of any other State; nor any State be formed by the Junction of two or more States, or Parts of States, without the Consent of the Legislatures of the States concerned as well as of the Congress.

The Congress shall have Power to dispose of and make all needful Rules and Regulations respecting the Territory or other Property belonging to the United States; and nothing in this Constitution shall be so construed as to Prejudice any Claims of the United States, or of any particular State.

Section 4: The United States shall guarantee to every State in this Union a Republican Form of Government, and shall protect each of them against Invasion; and on Application of the Legislature, or of the Executive (when the Legislature cannot be convened), against domestic Violence.

ARTICLE V

The Congress, whenever two thirds of both Houses shall deem it necessary, shall propose Amendments to this Constitution, or, on the Application of the Legislatures of two thirds of the several States, shall call a Convention for proposing Amendments, which, in either Case, shall be valid to all Intents and Purposes, as Part of this Constitution, when ratified by the Legislatures of three fourths of the several States, or by Conventions in three fourths thereof, as the one or the other Mode of Ratification may be proposed by the Congress; Provided that no Amendment which may be made prior to the Year One thousand eight hundred and eight shall in any Manner affect the first and fourth Clauses in the Ninth Section of the first Article; and that no State, without its Consent, shall be deprived of its equal Suffrage in the Senate.

ARTICLE VI

All Debts contracted and Engagements entered into, before the Adoption of this Constitution, shall be as valid against the United States under this Constitution, as under the Confederation.

This Constitution, and the Laws of the United States which shall be made in Pursuance thereof; and all Treaties made, or which shall be made, under the Authority of the United States, shall be the supreme Law of the Land; and the Judges in every State shall be bound thereby, any Thing in the Constitution or Laws of any State to the Contrary notwithstanding.

The Senators and Representatives before mentioned, and the Members of the several State Legislatures, and all executive and judicial Officers, both of the United States and of the several States, shall be bound by Oath or Affirmation, to support this Constitution; but no religious Test shall ever be required as a Qualification to any Office or public Trust under the United States.

ARTICLE VII

The Ratification of the Conventions of nine States, shall be sufficient for the Establishment of this Constitution between the States so ratifying the Same.

Attest William Jackson Secretary

Done in Convention by the Unanimous Consent of the States present the Seventeenth Day of September in the Year of our Lord one thousand seven hundred and Eighty seven and of the Independence of the United States of America the Twelfth In witness whereof We have hereunto subscribed our Names,

Go. Washington Presidt and deputy from Virginia
Delaware: Geo: Read, Gunning Bedford jun, John Dickinson, Richard Bassett, Jaco: Broom
Maryland: James McHenry, Dan of St Thos. Jenifer, Danl. Carroll
Virginia: John Blair—, James Madison Jr.
North Carolina: Wm. Blount, Richd. Dobbs Spaight, Hu Williamson
South Carolina: J. Rutledge, Charles Cotesworth Pinckney, Charles Pinckney, Pierce Butler
Georgia: William Few, Abr Baldwin
New Hampshire: John Langdon, Nicholas Gilman
Massachusetts: Nathaniel Gorham, Rufus King
Connecticut: Wm. Saml. Johnson Roger Sherman
New York: Alexander Hamilton
New Jersey: Wil: Livingston, David Brearley, Wm. Paterson, Jona: Dayton
Pennsylvania: B Franklin, Thomas Mifflin, Robt. Morris, Geo. Clymer, Thos. FitzSimons, Jared Ingersoll, James Wilson, Gouv Morris

Amendments to the Constitution

The first 10 amendments to the Constitution were ratified December 15, 1791, and form what is known as the "Bill of Rights."

AMENDMENT I

Congress shall make no law respecting an establishment of religion, or prohibiting the free exercise thereof; or abridging the freedom of speech, or of the press; or the right of the people peaceably to assemble, and to petition the Government for a redress of grievances.

AMENDMENT II

A well regulated Militia, being necessary to the security of a free State, the right of the people to keep and bear Arms, shall not be infringed.

AMENDMENT III

No Soldier shall, in time of peace be quartered in any house, without the consent of the Owner, nor in time of war, but in a manner to be prescribed by law.

AMENDMENT IV

The right of the people to be secure in their persons, houses, papers, and effects, against unreasonable searches and seizures, shall not be violated, and no Warrants shall issue, but upon probable cause, supported by Oath or affirmation, and particularly describing the place to be searched, and the persons or things to be seized.

AMENDMENT V

No person shall be held to answer for a capital, or otherwise infamous crime, unless on a presentment or indictment of a Grand Jury, except in cases arising in the land or naval forces, or in the Militia, when in actual service in time of War or public danger; nor shall any person be subject for the same offence to be twice put in jeopardy of life or limb; nor shall be compelled in any criminal case to be a witness against himself, nor be deprived of life, liberty, or property, without due process of law; nor shall private property be taken for public use, without just compensation.

AMENDMENT VI

In all criminal prosecutions, the accused shall enjoy the right to a speedy and public trial, by an impartial jury of the State and district wherein the crime shall have been committed, which district shall have been previously ascertained by law, and to be informed of the nature and cause of the accusation; to be confronted with the witnesses against him; to have compulsory process for obtaining witnesses in his favor, and to have the Assistance of Counsel for his defence.

AMENDMENT VII

In suits at common law, where the value in controversy shall exceed twenty dollars, the right of trial by jury shall be preserved, and no fact tried by a jury, shall be otherwise reexamined in any Court of the United States, than according to the rules of the common law.

AMENDMENT VIII

Excessive bail shall not be required, nor excessive fines imposed, nor cruel and unusual punishments inflicted.

AMENDMENT IX

The enumeration in the Constitution, of certain rights, shall not be construed to deny or disparage others retained by the people.

AMENDMENT X

The powers not delegated to the United States by the Constitution, nor pro hibited by it to the States, are reserved to the States respectively, or to the people.

AMENDMENT XI

Passed by Congress March 4, 1794. Ratified February 7, 1795. A portion of Article III, Section 2, was modified by the Eleventh Amendment.

The Judicial power of the United States shall not be construed to extend to any suit in law or equity, commenced or prosecuted against one of the United States by Citizens of another State, or by Citizens or Subjects of any Foreign State.

AMENDMENT XII

Passed by Congress December 9, 1803. Ratified June 15, 1804. A portion of Article II, Section 1, was superseded by the Twelfth Amendment. A portion of the Twelfth Amendment was superseded by Section 3 of the Twentieth Amendment.

The Electors shall meet in their respective states and vote by ballot for President and Vice-President, one of whom, at least, shall not be an inhabitant of the same state with themselves; they shall name in their ballots the person voted for as President, and in distinct ballots the person voted for as Vice-President, and they shall make distinct lists of all persons voted for as President, and of all persons voted for as Vice-President, and of the number of votes for each, which lists they shall sign and certify, and transmit sealed to the seat of the government of the United States, directed to the President of the Senate;—the President of the Senate shall, in the presence of the Senate and House of Representatives, open all the certificates and the votes shall then be counted;—The person having the greatest number of votes for President, shall be the President, if such number be a majority of the whole number of Electors appointed; and if no person have such majority, then from the persons having the highest numbers not exceeding three on the list of those voted for as President, the House of Representatives shall choose immediately, by ballot, the President. But in choosing the President, the votes shall be taken by states, the representation from each state having one vote; a quorum for this purpose shall consist of a member or members from two-thirds of the states, and a majority of all the states shall be necessary to a choice. *And if the House of Representatives shall not choose a President whenever the right of choice shall devolve upon them, before the fourth day of March next following, then the Vice-President shall act as President, as in case of the death or other constitutional disability of the President.*—The person having the greatest number of votes as Vice-President, shall be the Vice-President, if such number be a majority of the whole number of Electors appointed, and if no person have a majority, then from the two highest numbers on the list, the Senate shall choose the Vice-President; a quorum for the purpose shall consist of two-thirds of the whole number of Senators, and a majority of the whole number shall be necessary to a choice. But no person constitutionally ineligible to the office of President shall be eligible to that of Vice-President of the United States.

AMENDMENT XIII

Passed by Congress January 31, 1865. Ratified December 6, 1865. A portion of Article IV, Section 2, was superseded by the Thirteenth Amendment.

Section 1: Neither slavery nor involuntary servitude, except as a punishment for crime whereof the party shall have been duly convicted, shall exist within the United States, or any place subject to their jurisdiction.

Section 2: Congress shall have power to enforce this article by appropriate legislation.

AMENDMENT XIV

Passed by Congress June 13, 1866. Ratified July 9, 1868. A portion of Article I, Section 2, was modified by Section 2 of the Fourteenth Amendment. A portion of the Fourteenth Amendment was modified by Section 1 of the Twenty-sixth Amendment.

Section 1: All persons born or naturalized in the United States, and subject to the jurisdiction thereof, are citizens of the United States and of the State wherein they reside. No State shall make or enforce any law which shall abridge the privileges or immunities of citizens of the United States; nor shall any State deprive any person of life, liberty, or property, without due process of law; nor deny to any person within its jurisdiction the equal protection of the laws.

Section 2: Representatives shall be apportioned among the several States according to their respective numbers, counting the whole number of persons in each State, excluding Indians not taxed. But when the right to vote at any election for the choice of electors for President and Vice-President of the United States, Representatives in Congress, the Executive and Judicial officers of a State, or the members of the Legislature thereof, is denied to any of the male inhabitants of such State, *being twenty-one years of age,* and citizens of the United States, or in any way abridged, except for participation in rebellion, or other crime, the basis of representation therein shall be reduced in the proportion which the number of such male citizens shall bear to the whole number of male citizens twenty-one years of age in such State.

Section 3: No person shall be a Senator or Representative in Congress, or elector of President and Vice-President, or hold any office, civil or military, under the United States, or under any State, who, having previously taken an oath, as a member of Congress, or as an officer of the United States, or as a member of any State legislature, or as an executive or judicial officer of any State, to support the Constitution of the United States, shall have engaged in insurrection or rebellion against the same, or given aid or comfort to the enemies thereof. But Congress may by a vote of two-thirds of each House, remove such disability.

Section 4: The validity of the public debt of the United States, authorized by law, including debts incurred for payment of pensions and bounties for services in suppressing insurrection or rebellion, shall not be questioned. But neither the United States nor any State shall assume or pay any debt or obligation incurred in aid of insurrection or rebellion against the United States, or any claim for the loss or emancipation of any slave; but all such debts, obligations and claims shall be held illegal and void.

Section 5: The Congress shall have the power to enforce, by appropriate legislation, the provisions of this article.

AMENDMENT XV

Passed by Congress February 26, 1869. Ratified February 3, 1870.

Section 1: The right of citizens of the United States to vote shall not be denied or abridged by the United States or by any State on account of race, color, or previous condition of servitude—

Section 2: The Congress shall have the power to enforce this article by appropriate legislation.

AMENDMENT XVI

Passed by Congress July 12, 1909. Ratified February 3, 1913. A portion of Article I, Section 9, was modified by the Sixteenth Amendment.

The Congress shall have power to lay and collect taxes on incomes, from whatever source derived, without apportionment among the several States, and without regard to any census or enumeration.

AMENDMENT XVII

Passed by Congress May 13, 1912. Ratified April 8, 1913. Portions of Article I, Section 3, were modified by the Seventeenth Amendment.

The Senate of the United States shall be composed of two Senators from each State, elected by the people thereof, for six years; and each Senator shall have one vote. The electors in each State shall have the qualifications requisite for electors of the most numerous branch of the State legislatures.

When vacancies happen in the representation of any State in the Senate, the executive authority of such State shall issue writs of election to fill such vacancies: Provided, That the legislature of any State may empower the executive thereof to make temporary appointments until the people fill the vacancies by election as the legislature may direct.

This amendment shall not be so construed as to affect the election or term of any Senator chosen before it becomes valid as part of the Constitution.

AMENDMENT XVIII

Passed by Congress December 18, 1917. Ratified January 16, 1919. Repealed by the Twenty-first Amendment.

Section 1: After one year from the ratification of this article the manufacture, sale, or transportation of intoxicating liquors within, the importation thereof into, or the exportation thereof from the United States and all territory subject to the jurisdiction thereof for beverage purposes is hereby prohibited.

Section 2: The Congress and the several States shall have concurrent power to enforce this article by appropriate legislation.

Section 3: This article shall be inoperative unless it shall have been ratified as an amendment to the Constitution by the legislatures of the several States, as provided in the Constitution, within seven years from the date of the submission hereof to the States by the Congress.

AMENDMENT XIX

Passed by Congress June 4, 1919. Ratified August 18, 1920.

The right of citizens of the United States to vote shall not be denied or abridged by the United States or by any State on account of sex.

Congress shall have power to enforce this article by appropriate legislation.

AMENDMENT XX

Passed by Congress March 2, 1932. Ratified January 23, 1933. A portion of Article I, Section 4, was modified by Section 2 of the Twentieth Amendment. In addition, a portion of the Twelfth Amendment was superseded by Section 3 of the Twentieth Amendment.

Section 1: The terms of the President and the Vice President shall end at noon on the 20th day of January, and the terms of Senators and Representatives at noon on the 3d day of January, of the years in which such terms would have ended if this article had not been ratified; and the terms of their successors shall then begin.

Section 2: The Congress shall assemble at least once in every year, and such meeting shall begin at noon on the 3d day of January, unless they shall by law appoint a different day.

Section 3: If, at the time fixed for the beginning of the term of the President, the President elect shall have died, the Vice President elect shall become President. If a President shall not have been chosen before the time fixed for the beginning of his term, or if the President elect shall have failed to qualify, then the Vice President elect shall act as President until a President shall have qualified; and the Congress may by law provide for the case wherein neither a President elect nor a Vice President shall have qualified, declaring who shall then act as President, or the manner in which one who is to act shall be selected, and such person shall act accordingly until a President or Vice President shall have qualified.

Section 4: The Congress may by law provide for the case of the death of any of the persons from whom the House of Representatives may choose a President whenever the right of choice shall have devolved upon them, and for the case of the death of any of the persons from whom the Senate may choose a Vice President whenever the right of choice shall have devolved upon them.

Section 5: Sections 1 and 2 shall take effect on the 15th day of October following the ratification of this article.

Section 6: This article shall be inoperative unless it shall have been ratified as an amendment to the Constitution by the legislatures of three-fourths of the several States within seven years from the date of its submission.

AMENDMENT XXI

Passed by Congress February 20, 1933. Ratified December 5, 1933.
Repealed the Eighteenth Amendment.

Section 1: The eighteenth article of amendment to the Constitution of the United States is hereby repealed.

Section 2: The transportation or importation into any State, Territory, or Possession of the United States for delivery or use therein of intoxicating liquors, in violation of the laws thereof, is hereby prohibited.

Section 3: This article shall be inoperative unless it shall have

been ratified as an amendment to the Constitution by conventions in the several States, as provided in the Constitution, within seven years from the date of the submission hereof to the States by the Congress.

AMENDMENT XXII

Passed by Congress March 21, 1947. Ratified February 27, 1951.

Section 1: No person shall be elected to the office of the President more than twice, and no person who has held the office of President, or acted as President, for more than two years of a term to which some other person was elected President shall be elected to the office of President more than once. But this Article shall not apply to any person holding the office of President when this Article was proposed by Congress, and shall not prevent any person who may be holding the office of President, or acting as President, during the term within which this Article becomes operative from holding the office of President or acting as President during the remainder of such term.

Section 2: This article shall be inoperative unless it shall have been ratified as an amendment to the Constitution by the legislatures of three-fourths of the several States within seven years from the date of its submission to the States by the Congress.

AMENDMENT XXIII

Passed by Congress June 16, 1960. Ratified March 29, 1961.

Section 1: The District constituting the seat of Government of the United States shall appoint in such manner as Congress may direct:

A number of electors of President and Vice President equal to the whole number of Senators and Representatives in Congress to which the District would be entitled if it were a State, but in no event more than the least populous State; they shall be in addition to those appointed by the States, but they shall be considered, for the purposes of the election of President and Vice President, to be electors appointed by a State; and they shall meet in the District and perform such duties as provided by the twelfth article of amendment.

Section 2: The Congress shall have power to enforce this article by appropriate legislation.

AMENDMENT XXIV

Passed by Congress August 27, 1962. Ratified January 23, 1964.

Section 1: The right of citizens of the United States to vote in any primary or other election for President or Vice President, for electors for President or Vice President, or for Senator or Representative in Congress, shall not be denied or abridged by the United States or any State by reason of failure to pay poll tax or other tax.

Section 2: The Congress shall have power to enforce this article by appropriate legislation.

AMENDMENT XXV

Passed by Congress July 6, 1965. Ratified February 10, 1967. A portion of Article II, Section 1, was modified by the Twenty-fifth Amendment.

Section 1: In case of the removal of the President from office or of his death or resignation, the Vice President shall become President.

Section 2: Whenever there is a vacancy in the office of the Vice President, the President shall nominate a Vice President who shall take office upon confirmation by a majority vote of both Houses of Congress.

Section 3: Whenever the President transmits to the President pro tempore of the Senate and the Speaker of the House of Representatives his written declaration that he is unable to discharge the powers and duties of his office, and until he transmits to them a written declaration to the contrary, such powers and duties shall be discharged by the Vice President as Acting President.

Section 4: Whenever the Vice President and a majority of either the principal officers of the executive departments or of such other body as Congress may by law provide, transmit to the President pro tempore of the Senate and the Speaker of the House of Representatives their written declaration that the President is unable to discharge the powers and duties of his office, the Vice President shall immediately assume the powers and duties of the office as Acting President.

Thereafter, when the President transmits to the President pro tempore of the Senate and the Speaker of the House of Representatives his written declaration that no inability exists, he shall resume the powers and duties of his office unless the Vice President and a majority of either the principal officers of the executive department or of such other body as Congress may by law provide, transmit within four days to the President pro tempore of the Senate and the Speaker of the House of Representatives their written declaration that the President is unable to discharge the powers and duties of his office. Thereupon Congress shall decide the issue, assembling within forty-eight hours for that purpose if not in session. If the Congress, within twenty-one days after receipt of the latter written declaration, or, if Congress is not in session, within twenty-one days after Congress is required to assemble, determines by two-thirds vote of both Houses that the President is unable to discharge the powers and duties of his office, the Vice President shall continue to discharge the same as Acting President; otherwise, the President shall resume the powers and duties of his office.

AMENDMENT XXVI

Passed by Congress March 23, 1971. Ratified July 1, 1971. A portion of the Fourteenth Amendment, Section 2, was modified by Section 1 of the Twenty-sixth Amendment.

Section 1: The right of citizens of the United States, who are eighteen years of age or older, to vote shall not be denied or abridged by the United States or by any State on account of age.

Section 2: The Congress shall have power to enforce this article by appropriate legislation.

AMENDMENT XXVII

Originally proposed Sept. 25, 1789. Ratified May 7, 1992.

No law, varying the compensation for the services of the Senators and Representatives, shall take effect, until an election of representatives shall have intervened.

TIMELINE

ABBREVIATIONS:

A = Administration
AM = Anti-Masonic
D= Democratic
DR = Democratic-Republican
F = Federalist
J = Jacksonian
NR = National Republican
O= Other
Opp. = Opposition
R= Republican
W = Whig

YEAR	PRESIDENT	CONGRESS	US HISTORY	LEGISLATION
1787			Constitutional Convention, Independence Hall, Philadelphia	Northwest Ordinance
1788			Congress picks New York City as site of government	
1789	George Washington: 1789–1797 (Nonpartisan)	1st 1789–1791 Senate: 17 F; 9 Opp. House: 38 F; 26 Opp.	House of Representatives, Senate, executive branch organized, Supreme Court is established George Washington inaugurated in New York City Pres. Washington signs first act of Congress	Judiciary Act Tariff Act of 1789
1790			1st census: U.S. population 3,929,214 Congress meets in Philadelphia, new temporary capital Congress submits Bill of Rights to states for ratification Supreme Court meets for the first time	Copyright Act of 1790 Naturalization Act Patent Act Southwest Ordinance
1791		2d 1791–1793 Senate: 16 F; 13 DR House: 37 F; 33 DR	Bill of Rights ratified	Bank of the United States
1792			U.S. Mint established through Coinage Act New York Stock Exchange organized Cornerstone to White House laid	Coinage Act of 1792
1793		3d 1793–1795 Senate: 17 F; 13 DR House: 57 DR; 48 F	Cotton gin invented by Eli Whitney	Anti-Injunction Act Fugitive Slave Act of 1793

YEAR	PRESIDENT	CONGRESS	US HISTORY	LEGISLATION
1794			Excise tax on distilled liquor causes Whiskey Rebellion Creation of U.S. Navy authorized by Congress	
1795		4th 1795–1797 Senate: 19 F; 13 DR House: 54 F; 52 DR	Eleventh Amendment goes into effect (limits judicial powers) First state university, University of North Carolina, opens	
1796			*Hylton v. United States* is first Supreme Court case that upholds an act of Congress George Washington's farewell address is published, but never delivered as speech	
1797	John Adams: 1797–1801 (Federalist)	5th 1797–1799 Senate: 20 F; 12 DR House: 58 F; 48 DR	Congress creates 80,000 member militia	
1798			Undeclared war with France begins (conflict ends 1800) Rebellion in Haiti ends slavery there; many white Haitians flee to U.S., increasing fears among whites of slave rebellion and French revolution	Alien and Sedition Acts
1799		6th 1799–1801 Senate: 19 F; 13 DR House: 64 F; 42 DR		
1800			2d census: U.S. population 5,308,483 Library of Congress established Site of government moves to Washington, DC	
1801	Thomas Jefferson: 1801–1809 (Democratic-Republican)	7th 1801–1803 Senate: 18 DR; 13 F House: 69 DR; 36 F		Judiciary Act of 1801
1802				
1803		8th 1803–1805 Senate: 25 DR; 9 F House: 102 DR; 39 F	*Marbury v. Madison* is first Supreme Court case that declares an act of Congress unconstitutional Lewis and Clark expedition begins Louisiana Purchase (U.S. purchased about 828,000 square miles between the Mississippi River and Rocky Mountains from France, for $15 million)	
1804			Twelfth amendment ratified (separate ballots for president and vice president)	

YEAR	PRESIDENT	CONGRESS	US HISTORY	LEGISLATION
1805		9th 1805–1807 Senate: 27 DR; 7F House: 116 DR; 25 F		
1806				
1807		10th 1807–1809 Senate: 28 DR; 6 F House: 118 DR; 24 F	Steamboat (Robert Fulton's *Clermont*) completes round trip from New York to Albany in 62 hours, first practical steamboat trip Importation of slaves into the U.S. prohibited	Prohibition of the Slave Trade
1808			Anthracite coal first used as stove fuel in Pennsylvania	
1809	James Madison: 1809–1817 (Democratic-Republican)	11th 1809–1811 Senate: 28 DR; 6 F House: 94 DR; 48 F	Supreme Court case *United States v. Peters* affirms federal government power over states	Nonintercourse Act
1810			3d census: U.S. population 7,239,881 Revolt against Spanish by southern expansionists results in the U.S. gaining territory in the south	
1811		12th 1811–1813 Senate: 30 DR; 6 F House: 108 DR; 36 F	Non-intercourse policy against Great Britain renewed Senate declines to renew charter of Bank of the United States Construction of Cumberland Road begins (completed 1818; Cumberland, MD, to Wheeling, WV)	
1812			First war-bond issue; first interest-bearing U.S. Treasury notes are authorized War is declared on Great Britain (War of 1812, 1812–1814)	
1813		13th 1813–1815 Senate: 27 DR; 9 F House: 112 DR; 68 F	Creek War with Indian nations in southern United States	
1814			Peace treaty signed ending Creek War; Americans led to victory over Native Americans by Gen. Andrew Jackson Treaty of Ghent (Belgium) signed ending war with Britain	
1815		14th 1815–1817 Senate: 25 DR; 11 F House: 117 DR; 65 F	Treaties signed with Algiers, Tunis, and Tripoli ending piracy on U.S. ships	

YEAR	PRESIDENT	CONGRESS	US HISTORY	LEGISLATION
1816			Second Bank of United States is created	
1817	James Monroe: 1817–1825 (Democratic-Republican)	15th 1817–1819 Senate: 34 DR; 10 F House: 141 DR; 42 F	First Seminole War begins; Andrew Jackson named as commander of U.S. forces	
1818			Seminole War ends after American capture of St. Marks and Pensacola, FL	
1819		16th 1819–1821 Senate: 35 DR; 7 F House: 156 DR; 27 F	Adams-Onis treaty signed with Spain; Spain cedes East Florida to U.S., ends claim on West Florida Financial panic of 1819, economic recession begins First American savings banks open and begin paying interest on deposits	
1820			4th census: U.S. population 9,638,453	Missouri Compromise
1821		17th 1821–1823 Senate: 44 DR; 4 F House: 158 DR; 25 F	Republic of Liberia founded by American Colonization Society as haven for freed African-American slaves Sante Fe trail opened (Independence, MO, to Sante Fe, NM)	
1822			Planned slave revolt in Charleston, SC, blocked	
1823		18th 1823–1825 Senate: 44 DR; 4 F House: 187 DR; 26 F	In annual message to Congress, Pres. Monroe lays out what will become known as the Monroe Doctrine Treaties signed with Osage and Kansa Indian nations that cede lands in present-day Kansas, Oklahoma, and Missouri to the U.S. Great Britain abolishes slavery in its territories	
1824			Supreme Court case *Gibbons v. Ogden* upholds Congress's power to regulate interstate commerce	
1825	John Quincy Adams: 1825–1829 (Democratic-Republican)	19th 1825–1827 Senate: 26 A; 20 J House: 105 A; 97 J	Erie canal opens between Buffalo, NY, and New York City	
1826			John Stevens demonstrates use of first steam locomotive in Hoboken, NJ	

YEAR	PRESIDENT	CONGRESS	US HISTORY	LEGISLATION
1827		20th 1827–1829 Senate: 28 J; 20 A House: 119 J; 94 A	Mechanics Union of Trades Association, first central labor union, is created in Philadelphia	
1828			Treaty signed by United States and Mexico establishes Sabine River as common boundary	
1829	Andrew Jackson: 1829–1837 (Democratic)	21st 1829–1831 Senate: 26 D; 22 NR House: 139 D; 74 NR		
1830			5th census: U.S. population 12,860,702 Various Native American tribes sign treaties ceding western lands of present-day Iowa, Missouri, and Minnesota Mexico prohibits further settlement of Texas by Americans Baltimore & Ohio Railroad begins operation (first U.S. passenger railroad)	Indian Removal Act
1831		22d 1831–1833 Senate: 25 D; 21 NR; 2 O House: 141 D; 58 NR; 14 O	Nat Turner leads a slave rebellion in Virginia, is captured and executed along with 19 other blacks First U.S. built locomotive goes into service	
1832			Black Hawk War with Sac and Fox Indians; Creek nation cedes all its lands east of the Mississippi River to the United States; Seminoles cede lands in Florida Virginia legislature considers, but rejects, gradual termination of slavery	
1833		23d 1833–1835 Senate: 20 D; 20 NR; 8 O House: 147 D; 53 AM; 60 O	Oberlin College (Ohio) is first college in U.S. to adopt coeducation	
1834				
1835		24th 1835–1837 Senate: 27 D; 25 W House: 145 D; 98 W	Texas declares independence from Mexico; Mexico establishes military state in Texas Second Seminole War begins in response to attempts to remove Seminoles by force Cherokee nation cedes lands east of the Mississippi River	

YEAR	PRESIDENT	CONGRESS	US HISTORY	LEGISLATION
1836			Siege of the Alamo in San Antonio, TX, by Mexicans; entire garrison killed Mexican general Santa Anna captured at Battle of San Jacinto; Sam Houston installed as president of Republic of Texas	
1837	Martin Van Buren: 1837–1841 (Democratic)	25th 1837–1839 Senate: 30 D; 18 W; 4 O House: 108 D; 107 W; 24 O	Financial panic of 1837 leads to economic depression that lasts until 1842	
1838			Underground railroad becomes force in assisting slaves to reach the North and Canada Forced removal of Cherokee Indians from their native land in Georgia to Oklahoma begins (Trail of Tears)	
1839		26th 1839–1841 Senate: 28 D; 22 W House: 124 D; 118 W		
1840			6th census: U.S. population 17,063,353 Great National Pike completed (Cumberland, MD, to Vandalia, IL; formerly known as the Cumberland Road)	
1841	William Henry Harrison: 1841 (Whig) John Tyler: 1841–1845 (Whig)	27th 1841–1843 Senate: 28 W; 22 D; 2 O House: 133 W; 102 D; 6 O	First wagon train leaves for California from Independence, MO (47 people)	Bankruptcy Act of 1841
1842			Dorr's Rebellion in Rhode Island (demanded new state constitution guaranteeing equal voting rights) Settlement of Oregon begins via Oregon Trail Webster-Ashburton Treaty fixes northern border of U.S. in Maine and Minnesota	
1843		28th 1843–1845 Senate: 28 W; 25 D; 1 O House: 142 D; 79 W; 1 O		
1844			Treaty of Wanghia signed with China; opens five Chinese ports to American commerce Commercial telegraph service begins	
1845	James K. Polk: 1845–1849 (Democratic)	29th 1845–1847 Senate: 31 D; 25 W House: 143 D; 77 W; 6 O	Texas annexed by U.S.; Mexico breaks off relations with U.S.	

YEAR	PRESIDENT	CONGRESS	US HISTORY	LEGISLATION
1846			Mexican-American War begins (1846–1848) Treaty with Great Britain setting northern boundary of Oregon Territory at 49th parallel	
1847		30th 1847–1849 Senate: 36 D; 21 W; 1 O House: 115 W; 108 D; 4 O	Establishment of new government in California begins after treaty ends Mexican-American War hostilities there	
1848			Treaty of Guadelupe Hidalgo ends Mexican-American War California gold rush begins First women's rights convention in Seneca Falls, NY	
1849	Zachary Taylor: 1849–1850 (Whig)	31st 1849–1851 Senate: 35 D; 25 W; 2 O House: 112 D; 109 W; 9 O	Mormons establish state of Deseret after migration to Utah from Illinois (1846); Deseret becomes Territory of Utah in 1850	
1850	Millard Fillmore: 1850–1853 (Whig)		7th census: U.S. population 23,191,876	Compromise of 1850 Fugitive Slave Act of 1850
1851		32d 1851–1853 Senate: 35 D; 24 W; 3 O House: 140 D; 88 W; 5 O		
1852			Harriet Beecher Stowe publishes *Uncle Tom's Cabin*	
1853	Franklin Pierce: 1853–1857 (Democratic)	33d 1853–1855 Senate: 38 D; 22 W; 2 O House: 159 D; 71 W; 4 O	Commodore Matthew Perry arrives in Japan to deliver letter from the president, who wants to open trade Gadsden Purchase (southern areas of present-day Arizona and New Mexico)	
1854			Treaty of Kanagawa opens Japanese ports to the U.S. Large-scale immigration of Chinese begins First American oil company incorporated (Pennsylvania Rock Oil Co.)	Kansas Nebraska Act
1855		34th 1855–1857 Senate: 40 D; 15 R; 5 O House: 108 R; 83 D; 43 O	U.S. Court of Claims established Congress authorizes construction of telegraph line from Mississippi River to Pacific Ocean	

YEAR	PRESIDENT	CONGRESS	US HISTORY	LEGISLATION
1856			Violence in Kansas breaks out between pro- and anti-slavery factions over question of slavery; federal troops keep temporary peace	
1857	James Buchanan: 1857–1861 (Democratic)	35th 1857–1859 Senate: 36 D; 20 R; 8 O House: 118 D; 92 R; 26 O	Dred Scott case decided by Supreme Court (decision says Scott is not a citizen, therefore cannot sue in federal court; his residence in a free state does not make him free; Missouri Compromise is unconstitutional) Financial panic results from speculation in railroad securities and real estate	
1858				
1859		36th 1859–1861 Senate: 36 D; 26 R; 4 O House: 114 R; 92 D; 31 O	Kansas approves constitution making it a free state Harper's Ferry incident (abolitionist John Brown and 21 other men seize a U.S. Armory, are captured, Brown is hanged) First trip of a Pullman sleeping car on a railroad is completed	
1860			8th census: U.S. population 31,443,321 South Carolina is first state to secede from Union	
1861	Abraham Lincoln: 1861–1865 (Republican)	37th 1861–1863 Senate: 31 R; 10 D; 8 O House: 105 R; 43 D; 30 O	Confederate government created; Jefferson Davis elected president of the Confederacy Civil War begins (1861–1865) First transcontinental telegraph line is completed	Civil War Pensions First Confiscation Act
1862				Homestead Act Militia Act Morrill Land Grant Act Second Confiscation Act
1863		38th 1863–1865 Senate: 36 R; 9 D; 5 O House: 102 R; 75 D; 9 O	Pres. Lincoln issues Emancipation Proclamation Draft riots in New York City, about 1000 killed, some blacks lynched	Enrollment Act (Conscription Act)
1864			J. P. Morgan & Co. established	National Bank Act

YEAR	PRESIDENT	CONGRESS	US HISTORY	LEGISLATION
1865	Andrew Johnson: 1865–1869 (Democratic)	39th 1865–1867 Senate: 42 U; 10 D House: 149 U; 42 D	Gen. Robert E. Lee surrenders to Gen. U. S. Grant at Appomattox Court House Pres. Abraham Lincoln assassinated in Ford's Theater, Washington, DC Thirteenth Amendment is ratified (abolished slavery)	Freedmen's Bureau Act
1866			Reconstruction of the South begins Ku Klux Klan founded Fourteenth Amendment enacted by Congress (guarantees that no person is to be denied life, liberty, or pursuit of happiness by a state without due process of law) First refrigerated rail car built	Civil Rights Act of 1866
1867		40th 1867–1869 Senate: 42 R; 11 D House: 143 R; 49 D	U.S. purchases Alaska from Russia for $7.2 million National Grange is formed to protect farmer's interests	Reconstruction Acts (1867–1868)
1868			House of Representatives votes to impeach Andrew Johnson for violating the Tenure of Office Act after he tries to remove the secretary of war from office; Senate one vote short of two-thirds required for conviction	
1869	Ulysses S. Grant: 1869–1877 (Republican)	41st 1869–1871 Senate: 56 R; 11 D House: 149 R; 63 D	Congress enacts Fifteenth Amendment (makes it illegal to deprive a citizen of the right to vote based on race, color, or previous condition of servitude) National Woman Suffrage Association organized Freedmen's Bureau goes out of operation First transcontinental railroad completed with the joining of Union Pacific and Central Pacific railroads at Promontory, UT Knights of Labor (national labor union) formed	
1870			9th census: U.S. population 38,558,371 Justice Department is created Standard Oil Co. is incorporated	

YEAR	PRESIDENT	CONGRESS	US HISTORY	LEGISLATION
1871		42d 1871–1873 Senate: 52 R; 17 D 5 O House: 134 R; 104 D; 5 O	The Tweed Ring in New York City (led by Boss William Tweed of Tammany Hall) is broken up Race riots against Chinese in Los Angeles; 15 lynched Disastrous fire in Chicago destroys over 17,000 buildings, leaves 100,000 homeless	Ku Klux Klan Act Force Act
1872				Mail Fraud Statute Yellowstone National Park Act
1873		43d 1873–1875 Senate: 49 R; 19 D; 5 O House: 194 R; 92 D; 14 O	U.S. monetary policy shifts from bimetallic standard to gold standard Financial panic of 1873 results in New York Stock Exchange closing for ten days, substantial unemployment, and drastic fall in security prices Bethlehem Steel Co. begins operating	Coinage Act Comstock Act
1874				
1875		44th 1875–1877 Senate: 45 R; 29 D; 2 O House: 169 D; 109 R; 14 O		Civil Rights Act of 1875
1876			Battle of Little Bighorn in Montana; Col. George Custer and 266 are surrounded and killed in "Custer's last stand" Alexander Graham Bell receives patent for telephone, makes first telephone call	
1877	Rutherford B. Hayes: 1877–1881 (Republican)	45th 1877–1879 Senate: 39 R; 36 D; 1 O House: 153 D; 140 R	Federal troops withdraw from South in return for allowing Rutherford B. Hayes to become president in disputed election (Compromise of 1877) Strike on Baltimore & Ohio Railroad in protest of wage cuts leads to strikes on other railroads; 100,000 workers eventually involved	

YEAR	PRESIDENT	CONGRESS	US HISTORY	LEGISLATION
1878			First commercial telephone exchange opened, New Haven, CT	Bland-Allison Act Posse Comitatus Act
1879		46th 1879–1881 Senate: 42 D; 33 R; 1 O House: 149 D; 130 R; 14 O	First Woolworth five-and-dime store opens Incandescent electric lamp invented by Thomas Edison	
1880			10th census: U.S. population 50,155,783	
1881	James A. Garfield: 1881 (Republican) Chester A. Arthur: 1881–1885 (Republican)	47th 1881–1883 Senate: 37 R; 37 D; 1 O House: 147 R; 135 D; 11 O	Pres. Garfield shot and killed in Washington, DC, by disappointed office seeker Sitting Bull and Sioux surrender to U.S. Army Southern Pacific Railroad completed (New Orleans to Pacific) Tuskegee Institute founded by Booker T. Washington Western Union Telegraph Co. formed	
1882			First trust formed by Standard Oil Co. Severe strikes in iron and steel industry	Chinese Exclusion Act
1883		48th 1883–1885 Senate: 38 R; 36 D; 2 O House: 197 D; 118 R; 10 O	Brooklyn Bridge in New York City completed Northern Pacific Railroad completed	Civil Services Act (Pendleton Act)
1884			Statue of Liberty presented to U.S. by France (arrives in U.S. 1885, dedicated 1886) First tall building to use steel beams is erected (Home Insurance Building, Chicago) First large-scale electric street car system established in Richmond, VA First long-distance telephone service established between New York and Boston	
1885	Grover Cleveland: 1885–1889 (Democratic)	49th 1885–1887 Senate: 43 R; 34 D House: 183 D; 140 R; 2 O		
1886			Apache Indians (Southwest) surrender to U.S. Haymarket Massacre in Chicago American Federation of Labor (AFL) organized by 25 labor groups	

YEAR	PRESIDENT	CONGRESS	US HISTORY	LEGISLATION
1887		50th 1887–1889 Senate: 39 R; 37 D House: 169 D; 152 R; 4 O	Free mail delivery begins in cities of 10,000 or more The Interstate Commerce Commission, first U.S. regulatory commission, is created to regulate railroads	Indian General Allotment Act (Dawes Act) Interstate Commerce Act
1888			Department of Labor established	
1889	Benjamin Harrison: 1889–1893 (Republican)	51st 1889–1891 Senate: 39 R; 37 D House: 166 R; 159 D	Carnegie Steel Co. organized by Andrew Carnegie	
1890			11th census: U.S. population 62,979,766 Sioux Indians are defeated at Wounded Knee; last major battle of Indian wars	Sherman Antitrust Act
1891		52d 1891–1893 Senate: 47 R; 39 D; 2 O House: 235 D; 88 R; 9 O	Immigration and Naturalization Service is established	
1892			Ellis Island opens as an immigration receiving station	
1893	Grover Cleveland:1893–1897 (Democratic)	53d 1893–1895 Senate: 44 D; 38 R; 3 O House: 218 D; 127 R; 11 O	Free mail delivery extended to rural communities Stock market crash, financial panic of 1893 begins, 491 banks and 15,000 commercial institutions fail; economy in severe depression until 1897	
1894			American Railway Union strikes at Pullman plant in Chicago; federal injunction breaks strike	1894 Income Tax and the Wilson-Gorman Tariff Act
1895		54th 1895–1897 Senate: 43 R; 39 D; 6 O House: 244 R; 105 D; 7 O	Internal combustion engine patented; first automobile company started	
1896			Supreme Court upholds Louisiana law calling for "separate but equal" accommodations on public transportation in *Plessy v. Ferguson*	
1897	William McKinley: 1897–1901 (Republican)	55th 1897–1899 Senate: 47 R; 34 D; 7 O House: 204 R; 113 D; 40 O	Thomas Edison patents a movie camera First section of a U.S. subway opens, in Boston	

YEAR	PRESIDENT	CONGRESS	US HISTORY	LEGISLATION
1898			Spanish-American War begins and ends; Spain cedes Puerto Rico, Philippines, and Guam to U.S. and relinquishes all claims to Cuba	
1899		56th 1899–1901 Senate: 53 R; 26 D; 8 O House: 197 R; 151 D; 9 O	Filipino nationalists revolt against U.S. First Hague Conference held; 26 nations participate	
1900			12th census: U.S. population 76,212,168 U.S. announces Open Door Policy in China (opens Chinese markets to all nations)	Gold Standard Act
1901	Theodore Roosevelt: 1901–1909 (Republican)	57th 1901–1903 Senate: 55 R; 31 D; 4 O House: 197 R; 151 D; 9 O	Pres. McKinley assassinated in Buffalo, NY, by an anarchist	
1902			Pres. Roosevelt asks attorney general to bring first antitrust suit to dissolve a railroad holding company	National Reclamation Act Panama Canal Purchase Act
1903		58th 1903–1905 Senate: 57 R; 33 D House: 208 R; 178 D	Hay-Herran Treaty with Colombia provides for 100-year lease of 10-mile-wide strip across isthmus of Panama for canal Wright brothers demonstrate first motor-driven airplane	
1904			Muckraker Ida Tarbell publishes *The History of the Standard Oil Company* First section of New York City subway opens	
1905		59th 1905–1907 Senate: 57 R; 33 D House: 250 R; 136 D		
1906			Upton Sinclair publishes *The Jungle*, muckraking account of the meat-packing industry Dow Jones Industrial Average closes over 100 for the first time	Antiquities Act Pure Food and Drug Act
1907		60th 1907–1909 Senate: 61 R; 31 D House: 222 R; 164 D	Food and Drug Administration begins operation Financial panic of 1907 Indiana passes world's first compulsory sterilization law for "all confirmed criminals, idiots, rapists, and imbeciles" held in state institutions; 32 states eventually adopt such laws	

YEAR	PRESIDENT	CONGRESS	US HISTORY	LEGISLATION
1908			Bureau of Investigation formed (later to become FBI) Model T automobile introduced by Henry Ford, sells for $850	Federal Employers' Liability Act
1909	William Howard Taft:1909–1913 (Republican)	61st 1909–1911 Senate: 61 R; 32 D House: 219 R; 172 D	Congress passes Sixteenth Amendment (allows federal income tax; ratified 1913) NAACP created	Corporate Income Tax Act
1910			13th Census: U.S. population 92,228,496	Mann Act
1911		62d 1911–1913 Senate: 51 R; 41 D House: 228 D; 161 R; 1 O	Supreme Court orders dissolution of Standard Oil Co. as a monopoly; same goes for the American Tobacco Co. and the DuPont Co.	
1912				
1913	Woodrow Wilson: 1913–1921 (Democratic)	63d 1913–1915 Senate: 51 D; 44 R; 1 O House: 291 D; 127 R; 17 O	Seventeenth Amendment ratified (calls for popular election of senators) First drive-in gasoline station opens in Pittsburgh, PA Ford Motor Co. introduces conveyor-belt assembly-line production of cars	Federal Income Tax Act of 1913 Federal Reserve Act
1914			War breaks out in Europe; Woodrow Wilson issues neutrality proclamation Federal Trade Commission established Commercial traffic begins on Panama Canal Margaret Sanger launches *The Woman Rebel*, feminist magazine dedicated to birth control; is indicted for "inciting violence and promoting obscenity" (goes on to found first family planning clinic, 1916; American Birth Control League, precursor to planned parenthood, 1921)	Clayton Act Federal Trade Commission Act Narcotics Act
1915		64th 1915–1917 Senate: 56 D; 40 R House: 230 D; 196 R; 9 O	First transcontinental telephone call Film *Birth of a Nation* debuts and increases support for the new Ku Klux Klan	

YEAR	PRESIDENT	CONGRESS	US HISTORY	LEGISLATION
1916			Congress votes to increase size of army; authorizes 450,000 person national guard U.S. buys Danish West Indies In first half of year, nearly 2,100 strikes and lockouts occur First woman elected to House of Representatives (Jeanette Rankin, R-MT)	Keating-Owen Act National Park Service Act
1917		65th 1917–1919 Senate: 53 D; 42 R House: 216 D; 210 R; 6 O	U.S. declares war on Germany and on Austria-Hungary; first U.S. troops arrive in Europe Puerto Rico becomes U.S. territory	Espionage Act Selective Service Act Trading With the Enemy Act Vocational Education Act
1918			Woodrow Wilson outlines "Fourteen Points" for a peace program Armistice signed with Germany and Austria-Hungary Regular airmail service established (between Washington, DC, and New York City) Influenza epidemic kills around 20 million people worldwide; 548,000 die in U.S.	Sedition Act
1919		66th 1919–1921 Senate: 49 R; 47 D House: 240 R; 190 D; 3 O	Treaty of Versailles signed by Germany and Allies (excluding Russia) In *Schenck v. United States*, Supreme Court finds that free speech can be restricted in wartime, upholding Espionage and Sedition Acts Riots in Chicago, Washington, and many other cities	National Prohibition Act
1920			14th Census: U.S. population 106,021,537 Eighteenth Amendment goes into effect (Prohibition) Nineteenth Amendment goes into effect (women's suffrage) American Civil Liberties Union founded First commercial radio broadcasts	Merchant Marine Act Mineral Leasing Act

YEAR	PRESIDENT	CONGRESS	US HISTORY	LEGISLATION
1921	Warren G. Harding: 1921–1923 (Republican)	67th 1921–1923 Senate: 59 R; 37 D House: 301 R; 131 D; 1 O	Congress limits the number of immigrants from each country to 3 percent of the number of that foreign-born nationality living in U.S. First state sales tax levied (West Virginia)	
1922				
1923	Calvin Coolidge: 1923–1929 (Republican)	68th 1923–1925 Senate: 51 R; 43 D; 2 O House: 225 R; 205 D; 5 O	Pres. Harding dies in San Francisco during return trip from Alaska First transcontinental nonstop plane flight First sound-on-film motion picture (*Phonofilm*) shown in New York City	
1924			Regular transcontinental air service begins Annual immigration quota reduced to 2 percent of number of that foreign-born nationality living in U.S. Congress passes law making all Indians U.S. citizens First woman elected state governor (Nellie Tayloe Ross, D-WY)	Bonus Bill (Adjusted Compensation Act)
1925		69th 1925–1927 Senate: 56 R; 39 D; 1 O House: 247 R; 183 D; 4 O	National Aircraft Board created to investigate government's role in aviation	
1926			First liquid-fuel rocket demonstrated by Robert H. Goddard, Auburn, MA	
1927		70th 1927–1929 Senate: 49 R; 46 D; 1 O House: 237 R; 195 D; 3 O	Charles Lindbergh makes first New York–Paris nonstop flight	
1928				
1929	Herbert Hoover: 1929–1933 (Republican)	71st 1929–1931 Senate: 56 R; 39 D; 1 O House: 267 R; 167 D;1 O	Teapot Dome scandal (former secretary of state is found guilty of leasing government land for bribes) Stock market crash sets off Great Depression (1929–1939)	Migratory Bird Conservation Act
1930			15th census: U.S. population 123,202,624 Bank of the United States in New York closes; over 2,100 banks close between late 1929 and end of 1930	Smoot-Hawley Tariff Act

YEAR	PRESIDENT	CONGRESS	US HISTORY	LEGISLATION
1931		72d 1931–1933 Senate: 48 R; 47 D; 1 O House: 220 R; 214 D; 1 O		
1932			Bonus March on Washington, DC (WWI veterans demand early payment of their bonus) First woman elected to U.S. Senate (Hattie W. Caraway, D-AR)	Federal Home Loan Bank Act Norris-LaGuardia Act
1933	Franklin D. Roosevelt: 1933–1945 (Democratic)	73d 1933–1935 Senate: 60 D; 35 R; 1 O House: 310 D; 117 R; 5 O	An estimated 25 percent of the workforce is unemployed First 100 days of Roosevelt administration marked by passage of much New Deal social and economic legislation U.S. officially goes off gold standard Congress passes legislation providing for independence of the Philippine Islands after 12 years U.S. recognizes U.S.S.R. Twentieth Amendment ratified (moves presidential inauguration and beginning of congressional term to January; were previously in March) Twenty-first Amendment goes into effect (repeals Eighteenth Amendment)	Agricultural Adjustment Act Farm Credit Act Federal Deposit Insurance Act Glass-Steagall Act National Industrial Recovery Act Securities Act of 1933 Tennessee Valley Authority Act
1934			Dust storms in Midwest blow thousands of tons of topsoil away (Dust Bowl) Longshoremen strike in San Francisco leads to first general strike in the U.S.	Communications Act Gold Reserve Act Indian Reorganization Act Securities Exchange Act
1935		74th 1935–1937 Senate: 69 D; 25 R; 2 O House: 319 D; 103 R; 10 O	George H. Gallup founds Institute of Public Opinion, which holds Gallup polls First U.S. Savings Bonds issued Committee of Industrial Organization, precursor to Congress of Industrial Organizations (CIO), created	Aid to Dependent Children Motor Carrier Act National Labor Relations Act Neutrality Acts (1935–1939) Public Utility Holding Company Act Social Security Act Soil Conservation and Domestic Allotment Act
1936				Commodity Exchange Act Rural Electrification Act Walsh-Healey Public Contracts Act

YEAR	PRESIDENT	CONGRESS	US HISTORY	LEGISLATION
1937		75th 1937–1939 Senate: 76 D; 16 R; 4 O House: 331 D; 89 R; 13 O	First African-American federal judge (William H. Hastie) Pres. Roosevelt's plan to increase number of Supreme Court justices from 9 to 16 is defeated	United States Housing Act
1938			House Committee on Un-American Activities created to investigate subversive activities Federal minimum wage established	Civil Aeronautics Act Fair Labor Standards Act Federal Food, Drug, and Cosmetic Act Natural Gas Act
1939		76th 1939–1941 Senate: 69 D; 23 R; 4 O House: 261 D; 164 R; 4 O	U.S. declares neutrality in World War II Scientists, including Albert Einstein, warn Pres. Roosevelt of possibility of atomic bomb	Federal Unemployment Tax Act Hatch Act
1940			16th census: U.S. population 132,164,569 Congress approves first peace-time draft	
1941		77th 1941–1943 Senate: 66 D; 28 R; 2 O House: 268 D; 162 R; 5 O	First commercial television license issued to NBC Japanese attack on Pearl Harbor U.S. enters World War II	Lend-Lease Act Public Debt Act
1942			Manhattan Project organized for production of atomic bomb 10,000 Japanese-Americans on West Coast are relocated to camps in the interior	
1943		78th 1943–1945 Senate: 58 D; 37 R; 1 O House: 218 D; 208 R; 4 O	Building of Pentagon (to house Department of Defense) completed	
1944			Conference at Dumbarton Oaks, Washington, DC, lays groundwork for United Nations First large scale digital computer completed by IBM, given to Harvard University	Veterans' Preference Act

YEAR	PRESIDENT	CONGRESS	US HISTORY	LEGISLATION
1945	Harry S. Truman: 1945–1953 (Democratic)	79th 1945–1947 Senate: 56 D; 38 R; 1 O House: 242 D; 190 R; 2 O	Pres. Roosevelt dies suddenly while on vacation First atomic bomb detonated successfully in New Mexico Germany agrees to unconditional surrender; German occupational zones established Pres. Truman orders dropping of two atomic bombs on Japanese cities of Hiroshima and Nagasaki; Japan quickly surrenders; U.S. begins occupation United Nations is formed as representatives of 50 nations meet in San Francisco Nuremberg War Crimes Trials begin Lend-Lease program ends	Export-Import Bank Act United Nations Participation Act
1946			U.S. gives Philippine Islands independence U.N. General Assembly holds first session World Bank organizes	Administrative Procedure Act Atomic Energy Act Employment Act of 1946 Farmers Home Administration Act Federal Tort Claims Act Foreign Service Act Hill-Burton Act Hobbs Anti-Racketeering Act Richard B. Russell National School Lunch Act
1947		80th 1947–1949 Senate: 51 R; 45 D House: 245 R; 188 D; 1 O	The president pledges aid to Greece and Turkey (to prevent the spread of communism), known as the "Truman Doctrine" U.S. Army, Navy, and Air Force combined into Defense Department; Joint Chiefs of Staff and National Security Council created (National Security Act)	National Security Act Taft-Hartley Act
1948			U.S.S.R. blockades Allied sectors of Berlin; U.S. and British airlift food and coal into city (blockade ends in 1949) Universal Declaration on Human Rights adopted by U.N. General Assembly Israel declared an independent state Executive order issued by Pres. Truman outlawing racial segregation in armed forces Organization of American States formed by 21 Western Hemisphere nations	Economic Cooperation Act (Marshall Plan) United States Information and Educational Exchange Act Federal Water Pollution Control Act

YEAR	PRESIDENT	CONGRESS	US HISTORY	LEGISLATION
1949		81st 1949–1951 Senate: 54 D; 42 R House: 263 D; 171 R; 1 O	North Atlantic Treaty signed; NATO created	Central Intelligence Agency Act
1950			17th census: U.S. population 151,325,798 Korean War begins when North Korea invades South Korea; U.S. leads U.N. troops Thirty-five military advisers, along with arms and supplies, sent to South Vietnam to aid anti-Communist government Army seizes railroads to prevent general strike (ordered by Pres. Truman)	Federal Civil Defense Act
1951		82d 1951–1953 Senate: 49 D; 47 R House: 234 D; 199 R; 1 O	Twenty-second Amendment ratified (sets a maximum of two terms for the presidency) Credit card is introduced by Franklin National Bank of New York	Mutual Security Act
1952			First hydrogen bomb tested Pres. Truman orders seizure of steel mills to prevent strike; Supreme Court rules seizure is unconstitutional Ralph Ellison's novel *Invisible Man* published	Immigration and Nationality Act
1953	Dwight D. Eisenhower: 1953–1961 (Republican)	83d 1953–1955 Senate: 48 R; 47 D; 1 O House: 221 R; 211 D; 1 O	Armistice signed in Korea	Outer Continental Shelf Lands Act Small Business Act
1954			Supreme Court rules that racial segregation in public schools violates the Fourteenth Amendment (*Brown v. Board of Education of Topeka, Kansas*) Senator Joseph McCarthy conducts televised hearings concerning Communists in the U.S. government and Democratic Party Southeast Treaty Organization created First atomic-powered submarine is launched	Communist Control Act Federal National Mortgage Association Charter Act Internal Revenue Act of 1954

YEAR	PRESIDENT	CONGRESS	US HISTORY	LEGISLATION
1955		84th 1955–1957 Senate: 48 D; 47 R; 1 O House: 232 D; 203 r	American occupation of Germany ends U.S. agrees to help train South Vietnamese Army Rosa Parks refuses to give up her seat to a white man on a bus in Montgomery, AL; this leads to a boycott of buses and to Supreme Court decision that outlaws segregation in public transportation AFL and CIO, two largest labor organizations in U.S., merge McDonald's fast-food chain founded	National Housing Act (Capehart Act)
1956			Commercial telephone service over transatlantic cable begins Minimum wage raised to $1 per hour Dow Jones Industrial Average closes over 500 for the first time	Highway Act of 1956
1957		85th 1957–1959 Senate: 49 D; 47 R House: 233 D; 200 R	Southern Christian Leadership Conference founded, Martin Luther King, Jr., president	Civil Rights Act of 1957
1958			National Aeronautics and Space Administration (NASA) created	Federal Aviation Act National Aeronautics and Space Act
1959		86th 1959–1961 Senate: 64 D; 34 R House: 283 D; 153 R	Nikita Khrushchev, Soviet premier, visits U.S.	
1960			18th Census: U.S. population 179,323,175 Russia announces it shot down an American U-2 spy plane; President Eisenhower says he authorized the flight Sit-ins begin when 4 black college students refuse to move from a Woolworth lunch counter in Greensboro, NC Student Non-Violent Coordinating Committee established	

YEAR	PRESIDENT	CONGRESS	US HISTORY	LEGISLATION
1961	John F. Kennedy: 1961–1963 (Democratic)	87th 1961–1963 Senate: 65 D; 35 R House: 263 D; 174 R	Bay of Pigs invasion by Cuban exiles is crushed Peace Corps created by executive order; legislation follows Twenty-third Amendment ratified (allows residents of District of Columbia to vote for president) Minimum wage raised to $1.25 per hour	Arms Control and Disarmament Act Foreign Assistance Act Peace Corps Act
1962			Cuban missile crisis (Soviet missile buildup in Cuba) Cesar Chavez organizes National Farm Workers Association John Glenn becomes first U.S. astronaut to orbit the Earth	Bribery Act
1963	Lyndon B. Johnson: 1963–1969 (Democratic)	88th 1963–1965 Senate: 67 D; 33 R House: 258 D; 177 R	Pres. Kennedy is assassinated in Dallas, TX Dr. Martin Luther King gives "I have a dream" speech during March on Washington for equal rights, Washington, DC Ninety-nine nations, including U.S., U.S.S.R., and Great Britain agree to limited Nuclear Test Ban Treaty	Clean Air Act Equal Pay Act
1964			Pres. Johnson announces air attacks on Vietnam; Gulf of Tonkin Resolution passed by Congress gives the president broad authority for military action in Vietnam Three civil rights workers murdered in Philadelphia, MS; 21 white men arrested, 7 convicted of conspiracy in killings Twenty-fourth Amendment ratified (bars poll tax in federal elections)	Civil Rights Act of 1964 Economic Opportunity Act Food Stamp Act Urban Mass Transportation Act

YEAR	PRESIDENT	CONGRESS	US HISTORY	LEGISLATION
1965		89th 1965–1967 Senate: 68 D; 32 R House: 295 D; 140 R	First combat troops land in South Vietnam (125,000 total troops in Vietnam by year's end) Malcolm X assassinated in New York City Civil rights activists march 54 miles from Selma to Montgomery, AL	Elementary and Secondary Education Act Federal Cigarette Labeling and Advertising Act Higher Education Act Highway Beautification Act Housing and Urban Development Act Medicaid Act Medicare Act National Emissions Standard Act Solid Waste Disposal Act Voting Rights Act
1966			More than 10,000 protest Vietnam War in front of White House National Organization for Women (NOW) established	Freedom of Information Act Highway Safety Act National Historic Preservation Act National Traffic and Motor Vehicle Safety Act National Wildlife Refuge System Administration Act
1967		90th 1967–1969 Senate: 64 D; 36 R House: 246 D; 187 R	First African-American Supreme Court justice (Thurgood Marshall) Blacks riot in Newark, NJ, and Detroit, MI Twenty-fifth Amendment ratified (sets up presidential succession scheme)	Age Discrimination in Employment Act Public Broadcasting Act
1968			Martin Luther King, Jr., and Robert Kennedy are assassinated Lyndon B. Johnson announces that he will not seek reelection	Alcoholic and Narcotic Rehabilitation Act Fair Housing Act Gun Control Act Indian Civil Rights Act Omnibus Crime Control and Safe Streets Act
1969	Richard M. Nixon: 1969–1974 (Republican)	91st 1969–1971 Senate: 57 D; 43 R House: 245 D; 189 R	Peace talks to end Vietnam War begin; 250,000 protest war in Washington, DC U.S. astronauts land on moon	Consumer Credit Protection Act National Environmental Policy Act Truth in Lending Act
1970			19th Census: U.S. population 203,302,031 Four students at Kent State College in Ohio are killed during an antiwar demonstration First draft lottery since WWII is held Intel introduces its first computer memory chip	Controlled Substances Act Occupational Safety and Health Act Organized Crime Control Act Plant Variety Protection Act Rail Passenger Service Act

YEAR	PRESIDENT	CONGRESS	US HISTORY	LEGISLATION
1971		92d 1971–1973 Senate: 54 D; 44 R; 2 O House: 254 D; 180 R	Pentagon Papers, classified documents on Vietnam War leaked to the press, published in newspapers Amtrak begins operation Twenty-sixth Amendment ratified (lowers voting age to 18)	Alaska Native Claims Settlement Act Federal Election Campaign Act
1972			Pres. Nixon makes historic visits to China and U.S.S.R. Peace talks on Vietnam War begin and then stall Strategic Arms Limitation Treaty I signed with U.S.S.R. Five men are arrested for breaking into Democratic National Headquarters at the Watergate building in Washington, DC, beginning a series of events that would lead to Richard Nixon's resignation Dow Jones Industrial Average closes over 1,000 for the first time	Federal Advisory Committee Act Marine Mammal Protection Act Title IX, Education Amendments
1973		93d 1973–1975 Senate: 56 D; 42 R; 2 O House: 239 D; 192 R; 1 O	Cease fire signed between U.S., South Vietnam, and North Vietnam OPEC oil embargo (Arab countries ban oil exports to U.S. because of U.S. support to Israel in Arab-Israeli War) In *Roe v. Wade* Supreme Court rules that a state cannot prevent a woman from having an abortion in the first six months of pregnancy	Domestic Volunteer Service Act (VISTA) Endangered Species Act War Powers Resolution
1974	Gerald R. Ford: 1974–1977 (Republican)		House of Representatives authorizes an impeachment investigation of Pres. Nixon, votes and approves three impeachment articles; Nixon resigns Work begins on Alaskan oil pipeline Minimum wage raised to $2.00 per hour	Congressional Budget and Impoundment Control Act Employee Retirement Income Security Act Juvenile Justice and Delinquency Prevention Act Legal Services Corporation Act Privacy Act Safe Drinking Water Act Trade Act of 1974

YEAR	PRESIDENT	CONGRESS	US HISTORY	LEGISLATION
1975		94th 1975–1977 Senate: 61 D; 37 R; 2 O House: 291 D; 144 R	Remaining U.S. military evacuated from Vietnam after the shelling of Saigon by Communist forces; South Vietnam surrenders unconditionally to the Viet Cong U.S. military academies open to women Minimum wage raised to $2.10 per hour	Individuals with Disabilities Education Act Hazardous Materials Transportation Act
1976			Homestead Act of 1862 repealed for all states except Alaska Apple I desktop computer introduced Minimum wage raised to $2.30 per hour	Copyright Act of 1976 Federal Land Policy and Management Act Government in the Sunshine Act National Forest Management Act Toxic Substances Control Act
1977	James E. Carter: 1977–1981 (Democratic)	95th 1977–1979 Senate: 61 D; 38 R; 1 O House: 292 D; 143 R	Agreement between U.S. and Canada for oil pipeline from Alaska to continental U.S. Pres. Carter pardons most Vietnam War draft evaders Microsoft corporation is formed	Community Reinvestment Act Department of Energy Organization Act Foreign Corrupt Practices Act International Emergency Economic Powers Act Surface Mining Control and Reclamation Act
1978			Deregulation of the airline industry Minimum wage raised to $2.65 per hour	Bankruptcy Act of 1978 Civil Service Reform Act Contract Disputes Act Ethics in Government Act Foreign Intelligence Surveillance Act National Energy Conservation Policy Act Nuclear Non-Proliferation Act Pregnancy Discrimination Act Whistleblower Protection Laws
1979		96th 1979–1981 Senate: 58 D; 41 R; 1 O House: 276 D; 157 R	Sixty-three U.S. citizens taken hostage when Iranian militants seize U.S. embassy in Tehran; black and women hostages released in just over two weeks Nuclear accident (partial meltdown) at Three Mile Island, Middletown, PA Minimum wage raised to $2.90 per hour	

YEAR	PRESIDENT	CONGRESS	US HISTORY	LEGISLATION
1980			20th Census: U.S. population 226,542,203 Military mission to rescue U.S. hostages in Iran fails Residents are evacuated from homes in Love Canal, Niagara Falls, NY, a former toxic waste dump Minimum wage raised to $3.10 per hour	Comprehensive Environmental Response, Compensation, and Liability Act Drug Abuse Prevention, Treatment, and Rehabilitation Act Fish and Wildlife Conservation Act Paperwork Reduction Act Regulatory Flexibility Act Staggers Rail Act
1981	Ronald W. Reagan: 1981–1989 (Republican)	97th 1981–1983 Senate: 53 R; 46 D; 1 O House: 242 D; 189 R	Iran releases remaining 52 U.S. hostages First manned space shuttle (*Columbia*) launched into space Nationwide strike by Professional Air Traffic Controllers Association; most controllers are fired Sandra Day O'Connor becomes first woman Supreme Court justice Minimum wage raised to $3.35 per hour	
1982			Equal Rights Amendment to Constitution defeated (would assure equal rights regardless of sex) Unemployment reaches 10.8 percent of the labor force, highest since 1940 U.S. and Soviet Union hold arms control talks in Geneva, Switzerland	Nuclear Waste Policy Act
1983		98th 1983–1985 Senate: 54 R; 46 D House: 268 D; 167 R	Soviet Union shoots down a Korean Airlines plane, killing all 269 passengers, including 52 Americans U.S. Embassy in Beirut is bombed, killing 17 U.S. citizens; a truck bomb kills 241 Americans at a U.S. Marine compound in Beirut	
1984			Truck filled with explosives strikes U.S. Embassy annex in Beirut; U.S. Marines are withdrawn from Beirut As a result of an antitrust settlement, AT&T gives up 22 local Bell System telephone companies	Counterfeit Access Device and Computer Fraud and Abuse Act Hazardous and Solid Waste Amendments Sentencing Reform Act

YEAR	PRESIDENT	CONGRESS	US HISTORY	LEGISLATION
1985		99th 1985–1987 Senate: 53 R; 47 D House: 253 D; 182 R	U.S. and Soviet Union hold arms control talks in Geneva	Balanced Budget and Emergency Deficit Control Act (Gramm-Rudman-Hollings Act)
1986			Pres. Reagan signs secret order authorizing sale of arms to Iran; Lt. Col. Oliver North is dismissed when it is learned that some proceeds from the arms sales helped finance Nicaraguan Contras Space shuttle *Challenger* explodes in air after liftoff, killing entire crew	Anti-Drug Abuse Act Electronic Communications Privacy Act Emergency Planning and Community Right-To-Know Act Immigration Reform and Control Act Tax Reform Act
1987		100th 1987–1989 Senate: 55 D; 45 R House: 258 D; 177 R	Iran-Contra hearings in Congress last about three months U.S. and U.S.S.R. sign treaty banning medium- and short-range missiles Dow Jones Industrial Average closes over 2,000 for the first time	Computer Security Act McKinney-Vento Act
1988			Senate approves free trade agreement made with Canada (1987), all tariffs between the two countries will be eliminated by 1999	Civil Liberties Act Indian Gaming Regulatory Act
1989	George H. W. Bush: 1989–1993 (Republican)	101st 1989–1991 Senate: 55 D; 45 R House: 260 D; 175 R	Oil tanker, *Exxon Valdez*, runs aground on a reef in Prince William Sound, off the coast of Alaska, creating largest oil spill in American history Failing savings and loan industry receives $159 million bailout legislated by Congress 20,000 U.S. troops invade Panama, overthrow regime of Manuel Noriega Minimum wage raised to $4.25 per hour	Flag Protection Act
1990			21st census: U.S. population 249,632,692 U.N. forces begin air attacks on Iraq, after Iraq invades Kuwait	Administrative Dispute Resolution Act Americans with Disabilities Act Negotiated Rulemaking Act Oil Pollution Act

YEAR	PRESIDENT	CONGRESS	US HISTORY	LEGISLATION
1991		102d 1991–1993 Senate: 56 D; 44 R House: 267 D; 167 R; 1 O	First Persian Gulf War begins and ends, freeing Kuwait from Iraqi occupation U.S.S.R. is formally dissolved, effectively ending the Cold War Dow Jones Industrial Average closes over 3,000 for the first time	
1992			Representatives from Canada, Mexico, and U.S. approve draft agreement establishing free trade among the three nations in 15 years Riots in south-central Los Angeles after a jury acquits four white police officers on charges of brutality against a black man, Rodney King Twenty-seventh Amendment is ratified (legislated pay raises for congress don't take effect until a new Congress is convened)	Weapons of Mass Destruction Control Act
1993	William J. Clinton: 1993–2001 (Democratic)	103d 1993–1995 Senate: 56 D; 44 R House: 258 D; 176 R; 1 O	Bomb explodes in parking garage beneath World Trade Center, killing 6 people Twenty U.S. soldiers are killed in Mogadishu, Somalia, in an effort to protect food shipment and distribution to the population Second Strategic Arms Reduction Treaty signed with Russia U.S. and 117 other countries agree to GATT (General Agreement on Tariffs and Trade), to be signed in 1995, will remove export barriers and tariffs on thousands of products	Brady Handgun Violence Protection Act Family and Medical Leave Act NAFTA Implementation Act Religious Freedom Restoration Act
1994			U.S. and North Korea sign agreement that allows for U.N. inspection of North Korea nuclear facilities Republicans win control of Congress for the first time since 1952; Newt Gingrich to become Speaker of the House (1995–1999)	Community Development Banking and Financial Institutions Act Federal Blackmail Statute Freedom of Access to Clinic Entrances Act Violence Against Women Act Violent Crime Control and Law Enforcement Act

YEAR	PRESIDENT	CONGRESS	US HISTORY	LEGISLATION
1995		104th 1995–1997 Senate: 52 R; 48 D House: 230 R; 204 D; 1 O	U.S. troops arrive in Balkans as part of U.N. force, mission is to halt years of fighting in Bosnia Bombing of Oklahoma City Federal Building, killing 160 people Dow Jones Industrial Average closes over 4,000 (Feb.) and 5,000 (Nov.) for the first time	Lobbying Disclosure Act
1996			Nineteen U.S. military personnel die, several hundred wounded, in bombing of military complex near Dhahran, Saudi Arabia Minimum wage raised to $4.75 per hour Dow Jones Industrial Average closes over 6,000 for the first time	Antiterrorism and Effective Death Penalty Act Communications Decency Act Defense of Marriage Act Food Quality Protection Act Personal Responsibility and Work Opportunity Reconciliation Act
1997		105th 1997–1999 Senate: 55 R; 45 D House: 226 R; 208 D; 1 O	Settlement for $368.5 billion reached between four major tobacco companies and several state attorneys general (a $200 billion settlement with 46 states would happen in 1998) Minimum wage raised to $5.15 Dow Jones Industrial Average closes over 7,000 (Feb.) and 8,000 (July) for the first time	
1998			House of Representatives approves two articles of impeachment against Pres. Clinton for perjury and obstruction of justice; he is accused of lying under oath about his relationship with a White House intern Newt Gingrich steps down as Speaker of the House and leaves Congress amid ethics charges and poor results in the midterm congressional elections Dow Jones Industrial Average closes over 9,000 for the first time	Children's Online Privacy Protection Act Taxpayer Bill of Rights III

YEAR	PRESIDENT	CONGRESS	US HISTORY	LEGISLATION
1999		106th 1999–2001 Senate: 54 R; 46 D House: 222 R; 208 D; 1 O	Two students of Columbine High School in Littleton, CO, open fire and kill 12 students and a teacher, then commit suicide; at least 4 other school shootings occur during the year Pres. Clinton impeached but not convicted; investigation led by independent council Kenneth Starr reveals much about Clinton's sexual indiscretions Dow Jones Industrial Average closes over 10,000 (Mar.) and 11,000 (May) for the first time	
2000			Disputed results in the presidential election, centering around election results and ballot irregularities in Florida, lead to a Supreme Court decision that does not allow a vote recount to proceed in that state; George W. Bush declared winner over Al Gore, who won the popular vote U.S.S. *Cole*, an American ship, is bombed by terrorists while refueling in Yemen; 17 sailors killed, 39 injured in the blast "Dot com" boom experienced throughout the late 1990s begins to go bust, starting with the bursting of the stock market "bubble" in March; 4 of the 10 greatest point losses on the Dow Jones Industrial Average occur this year (3 of the 10 greatest point increases occur as well)	Electronic Signatures in Global and National Commerce Act

YEAR	PRESIDENT	CONGRESS	US HISTORY	LEGISLATION
2001	George W. Bush: 2001– (Republican)	107th 2001–2003 Senate: 50 D; 49 R; 1 O House: 222 R; 211 D; 1 O	On September 11, the U.S. comes under terrorist attack when two hijacked planes fly into the towers of the World Trade Center in New York, another plane flies into the Pentagon, and a fourth crashes in Pennsylvania Letters containing Anthrax spores, sent to congressmen and journalists, contaminate the U.S. mail system U.S. begins bombing of Afghanistan to oust the Taliban (Islamic fundamentalist party in power) and capture Osama Bin Laden (leader of Al-Qaeda, the group thought responsible for the September 11 attacks); Taliban removed from power, Bin Laden not captured	No Child Left Behind Act USA Patriot Act
2002			The Enron Corporation collapses as a scandal regarding the company's accounting practices emerges, its share prices plummet and the company declares bankruptcy; other similar corporate scandals follow Bush administration begins to announce an aggressive policy toward Iraq, including the possibility of a "preemptive" strike with the aim of "regime change"; U.N. passes resolution sending weapons inspectors to Iraq; Congress passes resolution authorizing the president to use military force in Iraq	Born-Alive Infants Protection Act Department of Homeland Security Act

YEAR	PRESIDENT	CONGRESS	US HISTORY	LEGISLATION
2003		108th 2003-2005 Senate: 51 R; 48 D; 1 O House: 229 R; 205 D; 1 O	Although U.N. weapons inspectors are still at work, U.S., Britain, and allies declare that Iraq has not disarmed and is in violation of a U.N. resolution passed in November 2002; U.S. is unable to get U.N. approval for the use of force against Iraq because of international opposition; U.S. and a "coalition of the willing" attack Iraq without U.N. approval and win war easily; after Pres. Bush declares an end to major combat a guerilla war ensues; reconstruction of Iraq's infrastructure proves to be more costly than thought; as of five months after Bush's declaration of victory, banned weapons—the major rationale for the war—had not been found Space shuttle *Columbia* breaks apart during reentry killing all seven crew members; independent investigation of accident lasts nearly seven months and concludes that flaws in NASA's management and culture were underlying causes of the disaster In California, a petition gathers enough signatures to force a recall election for governor (incumbent is Gray Davis [D]); 135 candidates to appear on ballot, including actor Arnold Schwarzenegger (R) Massive, rolling blackout across northern Midwest, Canada, and northeastern U.S. results in 50 million people losing power	

Glossary

abate: to reduce in amount; put an end to; make void or annul

abet: to actively, knowingly, and intentionally assist another in the committing (or attempt) of a crime

abolitionist: one favoring principles or measures fostering the end of slavery

absolute: complete, pure, free from restriction or limitation

adherent: a follower of a leader or party, or a believer in a cause

adjournment: the closing, or end, of a session

adjudicate: to settle something judicially

adjudicated: a matter or controversy that has already been decided through judicial procedure

adjudication: the act of settling something judicially

adjudicatory: having to do with the process of settling something judicially

adverse: contrary to one's interests; harmful or unfavorable

aggrieved: suffering physical injury or a loss of one's property interest, monetary interest, or personal rights

agrarian: having to do with farming or farming communities and their interests

alien: a citizen of another country

alternative dispute resolution: any means of settling disputes outside of the courtroom, typically including arbitration, mediation, early neutral evaluation, and conciliation

amend: to alter or change

antitrust: laws protecting commerce and trade from monopolistic restraints on competition

appellate: a court having jurisdiction to review the findings of lower courts

appoint: to select someone to fill an office or position

apportion: to divide and assign according to a plan

appropriate: to set aside for or assign to a particular purpose or group

arbitrate: to resolve disagreements whereby parties choose a person or group of people familiar with the issues in question to hear and settle their dispute

arbitration the settling of a dispute by a neutral third party

Articles of Confederation: first constitution of the United States (in effect 1781–1789); it established a union between the thirteen states, but with a weak central government

B

bipartisan: involving members of two parties, especially the two major political parties

blacklist: a list of persons who are to be denied employment

block grant: an unrestricted grant of federal money to state and local governments to support social welfare programs

bondage: a state of being involuntarily bound or subjugated to someone or something

boycott: to refuse to purchase goods or services from a specific company

C

capitulate: to surrender under specific conditions; to give up resistance

carcinogenic: cancer-causing

cause of action: reason or ground for initiating a proceeding in court

censor: to restrict the expression of something considered objectionable

charter: document that creates a public or private corporation and outlines the principles, functions, and organization of the corporate body

checks and balances: the limiting powers that each branch of government has over the other two. (The government is divided into three branches: legislative, executive, and judicial, each with distinct powers.)

civil action: a lawsuit brought to protect an individual right or redress a wrong, as distinct from criminal proceedings

civil disobedience: nonviolent protest

civil libertarian: one who is actively concerned with the protection of the fundamental freedoms guaranteed to the individual in the Bill of Rights

civil penalties: fines or money damages imposed as punishment

Civil Rights movement: the movement to win political, economic, and social equality for African Americans

class action: a lawsuit brought by a representative member of a large group of people who have suffered the same injury or damages

Cold War: a conflict over ideological differences carried on by methods short of military action and usually without breaking off diplomatic relations; usually refers to the ideological conflict between the U.S. and former U.S.S.R.

collateral: property put up by a borrower to secure a loan that could be seized if the borrower fails to pay back the debt

collective bargaining: a method of negotiations, usually between employees and an employer, in which a representative negotiates on behalf of an organized group of people

commerce: the large-scale exchange of goods, involving transportation from one place to another

commerce clause: the provision of the U.S. Constitution (Article I, section 8, clause 3) that gives Congress exclusive powers over interstate commerce—the buying, selling, or exchanging of goods between states

commodity: an article of trade or commerce that can be transported; especially an agricultural or mining product

common law: a system of laws developed in England—and later applied in the U.S.—based on judicial precedent rather than statutory laws passed by a legislative body

communism: an economic and social system characterized by the absence of classes and by common ownership of the means of production and subsistence

comply: to act in accordance with a wish, request, demand, rule, order, or statute

constraint: a restriction

consumer credit information: credit experiences, such as your bill-paying history, the number and type of accounts you have, late payments, collection actions, outstanding debt, and the age of your accounts

consumption tax: tax imposed on outlay for goods and services

contempt: disobedience of a court's order; interference with the court's operation

Continental Congress: the first central governing body of the United States (1774–1789)

contract: a formal agreement, usually in writing, between two or more parties that can be legally enforced

conventional mortgage: a home mortgage loan that is not federally insured

D

de novo: (Latin) anew, a second time; the same as if it had not been heard before

debtor: one who owes payment or other performance on an obligation; anyone liable on a claim

decedent: one who has died; the deceased

deduction: an amount subtracted from the amount of income that is used to calculate income tax due

default: the failure by the borrower to comply with the terms of the loan, usually the failure to make payments

defaulter: one who fails to comply with the terms of a loan or contract, usually by failing to make payments on a debt

defendant: one against whom a legal action is brought

deflation: a general decline in the prices of goods and services

demagogue: a leader who obtains power by means of impassioned appeals to the emotions and prejudices of the populace

dependency: a territory under the jurisdiction of a sovereign nation

detain: to keep in custody or temporary confinement

directors: those who establish the policies of the corporation

discharge petition: a method for moving a bill from a committee to the floor of the House when a committee refuses to do so itself. The bill must have been held by a committee for at least thirty legislative days, and half of the House membership must sign the petition for release that is filed

disclosure: obligation of parties to reveal material facts deemed necessary for one to make an informed decision

discount window: a lending facility available to member banks of the Federal Reserve System

dividend: a payment made by a company, based on its earnings, to its shareholders

dogma: an established opinion expressed as an authoritative statement

draconian: severe, harsh

Dust Bowl: a semiarid region in the south-central United States where the topsoil was lost by wind erosion in the mid-1930s

E

egalitarian: marked by a belief in human equality

electorate: the body of people qualified to vote

emancipate: to free from another's control, restraint, or bondage

embargo: a prohibition on commerce with a particular country for political or economic reasons

encroach: to infringe upon or violate

equal protection: Constitutional guarantee that prevents states from denying a person or class of persons from the same protection under the law as those enjoyed by other persons or classes of persons

espionage: the act of spying on the government to obtain secret information

ex officio: (Latin) from office, by virtue of office; powers may be exercised by an officer which are not specifically conferred upon him, but are necessarily implied in his office

excise tax: a tax levied on the manufacture or sale of specific—usually non-essential—commodities such as tobacco or liquor

executive order: an order issued by the president that has the force of law

exorbitant: an amount that far exceeds what is fair or customary

extortion: the obtaining of money (or other concessions) by force or intimidation

F

faction: a party or group united by a common cause

Federal Register: a newspaper published daily by the National Archives and Records Administration to notify the public of federal agency regulations, proposed rules and notices, executive orders, and other executive branch documents

federal securities laws: federal securities laws include the Securities Act of 1933, the Securities Exchange Act of 1934, and various rules and regulations under these acts. These acts regulate the offer and sales of securities as well as secondary markets for securities. They require numerous disclosures and prohibit deceptive practices

federalism: a system of political organization; a union formed of separate states or groups that are ruled by a central authority on some matters but are otherwise permitted to govern themselves independently

felony: a crime punished with a lengthy prison sentence (more than one year) or the death penalty

filibuster: a tactic involving unlimited debate on the floor of the Senate designed to delay or prevent legislative action

fiscal year: the term used for a business's accounting year; the period is usually twelve months which can begin during any month of the calendar year

foreclosure: when a person defaults on (fails to pay) a mortgage debt, the owner's legal right to the property is terminated. The real estate may be sold at an auction by the creditor; the money raised is then put toward the mortgage debt

forfeiture: the loss of something (property, assets) as a result of breaking the law

free expression: the right to state opinions without interference or censorship

freedman: one freed from slavery

G

garnish: process whereby one's property or money that is in the possession of a third party is paid to another to satisfy one's debt

gold standard: a monetary standard under which the basic unit of currency is equal in value to and can be exchanged for a specified amount of gold

graduated rate schedule: tax structured so that the rate increases as the amount of taxpayer income increases

grassroots: originating or operating at the basic level of society

Great Depression: the longest and most severe economic depression in American history (1929–1939); its effects were felt throughout the world

Great Society: broad term for the domestic programs of President Lyndon B. Johnson, in which he called for "an end to poverty and racial injustice

gross domestic product: the total market value of goods and services produced within a nation in a given time period (usually one year)

H

habeas corpus: (Latin, "you should have the body") a written order to bring a prisoner in front of a judge, to determine whether his or her detention is lawful

high-rate mortgages: a mortgage with a high interest rate because it is perceived to be a higher risk based on the purchaser's credit history

I

illiquid: incapable of being readily converted to cash

immigrant: one who comes to a country to take up permanent residence

immunity: protection from legal action

impair: to lessen or reduce

impeach: to set up a formal hearing on charges of high crimes and misdemeanors which could result in removal from office

imperial presidency: a powerful president who is being belligerent internationally, being intrusive domestically, and running roughshod over another branch of government

import: to bring in merchandise from another country as part of a commercial business

individual retirement account (IRA): an account into which a person can deposit up to a certain amount of money annually without being taxed until either retirement or early withdrawal (withdrawal when the person is under a certain age)

inflation: a general rise in the prices of goods and services

infringe: to exceed the limits of; to violate

ingress: a means or place for entering

injunctive relief: a court order that requires a person to refrain from doing something; the order guards against future damages rather than remedies past damages

insurgent: one who revolts against authority; especially a member of a political party who rebels against its leadership

insurrection: a rebellion against a government or civil authority

interest expense: the money a corporation or individual pays out in interest on loans

interest rate: the fee for borrowing money, expressed as a percentage of the amount borrowed

interstate commerce: trade involving the transportation of goods from one state to another, or the transfer of property between a person in one state and a person in another

interventionism: a policy of getting involved in international affairs through membership in international organizations and multinational alliances

invidious: tending to arouse ill will or animosity; an offensive or discriminatory action

involuntary servitude: forced service to a master

isolationism: a policy of not getting involved in international affairs

J

Jim Crow: the systematic practice of segregating and suppressing African Americans; the name is from a character in a nineteenth-century minstrel show

judgment debtor: one who owes money as a result of a judgment in favor of a creditor

judicial: having to do with judgments in courts of law or with the administration of justice

judicial decree: the ruling of a court

jurisdiction: the territory or area within which authority may be exercised

L

labor union: an organization of workers whose main purpose is to collectively bargain with employers about the terms and conditions of employment

laissez-faire: a doctrine opposing governmental interference in economic affairs beyond the minimum necessary for the maintenance of peace and property rights

lame-duck: an elected officer holder who is to be succeeded by another; in the case of Congress, the time it is in session between the November elections and the convening of the new Congress the following year

legal tender: an offer of money in the form of coin, paper money, or another circulating medium that the law compels a creditor to accept in payment of a debt

liability: an obligation, responsibility, or duty that one is bound by law to perform

libel: the publication of statements that wrongfully damage another's reputation

libertarian: one who upholds the principles of absolute and unrestricted liberty and strongly opposes any government-imposed restrictions

licentious: lacking moral discipline or sexual restraint

lien: legal claim to property by a creditor (one who makes a loan) as a condition of a contract

life estate: an estate that lasts for the duration of the life of the person holding it

litigation: a lawsuit

lobby: to try to persuade the legislature to pass laws and regulations that are favorable to one's interests and to defeat laws that are unfavorable to those interests

lockout: the withholding of work from employees by management, to get them to agree to certain terms and conditions

long-term capital gains: profit made on the sale or exchange of a capital asset (usually stock or real estate) that has been owned for more than twelve months

loophole: a means of evading or escaping an obligation or enforcement of a law or contract

M

mandate: an order or requirement

marginal rates: the total percentage of tax one pays on one's income, taking into account all the separate taxes levied on one's wages or salary

Mason-Dixon line: the boundary line between Pennsylvania on the north and Maryland on the south which, before the end of slavery, was the line between the slave and the free states

median: the middle value in a distribution, above and below which lie an equal number of values

migrate: to move from one place to another

militia: a part-time army made up of ordinary citizens

mirabile dictu "wonderful to relate"

monopoly: exclusive control of a market by one company, often marked by the controlling of prices and exclusion of competition

moratorium: a legally required suspension of activity

mortgage loan: a loan to purchase real estate; the real estate purchased with the loan usually serves as collateral against default

muckraker: one who tries to find and expose real or alleged evidence of corruption

multilateral: undertaken by multiple persons, parties, or entities, in conjunction with one another

N

nadir: lowest point

naturalize: to grant the privileges and rights of citizenship

necessary and proper clause: provision in the U.S. Constitution (Article I, section 8, clause 18) that authorizes Congress to pass laws needed in order to exercise its constitutional powers

negotiate: to deal or bargain with another as in the preparation of a treaty or contract

New Deal: the legislative and administrative program of President Franklin D. Roosevelt designed to promote economic recovery and social reform (1933–1939)

nominate: to propose one for appointment to office

nonprofit: an organization whose business is not conducted or maintained for the purpose of making a profit but is usually aimed at providing services for the public good

nonpunitive: not having the character of punishment or penalty

notice and disclosure requirements: in contracts and other transactions, the law requires that key provisions and penalties be disclosed in plain English so a consumer can make an informed decision

null and void: having no legal force; invalid

O

obscene: morally offensive; designed to degrade or corrupt

offender: one who breaks a rule or law

omnibus: including many things at once

OPEC oil embargo: in October 1973, the Organization of Petroleum Exporting Countries (OPEC) banned oil exports to the United States because the United States sold arms to Israel during the Arab-Israeli War of 1973

open market operations: purchases and sales of government securities by the Federal Reserve Bank, designed to control the money supply and short-term interest rates

opining: to hold or state as an opinion

ordinance: a law

originate: a loan is originated when the loan is first made by the lender to a borrower. The origination function includes taking the borrower's loan application, checking the borrower's credit history and employment, obtaining an appraisal of valuation of the home, and funding the loan

override: if the President vetoes a bill passed by Congress, the bill can still become law if two-thirds of each house of Congress votes to override the veto

P

partisan: someone loyal to a particular party, cause, or person

paternalism: a policy or practice of treating or governing people in a fatherly manner especially by providing for their needs without giving them responsibility

penal: having to do with punishments or penalties

perjury: lying under oath or otherwise breaking an oath by not doing what was promised

personal consumption goods: goods purchased for personal use

photovoltaic: relating to the technology used to capture radiation (light) from the sun and turn it into electricity

plaintiff: one who brings legal action against another

populist: someone who identifies with and believes in the rights and virtues of the common people (often as the foundation of a political philosophy)

poverty line: level of personal or family income below which a person or family is classified as poor. The standard is set by the government

powers of appointment: the right to appoint or give away property

preemption when a conflict of authority arises between the federal and state governments, the federal government prevails

president-elect: one who has been elected president but has not yet begun his term of office

preventive relief: relief granted to prevent a foreseen harm

private litigation: a civil lawsuit (one brought to protect an individual right or redress a wrong), as distinct from criminal proceedings

private sector: the part of the economy that is not controlled by the government

Prohibition: period from 1919 to 1933, during which the making, transport, and sale of alcoholic beverages was illegal in the United States

promulgate: to make the terms of a law known by formal public announcement

proponent: an advocate

prosecute: to begin and carry on a lawsuit; to bring legal action against

protectionism: the use of tariffs to protect domestic industries from foreign competition

protectionist: advocating the use of tariffs to protect domestic industries from foreign competition

public held company: a corporation whose stock anyone can buy on a stock exchange

public offering: the making available of corporate stocks or bonds to the general public

pursuant: to execute or carry out in accordance with or by reason of something

Q

quid pro quo: (Latin, "something for something") an equal exchange or substitution

quorum: the number of members required to be present for a vote to take place

R

ratify: to formally approve; three-fourths of all states in the Union must approve an amendment for it becomes part of the Constitution

real income: income of an individual, organization, or country, after taking into consideration the effects of inflation on purchasing power

recession: a period of reduced economic activity, but less severe than a depression

Reconstruction: the political and economic reorganization and reestablishment of the South after the Civil War

redress: to make right what is wrong

refinance: to pay off existing loans with funds secured from new loans

Regulation Q: a banking regulation that prohibits paying interest on short-term deposits; the scope of this regulation has narrowed over time, so that most noncommercial deposits are unaffected

remedy: the means to compensate a person whose rights have been violated, which usually takes the form of money damages

repatriate: to return to the country of one's birth or citizenship

repeal: to revoke or cancel

rescind: to declare a contract void in its inception and to put an end to it as though it never existed

rescission provisions: provisions in a contract that, if they occur or fail to occur, allow the contract to be rescinded

resolution: a formal statement of opinion, intent, or will voted by an official body

reverse mortgage: a type of home mortgage under which an elderly homeowner is allowed a long-term loan in the form of monthly payments against his or her paid-off equity as collateral, repayable when the home is eventually sold

S

sabotage: the destruction of property or obstruction of an action intended to hinder the normal operations of a company or government

secede: to depart or withdraw from an organization

secondary market: the market that exists for an issue of stock after large blocks of shares have been publicly distributed, or items not obtained directly from the manufacturer

sectarian characteristic of a group following a specific doctrine or leader

securities: stocks, bonds, and certain other instruments of investment

security interest: a form of interest in property which provides that the property may be sold on default in order to satisfy the obligation for which the security interest is given; a mortgage is used to grant a security interest in real property

seditious: urging resistance to or overthrow of the government

seed money: money needed or provided to start a new project

self-incrimination: the giving of testimony that will likely subject one to criminal prosecution

separation of powers: the division of the government into three branches: legislative, executive, and judicial, each with distinct powers. This separation supports a system of checks and balances

Sexual Revolution: the liberalization of social and moral attitudes toward sex and sexual relations

slander: to make a false statement that defames and damages another's reputation

socialism: any of various economic and political theories advocating collective or governmental ownership and administration of the means of production and distribution of goods

sovereign: self-governing and independent

sovereign immunity: the doctrine that prevents bringing a lawsuit against the government without the government's consent

special session: an extraordinary or special session of Congress is called to meet in the interval between regular sessions

specie: money in the form of coins, usually in a metal with intrinsic value, such as gold or silver

speculate: to engage in the buying or selling of a commodity with the expectation (or hope) of making a profit

statute: a law enacted by the legislative branch of government

stipend: a fixed or regular payment, such as a salary for services rendered or an allowance

stipulate: to specify as a condition of an agreement

strike: to stop work in protest, usually so as to make an employer comply with demands

subpoena: a writ issued under authority of a court to compel the appearance of a witness at a judicial hearing

superannuated: retired or discharged because of age; obsolete; out of date

surveillance: the close observation of a person, place, or process

T

tariff: a tax imposed on goods when imported into a country

tax credit: a reduction in the amount an individual or corporation owes in taxes

tax shelter: a strategy or method that allows one to legally reduce or avoid tax liabilities

temperance: moderation in or abstinence from the consumption of alcohol

tender offer: a public offer to purchase shares of a specific corporation, usually at a price above what the market offers, in an attempt to accumulate enough shares to take control of the company

terminology: the vocabulary of technical terms and usages appropriate to a particular trade, science, or art

tort: any wrongdoing other than a breach of contract for which a civil lawsuit can be brought. Examples include physical injury, damage to property, and damage to one's reputation

tortuous: unlawful conduct that subjects a person to tort liability

totalitarian: the political concept that the citizen should be totally subject to an absolute state authority

treason: the offense of attempting to overthrow the government of one's own state or country

treaty: a binding international agreement

treaty clause: provision of the U.S. Constitution (Article II, section 2, clause 2) that grants the power to make treaties with foreign nations to the president, which are subject to approval by the Senate

truancy: skipping out of school

U

underwrite: to assume financial responsibility and risk for something

unilateral: undertaken by one person, party, or entity

United States Trade Representative (USTR): a cabinet-level official appointed by the president who has primary responsibility for directing U.S. trade policy and trade negotiations

unprecedented: not resembling something already in existence

unsolicited: not wanted or requested

V

veto: when the president returns a bill to Congress with a statement of objections

vigilante: a member of a self-appointed group of citizens who undertake law enforcement within their community without legal authority

W

waive: to give up voluntarily

waivers of immunity: legal statement that gives up the government's right to sovereign immunity (the doctrine that the government cannot be sued without its consent)

warrant: a document issued by a judge granting authority to do something

Watergate: the scandal following the break-in at the Democratic National Committee headquarters located in the Watergate apartment and office complex in Washington, D.C., in 1972

Court Case Index

Each entry has (in order): the case name and the year the act became law (in parenthesis). The numbers after the date denote the volume and page number(s) where information can be found in Major Acts of Congress.

V

W

Y

Z

Cumulative Index

Page numbers in boldface type indicate article titles; those in italic type indicate illustrations. The number preceding the colon indicates the volume number; the number after a colon indicates the page number.

A

B

G

I

J

K